"Richard E. Averbeck convincingly dem... the Old Testament to the New Testament so that the whole law provides guidance for the life of the Christian church and the believer. This profound and refreshing book is full of insights that enlighten, challenge, and inspire the reader."

Roy E. Gane, professor of Hebrew Bible and ancient Near Eastern languages at Seventh-day Adventist Theological Seminary, Andrews University, and author of *Old Testament Law for Christians*

"Thinking through how the law relates to the gospel is like trying to cut a path through the Amazon jungle. Many have offered an array of approaches to this question. This book on the law and the life of the church cuts a fresh and revealing path to the refreshment the gospel offers without demeaning the law that helped to show the way there. It also makes a serious case for how the law can help us even now by keeping its eye on covenants, promises, and the progress of revelation. Well done."

Darrell Bock, senior research professor of New Testament studies and executive director for cultural engagement at the Hendricks Center, Dallas Theological Seminary

"Does the law of Christ leave the Old Testament law behind? No! Explaining the law's function for ancient Israel, Averbeck shows its goodness and its unity—moral, civil, and ritual belong together—and its weakness, for only the Holy Spirit can purify and vivify hearts to display the sacrificial life Israel should have exemplified as a 'kingdom of priests.' Consolidating decades of study in Old Testament law, Averbeck cogently concludes we should be thinking how all of the laws, rituals, and sacrifices apply to Christian life. With honest exegesis, spiritual sensitivity, and personal testimony, he guides readers to a better answer than others have offered."

Alan Millard, emeritus professor of Hebrew and ancient Semitic languages at the University of Liverpool

"Undergirding this book is a lifetime of study by an internationally recognized specialist in Old Testament law as well as a published voice in the field of Christian spiritual formation. Clearly written and accessible to a wide audience, this balanced presentation is replete with helpful insights and will be my first recommended reading on the subject."

John Hilber, professor of Old Testament at McMaster Divinity College and author of *Old Testament Cosmology and Divine Accommodation*

"This remarkable study effectively and clearly places the Old Testament law in its context within the ancient world of covenant making and law, and within the flow of redemptive history. From this basis, Richard Averbeck gives the church a positive and understandable view of the Old Testament law as God's continuing good gift to his people. Anyone struggling with how the Christian should understand the Old Testament law should read this critically important book."

Sarah Dorsey Bollinger, assistant professor of biblical studies at Evangelical Seminary

"Drawing on his considerable expertise, Richard Averbeck provides an accessible and authoritative introduction to the complex and challenging issue of how Christians should approach the Old Testament law associated with the covenant God made with the Israelites at Mount Sinai. Delving into passages, some initially striking modern readers of the Old Testament as largely irrelevant, Averbeck affirms the importance of the whole of Scripture as the living and transforming Word of God. For anyone grappling with how the Old Testament law might be best approached from a Christian perspective, this study offers insightful and compelling guidance."

T. Desmond Alexander, senior lecturer in biblical studies and director of postgraduate studies at Union Theological College in Belfast, author of *Face to Face with God*

"Everything that Richard Averbeck writes edifies me, and this work does so in abundance. Here the full range of the blessings he has to offer is on bright display: his meticulous scholarship and attention to detail, his deep and wide knowledge of the Hebrew Bible and its context, his love for the whole Bible and his scrupulous determination to let that shape his theology, his sincere Christian faith, and his gentle disposition. In all of this he patiently lays out his reasoning for the positions he takes in a manner that is both rigorous and fair, serving as a kind and thoughtful guide. What better way to think through these challenging issues, and what better company could we ask? Here is a splendid feast for heart, mind, soul, and might, and I count it a privilege to commend it to you."

C. John "Jack" Collins, professor of Old Testament at Covenant Theological Seminary and author of *Did Adam and Eve Really Exist?*

"Do you have a friend who is an antinomian or, alternatively, a legalist? Maybe it's a family member or even the person who looks back at you in the mirror. Whatever the case, this is the book for them (and you!). Richard Averbeck has long been a leading scholar of biblical law in its ancient Near Eastern context—the doyen, in fact, of such studies within evangelical circles. In this thorough yet accessible volume, he shows how the entirety of biblical law is good and profitable for Christians. Even if readers find things to quibble with along the way, Averbeck repeatedly proves himself an authoritative and—most importantly—a faithful guide."

Brent A. Strawn, professor of Old Testament and professor of law at Duke University

"Richard Averbeck has contributed much on this topic in a large number of important scholarly publications. Over the years, he has taught scores of students and laypeople striving to understand better how Christians relate to the instructional materials of the Old Testament. Here he offers the fruit of all that work in a way that is accessible and easy to follow, which puts us all in his debt. The nature and relevance of the Old Testament 'law' has become a topic of a number of book-level treatments recently, and Averbeck's is among the best of the lot."

Bill T. Arnold, Paul S. Amos Professor of Old Testament Interpretation at Asbury Theological Seminary

"I have been waiting a long time for this book. Reading the Scriptures forward before he reads them backward, Dr. Averbeck has caught the spirit and tone of Israel's law and demonstrated its relevance and authority for Christians with unequaled clarity and brilliance. Explaining the goodness and weakness of Israel's law, chapter ten alone is worth the price of the book. This volume should be required reading not only in courses in the Hebrew Bible but especially in New Testament theology."

Daniel I. Block, Gunther H. Knoedler Professor Emeritus of Old Testament, Wheaton College Graduate School

"This book weds two of Averbeck's greatest passions: the Old Testament law and the maturity of the church. We are the beneficiaries of his exegetical craft, love of biblical theology, and respect for the historical context of Scripture. Regardless of one's tradition, Averbeck explains how the Levitical regulations were about worship and our ongoing service. Believers young and old now have access to the most holistic treatment on the subject for a generation. Here is the product of a lifetime of study; prepare yourself for a feast!"

Andrew J. Schmutzer, director of teaching, residency, and spiritual formation at New Covenant Church, Naperville, Illinois, and coauthor of *Between Pain and Grace: A Biblical Theology of Suffering*

"Richard Averbeck has spent his entire career studying biblical law, especially Leviticus, and helping Christian students understand its ongoing relevance. He rejects the traditional distinction between moral, civil, and ceremonial law, insisting instead that we must read it holistically. His worthy proposal is sure to generate further discussion on the specifics of law keeping today. Given its length and level of discourse, this book could serve as a helpful introduction to law in an upper-division college elective."

Carmen Joy Imes, associate professor of Old Testament at Biola University and author of *Bearing God's Name: Why Sinai Still Matters*

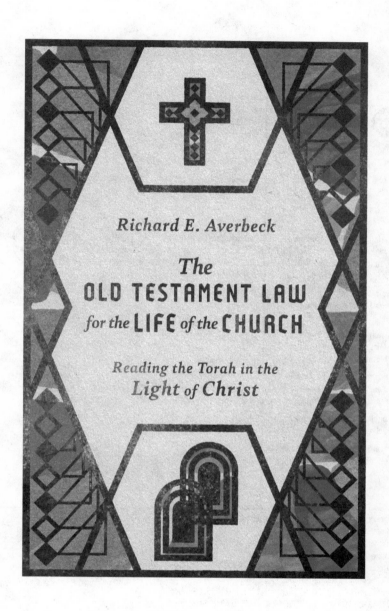

Richard E. Averbeck

The
OLD TESTAMENT LAW
for the LIFE of the CHURCH

Reading the Torah in the
Light of Christ

ivp
Academic
An imprint of InterVarsity Press
Downers Grove, Illinois

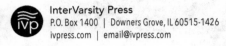

InterVarsity Press
P.O. Box 1400 | Downers Grove, IL 60515-1426
ivpress.com | email@ivpress.com

©2022 by Richard E. Averbeck

All rights reserved. No part of this book may be reproduced in any form without written permission from InterVarsity Press.

InterVarsity Press® is the publishing division of InterVarsity Christian Fellowship/USA®. For more information, visit intervarsity.org.

All Scripture quotations, unless otherwise indicated, are taken from The Holy Bible, New International Version®, NIV®. Copyright © 1973, 1978, 1984, 2011 by Biblica, Inc.™ Used by permission of Zondervan. All rights reserved worldwide. www.zondervan.com. The "NIV" and "New International Version" are trademarks registered in the United States Patent and Trademark Office by Biblica, Inc.™

A version of figure 1 and some content in chapter 2 previously appeared in *Israel, the Church, and the Middle East: A Biblical Response to the Current Conflict*, edited by Darrell L. Bock and Mitch Glaser. ©2018. Used by permission of Kregel Publications.

A version of figure 5 and some content in chapter 10 previously appeared in Richard E. Averbeck, "Spirit, Community, and Mission: A Biblical Theology for Spiritual Formation," *Journal of Spiritual Formation and Soul Care* 1, no. 1 (Spring 2008): 27-53.

Some content in chapter 8 is adapted from Richard E. Averbeck, "The Law and the Gospels, with Attention to the Relationship Between the Decalogue and the Sermon on the Mount/Plain," in *The Oxford Handbook of Biblical Law*, ed. Pamela Barmash (Oxford: Oxford University Press, 2019), 409-23.

The publisher cannot verify the accuracy or functionality of website URLs used in this book beyond the date of publication.

Cover design and image composite: David Fassett
Interior design: Daniel van Loon

ISBN 978-0-8308-4100-4 (print) | ISBN 978-0-8308-9954-8 (digital)

Printed in the United States of America ♾

Library of Congress Cataloging-in-Publication Data
Names: Averbeck, Richard E., author.
Title: The Old Testament law for the life of the church : reading the Torah
   in the light of Christ / Richard E. Averbeck.
Description: Downers Grove, IL : InterVarsity Press, 2022. | Includes
   bibliographical references and index.
Identifiers: LCCN 2022019796 (print) | LCCN 2022019797 (ebook) | ISBN
   9780830841004 (print) | ISBN 9780830899548 (digital)
Subjects: LCSH: Jewish law. | Bible. Pentateuch–Criticism, interpretation,
   etc. | Bible. Pentateuch–Relation to the New Testament. | Christianity
   and law. | Bible. New Testament–Criticism, interpretation, etc.
Classification: LCC BS1225.6.L3 A94 2022 (print) | LCC BS1225.6.L3
   (ebook) | DDC 222/.106–dc23/eng/20220610
LC record available at https://lccn.loc.gov/2022019796
LC ebook record available at https://lccn.loc.gov/2022019797

For my wife,

MELINDA,

who brought her love for God and his Word

into our love for one another and

into our life together

CONTENTS

PREFACE

IN MY SEMINARY STUDENT DAYS I remember very clearly a moment one day when I was walking down a particular hallway in the seminary building and it occurred to me: "Maybe God wants me to help the church with the Old Testament." Some years later I looked back on that day and came to the realization that this in fact had become the Lord's call on my life. It had somehow become my mission without my realizing it or making any intentional decision about it, at least none that I was aware of at the time. This book is an attempt to contribute in some small but meaningful way to fulfilling that mission. I offer it first to the Lord, and then to the church, and to you, the reader, in the hope that it will be helpful to you in your walk with Jesus day by day.

This book, therefore, is for the church and the believer. As I write, I am thinking primarily of pastors, the students I teach in training for the pastorate at Trinity Evangelical Divinity School, and the adult Bible fellowship I have taught weekly for twenty-five years in my home church. All of these are serious students of the Bible; some more trained than others, but all serious about it. The goal is to walk through the topic carefully, without assuming too much for these readers. Biblical scholars, therefore, are not at the forefront of my mind as I write, but the discussion depends on the scholarly work I have done on the subject over the past forty years and on the good work done by other scholars who have contributed to this area. We all stand on the shoulders of previous scholars, whether we agree with them or not.

The footnotes do not attempt to cover the immense volume of academic material written on the topic. My intention, however, is to provide enough coverage for curious readers to go further on their own, especially in the most recent literature. This, in turn, can lead them to earlier scholarly and/or popular literature. The treatment of technical matters (Hebrew, Greek, ancient Near Eastern context, complex theological debates, etc.) and opposing views will find its way into the discussion, of course, but in a way that should make them understandable to nonspecialists.

The approach to the topic taken here falls into three main parts. The first part of the book focuses on the biblical covenants as the overall foundation and context for the discussion of the Mosaic law in the Old Testament and the New Testament. Part two focuses on understanding the Old Testament law on its own terms, showing how it worked in its Old Testament context. This will include regular looks forward to the New Testament from the perspective of the Old Testament law. I am convinced that a good bit of the problem we have with the law for the church and the life of the believer derives from a poor understanding of the Mosaic law in the first place. The third part of the book will focus on understanding what the New Testament says about the law and looking back at the Old Testament from the New Testament point of view. I will take care to avoid imposing the Old Testament on the New Testament, or the New Testament on the Old Testament, to the best of my ability. I cannot and will not attempt to treat every detail of the law in this volume. There is simply too much of it. But I will seriously engage with the literary and historical-cultural context and the actual content of the law. Clarity is important here.

If this book helps believers and churches take a whole-Bible approach to their understanding and practice of the Christian life and ministry, it will have served my purpose in writing it. This is my hope and prayer. May the Lord Jesus Christ be praised!

ACKNOWLEDGMENTS

THE RESEARCH AND WRITING of this book has been in progress for over twenty-five years. Through that time I have benefited immeasurably from the students in my courses at Trinity Evangelical Divinity School (Deerfield, Illinois). I am in their debt and thank them for their sincere interest in the topic and willingness to consider lines of thinking that have sometimes been new to them. Their probing questions about the law itself and its significance for the church and believers today forced reconsiderations along the way.

One of the first of these students to take the study of the Mosaic law seriously was Bruce Wells. He is now one of the leading scholars today in the study of biblical law in its ancient Near Eastern context. Many of my other students have also written master's theses and PhD dissertations related to this topic over the years. Some are currently working on such projects.

Two previous research assistants, Neal Huddleston and Igor Swiderski, were especially helpful in gathering bibliography and doing their own writing on aspects of the topic. My current research and teaching assistant, Sai Madhava Venkata Gomatam (Joshua), has helped me in the final stages of the writing, editing, and indexing of this volume. I thank him for his faithful diligence.

A special note of thanks is due to Mitch Glaser, president and CEO of Chosen People Ministries, who interacted with various editions of the appendix on Jewish messianic believers and the Torah. His suggestions and recommendations have helped to keep me on track for this important segment of the church today. I also thank the members of the faculty interdisciplinary discussion group known as the Deerfield Dialogue Group, created and supported by the Henry Center for Theological Understanding. They have discussed my papers and tested my ideas about this topic many times over the past twenty years or so. I am solely responsible for the weaknesses that remain. I also thank editors Anna Gissing and Rebecca Carhart of InterVarsity Press, who have seen the manuscript through the various stages of production.

I thank my precious wife, Melinda, for her love and encouragement through the years leading to the publication of this book. The task has not been easy, but she has supported me with her prayers and faithful kindness through the whole process. Most of all I thank God the Father, Son, and Holy Spirit for his special grace and guidance in the pursuit of this important and controversial topic. My sincere hope and prayer is that he is pleased with what is said here.

ABBREVIATIONS

AB	Anchor Bible
ANET	*Ancient Near Eastern Texts Relating to the Old Testament*. Edited by James B. Pritchard. 3rd ed. Princeton, NJ: Princeton University Press, 1969.
AUSS	Andrews University Seminary Studies
BASOR	*Bulletin of the American Schools of Oriental Research*
BBRSup	Bulletin for Biblical Research Supplement Series
BECNT	Baker Exegetical Commentary on the New Testament
BKAT	Biblischer Kommentar, Altes Testament
BRev	*Bible Review*
BZABR	Beihefte zur Zeitschrift für Altorientalische und Biblische Rechtsgeschichte
CAD	*The Assyrian Dictionary of the Oriental Institute of the University of Chicago*. Chicago: The Oriental Institute of the University of Chicago, 1956–2006.
CBCS	Cornerstone Biblical Commentary Series
CBNTS	Coniectanea Biblica New Testament Series
COQG	Christian Origins and the Question of God
COS	*The Context of Scripture*. Edited by William W. Hallo and K. Lawson Younger Jr. 3 vols. Leiden: Brill, 1997–2002. Volume 4 supplements edited by K. Lawson Younger Jr. Leiden: Brill, 2017.
CTJ	*Calvin Theological Journal*
CUSAS	Cornell University Studies in Assyriology and Sumerology

ESV	English Standard Version
FAT	Forschungen zum Alten Testament
GMTR	Guides to the Mesopotamian Textual Record
HALOT	*The Hebrew and Aramaic Lexicon of the Old Testament.* Edited by Ludwig Koehler and Walter Baumgartner. Translated and edited under the supervision of Mervyn E. J. Richardson. 4 vols. Leiden: Brill, 1994–1999.
HBM	Hebrew Bible Monographs
HCOT	Historical Commentary on the Old Testament
ICC	International Critical Commentary
JAOS	*Journal of the American Oriental Society*
JBL	*Journal of Biblical Literature*
JETS	*Journal of the Evangelical Theological Society*
JSOTSup	Journal for the Study of the Old Testament Supplement Series
MC	Mesopotamian Civilizations
NAC	New American Commentary
NACSBT	New American Commentary Studies in Biblical Theology
NASB	New American Standard Bible
NICOT	New International Commentary on the Old Testament
NIDOTTE	*New International Dictionary of Old Testament Theology and Exegesis.* Edited by Willem A. VanGemeren. 5 vols. Grand Rapids, MI: Zondervan, 1997.
NIV	New International Version
NIVAC	New International Version Application Commentary
NRSV	New Revised Standard Version
NSBT	New Studies in Biblical Theology
OBO	Orbis Biblicus et Orientalis
PNTC	Pillar New Testament Commentary
SGBC	Story of God Bible Commentary
TAPS	Transactions of the American Philosophical Society

TDOT	*Theological Dictionary of the Old Testament*. Edited by G. Johannes Botterweck, Helmer Ringgren, and Heinz-Josef Fabry. Translated by John T. Willis and David E. Green. 15 vols. Grand Rapids, MI: Eerdmans, 1977–2006.
TOTC	Tyndale Old Testament Commentaries
TynBul	*Tyndale Bulletin*
VTSup	Vetus Testamentum Supplement Series
WAW	Writings from the Ancient World
WAWSup	Writings from the Ancient World Supplement Series
WBC	Word Biblical Commentary

INTRODUCTION

THE OLD TESTAMENT LAW is one of the major biblical and theological "problems" the church has had to deal with since it began. At the first church council the primary issue was whether or not "the Gentiles must be circumcised and *required to keep the law of Moses*" (Acts 15:5).[1] Even before this first Jerusalem council met, God had already gone to a great deal of trouble to convince Peter that Gentiles could put their faith in Christ, receive the Holy Spirit just as the Jews did at Pentecost, and be baptized in the name of Jesus Christ (Acts 10, esp. Acts 10:44-48). Of course, this caused serious concerns in the Jerusalem (Jewish) church (i.e., among "the circumcised believers"; Acts 11:2), since Peter had gone "into the house of uncircumcised men and ate with them" (Acts 11:3; cf. Acts 10:48: he stayed on "with them for a few days").

How could this be right? After all, had not God forbidden the Jews to eat with Gentiles and commanded them not to eat many of the foods that Gentiles would eat in order to keep them separate from all their corruptions? Leviticus 20:22-26 refers back to the clean and unclean animal regulations in Leviticus 11 that charge the Israelites to stay separate from the corrupting influence of the peoples round about them:

> *You must not live according to the customs of the nations I am going to drive out before you.* Because they did all these things, I abhorred them. . . . You must *therefore make a distinction between clean and unclean animals* and between unclean and clean birds. Do not defile yourselves by any animal or bird or

---

[1]Scriptural emphases here and throughout are the author's.

anything that moves along the ground—those that I have set apart as unclean
for you. You are to be holy to me because I, the LORD, am holy, and *I have set
you apart from the nations to be my own.* (Lev 20:23, 25-26; cf. Lev 18; 20; note
esp. Lev 18:3, 24-30; 20:1-22)

Of course, this was the point of the "large sheet" that was "let down
to earth" in Peter's vision (Acts 10:9-17). We will deal with Leviticus 11
and the Acts 10 incident in detail later in this book, but what we know
from Acts 11 is that Peter explained it to the Jewish believers in
Jerusalem and, in the end, they glorified God and concluded, "So then,
even to Gentiles God has granted repentance that leads to life"
(Acts 11:18).

This was all well and good to them, but nothing was said at the
time about how Gentile believers should live out their faith. That
brings us forward to Acts 15, where it is clear that many of the Jewish
believers were convinced that "the Gentiles must be circumcised
and required to obey the law of Moses" (Acts 15:5). In the meantime,
of course, the persecution that began with Stephen (Acts 7 with
Acts 8:1-3) had scattered believers in Jesus all over the known world
(Acts 11:19-30). And Saul, who had participated in the execution of
Stephen by stoning (Acts 7:58), had turned to Christ (Acts 9) and
gone with Barnabas on his first missionary journey (Acts 13–14). On
this journey, they went first to the synagogue (Acts 13:14-43), but
the main outcome was that God "had opened a door of faith to the
Gentiles" (Acts 14:27). This all led up to the first church council
in Acts 15.

The church, therefore, began as a movement within Judaism
made up of Jewish believers in Jesus as the Christ (in Hebrew,
Yeshuah Hammashiakh), and that movement continued with its
base in Jerusalem and even in the temple under the leadership of
James, the half-brother of Jesus (Acts 21:17-26). In the process, the
"wall of partition" between Jew and Gentile in the church was
broken down so that we are all one body in Christ Jesus (see, e.g.,
Gal 2; Eph 2). Over the centuries the perspective on all this has

changed because the church has become largely Gentile, rather than Jewish. Accordingly, we tend to look at things from a Gentile starting point, rather than the Jewish point of view from which the church began. This hinders our understanding of the New Testament perspective.

In one form or another, since those early days in Jerusalem the Old Testament law has been a subject of confusion, debate, and outright theological and ecclesiastical division. There is good reason for this: the way we deal with this particular issue has massive implications for the life of the individual Christian and the church as a whole. It effects both our orthodoxy (what we believe) and our orthopraxy (how we practice what we believe).

There has been a good deal written about this subject over the centuries. Much of it is well done and of enduring value. I will be standing on the shoulders of earlier scholars who have dared to enter these waters, including some of my own contemporary colleagues. One of the major problems with the way the discussion has been carried on, as I see it, is the tendency to write on the New Testament use of the Old Testament law without expending the necessary time and effort to know the law well in the first place in its Old Testament and Jewish context. This is one of the ways I hope to contribute to the discussion in the present volume.

The early chapters of this book, therefore, focus primarily on the Old Testament law: understanding its literary, historical, cultural, and theological context, its basic content, and how it was intended to function in ancient Israel. While we pursue these objectives, we will also look forward to the New Testament from the Old Testament perspective. The later chapters turn this around the other way. We will look back at the Old Testament law from the New Testament perspective, dealing with the core New Testament passages and themes. Our goal will be to understand how the Old Testament law does and does not come through into the New Testament for the church and the life of the believer.

THE "OLD" AND "NEW" TESTAMENTS

The topic of this book is, of course, part of the larger subject of the relationship between the Hebrew Bible (the "Old" or "First" Testament) and the Greek "New" (or "Second") Testament.[2] Note that even the terms *old* and *new* as used here can be taken in at least two different ways. For some "old" simply means that the Hebrew Bible is more ancient, but for others the terminology suggests that it is used up, worn out, set aside, and basically needs to be replaced by the "new." Some who hold the latter view nuance it more carefully than others, but the basic outcome is essentially the same. The main problem is that this perspective comes from exactly the opposite point of view held by the apostles and the people in the first-century church.

Like Jesus, most (if not all) of the New Testament writers were Jewish (Luke may be an exception).[3] The Bible of the New Testament church in the first century was the Old Testament, whether in Hebrew or translated into Greek (the Septuagint, or LXX), or perhaps Syriac, or some other language. Paul, the Jewish apostle to the Gentiles, wrote to Timothy, his half-Jewish protégé, whom he had left in charge of the largely Gentile church at Ephesus: "From infancy you have known the Holy Scriptures, which are able to make you wise for salvation through faith in Christ Jesus. All Scripture is God-breathed and is useful for teaching, rebuking, correcting and training in righteousness, so that the servant of God may be thoroughly equipped for every good work" (2 Tim 3:15-17).[4]

Timothy could rely on Scripture as his divine authority in teaching, exhorting, and training people to live in a godly way in Christ Jesus.

---

[2]David L. Baker, *Two Testaments, One Bible: A Study of the Theological Relationships Between the Old and New Testaments*, 3rd ed. (Downers Grove, IL: IVP Academic, 2010) was originally published in its first edition in 1976. It has been one of the most highly regarded discussions of the relationship between the Old Testament and the New Testament for the last four decades.
[3]See the discussion in E. E. Ellis, *The Gospel of Luke* (Grand Rapids, MI: Eerdmans, 1974), 51-53.
[4]For more detailed remarks on 2 Timothy 3 and 2 Peter passages treated here, see Richard E. Averbeck, "The Bible in Spiritual Formation," in *The Kingdom Life: A Practical Theology of Discipleship and Spiritual Formation*, ed. Alan Andrews (Colorado Springs, CO: NavPress, 2010), 279-81.

It is especially interesting that, according to the passage, he had known these writings "from his childhood" (2 Tim 3:15). This passage, therefore, is talking (at least primarily and most directly) about the Old Testament Scriptures, since the New Testament had not yet been written when Timothy was a child. It is also significant that Paul was near the end of his ministry when he penned these words, since 2 Timothy appears to be the last New Testament letter he wrote. Nevertheless, he still viewed the whole Old Testament as not only inspired but useful for instructing and guiding Christians. These were still inspired Scriptures as far as the apostle Paul was concerned. Second Peter 3:2, 15-16 extends this to the writings of the apostles and specifically to Paul's writings in the New Testament. They too are inspired Scripture.

Paul never came to the point of leaving the Old Testament behind in favor of the New Testament. Neither Jesus nor the apostles would have ever conceived of—or put up with—such a thing. Neither should we. We need the whole Bible. The New Testament relies heavily on the Old Testament. All the writers of the New Testament assumed that their readers were devoted to the Old Testament as the Scriptures of the church. To ignore the Old Testament is to misunderstand the New Testament. They wrote the New Testament with the Old Testament as their scriptural foundation. The shift between the Old Testament and New Testament, however, is very real. In the New Testament the apostles saw the Old Testament in light of the coming of the Messiah Jesus who was anticipated in it. The Holy Spirit had come at Pentecost as anticipated in Joel 2 and experienced in Acts 2. The kingdom of God had now taken the manifest form of the church, which increasingly came to recognize that both Jewish and Gentile believers in Jesus were now included in that kingdom as a unified whole.

It is interesting and important to observe, for instance, the number of Old Testament quotations in Hebrews 3–4. These culminate in the claim that such passages constitute the "word of God," which is "living and active. Sharper than any double-edged sword, it penetrates even to dividing soul and spirit, joints and marrow; it judges the thoughts and attitudes of the heart. Nothing in all creation is hidden from God's sight. Everything is uncovered and laid bare before the eyes of him to whom we must give account" (Heb 4:12-13). The Hebrew Old Testament Scriptures are alive and well, and full of meaning and importance for the New Testament believer. As noted above, some scholars prefer to call the "Old" Testament the "First" Testament, for example, to avoid the false notion that the Old Testament is old and worn out.

Old Testament passages such as Joshua 1:8 and Psalm 1:2 emphasize the central importance of study and meditation on the Old Testament law for the life of the believer. Joshua 1:8 exhorts Joshua, the new leader of Israel, to "keep this Book of the Law always on your lips; meditate on it day and night, so that you may be careful to do everything written in it. Then you will be prosperous and successful." Psalm 1 underlines the blessedness of the one "whose delight is in the law of the LORD, and who meditates on his law day and night" (Ps 1:2).

It is no coincidence that Joshua 1 and Psalm 1 occupy strategic positions in the Hebrew canon of the Old Testament. There are three sections: (1) the Law, or "instruction," also referred to as the Torah, the five books of Moses, or the Pentateuch; (2) the Prophets: the former prophets (Joshua through Kings, less Ruth) and the latter prophets (Isaiah through Malachi, less Lamentations and Daniel); and (3) the Writings: Psalms, Job, Proverbs, the five scrolls (Ruth, Song of Songs, Ecclesiastes, Lamentations, and Esther), Daniel, Ezra–Nehemiah, and Chronicles.

Note that Joshua 1 is the divide between the Torah and the Prophets, and Psalm 1 is the divide between the Prophets and the Writings. Thus, precisely at the seams of the three major units of the canon, both Joshua 1:8 and Psalm 1:2 emphasize the importance of meditation on the law of the Lord day and night as a way of life. The combination of expressions in these verses is unique in the Bible—intentionally so.

Another passage that highlights the importance of focusing on the law in life is Ezra 7, where Ezra himself first enters the scene. It presents him as "a teacher well versed [lit. 'quick, ready'] in the law of Moses, which the LORD, the God of Israel, had given." As a result, "the hand of the LORD his God was on him" (Ezra 7:6). Later verses expand on these points. In leading a contingent of pilgrims back to the land we are told that Ezra "arrived in Jerusalem on the first day of the fifth month, for the gracious [lit. 'good'] hand of his God was on him. For Ezra had devoted himself [lit. 'established his heart'] to the study [lit. 'to seek out' the meaning] and observance of [lit. 'to do'] the law of the LORD, and to teaching its decrees and laws in Israel" (Ezra 7:9-10). Who of us would not want "the good hand of God" on us? This thought and expression is a favorite one of the post-exilic writers (cf. Ezra 7:28; 8:18, 22, 31; Neh 2:8, 18). And notice the order of what Ezra had set his heart to do: first study the law, then practice it in his own life, and then, based on that, teach it in Israel. The sequence is important.

One could bring many more passages to bear on this point. For example, Psalm 119 is the longest "chapter" in the Bible, and all 176 verses are devoted specifically to the goodness and greatness of the law of God in the books of Moses. The point is that, if we are going to understand the New Testament well, we must make much of its Old Testament foundation and take it seriously as authoritative Scripture for the church. The Old Testament was the Bible of the New Testament church—and even of the authors of the New Testament. The books of Moses, in which we find the law, were the foundation that set the direction for the rest of the Old Testament—a concept that was never lost among the godly in ancient Israel. The New Testament writers argued from it and expected their readers to honor, value, study, practice, and teach it as authoritative for life and godliness. We need to do the same today. The question is, *How* do we do this? There are pitfalls here, as Paul noted in 1 Timothy 1:3-11 and other places (see chap. 9 below).

Theological Systems in the Discussion

For the writers of the New Testament the starting place was not the New Testament but the Old Testament. This has changed over the centuries. The church today is largely Gentile, not Jewish, although the messianic Jewish movement is gaining momentum. In the appendix, I will discuss the various approaches to the Old Testament law specifically in the life of the Jewish believer. Since the church is largely Gentile today, it has become natural to start with the New Testament rather than the Old Testament. On the one hand, this means that, in a sense, we come at the whole discussion backward. To some degree, we have to twist our minds around if we are going to think along with the New Testament writers as they encountered the issue of the Old Testament law in their day. On the other hand, the church lives in Christ under the new covenant (see, e.g., Jer 31:31-34 with Lk 22:20: "This cup is the *new covenant* in my blood, which is poured out for you"). The church has its most immediate footing in the work of Christ, the Pentecostal coming of the Holy Spirit, and the early development of the church. It is understandable, therefore, that the largely Gentile church of today would be more familiar with the New Testament than the Old Testament.

Over the centuries, a substantial body of literature has built up around the topic of the Old Testament law and the Christian, and the church has reached no stable consensus on the topic. The various approaches taken to the subject have tended to follow the tracks laid out by the particular theological perspective the scholar brings to the discussion.[5] In this regard, one of the most helpful summaries available is in a five views book published over twenty-five years ago.[6] The book covers the Reformed perspective, the theonomic Reformed approach, the dispensational view, and the modified Lutheran view.

---

[5]On this point I agree with Douglas J. Moo, "The Law of Christ as the Fulfillment of the Law of Moses: A Modified Lutheran View," in *The Law, the Gospel, and the Modern Christian*, ed. Wayne Strickland (Grand Rapids, MI: Zondervan, 1993), 320.

[6]Strickland, *The Law, the Gospel, and the Modern Christian*, later republished as Stanley N. Gundry, ed., *Five Views on the Law and Gospel* (Grand Rapids, MI: Zondervan, 1996).

This spectrum of views moves from those that give a greater signifi-cance to the use of the law in the church and the Christian life (Reformed and theonomic) to lesser significance (dispensational and Lutheran). There is also a fifth approach (The Law as God's Gracious Guidance for the Promotion of Holiness) that comes third in the se-quence in the book because, in a sense, it stands somewhere between the first two and the last two in its emphasis. I will treat this approach last and refer to it as the "guidance for holiness" view.

One of the crosscurrents in the discussion is the question of the threefold division of the Mosaic law into moral, civil (or judicial), and ceremonial law. Much depends on whether one considers this threefold division to be valid or not. The Reformed, theonomic, and guidance for holiness views accept it, but the dispensational and Lutheran views reject it. Making this division within the law avoids having to conclude that either the New Testament has abrogated the Old Testament law as a whole or that the whole law continues to apply to the New Testament church. One can just say, as many do, that the moral law applies but not the civil or ceremonial.[7]

Of course, there are variations even among scholars who fit gen-erally within one of the four major categories. There are also certain basic points that they all hold in common. First, almost all would say that the law was and is a good thing in one way or another (see, e.g., Rom 7:12, 14). Second, God did not give Israel the law as a means of obtaining eternal salvation. That comes only through Abrahamic faith (see esp. Gen 15:6 as treated in Rom 4 and Gal 3) and ultimately through faith alone in Jesus Christ alone (see, e.g., Eph 2:8-10).[8] Third, although there is disagreement about the validity of the threefold di-vision of the law into moral, civil, and ceremonial categories, virtually

---

[7]See, e.g., how this is articulated by Walter C. Kaiser Jr., "The Law as God's Gracious Guidance for the Promotion of Holiness," in Strickland, *The Law, the Gospel, and the Modern Christian*, 198-99.
[8]See the clarification with regard to false accusations against dispensationalism on this matter in Wayne Strickland, "The Inauguration of the Law of Christ with the Gospel of Christ: A Dispensational View," in Strickland, *The Law, the Gospel, and the Modern Christian*, 232-36 and n. 16.

everyone agrees that at least the ceremonial law has been abrogated in the New Testament because it has been fulfilled for us by Jesus Christ in his life, death, burial, resurrection, and ascension.

The Reformed view. The Reformed view follows the lines of the Westminster Confession of Faith.[9] It begins with the two main covenants of covenant theology: the covenant of works in the Garden of Eden (Gen 2) and the covenant of grace initiated as a response to the fall into sin (Gen 3). This approach favors continuity between the Old Testament and the New Testament, although there are two major administrations (i.e., dispensations) of the covenant of grace: law (OT) and gospel (NT). The threefold division between the moral, civil, and ceremonial law is a major feature of this view. The moral law amounts to the natural law moral order of God encapsulated in the Ten Commandments. Everything but the moral law is abrogated. The Holy Spirit does not replace the law but "opens people up to the law."[10] There are three purposes to the law: (1) conviction of sin: showing people that they are sinners so that they will seek God's grace; (2) restraint from sin: curbing the wickedness of the unjust out of fear of punishment; and (3) guidance for those who would live a godly life in Christ. The last is the highest function of the law.[11]

The theonomic view. The theonomic view is built on the Reformed foundation outlined above and is, in fact, sometimes referred to as the "theonomic Reformed" position.[12] It most naturally arises out of a postmillennial eschatological point of view because it argues for the gradual victory of the kingdom of God on earth before the return of Christ rather than after.[13] Essentially, theonomy holds to the threefold division of the law, but here the moral and civil/judicial law fall

---

[9]This summary is based on Willem A. VanGemeren, "The Law Is the Perfection of Righteousness in Jesus Christ: A Reformed Perspective," in Strickland, *The Law, the Gospel, and the Modern Christian*, 13-58.

[10]See VanGemeren, "A Reformed Perspective," 29, 37, 44-45, 47, 53, for these specifics.

[11]VanGemeren, "A Reformed Perspective," 53-57.

[12]This summary is based on Greg L. Bahnsen, "The Theonomic Reformed Approach to Law and Gospel," in Strickland, *The Law, the Gospel, and the Modern Christian*, 93-143.

[13]Bahnsen, "The Theonomic Reformed Approach," 121n18.

together under the category of moral law and are still obligatory; only the ceremonial law is abrogated. Since the moral law is universally valid, civil magistrates need to be guided and regulated by the moral law of God, including its penalties for misdeeds as found in the civil law.[14] As in the Reformed view, the moral law remains valid in the New Testament, except where God explicitly alters it.[15] By contrast, the dispensational and Lutheran views would argue that only the portions of the moral law that are repeated in the New Testament remain valid for the church.

The dispensational view. According to the dispensational approach, God gave the law to Israel to show his graciousness toward them, make provision for their approach to God and worship of him, and provide a means of governing the Israelite theocracy.[16] The law exposed sin and functioned as a tutor until the coming of Christ, but the law of Christ replaces it in the New Testament church.[17] There is no threefold division of the law. Jesus fulfilled the Old Testament law for us and thereby abolished it (Mt 5:17-19, as they interpret it), so even the moral law is inoperative in the church age in favor of the Spirit.[18] Nevertheless, one can still say that natural law appears in both the Mosaic law and the law of Christ. The Old Testament law no longer has a regulatory function but continues to have a revelatory function. That is what Paul refers to when he says the law is good (e.g., Rom 7:7-14).[19]

The Lutheran view. The Lutheran approach argues, similar to the dispensational view, that the New Testament writers relegate the Old Testament law to the redemptive historical period before the coming of Christ, so it is not directly applicable to us as Christians.[20] God gave the law to reveal his character to Israel, to supervise Israel before

---

[14]Bahnsen, "The Theonomic Reformed Approach," 125-28.
[15]Bahnsen, "The Theonomic Reformed Approach," 113.
[16]This summary is based on Strickland, "A Dispensational View," 229-79.
[17]Strickland, "A Dispensational View," 236-45
[18]Strickland, "A Dispensational View," 259-62.
[19]Strickland, "A Dispensational View," 276-79.
[20]This summary is based on Moo, "A Modified Lutheran View," 319-76.

Christ, and to imprison all people, including Israel, under sin. Here again the threefold division of the law is rejected.[21] In the New Testament, the law of Christ replaces the Old Testament law and does not consist of prescriptions and ordinances like those in the Old Testament law but the teaching and example of Christ and the apostles, the centrality of love, and the guidance of the Holy Spirit.[22] In this view, the law written on the heart in Jeremiah 31:33 is not the Mosaic law but the law as Jesus fulfilled it.[23] Individual commands from the law may be binding on the believer, but only those repeated within New Testament teaching for the church.[24]

The guidance for holiness view. The fifth approach (the third in order in the book) does not derive from the Westminster Confession and Reformed theology like the first two views presented above.[25] Nevertheless, its approach to the Old Testament law for the church and the Christian corresponds to that of Reformed theology and strenuously resists the dispensational and Lutheran positions. It maintains the threefold division of the law, and the "moral law" applies to the church and the Christian life.[26] The Decalogue and the holiness code (specifically Lev 18–19) offer a template for applying the Old Testament law today. This approach places a good deal of emphasis on Romans 10:4 as a reference to Christ as the *goal* toward which the whole law aimed, not the *termination* of the law.[27]

---

[21]Moo, "A Modified Lutheran View," 321-43.

[22]Moo, "A Modified Lutheran View," 343, 357, 368-69.

[23]Moo, "A Modified Lutheran View," 346-53.

[24]Moo, "A Modified Lutheran View," 376.

[25]This summary is based on Kaiser, "Guidance for the Promotion of Holiness," 177-99. This chapter is much shorter—only 22 pages compared to 45-60 for the others.

[26]Kaiser, "Guidance for the Promotion of Holiness," 188-90, 194-98. Joe M. Sprinkle, *Biblical Law and Its Relevance: A Christian Understanding and Ethical Application for Today of the Mosaic Regulations* (Lanham, MD: University Press of America, 2006), essentially follows Kaiser's approach. Roy E. Gane, *Old Testament Law for Christians: Original Context and Enduring Application* (Grand Rapids, MI: Baker Academic, 2017), does the same but in a different way. Both volumes are positive toward the law in the Christian life and are important and helpful for the church. The approach I take in this book is also positive toward the law but builds the argument in a very different way.

[27]Kaiser, "Guidance for the Promotion of Holiness," 180-88.

Summation and evaluation. The writers of all of these views, of course, attempt to support their arguments from careful exegesis and biblical-theological argumentation above all else. The question, therefore, becomes whether the writer's exegesis and biblical theology will carry the day. Many other helpful treatments of the subject have appeared in recent decades, many of which fit into one of the theological categories reviewed above to one degree or another. It is not my purpose to review them all in this introduction. Most of them will appear in appropriate places later in this book.

As for myself, I am convinced that the threefold division is neither legitimate nor helpful, from a biblical point of view, for resolving the issue of the application of the Old Testament law to the church and the believer. In fact, I will argue that the New Testament applies the whole law, including the so-called ceremonial parts to the church and the Christian life. It is not a matter of *whether* the Old Testament law applies but *how* the New Testament applies it.[28]

Yes, Jesus Christ our Lord died as God's divine sacrifice for our sins and so became our sacrificial substitute making eternal atonement for our sins (Rom 8:2-3). This was a once-for-all sacrifice and there is no more of this to come. We stand justified and fully acceptable to God the Father because of what Jesus his Son did for us, not because of any works we do to gain merit before God. Nevertheless, we are called to become like Christ in the way we live, and the Holy Spirit works in our lives to conform us to his image, all of which will eventually bring us to glory (Rom 8:26-30). We look forward to that day (Rom 8:31-39).

In the meantime, one biblical way of talking about the life that we are to live here and now is that it is sacrificial through and through. The church corporately (Eph 2:19-22) and the believer individually

---

[28]I and an old and dear friend and colleague of mine, David A. Dorsey, came upon this general approach independently but from different places and with different emphases. David died tragically from a long-term disease in 2014, but over twenty years earlier he wrote a seminal article on the topic: "The Law of Moses and the Christian: A Compromise," *JETS* 34 (1991): 321-34. He was never able to complete his full treatment of the topic, and we would not agree on everything or how to explain it, but our early ideas correspond well.

(1 Cor 6:18-20) are the temple of the Holy Spirit. Moreover, Jesus is the high priest (Heb 4–10) and the living cornerstone of this spiritual temple (1 Pet 2:4; cf. Eph 2:20). As his followers, we too are living stones built into a spiritual house in which we are also the living believer priests who offer the sacrifices in this temple (1 Pet 2:5), including our own bodies (Rom 12:1). In this way, even Isaiah 52:13–53:12, which looks forward to Jesus as the suffering servant who would die on the cross for us, also applies to believers who suffer unjustly in loving God and people (1 Pet 2:18-25).

Preview and Overview: Three Main Theses

Even while focusing on understanding the Old Testament law itself in the second part of the book, along the way we will naturally extend the discussion forward into the New Testament. A good deal of New Testament citation and discussion will find its way into the Old Testament discussion as a matter of course. In the discussion of the Old Testament law and the Christian it is just as important to look forward to the New Testament from the Old Testament perspective as it is to look back at the Old Testament from the point of view of the New Testament.

There are three interdependent biblical-theological theses that are essential to a full understanding of the law and its ongoing usefulness. Briefly stated the three theses are that the law is good, the law is weak, and the law is a unified whole. The second half of the book will focus on these three theses, working from the New Testament while also looking back at the Old Testament. The main concern here is that we must hold tenaciously to the truth and significance of *all three* theses *all the time* and *all at the same time* because all three correspond to significant statements about the law in both the Old Testament and the New.

Moreover, all three are still true in the application of the law today in the church and the Christian life. We must never lose hold of any of the three in any part of the conversation. The first two echo expressions found in Romans 7–8, but their truth permeates both Old Testament and New Testament Scripture. The last one derives from a combination of the straightforward reading of Old Testament law and the fact that, in any case, the New Testament uses all the different categories and dimensions of the law to inform and direct the Christian life and community. Again, even if one divides the laws into moral, civil, and ceremonial categories, the New Testament cites and applies specific laws and principles from all three categories to the life of the church and the believer.

Ultimately, thoroughgoing adherence to all three principles as the Bible articulates and relates each to the other will provide the matrix in which we can take the whole council of God seriously on the matter of the Old Testament law and the Christian. We need not—indeed must not—deny any part of the law full significance and authority in the church and the Christian life. As Jesus put it, "Until heaven and earth disappear . . . anyone who sets aside one of the least of these commands and teaches others accordingly will be called least in the kingdom of heaven, but whoever practices and teaches these commands will be called great in the kingdom of heaven" (Mt 5:18-19). He then goes on to explain what he means in the remainder of the Sermon on the Mount. Our goal here is to follow his lead faithfully since we are citizens of that "kingdom of heaven." We will treat this key passage in depth in chapter eight.

The law is good. First, the Old Testament law is good. It was good in the Old Testament; it was treated as good in the New Testament; and it will always be good. We need to be clear about the fact that "the law *is holy*, and the commandment *is holy, righteous and good.* . . . The law *is spiritual*" (Rom 7:12, 14; note the present tense). Furthermore, the Old Testament law was then and still today is not only "good" but also *useful* for the Christian (2 Tim 3:15-17). It applies to the life of the Christian today in a new covenant "written on the heart" sense, and it is the Holy Spirit who writes it there (see esp. Jer 31:31-34; Ezek 36:25-27; and the combination of both in 2 Cor 3:3-8).

Very few informed Christians would say that the law is actually bad, since the New Testament says it is good, but many will say that it is no longer good as a guide for the Christian life. They attempt to escape from the "old law" to the "new law" via the "law of Christ" (see 1 Cor 9:21; Gal 6:2; cf. also Jas 1:25; 2:8, 12; 2 Pet 3:2). The fact of the matter, however, is that Christ's commands to us correspond to the Old Testament to begin with. At the end of the day, the "law of Christ" is the way Christ mediates the Old Testament law to us. In fact, some of his clearest statements of basic principles of life in the kingdom of heaven ("the law of Christ") are direct quotes from the Old Testament. The most obvious example is the two greatest commandments, which all agree are part of the law of Christ: "'Love the Lord your God with all your heart and with all your soul and with all your mind.' This is the first and greatest commandment. And the second is like it: 'Love your neighbor as yourself'" (see Mt 22:37-38 and par.; cf. Deut 6:5; Lev 19:18). To this Jesus adds, "All the Law and the Prophets hang on these two commandments" (Mt 22:40). These two laws constitute the framework on which the whole Law and the Prophets hang (cf. also Mt 7:12). Unfortunately, many do not read the law this way, which means that they read it badly. Jesus says so!

The law is weak. Second, the law is weak; it always was weak; and it continues to be weak, as compared to the power of the Holy Spirit (e.g., Rom 8:3; Heb 7:18). On the one hand, it is true that "the law *is holy*, and the commandment *is holy, righteous and good*. . . . The law *is spiritual*" (Rom 7:12, 14). On the other hand, "I am unspiritual, sold as a slave to sin" (Rom 7:14). The implications are developed in Romans 8, "What the law was powerless to do in that it was *weakened* by the sinful nature, God did by sending his own Son in the likeness of sinful man to be a sin offering, in order that the righteous require-ments of the law might be fully met in us, who do not live according to the sinful nature but according to the *Spirit*" (Rom 8:3-4). In other words, the law was and still is also weak in that it never had the power in itself to change a human heart and motivate godly living. The strength, the power of the Christian life, comes not from the Old Testament law but from the continuing practice of *faith* through the work of the *Holy Spirit* in the *human spirit* (Rom 8:4-16; Gal 3:1-7; 1 Cor 2:10-13). There are certain things no law can do, not even God's law. The law has never had the power to change a human heart. Only the Holy Spirit can do that.

The same Holy Spirit who indwells and sanctifies us is also the one who inspired the writing of Scripture (2 Pet 1:21). It is natural, therefore, that the Spirit would continue to use the law as part of the Scripture that he himself made useful in very direct and directive ways for the Christian life (2 Tim 3:16-17). It is not fair to say that anyone who thinks the law is still authoritative for the Christian life is a "legalist." In point of fact, Jesus and the New Testament writers cited it as authoritative for us, so we have no right to discount it. Nevertheless, there is a major problem that was already recognized under the law in the Old Testament. It needed to be "written on the heart" (Jer 31:33), and only the Holy Spirit can do that (Ezek 36:26-27; cf. 2 Cor 3:3, 6). To have the law "written on the heart" is to live it from a heart purified and vivified by the Spirit of God doing his work in the human spirit. Unfortunately, it is quite possible to misuse the law, as some teachers did in the early church (1 Tim 1:7-8). One way of misusing it is to try to use it to do things that only the Holy Spirit has the power to do.

The law is one unified whole. Third and finally, the law is a unified whole. It is neither biblically correct nor useful in interpretation of the Bible to separate out one type of law from the others as a means of understanding the law or applying it today in the church and the Christian life. We should not be dividing it into "kinds of law"—for example, moral, civil, and ceremonial—and deciding what applies or does not apply to us based on that. The Bible does this nowhere. There is a better, more holistic and biblically sound, way of handling the law and its application today.

If it is true that the whole Law and Prophets hang on the two greatest commandments, then every element of the law supports or works out the implications of those two commandments in some way. Therefore, we need to understand and work out the details and implications of the fact that it is the whole, *unified* Mosaic law that is to be "written on the heart" of the new covenant believer, not just one aspect of it or another, or some combination thereof. The *whole* law applies to the Christian. As the Lord says it: "I will put my law in their minds and write it on their hearts" (Jer 31:33). This does not mean we should bring every specific law in the Old Testament over directly into the church and the Christian life. However, every law does contribute to some dimension of the law that, in turn, does indeed apply to the Christian life as part of the "law of Christ." We shall spend considerable time unpacking this point later in the book.

DIRECTIONS, PLANS, AND PROCEDURES

We will confront other biblical and theological issues along the way, of course, but focusing the discussion on these three main points will keep the topic as a whole in perspective. The law and the Christian is the kind of issue that can very easily get out of hand, as has been the case in many instances in the history of the church. In fact, even within the first-century New Testament period itself—during the apostolic age no less—it got so out of hand that the leaders of the church had to have a council about it (Acts 15). Peter and Paul themselves, two of the great apostles, were sometimes at odds with each other over this same matter (Gal 2:11-21).

I came at this topic originally from a focus on Leviticus, the center of the Pentateuch. It captured my attention way back in my seminary student days, forty-five years ago. My MDiv thesis in 1977 was on Leviticus 1:4 and atonement. Leviticus, and the law overall, has continued to be a main focus of my attention since that time. Along the way, God surprised me regularly! I had been accustomed to hearing and thinking that Jesus Christ fulfilled the sacrificial system in Leviticus through his death, burial, and resurrection—and he did! Yet, I kept on learning that there was more to it than that. In my study of the biblical theology of Leviticus God kept drawing my attention to how directly applicable the law is to our lives.

It became clear to me that it applies to how we see the church and our place in it, how we see the place of the church in the world, and how we are called to live as believers. For example, Christ gave himself as a sacrifice for me. If I am going to become like him, I must give myself as a sacrifice too, as he said, "Whoever wants to be my disciple must deny themselves and take up their cross daily and follow me" (Lk 9:23). I began to see the various dimensions of this kind of sacrifice in how Leviticus kept coming through into the New Testament (see, e.g., Rom 12:1; 1 Pet 2; and even Is 53 in 1 Pet 2).

Some have called this a "metaphorical" application. If that is the correct term, then we must distinguish it from mere "illustration" (i.e., not real application of the law, just an aesthetic ornamental picture), which is how some have treated it. Metaphor actually makes "real and substantial claims about reality" and is an important part of biblical theology as it applies to our lives.[29]

Others speak of "typological" application. The Jewish people practiced the sacrifices and offerings of the Old Testament in the New Testament world. Some, not all, elements of that background apply to the purpose and work of Christ in certain specific ways. Christ's sacrificial death, however, takes the Old Testament sacrifices to a new level "typologically." The Old Testament sacrifices function as the "type," and what Jesus did in sacrificing himself for us is the "antitype."[30]

As our Passover sacrifice, for example, Jesus did not become a literal lamb, and his blood was not applied to the doorposts of houses (Ex 12:1-30). Yet, he was still crucified at Passover time, and by his grace God applied Jesus' blood to the lives of those who put their trust in him, granting them his gift of eternal life (see, e.g., Lk 22:1-23 and par.; 1 Cor 5:7; 1 Pet 1:17). The fact that it is "typological" does not

---

[29]Ian Paul, "Metaphor," in *Dictionary for Theological Interpretation of the Bible*, ed. Kevin J. Vanhoozer (Grand Rapids, MI: Baker, 2005), 507-8.

[30]Daniel J. Treier, "Typology," in Vanhoozer, *Dictionary for Theological Interpretation*, 823-34.

make it any less true or important; quite the contrary. It underlines some of the features of the Old Testament sacrificial system that help us understand the wonders of what Jesus has done for us.

The point I am most concerned about here is that Jesus and the New Testament writers also apply some features of the Old Testament system of offerings to us as believers. No, we are not called to literally slaughter ourselves as a sacrifice on an altar, but we are called to offer ourselves up to God sacrificially in a way that is pleasing to him as we live our daily lives (Rom 12:1). The Old Testament sacrificial system applies to Jesus Christ typologically, and the same is true for us in Christ.

As I studied the Levitical sacrifices, I had the distinct sense that this was how the New Testament writers actually applied Leviticus as a guide to how to live the Christian life. They were reasoning from Leviticus to the Christian life: how we should think, feel, walk with God, and relate to others. This surprised me initially, and the surprises kept on coming as the exegetical and theological work continued.

Along the way, an important book was published—the one summarizing the five views of the law and the gospel discussed above. It dawned on me that what I was seeing in the Bible was not represented there. All the authors made good points and I gained much from reading them and seeing the back-and-forth discussion between them. Nevertheless, my exegetical and theological work was not taking me to any of those positions. Instead, I was feeling pushed to accept the notion that the whole Mosaic law comes through into the New Testament for application in the life of the church and the believer.

An ever-present danger is that a discussion like this could turn into a debate between theological systems rather than a sincere investigation of exegetical and theological issues on their own merit. We need to avoid this as much as possible. Focusing on these three aspects of the topic (the goodness, weakness, and unity of the law) brings us directly to the very center of the discussion in the larger world of biblical and theological studies. As noted above, we need to anchor the discussion of the law in its Old Testament context as the background for reading New Testament passages regarding the law. What is proposed here is that *the whole law was and still is good and profitable for the Christian and applies to the life of the Christian today in a new covenant way*. We need to think in terms of the *level* or the *kind* of application of the Old Testament Mosaic law, not the *limit* or *extent* of application.

One of the most troublesome problems in the ongoing debate regarding the Old Testament law and its application to the church and the believer is the tendency to choose one option from the first two theses above and deny the other. The fact is that both are true: *the law was and is both good and weak at the same time and at all times, including today*. It is essential to recognize and take fully into account the broad implications of both the enduring goodness as well as the essential weakness of the law. We need to hang on tightly to both of these truths with both hands if we are to articulate a thoroughly biblical approach to the law in its original Old Testament context, in the New Testament, and in its application to the life of the church and the believer.

With regard to the third main thesis, all those who divide the law into moral versus civil versus ceremonial commonly agree that the "moral" law applies to the church and the Christian at least on some level in some way. The applicability of the "civil" law is debated and continues to be a contentious subject among them. Everyone seems to agree, however, that the "ceremonial" law does not apply to the Christian life because Christ fulfilled the ceremonial aspects of the law for us when he died on the cross. There is a serious problem with this rationale. For example, did not Jesus fulfill the *whole* law for us, including also the "moral" and "civil" law, so that our righteousness before God comes by the imputation of Christ's righteousness to us, rather than our own supposed righteousness? The New Testament, however, clearly cites the law as instruction for us in many specific instances. We cannot ignore it.

As noted earlier in this introduction, although there are various units of law in the Torah, the categories of moral, civil, and ceremonial law never appear in the Bible. They are artificial and misleading. The Old Testament does not present the law this way, nor does the New Testament. In reality, the New Testament refers extensively to the so-called ceremonial regulations (e.g., the laws of the priesthood, the sacrificial system, the system of physical purity), sometimes in relation to the work of Jesus Christ as the new covenant sacrifice for us. Other times, however, it refers to them in relation to how we should live the Christian life (see, e.g., Rom 12:1; Heb 13:15-16; 1 Pet 2:4-10). From this point of view, the "ceremonial" law is as applicable to the Christian life as the "moral" law.

Over the years I have written a number of articles and essays on the Old Testament law, especially in Leviticus but also in the other parts. Most of them are rather technical. I have relied on this material in writing this book but have as much as possible avoided technical language, historical critical discussions, and such, without becoming overly simplistic or superficial. Much of the bibliography is excluded too, but the reader can go to the sources given in the footnotes for the original more technical discussions and further bibliography. My intention has been to write a book that would be helpful to scholars, but not only scholars. I have made every effort to write in such a way that my students at Trinity Evangelical Divinity School and other seminaries, the pastors that I know, and even the church people that attend my weekly adult Bible fellowship will be able to read and understand what I have written here. The people in the class are very serious about learning the Bible. They are good friends to have in the pursuit of the Lord. This is a book for such people.

The book falls into three main parts. After this introduction, part one includes chapters one and two on the covenants in the Bible. They will help the reader understand how the Old Testament law fits into the Mosaic covenant and how the various covenants relate to one another, especially how the Mosaic covenant relates to the new covenant. Part two includes chapters three through seven. These chapters take a relatively deep dive into the Old Testament law itself, beginning with its relationship to ancient Near Eastern law collections. From there we move to how the law fits into its narrative context, the relationships between the relatively parallel law collections within the Pentateuch, and a good look also at the tabernacle, sacrificial, and purity system. Part three consists of chapters eight through eleven, starting with Jesus and the law and continuing into the book of Acts. We then look at the Epistles from the perspective of the three theses discussed earlier in this introduction. The book ends with a short conclusion, followed by a relatively short reflection for Jewish Messianic believers in an appendix.

PART 1

COVENANT
and CONTEXT

One

COVENANTS IN THE OLD TESTAMENT

As discussed in the introduction, the approach taken in this volume will be, first, to lay a solid foundation for understanding the Old Testament law itself and how God intended it to work in its Old Testament context (parts 1 and 2). This will lead to a better understanding of how that law applies to the life of the church and the follower of Jesus the Christ according to the New Testament (part 3). We need a whole-Bible approach to this subject. The divine author, the Holy Spirit, was involved in the inspiration of both the Old and New Testament. Moreover, the same Holy Spirit dwells within us to bring the word that he himself inspired to bear on us in our own personal lives, our redemptive communities, and our mission in the world. This includes the Old Testament law. The Mosaic law is still God's word to us and for us.

This chapter and the next set the Mosaic law in its narrative and covenantal context. There can be no good understanding of the law of Moses without seeing how it fits into the Bible overall, both in terms of the biblical story as a whole and the progression of the biblical covenants through the story. Moreover, as we shall see throughout this book, this is of key significance for understanding how the law, which comes to us through the Mosaic covenant and fits most naturally within it, relates to the new covenant in the New Testament, church, and life of the believer. Of course, we cannot treat the covenants exhaustively here. That would require a major monograph, and there are already quite a number of them available.[1]

INTRODUCTION TO THE BIBLICAL METANARRATIVE

The larger biblical context of the law, of course, is the overall metanarrative of Scripture from creation through Old Testament history to its center in the life and work of Jesus Christ in the New Testament, and from there to the consummation that we look forward to even in the present day.[2] A metanarrative is a story that explains and provides a context for understanding and explaining all our other stories, whether personal, familial, communal, urban, rural, national, international, or universal. There is an old saying that history is really "his story"—that is, God's story. This story even extends beyond the pages of the Bible to include everything up to and beyond our present day. The Bible itself declares this. Our lives are trajectories from the Bible into today and forward into the future in one way or another.

The story that the Bible tells, therefore, is the story that we are all part of whether we know it or not and whether we like it or not. We have joined the story in progress, along the way, so to speak. The Bible tells the story in a way that focuses its primary attention on the main issues of the lives of all people of all time, ancient and modern. This is one way it connects directly to each of our personal stories.

The first eleven chapters of the Bible lay the primeval background for understanding our human predicament in this world. They level the ground of our human experience. These chapters tell us who God

---

[1]See footnotes 4-6 below for just a few of them.

[2]For a helpful introduction to the metanarrative of Scripture overall see Craig G. Bartholomew and Michael W. Goheen, *The Drama of Scripture: Finding our Place in the Biblical Story* (Grand Rapids, MI: Baker Academic, 2004). Stephen G. Dempster, *Dominion and Dynasty: A Theology of the Hebrew Bible*, NSBT 15 (Downers Grove, IL: InterVarsity Press, 2003), focuses primarily on the Old Testament story.

is and who we are. They also describe the nature of the world we live in and why life is the way it is. God originally designed us in his own image and likeness to have dominion in the world (Gen 1–2), but through the first human couple's violation of God's original design we, and our world, became corrupt (Gen 3–11). This leaves us in the midst of terrible struggles not just for dominion but even for survival—personal, emotional, relational, vocational, economic, and physical survival. These are unfortunate and sometimes excruciating realities in our world. We groan, and the rest of God's creation groans along with us. Paul reflects on this state of affairs in Romans 8:18-26.

The correspondence between the creation with corruption in Genesis 1–3 and the new creation without corruption in Revelation 21–22 provides the wider framework in which God's historical program of redemption and restoration fits. The parallels between the created paradise in Genesis 1–2 and the new heaven and earth in Revelation 21–22 are particularly instructive in this regard. The flowing waters (Rev 22:1) and the tree of life (Rev 22:2, 19) among other things reappear, and once again we will live in paradise. Similarly, contrast the fall and curses of Genesis 3 with the new heaven and earth in which there will "no longer . . . be any curse" (Rev 22:3)—no more tears, pain, and death (Rev 21:4). Thus, there is an envelope around the Bible: Genesis 1–3 and Revelation 21–22.

The rest of the Bible fits into this envelope not only in literary and theological terms but also historically. Moreover, eventually we are heading back to where we came from—in fact, to somewhere even better. In the meantime, we are part of the story, God's story, the history and the ongoing story that is above all "his story." The covenants that God has made with his people along the way provide an important framework and guide for understanding how God is working out his plan for the creation and its redemption. These covenants are of key importance for understanding the metanarrative of Scripture and history.

THE NOAHIC COVENANT(S)

The original creation mandate of Genesis 1:28 ("be fruitful and increase in number; fill the earth and subdue it") is renewed in Genesis 9:1-7 ("be fruitful and increase in number and fill the earth").[3] This provides the background for the Noahic covenant in Genesis 9:8-17. The Lord promises in covenant terms that he is committed to maintaining his involvement with all flesh, including humankind, within a relatively stable world order: "Never again will all life be cut off by the waters of a flood; never again will there be a flood to destroy the earth" (Gen 9:11; cf. Gen 8:21-22). In fact, he is committed to renewing all of it, eventually, in the form of the new heaven and earth.

The word *covenant* (Hebrew *bərît*) actually first appears in the Bible in Genesis 6:17-18 *before* the flood.[4] God declared to Noah, "I am going to bring floodwaters on the earth to destroy all life under the heavens. . . . I will establish my covenant with you, and you will enter the ark—you and your sons and your wife and your sons' wives with you." There have been several different interpretations of this first covenant passage. Some scholars are persuaded that the mention of "covenant" at Genesis 6:18 is "proleptic," referring forward to the Noahic covenant in Genesis 9 after the flood.[5]

---

[3]See the helpful treatment of these connections in Genesis 1–9 in Andrew J. Schmutzer, *Be Fruitful and Multiply: A Crux Thematic Repetition in Genesis 1–11* (Eugene, OR: Wipf & Stock, 2009).

[4]Here the focus will be on the Mosaic covenant (see below). Richard E. Averbeck, "Israel, the Jewish People, and God's Covenants," in *Israel, the Church, and the Middle East: A Biblical Response to the Current Conflict*, ed. Darrell L. Bock and Mitch Glaser (Grand Rapids, MI: Kregel, 2018), 21-37 offers a briefer discussion of the biblical covenants, focusing primarily on the Abrahamic covenant. The literature on the biblical covenants is immense. A recent comprehensive treatment in book form is Peter J. Gentry and Stephen J. Wellum, *Kingdom Through Covenant: A Biblical-Theological Understanding of the Covenants*, 2nd ed. (Wheaton, IL: Crossway, 2018). Even more recently, see the very fine volume by Daniel I. Block, *Covenant: The Framework of God's Grand Plan and Redemption* (Grand Rapids, MI: Baker Academic, 2021).

[5]See, e.g., Paul R. Williamson, *Sealed with an Oath: Covenant in God's Unfolding Purpose*, NSBT 23, ed. D. A. Carson (Downers Grove, IL: IVP Academic, 2007), 40, 59; and Paul R. Williamson, "Covenant," in *Dictionary of the Old Testament: Pentateuch*, ed. T. Desmond Alexander and David W. Baker (Downers Grove, IL: InterVarsity Press, 2003), 139-41. The same view is taken in, e.g., Scott W. Hahn, *Kinship by Covenant: A Canonical Approach to the Fulfillment of God's Saving Promises* (New Haven, CT: Yale University Press, 2009), 95-96.

Others argue that Genesis 6:18 looks back to the earlier chapters of Genesis rather than forward to the Noahic covenant in Genesis 9. According to this view, Genesis 6:18 is not referring to the initial making of a covenant with Noah, and neither is Genesis 9:8-17. Instead, "my covenant" in Genesis 6:18 (see also Gen 9:9, 11, 15) refers either to a "covenant of grace" made earlier between God and Adam and Eve in Genesis 3, after the fall, or a "covenant with creation" that God made by the very act of creating, beginning in Genesis 1:1.[6] The main argument for this approach is that the verb used in Genesis 6:18; 9:8-17 (Hebrew *hēqîm*) is not the verb commonly used for the initial making of a covenant (Hebrew *kārat*) in the expression *kārat bərît* (lit. "to cut a covenant"). The latter expression occurs about ninety times in the Old Testament. According to this view, therefore, Genesis 6 and Genesis 9 refer not to the making of a Noahic covenant but to confirming and upholding with Noah a previous covenant somehow established in Genesis 1-3.

In its immediate context, however, this verse most likely refers to the covenant commitment that God made with Noah to preserve him through the flood because of his righteousness amid that tragically corrupt generation (see Gen 6:5-8, 11-13).[7] The covenant is about entering the ark and surviving the flood. As for the verb in Genesis 6:18, if it refers to the maintenance of an earlier covenant commitment rather than the initiation of a new one, the most obvious candidate would be Noah's previous relationship with God before the flood, not a supposed covenant back in Genesis 1-3.[8] See Genesis 6:8-9: "Noah

---

[6]See esp. W. J. Dumbrell, *Covenant and Creation: An Old Testament Covenant Theology* (Milton Keynes: Paternoster, 1984), 11-43, esp. the summaries on pp. 25-33 and 41-43, followed by, e.g., Gordon J. McConville, "(bᵉrît), treaty, agreement, alliance, covenant," in *NIDOTTE* 1.748-49; Gentry and Wellum, *Kingdom Through Covenant*, 187-209 and the extensive literature cited there; and most recently, stated cautiously in Block, *Covenant*, 15-16, 45-46, but expanded in the remarks that follow there.

[7]See, e.g., the helpful remarks in Bruce K. Waltke, *An Old Testament Theology: An Exegetical, Canonical, and Thematic Approach* (Grand Rapids, MI: Zondervan, 2007), 284-85; Kenneth A. Mathews, *Genesis 1-11*, NAC (Nashville: Broadman & Holman, 1996), 366-68; Claus Westermann, *Genesis 1-11*, transl. John J. Scullion S. J. (Minneapolis: Augsburg, 1984), 422-23.

[8]See Gordon J. Wenham, *Genesis 1-15*, WBC (Waco, TX: Word, 1987), 175, and the especially helpful explanation in John Goldingay, *Old Testament Theology*, vol. 1: *Israel's Gospel* (Downers Grove, IL: IVP Academic, 2003), 173-75. See also the similar approach in Hahn, *Kinship by Covenant*, 95-96.

found favor in the eyes of the LORD. . . . Noah was a righteous man, blameless among the people of his time, and he walked faithfully with God."

Contrary to the argument of some scholars, however, the verb in Genesis 6:18 does sometimes occur for the initial making of a covenant.[9] For example, in Exodus 6:3-4 the Lord said to Moses: "I appeared to Abraham, to Isaac and to Jacob as God Almighty, but by my name the LORD I did not make myself known to them. I also *established* [Hebrew *hēqîm*] my covenant with them to give them the land of Canaan, where they lived as aliens." Here the Lord is not saying that back in the days of the patriarchs (centuries before Moses) he confirmed, fulfilled, or maintained a previous covenant with them to give them the land, which is what the corresponding argument would have to be if it would support the notion that Genesis 6 and Genesis 9 refer back to Genesis 1–3. No, he initiated this covenant with them back in those days. It is true that he also confirmed this covenant through the patriarchal generations, but Exodus 6:3-4 is referring to the fact that he "cut a covenant" back in the patriarchal days (Gen 15:18). In any case, extending the reference to a covenant in Genesis 6:18 back to Genesis 1–3 is a far stretch indeed. The term for covenant does not occur there and the exegetical and biblical-theological rationale for finding a covenant there has always been thin.

Exodus 6:5 goes on to say that now, in the days of Moses, "I have heard the groaning of the Israelites, whom the Egyptians are enslaving, and I have *remembered* my covenant." The link between God making a covenant and remembering it appears many times in the Old Testament. Consider, for example, Exodus 2:24-25, when Israel was in slavery in Egypt, "God heard their groaning and he *remembered* his covenant with Abraham, with Isaac and with Jacob. So God

---

[9]See also the remarks regarding the verb *hēqîm* with *bərît* in M. Weinfeld, "*bᵉrît*," in *TDOT* 2:260; and James Barr, "Some Semantic Notes on the Covenant," *Beitrage zur Alttestamentlichen Theologie: Festschrift für Walther Zimmerli zum 70. Geburtstag*, ed. H. Donner et al. (Göttingen: Vandenhoeck and Ruprecht, 1977), 33, contra Gentry and Wellum, *Kingdom Through Covenant*, 187-95.

looked on the Israelites and was concerned about them" (see also Lev 26:42, 45; Ps 105:8-9, 42, etc.). Of course, *remember* here does not mean the opposite of *forget*—as if God had previously forgotten—but rather something like the way we "remember" a person's birthday with gifts and a celebration.

The sequence of God establishing and then later remembering a covenant occurs back in Genesis 6–9 as well. The connection is especially clear in Genesis 9:8-16; the same verb (*hēqîm*) is used multiple times (Gen 9:9, 11, 17) for establishing the post-flood Noahic covenant (Gen 9:8-11). There he assigned the rainbow as the "sign" of the covenant so that, "Whenever I bring clouds over the earth and the rainbow appears in the clouds, I will *remember* my covenant between me and you and all living creatures of every kind. . . . Whenever the rainbow appears in the clouds, I will see it and *remember* the everlasting covenant" (Gen 9:14-16). This was clearly a covenant made after the flood because the rainbow appeared as the sign that such a flood would never happen again.

This brings us back to Genesis 6:18. Although the connection here is not as clear as in Genesis 9, the same sequence seems to occur again. God *established* the covenant in Genesis 6:18 to preserve them through the flood. Then we read in Genesis 8:1 that after all the flooding had occurred (Gen 7:17-24), "God *remembered* Noah and all the wild animals and the livestock that were with him in the ark, and he sent a wind over the earth, and the waters receded."[10] If this is the correct interpretation, we have two Noahic covenants in Genesis 6–9: one pre-flood covenant for getting them through the flood and then another post-flood covenant. The former was fulfilled in Noah's day, while the latter is still in effect and will remain so "for all generations to come" (Gen 9:11-12, 16). This perpetual commitment was anticipated in

---

[10]See Mathews, *Genesis 1-11*, 382-83. Umberto Cassuto, for example, rejects this connection because Gen 8:1 does not explicitly refer to remembering "the covenant," but this is an overly restrictive reading of the wording of the passage; *From Noah to Abraham*, trans. Israel Abrahams (Jerusalem: Magnes, 1964), 100.

Genesis 8:21-22, right after Noah exited the ark and made his sacrifice. God said: "As long as the earth endures, seedtime and harvest, cold and heat, summer and winter, day and night will never cease."

The Noahic covenant *is* the "creation covenant" in the Bible—the only one. God committed to maintain the natural world order until the generations of human history and his redemptive program have run their course, issuing in the new heaven and earth (see, e.g., Is 66:22-24; Rev 21–22). Until then, the natural order will never again devolve into the condition that it had in Genesis 1:2—a deep, dark watery abyss that covers the entire surface of the earth at great depth (see Gen 1:9-10 with Ps 104:6, and cf. Gen 7–8). There was no previous divine covenant in place to prevent this before the flood.

In the meantime, God has still stepped in to judge and guide his program at certain points along the way, as he did at the Tower of Babel (Gen 11), and in the "days of the Lord" described throughout biblical history. See, for example, Amos 5:18-27 for the exile of the northern kingdom into Assyria as a Day of the Lord and, similarly, Zephaniah 2:1-3 for the exile of the southern kingdom. The book of Revelation looks forward to the time when God will step in and set everything right for eternity.

Genesis 3–6 describes the corruption of God's design and plan for creation, beginning with the serpent's deception and the start of the cosmic battle in which we have found ourselves ever since (see, e.g., Rom 8:18-25; Eph 2:1-3; 6:10-20; Rev 12).[11] Since the time of the flood and the Noahic covenant, God has not brought another flood, as he promised, but has instead instituted a redemptive program, sometimes articulated through covenants that extend from Abraham through to the consummation in Revelation 19–20. This brings us to the background and meaning of the term *covenant* in the Old Testament.

---

[11]For the cosmic battle, see Richard E. Averbeck, "The Three 'Daughters' of Baal and Transformations of Chaoskampf in the Early Chapters of Genesis," in *Creation and Chaos: A Reconsideration of Hermann Gunkel's Chaoskampf Hypothesis*, ed. JoAnn Scurlock and Richard Beal (Winona Lake, IN: Eisenbrauns, 2013), 237-56.

TREATY AND COVENANT

Basically, a covenant is a solemn and formal means of expressing and a method of establishing and defining a relationship. There are at least two parties to a covenant (either individuals or groups) and, in one way or another, the issue at hand is always the manner in which they will practice relationship with each other.[12] When the term is used for the relationship between God and people it is intended to help us understand how the holy God does relationship with us as fallen sinful people.[13] Although it often goes unrecognized as such, it is essential to understand and keep in mind that covenant is a metaphor, a figure of speech, an analogy. The same terminology that God uses for his covenants with people in the Hebrew Bible also serves to designate a treaty, alliance, grant, loyalty oath, or something of that sort between people. It comes from that world and has analogs in the ancient Near Eastern world of the Old Testament.[14]

Much of biblical theology finds its expression through figures of speech. There are many of them that, like covenant, each carry a particular set of implications that are important to the context in which they appear and to biblical theology as a whole. Each takes a certain point of view on the relationship between God and people.

---

[12]Gary N. Knoppers, "Ancient Near Eastern Royal Grants and the Davidic Covenant: A Parallel?" *JAOS* 116 (1996): 696 summarizes his analysis of the biblical and ancient Near Eastern material with this basic conclusion: "covenant is a formal agreement involving two or more parties."

[13]R. Davidson, "Covenant Ideology in Ancient Israel," in *The World of Ancient Israel: Sociological, Anthropological and Political Perspectives*, ed. R. E. Clements (Cambridge: Cambridge University Press, 1989), 324 puts it this way: "bᵉrît in the Old Testament cannot be separated from the concept of relationships or the acts that lead to such relationships, and relationships of very varied types." See also the discussion in Richard E. Averbeck, "Law," in *Cracking Old Testament Codes: Essays in Honor of Richard D. Patterson*, ed. D. Brent Sandy and Ronald L. Giese Jr. (Nashville: Broadman & Holman, 1995), 116-19 and the earlier literature cited there. For a most recent treatment of the etymology of bᵉrît see now Dominique Charpin, *"Tu es de mon sang." Les alliances dans le Proche-Orient ancein* (Paris: College de France les Belles Lettres, 2019), 257-64 and 319 and the bibliography cited there. I thank Alan Millard for calling my attention to this treatment of the subject.

[14]See now esp. Samuel Greengus, "Covenant and Treaty in the Hebrew Bible and in the Ancient Near East," in *Ancient Israel's History: An Introduction to Issues and Sources*, ed. Bill T. Arnold and Richard S. Hess (Grand Rapids, MI: Baker Academic, 2014), 91-126. This is an excellent, up-to-date, and well-documented review of the primary and secondary literature related to this subject.

Vern Poythress, a well-known covenant theologian, refers to covenant as a recurring pattern in the Bible based on the explicit covenants there—specifically the Abrahamic, Mosaic, Davidic, and new covenants. He points out that "covenant theology" as a system expands the use of the term *covenant* wherever we find a "pattern of promise, command, human obedience or disobedience, and reward or punishment" in the Bible, so that it "sees all of God's relations with human beings in terms of the perspective of covenant."[15] In my view, this is too monolithic and simplistic to describe how God's revelation of himself and his purposes actually work.

As far as I am concerned, the treatment of these covenants here and below neither supports nor rejects, nor does it depend on, any of the main dogmatic theological systems. I intend no lack of respect in saying this. I have learned much from studying these systems, and I appreciate the good they have done and those committed to them. Moreover, I am fully aware that I do not stand outside of their influence, perhaps even in ways that I am not fully aware of. In any case, readers can and will make their own judgments about the equity of the discussion about the biblical material as it is presented here. The point is that the explanation of the covenants in the Bible that follows here depends on the explicit covenants in the Bible, not on any particular form of systematic theology.[16]

Some people think that when we speak of covenant as a metaphor, this makes it less real or relatively less important. This is a misunderstanding of what metaphor is and does, and how it works in Scripture.

---

[15]Vern S. Poythress, *Symphonic Theology: The Validity of Multiple Perspectives in Theology* (Grand Rapids, MI: Zondervan, 1987), 31. It is helpful to observe the interchange over this extended use of the term *covenant* between John H. Stek, "'Covenant' Overload in Reformed Theology," *CTJ* 29 (1994): 12-41, and Craig G. Bartholomew, "Covenant and Creation: Covenant Overload or Covenantal Deconstruction," *CTJ* 30 (1995): 11-33. Both are covenant theologians. Stek's critique provoked a negative reaction from Bartholomew, who raised some important objections. I would not agree with some of Stek's points about the nature of covenants and related matters but, in spite of Bartholomew's objections to the contrary, in my view, Stek has underlined a very real problem in covenant theology as a system.

[16]For brief remarks on covenant and dispensational theology in relation to this treatment of the biblical covenants, see Averbeck, "Israel, the Jewish People, and God's Covenants," 21-22.

Metaphor is a way of talking about a person, place, or thing that high-lights a certain feature (or features) of it and thereby makes it more concrete, real, and comprehensible. Such figures of speech pervade the Bible and are of central importance in a truly biblical theology.[17] For example, God is the father and we are his children. This has certain implications for how we should understand our relationship with the Lord, and certain passages of Scripture draw them out (e.g., Ps 103:13-14; Heb 12:4-13). Sometimes the Bible uses other kinds of familial language or images such as adoption (e.g., Rom 8:15-17, 31-39) or marriage (Jer 31:32, "though I was a husband to them"; cf. also, e.g., Hos 1–3 and Ezek 16:8-14). Similarly, he is the bridegroom and we are the bride (e.g., Rev 19:7-10; 21:2, 9).

Other metaphors include, for instance: The Lord is the shepherd and we are the sheep (e.g., Ps 23; Jn 10:1-18). He is the king and we are the people of his kingdom (e.g., Ps 2:8-9; Is 9:6-7; Mt 2; 4:17; 5:3, etc.; Rev 2:27; 12:5). He is the master and we are the servants/slaves (e.g., Lev 25:55; Is 52:13–53:12; 1 Pet 2:18-25). He is the head and we are the body (e.g., Rom 12:4-5; 1 Cor 12:12-31). He is the potter and we are the clay (e.g., Jer 18:1-12; Rom 9:21-23). The list goes on. That is the point.[18] These kinds of images are pervasive in Scripture and carry a great deal of significance for us as believers. We should not use one metaphor as the lens through which we view all the others or Scripture as a whole. Instead, we should let each of them add their own dynamic to our biblical theology on their own terms.

The term *bərît* occurs 285 times in the Hebrew Bible in the two major categories introduced above: between different people(s) and between God and people or people groups. Of course, this is not the only term for a covenant in the Bible. Sometimes, for example, "oath" (*'ālâ*; Deut 29:12) and "swearing an oath" (*šāba'*; Gen 21:31-32) can

---

[17]See the helpful summary of the current discussion of metaphor in Ian Paul, "Metaphor," in *Dictionary for Theological Interpretation of the Bible*, ed. Kevin J. Vanhoozer (Grand Rapids, MI: Baker, 2005), 507-10.

[18]A good brief introduction to reading the Bible theologically in this way is Poythress, *Symphonic Theology*.

stand for making a treaty/covenant or the content of it. Moreover, the concept sometimes appears where the term itself is not used (e.g., the Davidic covenant in 2 Sam 7:8-16 does not use the term, but Ps 89:34 and 132:12 use it in reference to the Davidic covenant).

The cultural institutional background of covenant is self-evident from very early in the patriarchal narratives.[19] The first instance is in Genesis 14:13, which reports that "Abram was living near the great trees of Mamre the Amorite, a brother of Eshcol and Aner, all of whom were allied with Abram." (This is the first occurrence of the term *covenant* after those referring to the Noahic covenants in Gen 6 and Gen 9 discussed above.) Rendered more literally, "They were the lords of the treaty [*bərît*] of Abram." They had what would best be called a "treaty" or an "alliance" that, among other things, required going to war as allies with Abram if or when the occasion should arise. In this case, foreign kings had invaded the land and taken "all the goods of Sodom and Gomorrah and all their food; . . . They also carried off Abram's nephew Lot and his possessions, since he was living in Sodom" (Gen 14:11-12). Abram's allies fulfilled their treaty obligation when they marched with him to Dan to conquer the foreign kings and bring back Lot, all the other people, and their possessions (Gen 14:13-16, 24). This incident took place before the first time God articulated his relationship with Abram in covenant terms in Genesis 15:7-21 (note esp. Gen 15:18: "On that day the LORD made a covenant with Abram"). Before Genesis 15, God's promises to Abram were all stated in terms of promise and obligation language (see Gen 12:1-3; 13:14-18; 15:1-6), not specifically treaty language.

There are also three other passages within the patriarchal narratives that show how they used covenant/treaty terminology on the human level: one for Abraham (Gen 21:27-32), one for Isaac (Gen 26:26-31),

---

[19]See Greengus, "Covenant and Treaty," 95-101 for such covenants in the ANE and the Bible. The application of the same terminology to the Noahic covenant (see above) before the patriarchal period only reflects the knowledge of the same ANE backgrounds by the writer, Moses; see Greengus, "Covenant and Treaty," 101-2.

and one for Jacob (Gen 31:44-54). Take the treaty with Isaac, for example. The people of Gerar had mistreated him (Gen 26:12-21), so he moved out of their territory (Gen 26:22-25). Afterward, Abimelech, the ruler of Gerar, and his officials came to make a treaty (*bərît*) with Isaac in order to overcome the ill feelings between them (Gen 26:26-27). The most pertinent elements of the scene are when Abimelech and his officials spoke to Isaac and Isaac responded accordingly, "'There ought to be a *sworn agreement* [lit. "oath"] between us—between us and you. Let us *make a treaty* [lit. "cut a covenant"] with you that you will do us no harm.' . . . Isaac then made a feast for them, and *they ate and drank*. Early the next morning the men *swore an oath* to each other. Then Isaac sent them on their way, and they left him in peace" (Gen 26:28-31). This is characteristic of such an arrangement in the Genesis patriarchal passages. Note in particular the swearing of the oath and the eating of the covenant meal. The treaty/covenant between Jacob and Laban in Genesis 31:44-54 also includes both swearing oaths and eating a meal together. The one between Abraham and Abimelech in Genesis 21:27-32, however, focuses on swearing oaths (in an interesting play on words) with no specific mention of eating a meal together.

Alongside the statement of the stipulations, swearing an oath and eating a meal together were the two most common customs associated with treaty or covenant making.[20] There are instances where there is no meal, or at least there is no explicit indication of one, but often both of them appear together in a covenant-making ritual procedure. They are complementary and emphasize the two major foci of such a bond. The oath gave the covenant bond a *commitment* focus. The meal put the focus on the *relationship* established between the parties. In the ancient Near Eastern world, people did not

---

[20]See the discussion of the ceremonial features of making covenants in Menahem Haran, "The *Bĕrît* 'Covenant': Its Nature and Ceremonial Background," in *Tehillah le-Moshe: Biblical and Judaic Studies in Honor of Moshe Greenberg*, ed. Mordechai Cogan et al. (Winona Lake, IN: Eisenbrauns, 1997), 203-19. See also Greengus, "Covenant and Treaty," 109-12.

normally eat together unless they had a committed relationship with one another. A covenant (or treaty) was first of all, and above all, a committed relational bond, whether between different individuals or groups of people (on the horizontal plane), or between God and people (on the vertical plane). In making his redemptive covenants, therefore, God used an available cultural institution as a metaphorical analogy that the people would have understood in that day. Then and now it lends a certain quality to his revelation of the way he does relationship with his people, fallen and corrupt though we all are.

THE MAKING OF REDEMPTIVE COVENANTS IN THE BIBLE

The Old Testament Mosaic law stands within the Mosaic covenant as the "words," or one might say the "stipulations," of the covenant (see, e.g., Ex 19:5; 24:7-8; Lev 26:9, 42-45; Deut 5:2-3; 29:1, 9). In turn, the Mosaic covenant provides the primary covenantal context for the Old Testament law. The legal regulations extend from Exodus 20 through Deuteronomy 26, and fit historically into the narrative of Israel's forty-year wilderness experience from Egypt to Sinai to Moab in the days of Moses. In turn, the Mosaic covenant is part of a much larger group of interrelated covenants between God and his people running through the Old Testament and into the New Testament. We will pay special attention to four of them—the Abrahamic, Mosaic, Davidic, and new covenants. The relationship between these covenants— especially the Mosaic and new covenants—is of special importance in the discussion of the Old Testament law in relation to the New Testament, the church, and the believer.

The discussion that follows will include some remarks on the ancient Near Eastern background of the treaties and covenants in the Bible, but a full treatment is beyond the scope of this book.[21] It is important to recognize that originally the Hebrew Bible spoke into

---

[21]See now esp. Greengus, "Covenant and Treaty," and all the primary and secondary literature cited there.

the ancient Near Eastern world. The ancient Israelites were ancient Near Eastern people. God approached them in their real-world context and communicated to them in ways that would have made sense to them in that time, place, and culture. The way the Mosaic covenant fits into and relates to the overall covenant program of God through history will provide an important underlying perspective for grasping the nature and makeup of the Old Testament law, how God intended it to work in ancient Israel, and how it relates to the new covenant in which we live today. We will focus our attention here on the making of the Abrahamic and Mosaic covenants, and then develop the relationships between all four redemptive covenants in the next chapter.

MAKING THE ABRAHAMIC COVENANT

God's call and commission of Abram in Genesis 12:1-3 is foundational to all that follows in the Abraham narratives, including the covenant enactment passages in Genesis 15 and Genesis 17 (recall that God did not change Abram's name to Abraham until Gen 17:5). The first of these focuses on the land promise, and the second on the seed promise (but does not exclude the land promise).[22] Genesis 15:7-21 is especially important for our purposes here. The previous unit is famous for the well-known finale in Genesis 15:6, "Abram believed the LORD, and he credited it to him as righteousness." The apostle Paul uses this passage in Galatians 3 and Romans 4 to argue for the basic gospel principle of salvation through justification by God's grace through faith, not by works—not even by the works called for in God's Old Testament law. God had not even revealed his law yet in the days of Abraham. In Genesis 15:6, Abram believed in God's promise of a multitude of descendants in the previous two verses, and God justified him based on that trust. Today we place our faith in the ultimate seed of Abraham, Jesus Christ our Lord. Similarly, circumcision does not bring salvific

---

[22]For a discussion of the permanence of the land promise see Averbeck, "Israel, the Jewish People, and God's Covenants," 28-30.

justification, since Genesis 15 comes before the institution of circumcision in Genesis 17.

The next few verses focus specifically on the land promise: "He also said to him, 'I am the LORD, who brought you out of Ur of the Chaldeans to give you this land to take possession of it.' But Abram said, 'O Sovereign LORD, how can I know that I will gain possession of it?'" This may sound to us like the opposite kind of response of that in Genesis 15:6, but God did not take offense. Abram was asking for a guarantee, and the making of the covenant that follows is just that. God had Abram divide animals into parts and set them across from each other (Gen 15:9-11). As sunset approached Abram fell into a deep, dark sleep (Gen 15:12), within which God spoke promises to him (Gen 15:13-16). This brings us to Genesis 15:17, "When the sun had set and darkness had fallen, a smoking firepot with a blazing torch appeared and passed between the pieces."

The relationship between the deep, dark sleep in Genesis 15:12 and the sunset and darkness in Genesis 15:17 is not clear. Either he remained in the condition of Genesis 15:12, or he became conscious to witness God passing between the parts of the animals to confirm the promise of the land (Gen 15:18-21). There is no explicit explanation of the "smoking firepot" and "blazing torch" (Gen 15:17). The ancient Israelite readers to whom Moses was writing, however, would likely have associated it with God's presence and guidance in their experience. They would recall the pillars of cloud by day and fire by night that led them out of Egypt and through the wilderness (e.g., Ex 13:21-22; 14:19, 24; 40:36-38; cf. Is 4:5), or the smoke, fire, and torch in his theophany at Mount Sinai, or perhaps both (Ex 19:18; 20:18; cf. Is 31:9).[23] God made the promises here, and he himself passed between the parts of the animals. Abram makes no commitments here; God does.[24]

---

[23]For the association with the Sinai theophany, see Seth D. Postell, "Abram as Israel, Israel as Abram: Literary analogy as Macro-Structural Strategy in the Torah," *TynBul* 67 (2016): 171-73.

[24]See, e.g., Nahum M. Sarna, *The JPS Torah Commentary: Genesis* (Philadelphia: Jewish Publication Society, 1989), 117, 359n20; Claus Westermann, *Genesis 12–36: A Commentary*, trans. John J.

There is a helpful parallel in Jeremiah 34. In that day the Lord had made a covenant with the Israelites to free their Hebrew brothers from slavery in the land. They broke the covenant (Jer 34:12-16). So the Lord proclaimed sarcastically that he would give them their "freedom" all right; that is, "'freedom' to fall by the sword, plague and famine" (Jer 34:17). The next verses are clear and to the point, "The men who have violated my covenant and have not fulfilled the terms of the covenant they made before me, I will treat *like the calf they cut in two and then walked between its pieces.* The leaders of Judah and Jerusalem, the court officials, the priests and all the people of the land *who walked between the pieces of the calf*" (Jer 34:18-19). The end result would be that "Their dead bodies will become food for the birds of the air and the beasts of the earth" (Jer 34:20).

It is significant that in Genesis 15:11, "birds of prey came down on the carcasses, but Abram drove them away." In Jeremiah 34:20 the carcasses that would be eaten by the birds and beasts are those of the dead men who had violated the covenant. The parts of the animals in Genesis 15:11, therefore, represent the Lord, since he was the only one who passed between the parts. Abram, therefore, would not allow the scavenger birds to eat them. He knew exactly what the Lord was doing here. This was a self-curse. By passing between the (parts of the) animals the Lord was saying something like this: if I do not keep this covenant oath with Abram, let me be chopped into parts like these animals and my carcass eaten by the scavenger birds and the wild beasts. We have parallels to similar practices in treaty texts from elsewhere in the ancient Near East.[25] For example, in a Mari text (eighteenth century BC), we read in a treaty-making context that an official had brought about an agreement "to kill a donkey between [*birīt*] the Hana people and the Idamaraz." In a later Neo-Assyrian text (eighth century BC) we read about a king making a treaty with a vassal by

---

Scullion S. J. (Minneapolis: Augsburg, 1985), 228; Allen P. Ross, *Creation and Blessing: A Guide to the Study and Exposition of the Book of Genesis* (Grand Rapids, MI: Baker, 1988), 312-13.
[25]Greengus, "Covenant and Treaty," 94-95, 110-11.

cutting up a lamb piece by peace and proclaiming sanctions like, "This head is not the head of a spring lamb. It is the head of Mati'ilu, it is the head of his sons, his magnates, the people of his land," if he does not keep the stipulations of the treaty.[26]

Thus, the procedure in Genesis 15 was a way of answering Abram's original question in Genesis 15:7 ("how can I know that I will gain possession of this land?"). It was a particular kind of covenant oath enactment meant to convince Abram that this was an irrevocable promise from God to him. When I was a child, we would sometimes make oaths with the expression, "cross my heart and hope to die." God was guaranteeing this covenant promise to Abram with an enactment that said essentially the same thing, but he was not playing around like we were as children.

For various reasons some have questioned this interpretation, as obvious as it is.[27] Among other things, they have thought that the notion of God taking part in a rite that would enact such a self-curse is sacrilegious. However, this is essentially what Jesus went through on the cross for us. He became a curse for us (Gal 3:13). Our God is a radical God. He goes to great lengths to have a relationship with us as fallen people. There is no covenant meal here in Genesis 15 because the whole point of the exercise was to guarantee the land promise to Abram by oath. The oath was the sole purpose of this covenant enactment. Both Genesis 15 and Jeremiah 34 refer to walking between the parts of cut up animals as a self-curse. There is no sacrificial procedure for the making of the Abrahamic covenant in Genesis 17. There the focus is on the covenant seed and land promises of God (Gen 17:2, 6-8) and Abraham's covenant obligations of obedience (Gen 17:1) and circumcision (Gen 17:9-14).

---

[26]See Greengus, "Covenant and Treaty," 110-11, and the more extensive literature cited there.

[27]I do not find Wenham's alternative explanation convincing. He argues that the parts of the animals were representative of the nation of Israel; Wenham, *Genesis 1-15*, 332-33. Richard Hess, "The Slaughter of the Animals in Genesis 15: Genesis 15:8-21 and Its Ancient Near Eastern Context," in *He Swore an Oath*, edited by R. S. Hess et al. (Grand Rapids, MI: Baker, 1994), 55-65, follows Wenham here.

As noted earlier, the most common terminology for making a covenant in the Old Testament is literally "to cut [*kārat*] a covenant [*bərît*]" (about 90 occurrences). The first occurrence of this expression in the Bible is Genesis 15:18, "On that day the LORD made [*kārat*, lit. 'cut'] a covenant [*bərît*] with Abram and said, 'To your descendants I give this land, from the river of Egypt to the great river, the Euphrates.'" Some think the "cutting" originally comes from the ritual procedure of cutting up the animals that Abram cut up in the ritual procedure (Gen 15:9-11, 17). The parallel passage in Jeremiah 34:18-20 is especially significant in this regard. Both *kārat* and *bərît* occur twice in Jeremiah 34:18, once in the combination *kārat bərît*, and then *kārat* as the verb for cutting up the calf. "Those who have violated my covenant [*bərît*] and have not fulfilled the terms of the covenant [*bərît*] they made [*kārat*] before me, I will treat like the calf they cut [*kārat*] in two and then walked between its pieces."

Others take *bərît* to derive from the Akkadian noun "*birītu*" clasp, fetter" (or *birit* "between" or *biritu* "space between") and *kārat bərît* as related to the Aramaic expression *gəzar adê* "to cut (i.e., 'determine') stipulations (for a treaty)" (cf. also Akkadian *adû/adê* "treaty, oath," which is related to the Hebrew *ʿēd/ ʿēdût/ ʿēdôt* "testimony," and in the plural, "covenant or contractual obligations").[28] In this case, the idiom "to cut a covenant" would mean "to establish (or determine) the obligations (or stipulations)" of a relationship between two persons or groups of persons. The verb meaning "to cut" in Semitic languages, and in other unrelated languages as well, can often mean to "determine" or "establish" boundaries or limitations. Consider even in English our

---

[28]See Weinfeld, "*bərît*," *TDOT* 2:257 and *HALOT* 790-91. For a very good discussion of all the biblical and ANE terminology for treaty/covenant and covenant making, see Kenneth A. Kitchen and Paul J. N. Lawrence, eds., *Treaty, Law and Covenant in the Ancient Near East*, 3 vols. (Wiesbaden: Harrasowitz, 2012), 2:233-44. For the expression *gəzar adê* in Aramaic, see the Sefire treaties; John C. L. Gibson, *Textbook of Syrian Semitic Inscriptions*, vol. 2: *Aramaic Inscriptions* (Oxford: Oxford University Press, 1975), p. 28 line 7. See also W. F. Albright, "The Expression for 'Making a Covenant' in Pre-Israelite Documents," *BASOR* 121 (February 1951): 21-22, and also the remarks in Peter C. Craigie, *The Book of Deuteronomy*, NICOT (Grand Rapids, MI: Eerdmans, 1976), 81, esp. n. 8. For the Akkadian terminology, see *CAD* vol. A part 1, 131-35 for *adû*; vol. B, 249-55 for *birīt(u)*; and vol. R, 347-55, esp. 353-54, for *riksu*, "bond."

expression "to cut a deal" or "to cut a contract." The Hebrew idiom "to cut a covenant," therefore, may derive from the concept of cutting in the sense of "determining"—in this case determining the stipulations of a covenant bond.

Perhaps at one stage the expression *kārat bərît* reflected the actual cutting up of the ritual animal for making a covenant, but then the derivation was lost and the expression came to mean "to cut (i.e., 'make') a covenant" (i.e., determine covenant obligations).[29] Of course, we cannot really determine the meanings that words or expressions had for their users through etymologies. We need to look at their usage in context, according to the way they contribute to the meanings of the passages in which they actually occur.

MAKING THE MOSAIC COVENANT

The ritual for the ratification of the Mosaic covenant in Exodus 24:1-11 is similar in some respects to that in Genesis 15, but very different in others. Here we have both a covenant oath (Ex 24:3-8) and a covenant meal (Ex 24:1-2, 9-11). Initially, God called Moses with "Aaron, Nadab and Abihu, and seventy of the elders of Israel" up on the mountain to worship him there together (Ex 24:1-2). In anticipation of that, Moses enacted a covenant oath ceremony with all Israel at the foot of the mountain (Ex 24:3-8). He told the people all the Lord's words and the laws of the covenant. The people responded, "Everything the LORD has said we will do" (Ex 24:3). So Moses wrote down what is referred to later in the passage as "the book of the covenant" (Ex 24:4, 7; essentially Ex 21–23). Then early the next morning he built an altar "and set up twelve stone pillars representing the twelve tribes of Israel" and offered burnt offerings and sacrificed peace offerings there.

Then we come to the actual oath ceremony. Moses took half the blood of the offerings and sacrifices and splashed it on the altar. The altar represented the Lord in the ritual procedure since what

---

[29]Greengus, "Covenant and Treaty," 94.

goes on the altar by nature goes to the Lord. Then, Moses read the book of the covenant to the people and they responded, "We will do everything the LORD has said; we will obey" (Ex 24:7). This, of course, is the covenant oath statement. After that Moses took the (other half of the) blood, splashed it on the people and said, "This is the blood of the covenant that the LORD has made with you in accordance with all these words" (Ex 24:8). Thus, blood from the same animals that he splashed on the altar he also splashed on the people, thereby binding the Lord and the people together in a blood covenant. The book of the covenant that Moses read in between the two blood manipulations constituted the terms (i.e., the stipulations) of the covenant commitment. There are differences, but this sounds quite similar to the Abba-El(AN) and Zimrilim treaty ritual and formula from the second millennium BC at Alalakh: "Abba-AN is under oath to Yarimlim, and also he cut the neck of a lamb. (He swore:) 'I shall never take back what I gave thee.' If in the days to come Yarimlim sins against Abba-AN . . . he [shall forfe]it his cities and territories. Further, if a successor of Yarimlim sins against Abba-AN . . ."[30]

Thus, they made a blood oath covenant with the Lord. It was only after the ceremony at the bottom of the mountain that Moses complied with the Lord's earlier command: "Moses and Aaron, Nadab and Abihu, and the seventy elders of Israel went up and saw the God of Israel" (Ex 24:9-10). Then at the very end we read, "they saw God, and they ate and drank" (Ex 24:11). This, of course, is the covenant ratification meal. The text does not actually say this, but the people would have been celebrating a covenant enactment banquet at the base of the mountain. This is what they would do with the meat from "fellowship (peace offering) sacrifices," as opposed to "burnt offerings,"

---

[30]Dennis J. McCarthy, S. J., *Treaty and Covenant: A Study in Form in the Ancient Oriental Documents and in the Old Testament*, rev. ed. (Rome: Biblical Institute Press, 1981), 307. No one would argue that the oath here is unconnected to the ritual cutting of the throat of the lamb. To split the oath off from the ritual is just as unlikely in Ex 24:6-8. See also other texts sighted in relation to this passage in Greengus, "Covenant and Treaty," 109-10.

which the altar fire would have completely consumed. Moses, Aaron and his two sons, and the seventy elders would have eaten some of the peace offering meat along with the accompanying drink and bread offering on the top of the mountain in the very presence of the Lord (cf. Num 15:1-16).

Covenant renewals appear several times in the Old Testament. The first of these comes as a result of the golden calf debacle referred to above (Ex 32–34; note esp. Ex 34:10, 27-29). The next is the renewal of the original Mosaic covenant with a new generation of Israelites in Moab after forty years in the wilderness, as recounted in the book of Deuteronomy. There is some dispute over whether Deuteronomy ratifies a new covenant with Israel in Moab, forty years after the one made at Sinai, or renews that earlier covenant.[31] In my view, it renews the covenant at Sinai in anticipation of entering into the land. Deuteronomy 26:18-19 clearly echoes Exodus 19:5-6, the latter at the very beginning of the law at Sinai and the former at the very end of the law in Moab (i.e., the legal regulations end with Deut 26):

> "Now if you obey me fully and keep my covenant, then out of all nations you will be *my treasured possession*. Although the whole earth is mine, you will be for me a kingdom of priests and *a holy nation*." These are the words you are to speak to the Israelites. (Ex 19:5-6)

> And the LORD has declared this day that you are his people, *his treasured possession as he promised*, and that you are to keep all his commands. He has declared that he will set you in praise, fame and honor high above all the nations he has made and that you will be *a people holy* to the LORD your God, *as he promised*. (Deut 26:18-19)

The use of common expressions between them ("treasured possession" and "holy nation/people") suggests that Deuteronomy 26:18-19 echoes Exodus 19:5-6, and the twofold note "as he promised" supports this understanding. In other words, the end of the law echoes its

---

[31]Greengus, "Covenant and Treaty," 112-18, argues that it is a new divine covenant with the next generation of Israel.

beginning, thus creating the larger canonical framework for the law as a whole in the Pentateuch.[32]

The differences between the law as given at Sinai in Exodus and Leviticus as opposed to the law in Deuteronomy are due to three major factors. First, the giving of the law at Sinai still had to anticipate the travel from Sinai to the Promised Land, although at that point this was not expected to be more than a month or two. In Deuteronomy they had already arrived in Moab, just across the Jordan River, anticipating their entry into the Promised Land, but this was forty years later. This required certain adjustments to the regulations. For example, Leviticus 17:1-7 requires that, while they travel through the wilderness and dwell together around the tabernacle, they must be sure to slaughter domesticated animals for food only at the tabernacle so that they could offer their blood and fat on the altar to the Lord. This would avoid illegitimate sacrifice in the wilderness. Deuteronomy 12, however, allows for "profane" slaughter of domesticated animals as long as they poured out the blood on the ground as they did with wild game. Since they would be spread out in the land, God did not require them to take a long trip to where the tabernacle was located whenever they wanted to have meat for dinner (Deut 12:16-25).[33]

Second, on the one hand, the Lord gave the law through Moses as the mediator at Sinai. On the other hand, Moses was "preaching" the law to the second generation of the Israelite nation in Moab, urging them to obey God's law after they entered into the Promised Land: "East of the Jordan in the territory of Moab, Moses began to *expound* this law" (Deut 1:5). In Exodus and Leviticus, he was functioning as

---

[32]For a much more detailed explanation, see Richard E. Averbeck, "The Egyptian Sojourn and Deliverance from Slavery in the Framing and Shaping of the Mosaic Law," in *"Did I Not Bring Israel Out of Egypt?" Biblical, Archaeological, and Egyptological Perspectives on the Exodus Narratives*, BBRSup, ed. James Hoffmeier, Alan Millard, and Gary Rendsburg (Winona Lake, IN: Eisenbrauns, 2016), 144-50.

[33]See Richard E. Averbeck, "The Cult in Deuteronomy and Its Relationship to the Book of the Covenant and the Holiness Code," in *Sepher Torath Mosheh: Studies in the Composition and Interpretation of Deuteronomy*, ed. Daniel I. Block and Richard L. Schultz (Peabody, MA: Hendrickson, 2017), 232-60, for a full discussion.

the priest. He served as a priest, for example, when he performed the ritual procedures for ordaining the Aaronic priesthood (Lev 8; cf. also Ex 24:3-8). In Deuteronomy, he functioned as a prophet, preaching obedience to the law given at Sinai. The word *expound* means to explain and elucidate. This is why the book consists largely of first-person speeches by Moses. For example, Deuteronomy 1:5 introduces the speech that runs through the first part of the historical prologue to Deuteronomy 3:29 (see also Deut 4:1; 5:1; 6:1; 8:1; 11:26; 27:1; 29:2; 30:1, 11; 31:1, 30; 33:1-2). He was not "legislating" the law a second time but preaching the revelation that he had previously mediated at Sinai, expanding and emphasizing elements of it as he went, as good preachers do. If one wants to know how to preach the law, Moses provides us with a good pattern to follow.

Third, although the book of Deuteronomy consists largely of expository first-person speeches by Moses at the end of his life, many have argued it also follows quite closely the pattern of a second-millennium BC Hittite suzerain vassal treaty. Exodus 19–24 does not. The latter is a covenant-making narrative with documents inserted into it (i.e., the Ten Commandments in Ex 20:1-17 and the book of the covenant in Ex 21–23; cf. Ex 24:4, 7). There has been a good deal of scholarly discussion about the structure of Deuteronomy, its relationship to the vassal treaties, and its implications for dating and interpreting the book.[34]

It seems to me that we should take this comparative background seriously, though it is not a hard and fast comparison. Deuteronomy also has its own special features. In any case, as a covenant document similar in form to the extant second-millennium Hittite suzerain

---

[34]For a brief summary see K. A. Kitchen, *On the Reliability of the Old Testament* (Grand Rapids, MI: Eerdmans, 2003), 283-312; and for a more detailed treatment, citing all the documents available, see Kitchen and Lawrence, *Treaty, Law and Covenant in the Ancient Near East*, 3:93-214. See now also the careful analysis in Neal A. Huddleston, "Ancient Near Eastern Treaty Traditions and Their Implications for Interpreting Deuteronomy," and K. Lawson Younger Jr. and Neal A. Huddleston, "Challenges to the Use of Ancient Near Eastern Treaty Forms for Dating and Interpreting Deuteronomy," both in Block and Schultz, *Sepher Torath Mosheh*, 30-77 and 78-109 respectively. See also Greengus, "Covenant and Treaty," 112-18.

vassal treaties, Deuteronomy falls into six major sections, with variations in how scholars see the details: title/preamble (Deut 1:1-5), historical prologue (Deut 1:6–3:29), stipulations (Deut 4:1–26:19), depositing and reading the text (Deut 31:9-26), witnesses (Deut 31:19–32:47), and blessings and curses (Deut 28). Exodus 19–24 does not display this pattern to any significant degree. Some extend the view to reach from Exodus 20 to Leviticus 26:46, "These are the decrees, the laws and the regulations that the LORD established at Mount Sinai between himself and the Israelites through Moses."[35] This would enable a stronger comparison.

The main point here, however, is that Moses apparently enacted the covenant with the second generation through some kind of ritual process similar to Exodus 24:1-11. Deuteronomy 26:16-17 seems to suggest this: "You have declared this day that the LORD is your God and that you will walk in obedience to him. . . . And the LORD has declared this day that you are his people, his treasured possession." Deuteronomy 29:1, 12 are even more to the point when they refer to "a covenant the LORD is making with you this day and sealing with an oath" (cf. also Deut 29:15 "making this covenant, with its oath").[36] The text simply says that God was making a covenant with the people but, as argued above, it was actually a renewal of the one made earlier, soon after they arrived at Sinai forty years earlier. The same terminology appears, for example, near the end of Joshua's life when he warned the people against violating the Mosaic covenant (Josh 23:16), leading directly into a renewal of the same covenant (Josh 24; see esp. Josh 24:25). Similarly, even though the term *covenant* does not appear, when Samuel drew the people together at Gilgal in 1 Samuel 12 to "renew the kingship" (1 Sam 11:14), it was a renewal of their commitment to covenant faithfulness (cf. also 2 Chron 15:10-15; 29:10, etc.).[37]

---

[35]See, e.g., Kitchen, *Reliability of the Old Testament*, 284.

[36]Averbeck, "The Egyptian Sojourn and Deliverance from Slavery," 144-47.

[37]J. Robert Vannoy, *Covenant Renewal at Gilgal: A Study of 1 Samuel 11:14–12:25* (Cherry Hill, NJ: Mack, 1978). See Greengus, "Covenant and Treaty," 118-25, for a more complete review of covenant renewals in the Hebrew Bible.

CONCLUSION

There is a fascinating connection between the ratification of the Mosaic covenant in Exodus 24 and the Lord's Supper in the New Testament. We can see this especially in Luke 22:14-20 (cf. the parallels in Mt 26:26-30; Mk 14:22-26; 1 Cor 11:23-26). As is clear from the context, the Lord's Supper took place as part of Jesus' last celebration of the Passover (Lk 22:7-13). Near the end of the Passover meal Jesus did what we call "ritualization." He created a new ritual from the Passover ritual—namely, what we now call the Lord's Supper, or the Last Supper, or the Eucharist, depending on which term one prefers or the church traditions associated with it. He begins by taking some bread, giving thanks, breaking it, and handing it to them, saying, "This is my body given for you; do this in remembrance of me" (Lk 22:19). After they were finished eating the bread, he took the cup and said, "This cup is the new covenant in my blood, which is poured out for you" (Lk 22:20).

For our purposes, what is especially striking is the correspondence of the new covenant ritual in Luke 22 to the ritual for the ratification of the Mosaic covenant in Exodus 24. It would have been hard for a first-century Jew to miss the connection. The bread corresponds to the eating of the covenant meal on the mountain (Ex 24:9-11). Perhaps it is even significant that in Luke 22 they were in an "upper room" (Lk 22:12). The cup of wine corresponds to the blood ritual in Exodus 24:6-8. In fact, the statement that Jesus made echoes that of Moses: "This is the blood of the covenant that the LORD has made with you" (Ex 24:8). As Jesus said it: "This cup is the new covenant in my blood" (Lk 22:20). Of course, there are differences too. Jesus, for example, was using wine to represent his blood, anticipating his death on the cross as the new covenant sacrifice. The sacrifices in Exodus 24 were real blood sacrifices, like Jesus' own bloody sacrifice would be on the cross, which is what he was anticipating. In Exodus 24 they were also eating the meat of actual animals, not just bread. The point is that Moses offered sacrifices that ratified the Mosaic covenant, and

Jesus was about to offer himself as the sacrifice of the new covenant, a better sacrifice (see, e.g., Heb 9:23).

The Lord's Supper, therefore, is essentially a covenant oath (the wine as blood; cf. Ex 24:6-8) and a covenant meal (the bread; cf. Ex 24:9-11). Jesus meant us to practice it regularly as a means of covenant renewal and recommitment to the Lord and to one another in the Lord. This is the main reason Paul was so concerned about how they were practicing the Lord's Supper at Corinth (1 Cor 11:17-34). It is no small matter. There are two sides to the practice of the Lord's Supper. On the one hand, it is about looking back in remembrance of what Jesus did for us on the cross. At the same time, we look forward and commit our life to fulfilling our new covenant obligations to God and one another. It is a covenant renewal ritual.

Our God is an extreme God. He went to great lengths to redeem us through the blood sacrifice of his own eternal Son. The sacrifice of Jesus the Christ ratified the new covenant in which we have eternal life and an ongoing personal relationship with God. We practice the Lord's Supper as a regular renewal of our commitment to live faithfully before the Lord in this world here and now.

Two

THE NATURE AND PROGRESSION OF THE REDEMPTIVE COVENANTS

THE PREVIOUS CHAPTER INTRODUCED treaty and covenant in the Bible and the ancient Near East. We also paid special attention to the making of the Abrahamic and Mosaic covenants, and the connection of the latter to the making of the new covenant. In the present chapter, we turn our attention specifically to the substance of the four main redemptive covenants in the Old Testament: the Abrahamic, Mosaic, Davidic, and new covenants. We will also deal with the relationships between these four covenants, their progression through the canon, and the ways all four of them come through into the New Testament.[1]

There are, of course, other important covenants in the Old Testament. We discussed the Noahic covenant in the previous chapter. Another would be God's perpetual covenant commitment to the priests (Num 18:19: "a covenant of salt"; cf. Lev 2:13; and 2 Chron 13:5 for the covenant with David) and the Levites (Neh 13:29; Jer 33:20-25;

---

[1]Some of the material here is covered from a different perspective in Richard E. Averbeck, "Israel, the Jewish People, and God's Covenants," in *Israel, the Church, and the Middles East: A Biblical Response to the Current Conflict*, ed. Darrell L. Bock and Mitch Glaser (Grand Rapids, MI: Kregel, 2018), 30-37.

Mal 2:1-9), and especially Phinehas, one of the four sons of Aaron, the high priest (Num 25:12-13). The perpetual covenant between God and Phinehas continues all the way through the Old Testament and beyond in the form of the high priesthood of the Zadokites, descendants of Phinehas, in the restored temple of Ezekiel 40–48 (see Ezek 44:15 with 1 Chron 6:4-8, 48-53).[2] According to Jeremiah 33:14-26, this covenant with the Levitical priests is on the same level as the one with David. Neither of these families will ever lack a representative as long as the heaven and earth remain in place.[3] The expressions of perpetuity here resemble those for the new covenant (Jer 31:35-37; cf. also the Noahic covenant in Gen 8:22).

Other passages use the term *covenant* for other kinds of personal relationships and alliances such as the one between Jonathan and David (1 Sam 18:3; 20:8; 23:18). Here the connection between covenant (*bərît*) and relational loyalty (*ḥesed*) appears: "As for you (Jonathan), show kindness [*ḥesed*] to your servant [David], for you have brought him into a covenant with you before the LORD" (1 Sam 20:8). The opposite of such loyalty in a covenant relationship appears in the passage about marriage as a covenant in Malachi 2:14: "The LORD is the witness between you and the wife of your youth. You have been unfaithful [*bāgad*], though she is your partner, the wife of your marriage covenant [lit. 'the woman/wife of your covenant']." Marriage as a covenant is also seen in Proverbs 2:16-17. The marriage covenant as a metaphor for the Lord's relationship with Israel appears, for example, in Hosea 1–3, Jeremiah 31:32, and Ezekiel 16:8, 20-22.[4] Many more passages show these connections in various kinds

---

[2]For a concise but relatively detailed discussion of the history of the Aaronic priesthood, including the priestly covenant with Phinehas, see Richard E. Averbeck, "Priest and Priesthood," in *The Evangelical Dictionary of Biblical Theology*, ed. Walter A. Elwell (Grand Rapids, MI: Baker, 1996), 632-38, esp. 635-36.

[3]See Samuel Greengus, "Covenant and Treaty in the Hebrew Bible and in the Ancient Near East," in *Ancient Israel's History: An Introduction to Issues and Sources*, ed. Bill T. Arnold and Richard S. Hess (Grand Rapids, MI: Baker Academic, 2014), 103-6. The Jer 33:14-26 passage appears in the Hebrew Bible, but not in the LXX.

[4]See the full treatment in G. P. Hugenberger, *Marriage as a Covenant: A Study of Biblical Law and Ethics Governing Marriage, Developed from the Perspective of Malachi* (Leiden: Brill, 1994).

of committed relationships. It is not our purpose to review all of them here. Our main concern in the present chapter is the nature and progression of the four redemptive covenants and the relationships between them.

PERMANENT PROMISE AND ONGOING OBLIGATION

It is often argued that certain of the major covenants were conditional or administrative—that is, placing obligations on the people involved. Some put the Mosaic covenant in this category, and some even put the new covenant here in certain cases. Conversely, other covenants were unconditional or promissory—not placing obligations on the people involved. Usually the Abrahamic and Davidic covenants are viewed this way.[5]

There are several serious problems with this approach. First, it simply does not work scripturally. As we consider the covenant passages below, it will become clear that the supposed conditional covenants are sometimes stated unconditionally and, conversely, the supposed unconditional covenants are sometimes stated conditionally.[6] Thus, we get tangled up with the way the Bible actually talks about the covenants in certain passages. At a minimum, dividing the covenants along conditional versus unconditional lines is misleading and takes the discussion in unhelpful directions.

Second, in spite of arguments to the contrary, this conditional versus unconditional distinction does not work with the analogues (i.e., comparative literature) from the ancient Near East. Some have argued that ancient Near Eastern kings made royal grants to subordinates without any obligations required of them. Based on this

---

[5]See, e.g., Thomas Edward McComiskey, *The Covenants of Promise: A Theology of the Old Testament Covenants* (Grand Rapids, MI: Baker, 1985). Several negative critiques of McComiskey's book appeared quite soon after its publication. See, e.g., Meredith Kline's book review in *JETS* 30 (1987): 77-80.

[6]See esp. Bruce K. Waltke, "The Phenomenon of Conditionality Within the Unconditional Covenants," and William J. Dumbrell, "The Prospect of Unconditionality in the Sinaitic Covenant," in *Israel's Apostasy and Restoration: Essays in Honor of Roland K. Harrison*, ed. A. Gileadi (Grand Rapids, MI: Baker, 1988), 123-39 and 141-55, respectively.

supposed distinction, certain of the covenants, specifically the Abrahamic and Davidic covenants, are seen to be promissory, with no obligations imposed on the recipient of the covenant grant.[7] But this is simply not how royal grants worked in the first place.[8]

In light of these realities, we need to abandon the supposed conditional versus unconditional distinction between the covenants. There is a better way. All four redemptive covenants have two sides: permanent promise and ongoing obligation. This is not to say that all the passages related to these covenants put equal emphasis on both. There is a great deal of flexibility in this regard. It all depends on the purpose of the covenant or covenant-making procedure in its particular historical and textual context. In any case, this combination of permanent promise and ongoing obligation is what the verses inserted under the covenants in the umbrella chart (see figure 1) are intended to illustrate. The point is that the *promises* assure the enduring nature of a covenant relationship no matter what may happen, while the *obligations* focus on the importance of faithfulness to God in order to experience the Lord's blessings within the covenant relationship (as opposed to his chastisement, the curses). Like good relationships everywhere in all times, all four redemptive covenants consist of a combination of permanent promise along with ongoing obligation.

God built elements of both promise (yielding peace in the relationship) and obligation (yielding purpose in the relationship) into the very organic nature of his redemptive covenant program. Neither of these elements makes good covenant sense without the other. Numerous

---

[7] See esp. Moshe Weinfeld, "The Covenant of Grant in the Old Testament and in the Ancient Near East," *JAOS* 90: 184-203; "The Loyalty Oath in the Ancient Near East," *UF* 9 (1976): 379-414; and "b^erît," in *TDOT* 2:253-79. Peter J. Gentry and Stephen J. Wellum, *Kingdom Through Covenant: A Biblical-Theological Understanding of the Covenants*, 2nd ed. (Wheaton, IL: Crossway, 2018), 161-67, seem to accept the distinction between ancient Near Eastern grants and treaties and their importance to distinctions between the redemptive covenants. However, they are also rightly concerned that we not impose this ANE analogue on the biblical covenants in an artificial way that overrides the covenants as the Bible presents them.

[8] See the full review and critique of Weinfeld's proposal in Gary N. Knoppers, "Ancient Near Eastern Royal Grants and the Davidic Covenant: A Parallel?" *JAOS* 116 (1996): 670-97; and Richard S. Hess, "The Book of Joshua as a Land Grant," *Biblica* 83 (2002): 493-95, 505-6.

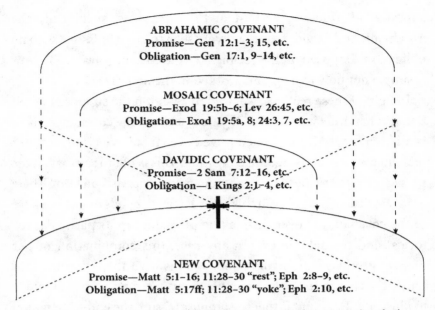

NOTE: Both promise (yielding peace) and obligation (yielding purpose) are built into the very organic nature of God's redemptive program. One makes no sense and will not work without the other. Our "rest" depends upon the combination of the two.

Figure 1. Redemptive covenant structure in the Bible

passages in Scripture highlight this in one way or another. The discussion below will bear that out. We need both a solid place to stand in our relationship with God (permanent promise) and a direction to take in living out our relationship with him (ongoing obligation).

THE PROGRESSION OF THE REDEMPTIVE COVENANTS

The umbrella structure of the covenant chart (figure 1) illustrates the progressive historical development of the covenants and the interrelationships between them. The Abrahamic covenant (ca. 2050 or 1850 BC) takes historic priority over the Mosaic covenant (ca. 1445 or 1270 BC),[9] and the Mosaic covenant over the Davidic covenant

---

[9]The optional dates for the Abrahamic and Mosaic covenants depend on how one interprets the 480 years of 1 Kings 6:1: "In the four hundred and eightieth year after the Israelites had come out of Egypt, in the fourth year of Solomon's reign over Israel . . . he began to build the temple of the

(ca. 1000 BC). Each functions under the umbrella of the previous covenant. Ancient Israel had never existed as an independent nation in need of independent self- (or theocratic) regulation before the time of Moses and the exodus. They had grown from a family into a nation while in Egypt, where they were under the Egyptian government both before and during their slavery (Ex 1–2).

There would have been no Mosaic covenant without the Abrahamic covenant. The deliverance from Egypt and all that followed depended on the previous commitment to the patriarchs: "The Israelites groaned in their slavery and cried out, and their cry for help because of their slavery went up to God. God heard their groaning and he remembered his covenant with Abraham, with Isaac and with Jacob. So God looked on the Israelites and was concerned about them" (Ex 2:23-25; see also Ex 3:6). The covenant made at Sinai was a natural and necessary extension of the Lord's commitment to the patriarchs, which included a commitment to their descendants. The constituents of the Mosaic covenant were to have "Abrahamic faith" in the Lord as the foundation for faithfulness to the Lord as a people under the Mosaic covenant.

Similarly, there would be no Davidic covenant without the previous Abrahamic and Mosaic covenants. The Davidic kings were to rule according to the Mosaic law, as those who also had Abrahamic faith. The Mosaic covenant makes no sense without the Abrahamic, and the Davidic covenant makes no sense without both the Abrahamic and Mosaic covenants. The new covenant (anticipated ca. 600 BC in Jer 31:31-40 and inaugurated by Jesus ca. AD 30) draws on the three previous covenants and brings them all to fulfillment in the New Testament for the church and the believer.

LORD," and the reading of Ex 12:40. The Hebrew text of Ex 12:40 reads, "Now the length of time the Israelite people lived in Egypt was 430 years." The Samaritan Pentateuch and the Septuagint (Greek) translation (LXX) read instead, "in the land of Canaan and in the land of Egypt." The latter reading would include the patriarchal age in the 430 years and thus bring the date of the patriarchs down by about 215 years. For a careful discussion of the date of the exodus, see John H. Walton, "Exodus, Date of," in *Dictionary of the Old Testament: Pentateuch*, ed. T. Desmond Alexander and David W. Baker (Downers Grove, IL: IVP Academic, 2003), 258-72.

The Abrahamic, Mosaic, Davidic, and new covenants, as a set, therefore, build one on the other so that none of them eliminates the Lord's previous covenantal commitments and expectations. This is so in spite of the fact that they vary in terms of emphasis because of the situation in which they were enacted and the purpose of each particular covenant in its historical-redemptive context. As Paul puts it in Galatians 3:15-17,

> Brothers, let me take an example from everyday life. Just as no one can set aside or add to a human covenant that has been duly established, so it is in this case. The promises were spoken to Abraham and to his seed. Scripture does not say "and to seeds," meaning many people, but "and to your seed," meaning one person, who is Christ. What I mean is this: The law, introduced 430 years later, does not set aside the covenant previously established by God and thus do away with the promise.

The key point here is that this passage explicitly states a general principle (Gal 3:15) and then specifically applies it to the relationship between the Abrahamic and Mosaic covenants, and the law embedded in the latter (Gal 3:16-17). It does not bring the Davidic and new covenants into the picture, but the general principle still applies since it is, in fact, a general principle.

None of these covenants, therefore, sets aside the previous ones as one succeeds the other, but they build together into a compilation of God's ongoing covenantal commitments and his expectations for those who commit to him in those covenants. Our goal here is to understand exactly how the text articulates this and to follow through on its implications for how the Old Testament law applies to the church and the Christian life. The dotted lines with arrows pointing downward alongside the umbrellas from the Abrahamic, Mosaic, and Davidic covenants to the new covenant illustrate that all the previous covenants find their ultimate fulfillment in the new covenant. In other words, the accumulated effect of the promises and obligations of all three of these previous covenants come to fruition in the new covenant in one way or another. Christ is the ultimate "seed" of Abraham

(Gal 3:16),[10] and we are the children of Abraham by faith (e.g., Jn 8:31-39; Rom 4:9-16, esp. v. 16; Gal 3:7, 29). Christ is our Davidic king (e.g., Mt 2:2; 3:2; 4:17, 23; 5:3; 21:1-11; Acts 1:6; 3:17-26; 15:12-19; Col 1:13), and at the appropriate time he will bring his kingship to full and obvious manifestation on this earth (Rev 19–20, esp. Rev 20:6).

A similar continuity applies to the Mosaic covenant in relation to the new covenant. On the one hand, the discontinuity between them is made obvious in the shift from Jeremiah 31:31 to the next verse, where the Lord says that the new covenant "will *not* be like the covenant I made with their forefathers when I took them by the hand to lead them out of Egypt" (Jer 31:32). On the other hand, the Lord says only a verse later, "I will put *my law* in their minds and write it on their hearts. *I will be their God, and they will be my people*" (Jer 31:33). In other words, the Old Testament law, which is embedded in the Mosaic covenant, is *not* left behind in the new covenant. The "law" here is certainly the Mosaic law, just as the covenant in Jeremiah 31:32 is the Mosaic covenant. Jeremiah had focused on the concern for faithfulness to the covenant law in his ministry. Furthermore, the particular expression of identity and relationship between God and his people in the latter part of Jeremiah 31:32, commonly called the "covenant formulary," is constantly repeated in the Mosaic covenant context from beginning to end (see Ex 6:7; and esp. Ex 19:5-6).[11]

The Abrahamic covenant originally applied to the family of Abraham, not a nation, so the promises and obligations of that covenant were

---

[10]Paul's argument from the singular "seed" in Gal 3:16 has troubled commentators because of the well-known fact that "seed" in Genesis is commonly collective plural (e.g., Gen 13:16; 17:8-9). See the remarks in Ernest de Witt Burton, *The Epistle to the Galatians*, ICC (Edinburgh: T&T Clark, 1921), 181-82; and F. F. Bruce, *Galatians: A Commentary on the Greek Text* (Grand Rapids, MI: Eerdmans, 1982), 171-73. The best solution is that which the patriarchal narratives themselves suggest. According to Gen 17, Abraham was made to be fully aware that only *one* of his immediate "seed" was the "seed of promise" (see esp. Gen 17:18-19, 21, and Gen 21:12)—not Ishmael but Isaac. This pattern continues all the way through biblical history until Christ, who is both the ultimate seed of David and, in turn, the consummate seed of Abraham; see the helpful remarks in Bruce, *Galatians*, 172-73.

[11]See Rolf Rendtorff, *The Covenant Formulary: An Exegetical and Theological Investigation* (Edinburgh: T&T Clark, 1998).

suitable for a family. However, since the time of the patriarchs, the family of Abraham had grown into a nation and had therefore come to need guidance for their faith as a nation, not just as a family. When the Lord made the covenant with them at Sinai, he was deeply concerned about the continuation of "Abrahamic faith" within the nation as the basis of Mosaic covenant faithfulness. The Abrahamic covenant was and continues to be the historical foundation of God's redemptive program for all humanity (see Gen 12:3: "all peoples on earth will be blessed through you"). The patriarchal covenant, however, did not have the features that were necessary to regulate an entire nation on all levels. The Mosaic covenant fulfilled the need for promises and obligations that would be suitable for this purpose. The covenant made at Sinai was a natural and necessary extension of the Lord's commitment to the patriarchs, which included a commitment to their descendants.

So the Abrahamic family grew into a nation—a theocratic nation that needed guidance and regulation by God on the national, not just the family, level. The Mosaic covenant provided a sort of national constitution that included a legal system. It also included a worship system precisely because Israel was to be a theocratic nation, ruled by God. Nevertheless, eventually the nation would need a human king even though it was a theocratic nation. Deuteronomy 17:14-20 anticipated this reality, which came to legitimate fulfillment in the Davidic covenant (2 Sam 7). As an Abrahamic believer (Gen 15:6), the Davidic king was to rule according to the Mosaic law (Deut 17:18-20). The family had grown into a nation that needed a king—and a particular kind of king (Deut 17:14-17; not one like they requested in 1 Sam 8). The progression was as natural and necessary as the law that arose within it. The book of Judges highlights this need for a king, "In those days Israel had no king; everyone did as they saw fit" (Judg 17:6; cf. Judg 18:1; 19:1; 21:25).

THE ABRAHAMIC COVENANT

God reconfirmed his promises to Abram throughout the patriarchal narratives, from generation to generation, and throughout the Old

Testament and in the New Testament as well. It all began with the call and commission of Abram in Genesis 12:1-3. The commission was a call to express a radical faith in the Lord. God promised him a "land" (Gen 12:1, 7), a "seed" (Gen 12:2), and a special "blessing" (Gen 12:3), which would exceed that of any nation and is, in fact, the foundation for God blessing all the nations. All depended on Abram's willingness to step out and take on a new life in a new place with no security except the promises of God.

Abraham's steps of faith led to numerous encounters between him and the Lord through the years. Some of those encounters continue the promise/faith/blessing motif (e.g., Gen 13:14-18; 15:1-6; and esp. Gen 22:15-19). There are also restatements of this to Isaac (Gen 26:23-25) and Jacob (Gen 28:10-17; 35:9-12). In other encounters, the covenant motif was explicit and fully developed, and we find both permanent promise and ongoing obligation clearly expressed. Genesis 15:7-21 expresses permanent promise with regard to the inheritance of the land. God passes between the parts of the animals to assure Abram of the promise of the land for his descendants. In Genesis 17 as well God expounds on the permanent promises: the seed and the blessing (Gen 17:2-7, 15-22), and the land (Gen 17:8).

In Genesis 17 the ongoing obligations of the covenant rise to prominence alongside the permanent promises. In Genesis 17:1-2 the Lord commands Abraham, "I am God Almighty; walk before me and be blameless, in order that I may confirm my covenant between me and you, and greatly increase your numbers" (my translation). There is obligation here. This is further clarified later in the same chapter in the regulations for circumcision: "Then God said to Abraham, 'As for you, you must keep my covenant, you and your descendants after you for the generations to come'" (Gen 17:9; cf. Gen 17:13-14). Here circumcision is called a covenant but also referred to as "the sign of the covenant between me and you" (Gen 17:11), referring to the larger Abrahamic covenant of which it is a part. This is an obligatory part of the Abrahamic covenant: "Any uncircumcised male, who has not been circumcised in the flesh, will be cut off from his people; he has broken my covenant" (Gen 17:14). Clearly, the Abrahamic covenant is not a covenant of promise with no obligations on the part of Abraham and his descendants.

Circumcision as a "sign" of the Abrahamic covenant makes perfectly good sense. The sign appears at the place associated with the promise, the place of the "seed." The rainbow for the "sign" of the Noahic covenant is similar (Gen 9:12-17). The sign is of a certain kind and put in an appropriate place for the focus of the covenant: the rainbow in the sky, the place from which came the rain that flooded the earth. To my knowledge, there is no specific sign designated in the text for the Davidic and new covenants, but the sign of the Mosaic covenant is also especially appropriate: "You must observe my Sabbaths. This will be a sign between me and you for the generations to come, so you may know that I am the LORD, who makes you holy" (Ex 31:13, 17; Ezek 20:12, 20). Like circumcision, the text also refers to the Sabbath as a covenant in and of itself (Ex 31:16). The Sabbath marked Israel as a nation sanctified to the Lord; a nation that rested every seventh day, including all people, no matter what their status may be, slave or free, native or alien, and the animals too (cf. Ex 20:8-11; Deut 5:12-15). Faithful Israelites were to take the Sabbath seriously (e.g., Num 15:32-36; Isa 58:13-14; Jer 17:19-27).

THE MOSAIC COVENANT

The subject of the Sabbath, of course, brings us to the Mosaic covenant. No one has trouble recognizing that there are ongoing obligations in this covenant. We will deal with some of the laws in detail in the next few chapters, although we cannot treat them all in this volume. What is important for now is to recognize the close connection between faith, love, and obedience. The Lord wanted the people of Israel to put their trust in him by committing to an exclusive covenant with him as their only God. This covenant bond included both promises and obligations: from God to Israel (the permanent promises) and from Israel to God (the ongoing obligations). Sometimes the text connects obedience to the obligations directly to love for God, as in the Great Shema: "Hear, O Israel: The LORD our God, the LORD is one. Love the LORD your God with all your heart and with all your soul and with all your strength. These commandments that I give you today are to be upon your hearts" (Deut 6:4-6). Consider also, for example, "The LORD your God will circumcise your hearts and the hearts of your descendants, so that you may love him with all your heart and with all your soul, and live. You will again obey the LORD and follow all his commands I am giving you today" (Deut 30:6, 8).

This comes through in some places in the same way in the New Testament. Even Abraham's faith is shown by his works, according to James: "Show me your faith without deeds, and I will show you my faith by what I do" (Jas 2:18); and then, "Was not our ancestor Abraham considered righteous for what he did when he offered his son Isaac on the altar? You see that his faith and his actions were working together, and his faith was made complete by what he did. And the Scripture was fulfilled that says, 'Abraham believed God, and it was credited to him as righteousness,' and he was called God's friend" (Jas 2:21-23). Jesus comes right out and says it this way: "Whoever has my commands and obeys them, he is the one who loves me. He who loves me will be loved by my Father, and I too will love him and show myself to him" (Jn 14:21). God has always been after the same thing from everyone: a genuine faith in him that issues itself in a love, which in turn shows itself in the kind of works that glorify God (Mt 5:14-16, esp. v. 16).

What is of special interest in light of the discussion of conditionality at the beginning of this chapter, however, is that the Lord states the initial offer of the Mosaic covenant when they arrive at Sinai conditionally: "Now *if* you obey me fully and keep my covenant, *then* out of all nations you will be my treasured possession. Although the whole earth is mine, you will be for me a kingdom of priests and a holy nation" (Ex 19:5-6). The question that arises for the Mosaic covenant, therefore, is whether the Lord's covenant promises are permanent and guaranteed, or whether this and other passages tell us the promises are conditioned on obedience to the covenant obligations.

Part of the overarching problem here, of course, is that if God is not committed permanently to the Mosaic covenant with the descendants of Abraham, then how can his commitment to Abraham have permanent promise, since one of the core Abrahamic promises is the perpetuity of God's blessing on his descendants? God said, "I will establish my covenant as an everlasting covenant between me and you and your descendants after you for the generations to come, to be your God and the God of your descendants after you" (Gen 17:7). Since the Israelites were Abraham's seed and God was already committed to Abraham and his seed, on the one hand, it would seem that in some sense the promises of the Mosaic covenant must be as permanent as those of the Abrahamic covenant. On the other hand, according to the blessings and curses attached to the Mosaic covenant, if the Israelites were obedient, they would receive blessings from the Lord, but if they were disobedient, they would receive the curses instead (Lev 26 at Sinai; Deut 28 in Moab forty years later).

Leviticus 26:40-45 helps us here. These verses come at the conclusion to the covenant at Sinai, right after the blessings (Lev 26:3-13) and curses (Lev 26:14-39). A colophon (i.e., statement of content and composition) follows immediately, "These are the decrees, the laws and the regulations that the LORD established on Mount Sinai between himself and the Israelites through Moses" (Lev 26:46). In Leviticus 26:40-44 the Lord proclaimed his permanent commitment to Israel even though they would be in exile from the land for their lack of faithfulness to the Mosaic covenant obligations. Earlier, in the curses, God had warned that if they did not obey the covenant law, he would take them into exile and the land would have its sabbaths during their exile (Lev 26:33-35; see the sabbatical year regulations in Lev 25:1-7). His purpose for taking them into exile would be to chastise them. They would turn back and "confess their sins and the sins of their ancestors—their unfaithfulness and their hostility toward me, which made me hostile toward them so that I sent them into the land of their enemies—then when their uncircumcised hearts are humbled and they pay for their sin, I will remember my covenant with Jacob and my covenant with Isaac and my covenant with Abraham, and I will remember the land" (Lev 26:40-42).

Thus, the Abrahamic covenant will remain intact. God will "remember" it even though they are in exile. When they are in exile, the land will have its Sabbaths and "they will pay for their sins because they rejected my laws and abhorred my decrees" (Lev 26:43). Nevertheless, "in spite of this, when they are in the land of their enemies, I will not reject them or abhor them so as to destroy them completely, breaking my covenant with them. I am the LORD their God" (Lev 26:44). Even though they have broken the covenant, God will not. He is not fickle, even though they are. When God commits, he commits—and he stays committed. It is part of his character. His program and the way he works it out flow directly from his character.

The following verse tells us that this permanence applies not only to the Abrahamic covenant but also to the Mosaic covenant: "For their sake I will remember the covenant with their ancestors whom I brought out of Egypt in the sight of the nations to be their God. I am the LORD" (Lev 26:45). This can only refer to the ancestors who were directly involved in the exodus from Egypt and, therefore, the historical establishment of the Mosaic covenant at Sinai.[12] The historical and theological rationale is that the Mosaic covenant is a natural extension of the Abrahamic covenant and as a result carries the promises of the latter forward into the future of Israel as a nation. In this sense the Mosaic covenant promises of God are as permanent as the Abrahamic promises. Again, even though they have broken the covenant, God will not.

---

[12]See, e.g., John E. Hartley, *Leviticus*, WBC (Dallas: Word, 1992), 471.

This is a very important point. One of the key related Hebrew words is *ḥesed*. Note, for example, this quality in God as it is put in Deuteronomy 7:9, 12: "Know therefore that the LORD your God is God; he is the faithful God, keeping his covenant of love [lit. 'keeping his covenant and his *ḥesed*'] to a thousand generations of those who love him and keep his commands. . . . If you pay attention to these laws and are careful to follow them, then the LORD your God will keep his covenant of love (lit. 'will keep his covenant and his *ḥesed*') with you, as he swore to your forefathers."

This is an essential element in his ability and willingness to forgive us for our sin and stay in relationship with us in spite of our fallen, sinful condition. This becomes clear in the recovery from the golden calf catastrophe in Exodus 32–34 in the shadow of Mount Sinai. When the Lord proclaimed his own name—his quality of character—that will allow him to remake the covenant, he began this way: "The LORD, the LORD, the compassionate and gracious God, slow to anger, abounding in love [Hebrew *ḥesed*] and faithfulness, maintaining love to thousands, and forgiving wickedness, rebellion and sin" (Ex 34:6-7). Actually, the second half of Exodus 34:6 is repeated a number of times in similar contexts (see, e.g., Num 14:18; Neh 9:17; Ps 86:5, 15; 103:8; Joel 2:13; Jon 4:2). This does not mean he does not chastise his covenant people for their sinful behavior (see, e.g., Ex 34:7), but his loyalty to them keeps his willingness to forgive them available when repentance comes.

The eventual complete fulfillment of the Mosaic covenant will come in association with the outworking of the new covenant. Look at the major new covenant passage in Jeremiah 31:31-37 and note the especially emphatic statement of God's permanent loyalty to the physical seed of Abraham (Jer 31:35-37), which calls us back again to the original Abrahamic covenant as well. There is a clearly expressed discontinuity between the Mosaic and new covenants. As the Lord puts it, the time is coming "when I will make a new covenant with the house of Israel and with the house of Judah. *It will not be like* the covenant I made with their ancestors when I took them by the hand to lead them out of Egypt" (Jer 31:31-32). Therefore, it is probably best not to refer to the new covenant as the "renewed" covenant.[13] One can see why this is attractive to some scholars, but the text speaks in quite opposite terms about the transition from the one covenant to the other.

At the same time, like the continuity of the Abrahamic covenant commitment to his descendants in the Mosaic covenant, the obligations of the Mosaic law continue into the new covenant. This becomes clear in the next verse: "This is the covenant I will make with the house of Israel after that time. . . . I will put my law in their minds (lit. 'within them') and write it on their hearts. I will be their God, and they will be my people" (Jer 31:33). The Old Testament law is not left behind in the new covenant, so by nature it is not to be left behind in the church and the Christian life, since our covenant with God is the new covenant.

The Davidic Covenant

In the meantime, there are also permanent promises and ongoing obligations in the Davidic covenant. As we have already explained, the Davidic covenant fits under the umbrella of the Abrahamic and Mosaic covenants. The family has grown into a nation that needs a king. This is a dynastic covenant; a promise of a perpetual dynasty to rule on the throne of Israel, God's kingdom people. It is a permanent promise to David and his descendants as numerous passages make clear. In 2 Samuel 7, for instance, David had determined that it was time for him to build a house for the Lord since he himself was living in a palace and there was rest in the land from all their enemies (2 Sam 7:1-4). The Lord's response was that David was not going to build a house for him, but he (the Lord) was going to build a house for David, a dynastic house (2 Sam 7:5-11, esp. v. 11). The Lord then declares, among other things, that his son who takes the throne after

---

[13]See also F. B. Huey Jr., *Jeremiah, Lamentations* (Nashville: Broadman & Holman, 1993), 280-81 and n. 50 and the literature cited there.

him will build a house for the Lord and, finally, "Your house and your kingdom will endure forever before me; your throne will be established forever" (2 Sam 7:16). The permanent promise is clear. Although the term *covenant* never appears in 2 Samuel 7 or in the parallel passage in 1 Chronicles 17, other passages refer back to the Lord's promise to David in 2 Samuel 7 as an enduring covenant (see, e.g., 2 Sam 23:5; Ps 89:3-4, 28-37; 132:12).

The ongoing obligations and permanent promises fit together. Referring to David's son, Solomon, the Lord promises, "I will be his father, and he will be my son. When he does wrong, I will punish him with the rod of men, with floggings inflicted by men. But my love will never be taken away from him, as I took it away from Saul, whom I removed from before you" (2 Sam 7:14-15). In other words, the Lord expected David's son to rule according to the Lord's will. After all, the Lord was the theocratic king. The regulations for the human king given in the Mosaic law require that the king write his own copy of the scroll of law belonging to the Levitical priests, the custodians of the law (Deut 17:18). He was to keep it with him and read it all his life "so that he may learn to revere the LORD his God and follow carefully all the words of this law and these decrees and not consider himself better than his brothers and turn from the law to the right or to the left" (Deut 17:19-20). The passage concludes, "Then he and his descendants will reign a long time over his kingdom in Israel" (Deut 17:20). The obligations of the dynastic covenant, therefore, are clear.

Interestingly enough, like the Mosaic covenant, one could also articulate the Davidic covenant conditionally. When David was on his deathbed in 1 Kings 2:1-4, he gave a charge to Solomon his son, who was about to take the throne:

> Observe what the LORD your God requires: Walk in obedience to him, and keep his decrees and commands, his laws and regulations, as written in the law of Moses. Do this so that you may prosper in all you do and wherever you go and that the LORD may keep his promise to me: "*If* your descendants watch how they live, *and if* they walk faithfully before me with all their heart and

soul, you will never fail to have a successor on the throne of Israel."
(1 Kings 2:3-4; cf. also 1 Kings 9:3-9; Ps 132:10-12)

In this case, one of the covenants often regarded as unconditional is treated as conditional. It reinforces the obligation side of the Davidic covenant as David himself understood it. So again, there is good reason not to classify the redemptive covenants as conditional or unconditional. Moreover, the urgency for the king to rule according to the Mosaic law in this passage once again affirms the same point in Deuteronomy 17:16-18, as noted above. The Davidic covenant, therefore, fits under the umbrella of the Mosaic covenant and, in turn, under the umbrella of the Abrahamic covenant. The Davidic king must put his personal trust in the Lord just as Abraham did and therefore rule the nation of Israel according to the Lord's will as expressed in the Mosaic law. The perpetuity of the Davidic covenant is part of the new covenant plan too, according to Jeremiah 33:14-26.

THE NEW COVENANT

Jeremiah anticipated the new covenant (Jer 31:31-37; cf. also Jer 32:36-44; Ezek 36:22-28) and Jesus inaugurated it through his death on the cross (see, e.g., Lk 22:19-20; 1 Cor 11:23-25; 2 Cor 3:3-8; Heb 8:6-13). The chart of the redemptive covenants in figure 1 has a cross at the apex of the new covenant umbrella with diagonal and crossing dotted lines running through it from above to below. This represents a kind of lens through which the Old Testament covenant promises and obligations come through into the New Testament in transformed ways suitable to the nature of the new covenant. In the discussion of the making of the Mosaic covenant, we noted that there were differences between the law as the Lord gave it at Sinai (Exodus and Leviticus) and its proclamation in Moab forty years later (Deuteronomy). One example is the slaughtering of domesticated animals as sacrifices to the Lord only at the tabernacle in Leviticus 17:1-7, as opposed to profane sacrifice anywhere in the land in Deuteronomy 12:12-25. This was necessary because in Deuteronomy they were about to enter, conquer, and occupy the land of Canaan. They would not continue to live together in tents around the tabernacle with easy access to it as they traveled through the wilderness.[14]

There is an even more substantial shift from life under the Mosaic covenant to life under the new covenant. Ancient Israel was a nation. The church is not. We live as communities of faith amid all the nations of the earth and, in many ways, under the supervision of the governments of those nations (see, e.g., Rom 13:1-10; cf. Titus 3:1; 1 Pet 2:13-17). Yes, we are citizens of heaven (Phil 3:17-21) and ambassadors here (2 Cor 5:16-21), but we do not have secular governmental powers in the church, except as the governmental powers grant them to us as citizens of our country. Moreover, we live now after the death, burial, and resurrection of Christ, not in anticipation of it, and after the special pouring out of the Holy Spirit on the Day of Pentecost (Acts 2; cf. Joel 2). These historical realities have a great deal of impact on how the Mosaic law does and does not come through into the New Testament for the life of the church and the believer. Thus, there is transformation of the law in the new covenant context as represented by the diagonal dotted lines that run through the cross at the apex of the new covenant umbrella in the chart.

The way the Mosaic law applies in the church and the Christian life, therefore, depends largely on the nature of the relationship between and the shifts from the Mosaic covenant to the new covenant. We have now moved from a theocratic kingdom on earth to a theocratic kingdom of heaven that crosses all the boundaries between earthly kingdoms, from the writing of the law on tablets of stone to the writing of it on human hearts, and so on. Some elements of the Old Testament law do not fit directly into the new covenant context. For a simple example, consider "You shall not murder" (Ex 20:13). This, of course, fits as well under the new covenant as under the Mosaic, but according to Exodus 21:12, "Anyone who strikes a man and kills

---

[14]See Averbeck, "The Cult in Deuteronomy," 235-36, 239-41, 254-56.

him shall surely be put to death." Since, unlike Israel under the Mosaic covenant, the church under the new covenant does not serve as the civil government, it would not be appropriate to take a murderer out into the church parking lot and stone him to death on Sunday morning. We need to leave the punishment of murderers up to the civil authorities (see, e.g., Rom 13:1-7).

Jeremiah 31:31-34 tells us that the law is written on the heart of new covenant believers (Jer 31:33). In the context, this means that "no longer will they teach their neighbor, or say to one another, 'Know the LORD,' because they will all know me, from the least of them to the greatest" (Jer 31:33-34). The Mosaic covenant was such that Israelite children were born into it—the males circumcised on the eighth day. As they grew up, therefore, it was important to teach them to "know the Lord." This was an essential element of the festival system and the lifestyle of the pious household, among other things (see, e.g., Ex 13:8-10, 14-16; Deut 6:4-9).

Through the prophet Jeremiah, the Lord also calls attention to the theme of circumcision of the heart found already in the Mosaic law (e.g., Lev 26:41; Deut 10:16; 30:6). He uses it to exhort the people of the day: "Break up your unplowed ground and do not sow among thorns. Circumcise yourselves to the LORD, circumcise your hearts" (Jer 4:3-4). The more extended passage in Jeremiah 9:23-26 clarifies the point of the image: "Let not the wise boast of their wisdom or the strong boast of their strength or the rich boast of their riches, but let the one who boasts boast about this: *that they have the understanding to know me*. . . . The days are coming . . . when I will punish all who are circumcised only in the flesh—Egypt, Judah, Edom. . . . For all these nations are really uncircumcised, and even the whole house of Israel is *uncircumcised in heart*." Circumcision of the heart amounts to truly knowing and understanding the Lord, and that is what the new covenant has always been all about (cf. the same image in Rom 2:28-29).

Jeremiah, however, had been dealing with a generation of Israelites who belonged to the covenant nation but, by and large, did not know the Lord. They had no real Abrahamic faith in the Lord even though they were born into a Jewish household, the males circumcised on the eighth day and, therefore, belonged to the national-level Mosaic covenant. The new covenant in Jeremiah 31 looks forward to a time when this would not be the case. Only those who know the Lord would be in new covenant with the Lord because, by definition, no one would belong to the new covenant who did not already have the Mosaic law written on the heart. That coming day would be a time when all the covenant people would know the Lord. What a breath of fresh air this would be for the Lord, and for Jeremiah too.

In 2 Corinthians 3, the apostle Paul combines Jeremiah 31 with Ezekiel 36. This brings the Holy Spirit into the discussion of the law and the Christian. Ezekiel 36 is largely a prophetic rebuke of Israel as a nation because they had profaned the holy name of the Lord "among the nations" (Ezek 36:22). The Lord was not about to leave it that way. No, he intended to act on behalf of his own name: "I will show the holiness of my great name. . . . Then the nations will know that I am the LORD . . . when I show myself holy through you before their eyes" (Ezek 36:23). How is he going to do that? Ezekiel 36:24-27 tell us:

> I will take you out of the nations; I will gather you from all the countries and bring you back into your own land. I will sprinkle clean water on you, and you will be clean; I will cleanse you from all your impurities and from all your idols. I will give you a *new heart* and *put a new spirit in you*; I will remove from you your *heart of stone* and give you a *heart of flesh*. And *I will put my Spirit in you* and move you to follow my decrees and be careful to keep my laws.

Like Jeremiah, Ezekiel sees a restoration coming, and it will happen through a coming of the Spirit that will transform the people and the nation as a whole. Bringing Ezekiel 36 and Jeremiah 31 together, Paul writes, "You show that you are a letter from Christ, the result of our ministry, *written not with ink but with the Spirit of the living God*" (2 Cor 3:3). The image here combines the Spirit in Ezekiel 36 with the writing of the law on the heart of Jeremiah: "not on tablets of stone but *on tablets of human hearts*" (2 Cor 3:3), making them "ministers of *a new covenant*" (2 Cor 3:6). Furthermore, this new covenant ministry is one "not of the letter but *of the Spirit*; for the letter kills, but *the Spirit gives life*" (2 Cor 3:6). The Spirit of Ezekiel 36 provides the background here, and perhaps this even includes an allusion to the life-giving power of the Spirit in the vision of dry bones (Ezek 37:7-9, 14; cf. also Ezek 11:14-21).

In effect, the apostle Paul binds together the work of the Spirit (Ezekiel) with the writing of the Mosaic law on the heart (Jeremiah). In fact, even Ezekiel himself binds them together in his own way: "I will put *my Spirit* in you and move *you to follow my decrees and be careful to keep my laws*" (Ezek 36:27). This is another way of talking about what Jeremiah 31 states in terms of writing the law on the heart. The law and the Spirit go together. One cannot have the Spirit without the Spirit bringing God's revealed law to bear on one's life. This is an integral part of the sanctifying work of the Holy Spirit. Once again, we are not leaving the Old Testament law behind in the new covenant, the New Testament, the church, or the Christian life.

SUMMARY AND CONCLUSION

Historically, God originally designed the Abrahamic covenant for a family, not a nation. Eventually, however, the family of Abraham grew into a nation. The Mosaic covenant expanded and extended the Abrahamic promises and obligations to the ancient nation of Israel. The law within the Mosaic covenant would serve their need for guidance as a theocratic nation under the rule of their God as their king. When the Lord made the covenant with them at Sinai, this assumed the continuation of Abrahamic faith within the nation as the basis of Mosaic covenant faithfulness. Similarly, the dynastic covenant with David depended on the Abrahamic and Mosaic covenants. The Davidic king was to rule according to the Mosaic law as one with Abrahamic faith. The *family* had grown into a *nation* that needed a *king*. The Abrahamic covenant was and continues to be the historical foundation of God's redemptive program for all people (Gen 12:3: "all peoples on earth will be blessed through you").

This redemptive covenant progression leads finally to the new covenant in Christ. The law of God in the Mosaic law is anything but left behind in the new covenant: "I will put my law within them and on their heart I will write it" (Jer 31:33). God suggests essentially the same thing with circumcision, which he initiated under the Abrahamic covenant: "circumcision is circumcision of the heart, by the Spirit, not by the written code" (Rom 2:29; cf. Gal 5:6 with Lev 26:41; Deut 10:16; Jer 4:4).

At this point, we can briefly anticipate the argument coming in part three of this book regarding the Old Testament law in the New Testament. What does the apostle Paul mean when he writes that we are not "under the law" (e.g., 1 Cor 9:20; Gal 3:23, 25; 4:4-5, 21)? To begin with, it means that we are no longer under "the curse of the law" (Gal 3:13; cf. Gal 3:10). The law cannot condemn us because we have been justified by God through accepting by faith the work of Jesus Christ on the cross. Moreover, the Mosaic law was never designed to give anyone spiritual life in the first place: "For if a law had been given that could impart life, then righteousness would certainly have come by the law" (Gal 3:21). The law was given as a guide to those who already had Abrahamic faith, whether in the Old Testament or the New Testament. Paul refers to it as a "tutor" (Gal 3:24-25), and we are no longer "under" a tutor.

Spiritual life comes through the work of the Holy Spirit in the person who has Abrahamic faith. From a biblical point of view, Abraham kept the law as a man of faith (Gen 15:6) before the Mosaic law had been given: "Abraham obeyed me and kept my charge, my commandments, my statutes and my laws" (Gen 26:5; cf., e.g., Deut 6:2; 11:1).[15] Similarly, we keep the law as people of Abrahamic

---

[15]See, e.g., the remarks in Tremper Longman III, *Genesis*, The Story of God Bible Commentary (Grand Rapids, MI: Zondervan, 2016), 341-42; Ross, *Creation and Blessing*, 458-59. Moses wrote the law long after Abraham was dead, but since he was a righteous man before God in his own

faith (Gal 3:14) even though we are not "under the law." As Paul puts it later in Galatians 5:14, "For the entire law is fulfilled in keeping this one command: 'Love your neighbor as yourself.'" Of course, this refers back to the second of Jesus' two great commandments (Mt 22:34-40 and par.). These two commandments are central to "the law of Christ" as Paul labels it in 1 Corinthians 9:21: "To those not having the law I became like one not having the law (though I am not free from God's law but am under *Christ's law*)."

Essentially, the "law of Christ" is the way Jesus mediates the Old Testament law to us in the new covenant in Christ. We have the Old Testament law "written on the heart." When Jesus gave the two great commandments, both of which come from the Old Testament law itself, he added at the end, "All the Law and the Prophets hang on these two commandments" (Mt 22:40; cf. the "golden rule" in Mt 7:12). God has always desired the same from everyone: a whole-hearted love for God and for people. The Ten Commandments and the entirety of the law given in the Pentateuch are all about how to live out the two great commandments as a nation of Abrahamic believers in their ancient context.

As noted above, the diagonal dotted lines that cross through the covenant chart indicate that the Old Testament covenants and their features enter the new covenant transformed by the work of the Messiah on the cross, the coming of the Spirit on Pentecost, and the nature of the new covenant community of faith. Naturally, there were changes made because the laws of the national covenant with Israel do not match the needs and nature of communities of faith living in all the various nations. In fact, as noted above, even in the Old Testament, the law itself changed within the Pentateuch to manage situational shifts that took place—for example, when the life of Israel in the wilderness shifted to life in the land after the conquest. The law always included a degree of flexibility through time, place, and

---

day, one could say that he was a keeper of the law in terms that the later Israelite readers, who had the law, would have understood.

circumstance in order to meet the needs of the covenant people. This is true in the New Testament as well.

The goal in the following chapters is to clarify why and how the Mosaic law continues as Scripture in the church—authoritative and important for how we live for Christ. As Paul wrote near the end of his life, "All Scripture [including the Old Testament law] is God-breathed and is useful for teaching, rebuking, correcting and training in righteousness, so that the servant of God may be thoroughly equipped for every good work" (2 Tim 3:16-17).

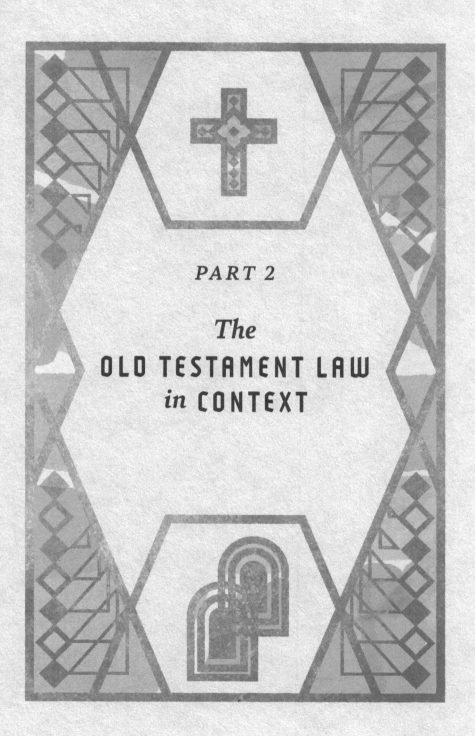

PART 2

The
OLD TESTAMENT LAW
in CONTEXT

Three

THE MOSAIC LAW COLLECTIONS AND THE REDEMPTIVE SETTING OF THE LAW

THE TWO PREVIOUS CHAPTERS treated the biblical covenants, especially the redemptive covenants (i.e., the Abrahamic, Mosaic, Davidic, and new covenants), and the relationships between them. They provide indispensable textual, historical, and theological background for understanding how the Mosaic law worked in the Old Testament and how it applies to the life of the church and the believer in Christ. The whole law is Scripture to us: authoritative, useful, and effective for us today (2 Tim 3:15-17) like the rest of the Bible. The question is not *whether* this or that part of the law applies to us but *how* it applies. The *how* often becomes clear when we look closely at what the New Testament Scriptures do with the various units and dimensions of the Mosaic law.

The first Bible of the New Testament church was the Old Testament. Initially, the apostles preached the gospel from the Hebrew Scriptures (usually translated into Greek), understanding it in light of what Jesus Christ had done in their day, the coming of the Holy Spirit at Pentecost, the extension of it to the Gentiles, and all the implications these hold for God's ongoing redemptive work in the world. The apostolic preaching in written form gradually built up the New Testament in the second half of the first century AD.

Many who read the New Testament do not have a thorough familiarity with the Old Testament, especially the Mosaic law. Much of the confusion about the application of the Mosaic law in the New Testament, the church, and the life of the believer arises from this lack of knowledge and basic misunderstanding of the Old Testament law itself. The goal in this and the following few chapters is to lay a solid foundation for reading the Old Testament law well on its own terms.

LAW AND LAW COLLECTIONS IN THE PENTATEUCH AND THE ANCIENT NEAR EAST

In English we commonly refer to the first five books of the Old Testament, the books of Moses, as the "Pentateuch" (from Greek *penta*, "five," plus *teuchos*, "book" or "implement"). In the Hebrew Bible, we refer to these books as the Torah, which Jesus refers to as the "the Law" or "the Law of Moses" (see, e.g., Mt 5:17; Lk 24:44). The Hebrew word means "law," but it also has the broader meaning of "instruction." This is important. The Torah is composed of many different genres of literature: law but also narratives, poems, genealogies, and so on. All of these different kinds of textual material "instruct," but they do it in different ways. Laws, for example, usually instruct very directly, telling people what to do or not do, sometimes depending on the circumstances, or how to judge different situations or the actions of others. Narratives, however, instruct readers by drawing them into the stories that they tell, causing the readers to reflect on their implications, often reflecting principles and patterns that appear in the law. The two are related but different. We do not, or at least should not, read narratives the same way we read laws, although they can both deal with the same kinds of issues in their own ways and instruct us accordingly.

There are five basic units of law in the Torah from Exodus to Deuteronomy:

1. *The Ten Commandments* (Ex 20:1-17, repeated with a few variations in Deut 5:6-21). The actual expression in Hebrew is the "ten words" (see Ex 34:28; Deut 4:13; 10:4; cf. also Deut 5:22), which is why we also sometimes refer to them as the "Decalogue" (from Greek *deka*, "ten," plus *logos*, "word").

2. *The book of the covenant* (Ex 21–23, or perhaps Ex 20:22–23:19, but the main body of regulations is limited to Ex 21:1–23:19). The actual Hebrew means "the scroll of the covenant" (see Ex 24:7). Some refer to it as the "covenant code."

3. *The priestly regulations* (Lev 1–16, made up of ritual, holiness, and purity regulations). These regulations speak from the perspective of the priests standing within the tabernacle looking out into the community (see, e.g., Lev 10:10-11). Some call this the "priestly code."

4. *The holiness regulations* (Lev 17–27, regulations for the holiness of the community). This section speaks from the perspective of standing out in the community looking in toward the tabernacle. Some refer to this as the "holiness code."[1]

5. *The Deuteronomic regulations* (Deut 12–26, spoken by Moses forty years later in Moab). Here Moses speaks as God's prophet to the nation of Israel, expounding the law (Deut 1:5). This was before they crossed the Jordan to conquer the land under the leadership of Joshua. Some call this the "Deuteronomic code."

Beyond this, there are also regulations for the tabernacle and an account of its fabrication in Exodus 26–31; 35–40, respectively, interrupted by the golden calf debacle in Exodus 32–34. Various additional regulations are also strewn throughout the book of Numbers (Num 1–9; 15; 18–19; 28–30; 35).

Although some use the term *code* to refer to one or the other of these law collections, this can be misleading. It suggests they are

---

[1]Note that God gave these first four to Israel through Moses at Sinai.

comprehensive legal collections, intended to cover everything needed to maintain the society in which they function. None of these biblical collections individually—and not even all of them put together—constitutes a complete set of laws. For one thing, too many necessary categories of law are missing for them to fulfill all the legal needs of ancient Israel. For example, there are no laws about rental of property or adoption in the Torah, even though other ancient Near Eastern law collections have them. The same is true for laws of marriage cancelation, the sale of chattel slaves, assault on dignity, hiring of boats and loss for negligence, agricultural lease and natural disaster, and so on.[2]

We will examine some of the regulations contained in these various law collections in detail in the following chapters, but it is not our plan or purpose to treat every specific regulation in the present volume. Some of the collections and, in fact, some of the specific regulations within them have whole books devoted to them. Thankfully, today there are many good resources available to consult on these details of the law. There are numerous exegetically and theologically based commentaries, and some very recent and relatively comprehensive collections of material from specialists in ancient Near Eastern and biblical law.[3]

Our main goal is to help the reader read and understand the Mosaic law better in its ancient Israelite context. The more detailed

---

[2]See the helpful remarks in William S. Morrow, *An Introduction to Biblical Law* (Grand Rapids, MI: Eerdmans, 2017), 34-45, esp. p. 36, and a more complete list and discussion in Samuel Greengus, *Laws in the Bible and in Early Rabbinic Collections: The Legacy of the Ancient Near East* (Eugene, OR: Cascade, 2011), 282-83.

[3]See esp. the two major works published recently by Oxford, drawing from the very best research in the field written by highly qualified scholars: Pamela Barmash, ed., *The Oxford Handbook of Biblical Law* (Oxford: Oxford University Press, 2019); and Brent A. Strawn, ed., *The Oxford Encyclopedia of the Bible and Law*, 2 vols. (Oxford: Oxford University Press, 2015). The reader will also find excellent bibliographies in these volumes if they desire to go further. Some of the most recent commentaries will be cited in the remarks on particular regulations later in this chapter and in the following chapters. Other recent volumes to consult include, e.g., Roy E. Gane, *Old Testament Law for Christians: Original Context and Enduring Application* (Grand Rapids, MI: Baker Academic, 2017); Raymond Westbrook and Bruce Wells, *Everyday Law in Biblical Israel: An Introduction* (Louisville, KY: Westminster John Knox Press, 2009); and Greengus, *Laws in the Bible*.

treatments of certain regulations serve to inform and model such reading.

ANCIENT NEAR EASTERN LAW COLLECTIONS AND THE PRACTICE OF LAW

The ancient Near Eastern cuneiform ("wedge-shaped" writing) law collections are preserved on clay tablets and on the black diorite stone stele of Hammurabi. The Laws of Ur-Namma (ca. 2100 BC) and Lipit-Ishtar (ca. 1930 BC) are in the Sumerian language. We have four of them in the Akkadian language: the Laws of Eshnunna (ca. 1770 BC), the Laws of Hammurabi (ca. 1750 BC), the Middle Assyrian Laws (ca. 1075 BC), and the Neo-Babylonian Laws (ca. 700–600 BC). There is also a collection of Hittite laws written sometime in the Late Bronze Age (1550–1200 BC).[4] There are many close parallels between these collections, especially the ones in Sumerian and Akkadian, and between them and the laws found in the biblical collections. This is not surprising since Akkadian was the political, diplomatic, and economic *lingua franca* of the entire ancient Near East from about 2000 to 600 BC; that is, from the time of the patriarchs through the entire history of ancient Israel in the preexilic period.

---

[4]See the brief introductions to these law collections and the ancient Near Eastern legal tradition as they relate to biblical law in Morrow, *Introduction to Biblical Law*, 37-40, and Westbrook and Wells, *Everyday Law in Biblical Israel*, 21-25. For the documents themselves in English translation, see COS 2:106-19 (Hittite), 332-61 (Akkadian), and 408-14 (Sumerian). For the most comprehensive analysis of these and other ancient Near Eastern legal texts, including some discussion of biblical law, see the extensive discussion by top scholars in the field in Raymond Westbrook, ed., *A History of Ancient Near Eastern Law*, 2 vols. (Leiden: Brill, 2003). The scholarly literature cited in COS 2 also provides access to more in-depth analyses of these laws. For a more recent and thorough edition of the earliest of these collections, see now Miguel Civil, "The Law Collection of Ur-Namma," in *Cuneiform Royal Inscriptions and Related Texts in the Schoyen Collection*, CUSAS 17, ed. A. R. George (Bethesda, MD: CDL Press, 2011), 221-86. No law collections have survived from ancient Egypt, perhaps because they wrote mainly on perishable writing materials, especially papyrus, not on clay that would naturally dry and harden for preservation. Hieroglyphic writing on the walls of pyramids and other tombs focused on issues of death and the afterlife. We have some legal documents on ostraca and papyri that have survived from Egypt, but nothing like what we have in cuneiform (Westbrook and Wells, *Everyday Law in Biblical Israel*, 21). For a good summary of what is available from Egypt, see now the essays by Richard Jasnow in Westbrook, *History of Ancient Near Eastern Law*, 1:93-140, 155-288; 2:777-818.

It is significant that none of the multitudes of cuneiform trial documents, contracts, or other kinds of judicial court records discovered
in excavations refer to any of these law collections. The consensus
among scholars, therefore, is that the law collections did not serve
statutory purposes. The most common view is that they reflect the
practice of "list science" common in the cuneiform scribal school
context.[5] From the earliest days of cuneiform writing in the late fourth
millennium BC through the following three millennia, the scribal
schools produced thematic lexical lists of professions, vessels, trees,
and objects made of wood, domestic animals, fish, birds, medical
symptoms and their diagnosis, and omens, for example.[6] Cuneiform
scribal schools spread throughout the ancient Near East and with
them such lists for the practice of the scribal profession. This was
their "science."[7]

In principle, the cuneiform law collections derive from this same
scribal list science applied to the practice of law. On the one hand,
they collected the results of legal practice in the courts and compiled them into lists and, on the other hand, as was the practice in
other kinds of lexical lists, some of the entries were more a function
of scribal imagination. They made them up as hypothetical legal
cases. The results are the kinds of regulations we find in the law collections. Officials and scribes collected, compiled, and inscribed the
laws, but the stele on which the Laws of Hammurabi appeared, for
example, was a monumental royal inscription erected to laud the
just rule of Hammurabi before the gods and his people—that is,
royal propaganda.[8]

---

[5]See, e.g., Westbrook and Wells, *Everyday Law in Biblical Israel*, 25-26; and Bruce Wells, "Law and
Practice," in *A Companion to the Ancient Near East*, ed. Daniel C. Snell (Malden, MA: Blackwell,
2005), 184-86.

[6]For a full treatment of the cuneiform lexical tradition, see now Niek Veldhuis, *History of the
Cuneiform Lexical Tradition*, GMTR 6 (Münster: Ugarit-Verlag, 2014).

[7]Francesca Rochberg, *Cuneiform Knowledge and the History of Science* (Chicago: University of
Chicago Press, 2016).

[8]See the careful analysis in Victor Hurowitz, *Inu Anum Ṣīrum: Literary Structures in the Non-
Juridical Sections of Codex Hammurabi* (Philadelphia: Occasional Publications of the Samuel
Noah Kramer Fund, 1994), and the remarks in Adele Berlin, "Numinous *Nomos*: On the

Many (partial) copies of these laws appear on clay tablets extant from excavations around the ancient Near East. It was a very conservative tradition preserved in essentially the same form with the same content over many centuries. They are *descriptive* of legal practice as it occurred in the courts, not *prescriptive* for that practice. The law collections, therefore, are reflective of "common" or "customary" law. The practice of "statutory" law in which lawyers and judges consult written codes for making decisions in court does not seem to have existed in the ancient Near East.[9] At the end of the day, the result is that cuneiform law collections are, to a significant degree, reflections of the customary law tradition as it applied in regular legal cases.

There are three models for explaining the relationship between the cuneiform law collections and the biblical law collections.[10] The *evolutionary* model sees the development of biblical law as largely independent in early Israel, except for some of the regulations taken up from the Canaanite culture around them.[11] The *literary* model takes the opposite view, arguing for a close literary dependence of the biblical law on the written cuneiform sources.[12] The *diffusion* model proposes that biblical law codes draw partly from the oral legal tradition and partly from the written cuneiform tradition that had spread throughout the ancient Near East. This created a common legal

---

Relationship between Narrative and law," in *"A Wise and Discerning Mind": Essays in Honor of Burke O. Long*, ed. Saul M. Olyan and Robert C. Culley (Providence, RI: Brown Judaic Studies, 2000), 27-28. See also Wells, "Law and Practice," 185.

[9]See the extensive discussion of common versus statutory law in the ancient Near East and up to today in Joshua A. Berman, *Inconsistency in the Torah: Ancient Literary Convention and the Limits of Source Criticism* (Oxford: Oxford University Press, 2017), 107-17. Berman shows how much of the historical critical approach to reading biblical law derives from our modern concept of statutory law and, therefore, is not appropriate for reading the Mosaic law. For a detailed and fully documented historical summary of the historical critical analysis of biblical law see Eckart Otto, "The Study of Law and Ethics in the Hebrew Bible/Old Testament," in *Hebrew Bible/Old Testament: The History of Its Interpretation*, vol. 3.2, ed. Magne Sæbø (Göttingen: Vandenhoeck & Ruprecht, 2015), 594-621.

[10]For this discussion, see esp. Westbrook and Wells, *Everyday Law in Biblical Israel*, 24-25.

[11]See, e.g., Otto, "The Study of Law and Ethics," 602-4 and the extensive lit. cited there.

[12]See, e.g., David P. Wright, *Inventing God's Law: How the Covenant Code of the Bible Used and Revised the Laws of Hammurabi* (Oxford: Oxford University Press, 2009).

tradition reflected also in the Israelite law collections since the ancient Israelites were ancient Near Eastern people too.[13]

Unlike the evolutionary model, the diffusion model takes the many parallels between cuneiform and biblical law fully into account, and unlike the literary model, the diffusion model does not require the writer of the biblical law to have an extensive written library of cuneiform law at his elbow as he composed the covenant code, for example. The common legal tradition suggested by the diffusion model comes through not only in the biblical law collections but also in biblical stories, such as in the way Boaz managed the legal issue of the kinsman redeemer in Ruth 4:1-10.[14] The elders in the city gate knew the legal principles and practices from regular application. No one had to look up or make reference to the regulation in Leviticus 25:25, for example.

The actual practice of law in the courts operated on the principle of the buildup of common-law tradition known and implemented by those in authority (elders, judges, kings, etc.). We have thousands of cuneiform and other court records from ancient Near Eastern legal proceedings.[15] These are helpful in that they give us a

---

[13]This is the view taken in Westbrook and Wells, *Everyday Law in Biblical Israel*. For a very helpful collection of the extensive writings on law in the ancient Near East and the Bible by the late Raymond Westbrook, see Bruce Wells and Rachel Magdalene, eds., *Law from the Tigris to the Tiber: The Writings of Raymond Westbrook*, 2 vols. (Winona Lake, IN: Eisenbrauns, 2009).

[14]See Morrow, *Introduction to Biblical Law*, 35-36, 41-43; and Westbrook and Wells, *Everyday Law in Biblical Israel*, 14. Two scholars who develop this principle of law in narrative and narrative as a source of law in the Old Testament are David Daube, *The Collected Works of David Daube*, vol. 3: *Biblical Law and Literature*, ed. Calum Carmichael (Berkeley: University of California Press, 2003); and Calum Carmichael, *Law and Narrative in the Bible: The Evidence of the Deuteronomic Laws and the Decalogue* (Ithaca, NY: Cornell University Press, 1985). The approach taken by Carmichael does not always yield convincing results. He proposes that the biblical law collections derive from the narratives. It is more likely that both draw independently from the common legal tradition dispersed far-and-wide in the ancient Near East. Neither is necessarily dependent on the other.

[15]See the helpful remarks on such sources in Wells, "Law and Practice," 186-87. There is a useful but limited selection of these in COS 3:19-32 (Egyptian), 55-60 (Hittite), 135-98 (Phoenician and Aramaic), 247-72, 283 (Akkadian), and 297-312 (Sumerian). For late Babylonian legal texts see now the new and very important treatment in F. Rachel Magdalene, Cornelia Wunsch, and Bruce Wells, *Fault, Responsibility, and Administrative Law in Late Babylonian Legal Texts*, MC 23 (University Park, PA: Eisenbrauns, 2019), and the extended bibliography there.

more realistic sense of the actual practice of law and legal proceedings in the ancient Near East. The law collections sometimes mention the need to bring such documents to prove one's case in a legal dispute. Such legal documentary proof, properly sealed and witnessed, would carry significant force in court proceedings. The Hebrew Bible also emphasizes the importance of witnesses and faithful and true testimony in court proceedings (e.g., Ex 20:16; Lev 5:1; Deut 17:6; 19:15).[16] Royal edicts also contribute to our understanding of the practice of law in ancient Near Eastern societies.[17] Kings issued these on occasion for specific temporary purposes such as debt release to relieve economic pressure on certain segments of the populace. They reflect concerns similar to those of the Jubilee regulations in Leviticus 25 and the seventh-year release of debt in Deuteronomy 15:1-11.

MOSAIC LAW AND COMMON LAW IN ANCIENT ISRAEL

The Bible tells us that the source of the law in the Pentateuch is the Lord God and that Moses is the mediator through whom God revealed it to Israel. In fact, God himself inscribed the Ten Commandments with his own finger on tablets of stone and delivered them to Moses on Mount Sinai (see Ex 31:18; 32:15-16; 34:27-28; Deut 4:13; 10:1-5). These are the primary principles of law for ancient Israel. In effect, all the other collections of law in the Pentateuch unpack the details of how God intended that they should live according to these ten principles in their ancient Near Eastern context.

The Mosaic law displays its core *ideals* in the Ten Commandments, but it was not *idealistic*. It was realistic for application to the life of ancient Israel in its real-world cultural context. In fact, in many instances, to read it well depends on a wider understanding of the political, sociological, familial, psychological, and economic realities of

---

[16]Bruce Wells, *The Law of Testimony in the Pentateuchal Codes*, BZABR 4 (Wiesbaden: Harrassowitz, 2004), discusses these matters in some detail.

[17]Wells, "Law and Practice," 188.

the world in which they lived, most of which are evident within the Bible itself. The administration of justice, of course, required consideration of all these important factors. Wisdom was essential to the whole process. The court in the city gate that Boaz convened in Ruth 4 is a good example. He knew the mitigating factors for all involved, including the economic realities of the other potential redeemer who was a nearer relative. Similarly, in the royal court, Solomon needed to be able to see through the situation presented to him by the two women, both of whom claimed the same baby as their own (1 Kings 3:16-28). Being sufficiently wise to discern and adjudicate this case showed the people that "he had wisdom from God to administer justice" (1 Kings 3:28). Ancient wisdom literature called for such qualities of judicial wisdom in the royal court.

The Lord intended that the Mosaic law serve as the foundation for such judicial wisdom in ancient Israel. The written law could not and did not intend to deal with every possible situation people faced, but it could provide ideals and precedents to guide the decisions of the judicial officers, whether they were local city elders (Deut 16:18-20), Levitical priestly judges (Deut 17:8-13), or kings (Deut 17:18-20). There is no reason to believe, however, that they distributed written copies of the law throughout ancient Israel for them to consult when they were judging cases. In reality, the ancient Near Eastern practice of "common law" in the courts was essentially the way the courts worked in ancient Israel too.

Common customary law was a matter of judicial cultural tradition that built up over time, generally passed on orally from generation to generation in local and regional contexts. The law collections and other legal materials written and preserved in the Sumerian and Akkadian cuneiform texts and other extant written sources provide a window into this common-law culture of the wider ancient Near East. It is not that these texts drove the judicial tradition but that the texts reflect the common-law legal tradition that was alive and well in that cultural world.

GORING OX LAWS IN THE OLD TESTAMENT
AND THE ANCIENT NEAR EAST

In principle, the Old Testament law is both in its world and against its world. It is not surprising that there are similarities between some of the regulations in the law of Moses and those found in other sources from the ancient Near Eastern world. After all, many of the same kinds of situations would come under consideration. The cultures varied, of course, but the evidence suggests that there were also common features, some of which come through in legal texts.

Consider, for instance, the goring ox laws in Exodus 21:28-32. This is a rather complex discussion, so we cannot cover all the details here. Oxen were regular work animals and everywhere present. Because they were so large and powerful, they could also be dangerous if they went wild and attacked people or other animals with their head and horns and trampled them into the ground (i.e., goring). This led to the need for regulations known as the goring ox laws.[18]

According to Exodus 21:28, "If an ox gores a man or his wife and he dies, the ox shall surely be stoned and his flesh shall not be eaten, but the owner of the ox is free from liability" (my translation). The ox was stoned (a form of execution) and could not be eaten because it murdered the person.[19] Although the Laws of Hammurabi §250 does not mention what would happen to an ox that gored a person to death, the ruling is similar in other ways: "If an ox gores to death a man while it is passing through the streets, that case has no basis for a claim."[20]

---

[18]For more details than can be considered here, see the discussions, e.g., in J. J. Finkelstein, *The Ox That Gored*, TAPS vol. 71 pt. 2 (Philadelphia: American Philosophical Society, 1981); Greengus, *Laws in the Bible*, 172-79; and Westbrook and Wells, *Everyday Law in Biblical Israel*, 27-31. Cornelius Houtman, *Exodus*, HCOT, vol. 3 (Leuven, Belgium: Peeters, 2000), 172-82, 184-85, offers a comprehensive discussion of the history of interpretation of the goring ox laws in Ex 21:28-32, 35-36 with extensive bibliography. See also the remarks in William H. C. Propp, *Exodus 19–40*, AB 2A (New York: Doubleday, 2006), 232-36.

[19]See the more complete explanation in Nahum M. Sarna, *Exodus*, JPS Torah Commentary (Philadelphia: Jewish Publication Society, 1991), 128.

[20]*COS* 2:350.

The next verse in Exodus reads, "But if the ox was (known to be) a gorer previously *and its owner was warned, but he does not guard it,* and the ox put a man or his wife to death, it shall be stoned and also its owner shall be put to death" (Ex 21:29, my translation). In this case, because of the previous warning, they would also hold the owner responsible and liable for the goring. He would suffer execution for criminal negligence. The same shift to liability for the same reason also appears in the next regulation in the Laws of Hammurabi: "If a man's ox is a known gorer, and *the authorities of his city quarter notify him that it is a known gorer, but he does not blunt(?) its horns or control his ox,* and that ox gores to death a member of the *awīlu*-class, he [the owner] shall give 30 shekels of silver."[21]

The owner is liable here as in Exodus 21:29, but the level of owner liability is not the same—the Bible requires execution, the Laws of Hammurabi monetary payment. If the ox had gored previously but the person had not died, then the ox would have gained the reputation as one that gored, but there would have been no stoning of the ox in that case.

Interestingly, the next regulation in the Bible reduces the liability from execution to a monetary payment, like in the Laws of Hammurabi: "If a ransom is imposed on him, he shall give (for the) redemption of his life according to all that is imposed on him" (Ex 21:30, my translation).[22] Here is an instance of flexibility of the Mosaic law at the discretion of the court. Not everything in the law is hard and fast. Apparently, either the court or the family of the deceased, or the two combined, could set a ransom payment that the owner of the ox would pay to avoid execution.

The next variant in the regulations for the goring ox draws again on the principle of graduated payment found in the Bible and common in the ancient Near East. Exodus 21:32 refers to the goring of a slave to death: "If the ox gores a male or female slave, he [the

---

[21]*COS* 2.350 for LH § 251 (emphasis added). An *awīlu* was a free citizen.
[22]See the details of interpretation here in Greengus, *Laws in the Bible*, 173-75.

owner] must pay thirty shekels of silver to his master, and the ox shall be stoned to death" (my translation).

Instead of execution or ransom, the master of the slave received monetary compensation for the loss of his slave. It is important to note that this principle of graduated payment according to the "life value of the victim . . . is indeed the principle that governs remedies for wrongful death in almost every jurisdiction today."[23] The gradation in payment has nothing do with anyone being any less of a person or of less worth as a person than someone else, even if they were a slave. It was a matter of economic possessions and resources, and potential for economic productivity.

We have seen that there are differences between the goring ox regulations in the Laws of Hammurabi and those found in the Bible. Nevertheless, it would be hard to deny that there was common customary law underlying all of them. There is no "borrowing" here from one source to the other. As the saying goes, "it was in the water" they drank. On the one hand, the Lord worked with Israel in its context. He did not create a completely different set of regulations from those found in the surrounding world but used the common customary law of the day as an underlying foundation for his revelation of the Mosaic law. On the other hand, he did not just adopt this common law tradition as it was either. His special concerns came through loud and clear. He was meeting them where they were in the cultural world but also taking them where they needed to go to become a nation that would show forth his character and glory in the world.

The apostle Paul applied another ox law to the church in 1 Corinthians 9:9 and 1 Timothy 5:18, "Do not muzzle an ox while it is treading out the grain," citing Deuteronomy 25:4. In 1 Timothy 5:18 he also adds an allusion to Deuteronomy 24:14-15 and Leviticus 19:13, "The worker deserves his wages." The point in both places is that this

---

[23]Finkelstein, *The Ox That Gored*, 31-32.

is not just about oxen but has application to those who devote themselves to hard labor in the service of the Lord in the church.

It is *mean* and *abusive* to muzzle an ox while it is walking in food.
Think of the ox straining at the muzzle to try to eat some of the grain.
It amounts to torturing the ox. Similarly, it is vicious and callous for
people in the church to benefit from the ministry and not supply the
needs of the minister. Moreover, by the nature of the case, to muzzle
the ox while it is threshing the grain promotes an abusive disposition
in the owner that could well transfer to other situations. It is about
the owner's character. It is about the personal character of Christians
in the church too.

DIVINE REVELATION AND THE MOSAIC LAW

Given this common customary law reality, according to the Hebrew
Bible, there are also some essential differences between the ancient
Near Eastern and ancient Israelite judicial practice. The first and most
important of these comes to the forefront in Exodus 18. Jethro, Moses'
father-in-law, had come to visit him at Sinai and brought Moses' wife
and two sons along with him. While he was there, he observed the
excessive burden Moses was bearing in judging all the people himself
(Ex 18:13-16). His advice to Moses was, "You must be the people's
representative before God and bring their disputes to him. Teach
them his decrees and instructions, and show them the way they are
to live and how they are to behave" (Ex 18:19-20). He also suggested
assigning other leaders to judge the people according to what God
revealed directly to Moses when he brought their cases to the Lord.[24]

Of course, the wisdom and uncompromising character of the
judges was of utmost importance in the just application of the law to
the people. As Jethro put it, "select capable [Hebrew *hayil* 'stalwart,

---

[24]For a very helpful review of the extensive biblical, rabbinic, and historical critical discussion
regarding the origin of the laws in the Pentateuch, see Ze'ev Weisman, "The Place of the People
in the Making of Law and Judgment," in *Pomegranates and Golden Bells: Studies in Biblical, Jewish
and Near Eastern Ritual, Law and Literature in Honor of Jacob Milgrom*, ed. David P. Wright et al.
(Winona Lake, IN: Eisenbrauns, 1995), 407-20.

competent, qualified'] men from all the people—men who fear God, trustworthy men who hate dishonest gain" (Ex 18:21; cf. the same emphasis in Deut 16:18-20). The law calls for the same basic character qualities in all Israelites (see, e.g., Ex 23:1-9; Lev 19). Moses saw the wisdom in Jethro's advice and proceeded to do just what he recommended: "He chose capable men from all Israel and made them leaders of the people, officials over thousands, hundreds, fifties and tens. They served as judges for the people at all times. The difficult cases they brought to Moses, but the simple ones they decided themselves" (Ex 18:25-26).

With certain necessary changes, this became the model after the death of Moses too. After they conquered and occupied the land, they were to hold court in the local city gates (Deut 16:18–17:7), but if they could not decide a particular case, they would bring it to the central sanctuary for judgment by the Levitical priests and judges who were there (Deut 17:8-13). Moses and Aaron were from the tribe of Levi (Ex 6:13-27), so the Levitical priests became the custodians of the Mosaic law (Deut 17:8-9; cf. Deut 17:18). Moreover, the Levites lived in cities distributed throughout the land (Num 35), which would support the spread of the knowledge of the law throughout the land, assuming these Levitical priests would remain faithful to the Lord and the Mosaic law.[25]

Of course, the historical reality is that they often did not remain faithful (see, e.g., Judg 17:5-12 with Ezek 44:10-16 and their association with judicial practice; Ezek 44:24). After the Babylonian exile, Ezra, an Aaronic Levitical priest (a Zadokite; Ezek 44:15-16), faithfully brought the Mosaic law to bear in postexilic Israel (Ezra 7:1-10): "Ezra set his heart to seek the law of the Lord and to practice [it], and teach statute and judgement in Israel" (Ezra 7:10). Under the governorship of

---

[25]Daniel I. Block, "'The Meeting Places of God in the Land': Another Look at the Towns of the Levites," in *Current Issues in Priestly and Related Literature: The Legacy of Jacob Milgrom and Beyond,* ed. Roy E. Gane and Ada Taggar-Cohen, SBL Resources for Bible Study (Atlanta: SBL Press, 2015), 93-121, esp. 100-120.

Nehemiah, he even read the law of Moses publicly and taught it with the assistance of other Levites (Neh 8:1-9).

According to the Pentateuch, this was not a new idea that the "legalist" Ezra conjured up late in the history of Israel. Moses commanded it already in his day:

> At the end of every seven years, in the year for canceling debts, during the Festival of Tabernacles, when all Israel comes to appear before the LORD your God at the place he will choose, you shall read this law before them in their hearing. Assemble the people—men, women and children, and the foreigners residing in your towns—so they can listen and learn to fear the LORD your God and follow carefully all the words of this law. Their children, who do not know this law, must hear it and learn to fear the LORD your God as long as you live in the land you are crossing the Jordan to possess. (Deut 31:10-13)

Since Julius Wellhausen in the nineteenth century there has been a common tendency in Old Testament scholarship to characterize postexilic Judaism as "legalistic"—instituting an oppressive use of the Mosaic law to impose excessive restrictions on people, supported by religious zeal and power. Ezra is supposed to have begun this trend.[26]

It is true that, during the period between the Old and New Testaments, certain sects of Judaism developed in this direction, leading to some of the tension between Jesus and the Jewish leaders of his day. Ezra, however, did not initiate it and was not part of it. He did not multiply restrictions beyond those that were already present in the Torah itself. He simply called the people to faithful obedience to their covenant with God through abiding by the laws of Moses— something they agreed to at the initiation of the covenant (Ex 24:3-8; cf. Ex 19:5-8). Many passages in the Torah call for faithfulness to the covenant law both in the courts and among the populace as a whole (see, e.g., Ex 34:11-26; Lev 10:10-11; Deut 4:1-8; with the passages on judicial law cited above).[27]

---

[26]See, e.g., the recent iteration of this view in Westbrook and Wells, Everyday Law in Biblical Israel, 29-31.

[27]See the full treatment of this issue in Ze'ev Weisman, "The Place of the People in the Making of Law and Judgment," 407-20.

Returning now to Exodus 18, Moses had been the only judge for all Israel according to his response to Jethro in this passage: "The people come to me to seek God's will. Whenever they have a dispute, it is brought to me, and I decide between the parties and inform them of God's decrees and instructions" (Ex 18:15-16). In Exodus, this took place at Sinai (Ex 18:5), but it is placed before the Sinai theophany and giving of the law in Exodus 19–24. In Moses' review of the Sinai history in Deuteronomy 1:6-18, however, it seems that the Jethro event actually took place just before they left Sinai to travel to the Promised Land. Compare Deuteronomy 1:6-7, "The LORD our God said to us at Horeb, 'You have stayed long enough at this mountain. Break camp and advance into the hill country of the Amorites,'" with Deuteronomy 1:9, "*At that time* I said to you, 'You are too heavy a burden for me to carry alone.'" In the context, the expression "at that time" refers back to the Lord's command to leave Sinai in Deuteronomy 1:6. Deuteronomy 1:19 begins immediately with the journey from Sinai to Kadesh Barnea. Thus, it appears that Jethro's visit took place around the time the Lord told Moses to leave Sinai to travel to the Promised Land.[28]

CASUISTIC AND APODICTIC LAW

Case law is one of two main kinds of legal regulations in the Mosaic law, often referred to as "casuistic" law.[29] It consists of legal precedents drawn from particular cases already adjudicated, usually stated in if/then format. It would not take long for precedents to accumulate and therefore be available for application to similar cases as they arose. From this background of experience in bringing cases before the Lord, Moses could instruct the new cadre of judges and they, in turn, could judge the people accordingly. If something new

---

[28]Also, the fact that the Samaritan Pentateuch inserted Deut 1:9-18 right after Ex 18:24 supports the understanding that Deut 1:9-18 belongs with the event described in Ex 18.

[29]See, e.g., the introduction to casuistic and apodictic law in Morrow, *Introduction to Biblical Law*, 74-75. In my view, "participial" law, as Morrow refers to it, belongs to the general category of casuistic law. See, e.g., Ex 21:12, "One who strikes a man and he dies, shall be put to death."

arose, Moses would go to the Lord for instruction on how to handle the matter.

As Jethro advised, "You must be the people's representative before God and bring their disputes to him" (Ex 18:19; cf. Ex 18:26). Exodus 33:7-11 seems to describe the regular procedure for Moses taking legal cases to the Lord but may also include other kinds of inquiries:

> Now Moses used to take a tent and pitch it outside the camp some distance away, calling it the "tent of meeting." Anyone inquiring of the LORD would go to the tent of meeting outside the camp. . . . As Moses went into the tent, the pillar of cloud would come down and stay at the entrance, while the LORD spoke with Moses. . . . The LORD would speak to Moses face to face, as one speaks to a friend. Then Moses would return to the camp, but his young aide Joshua son of Nun did not leave the tent.

This is not the same tent as the tabernacle, although both were "tents of meeting." The Lord met only with Moses at this tent but with Moses and all the people at the tabernacle tent (see, e.g., Lev 9:23-24). The former was located outside the camp, partway up the side of the mountain (cf. Ex 19:17, 21-22; 20:21, and the remarks on the Sinai theophany below). The latter was located in the middle of the camp with the tribes surrounding it.

"Apodictic" law is the other major kind of legal expression in ancient Israel. It consists of principles of law, whether positive or negative commands, such as the Ten Commandments (but by no means limited to them). Casuistic and apodictic regulations sometimes come in separate groups, but the two types also appear together, as for example in Exodus 23:1-9. Apodictic law does not normally declare a specific penalty for the crime committed if one violates it. For example, Leviticus 24:11 tells of the son of an Israelite woman who blasphemed by cursing the name of the Lord in a fight. This was a direct violation of the apodictic law in Exodus 22:28, "You must not curse God," in which case there was no indication of what to do if someone broke the command. The procedure, therefore, was for Moses to take the matter to the Lord to determine the punishment, which was to be execution by stoning (Lev 24:16; for similar procedures, see Num 9:1-14; 15:32-36; 27:1-11).[30]

PROGRESSIVE GROWTH OF THE MOSAIC LAW

The discussion above demonstrates that there was an ongoing, progressive growth of the Mosaic law from Sinai through the wilderness wanderings. Cases kept coming to Moses and he kept going to the Lord to resolve them. The procedures introduced in Exodus 18 continued not only while they were at Sinai but through the whole forty years. This is one of the reasons we have so many different collections and individual units of law lodged at various points from Exodus through Deuteronomy.

According to Exodus 19–24, God spoke the Ten Commandments directly to the people during his terrifying theophany at Sinai, but, at the request of the people, Moses became the mediator between them and God for the book of the covenant (Ex 21–23; cf. Ex 24:4, 7) and the rest of the law. Aside from the Ten Commandments, therefore, God proclaimed the first set of laws to Moses alone, many of which are in casuistic form. The placing of Exodus 18 before this, even though the event took place later, is strategic in a literary and judicial way. It suggests that the law began to grow case by case almost immediately after they arrived at Sinai, as the people brought cases to Moses for him to gain resolution directly from the Lord. The Lord initiated this when he appeared in the great and terrifying theophany.

This all took place in the wake of the Lord's deliverance from slavery in Egypt, which provides the redemptive setting and the framing and shaping ethos of the whole law, beginning with the first line of the Ten Commandments: "I am the LORD your God, who brought you out of Egypt, out of the land of slavery" (Ex 20:2). It continues with the first set of casuistic laws in the book of the covenant—namely, the debt slave regulations in Exodus 21:1-11. No other collection of laws in the

---

[30]See the helpful remarks in Baruch A. Levine, *Leviticus*, JPS Torah Commentary (Philadelphia: Jewish Publication Society, 1989), 166-67.

Bible or in the ancient Near East begins with slave law. This first set of casuistic regulations reveals how much the Mosaic law abides under the shadow of their deliverance from slavery. This is especially true for the book of the covenant but extends all the way to the last chapter of legal regulations in the Pentateuch (Deut 26).

The book of the covenant continues with various regulations, the main substance of which anticipates their movement from Sinai immediately to the land that God had promised them. The final section of the book of the covenant in Exodus 23:20-33 confirms their expectation to move immediately from Sinai to conquer and occupy the Promised Land and outlines God's plan to go before them and make them victorious. The regulations in Exodus 21:1–23:19, therefore, reflect the common customary law that would go into effect at that time. In the meantime, they lived as a large traveling camp of family, clan, and tribal people for whom Moses served as the chief judge, mediating God's law to them. It should not surprise us if the book of the covenant as we now have it expanded during this time, with the addition of the some of the precedents established through the process outlined in Exodus 18:15-16. Sinai was where the continued expansion of the law began after God revealed it in the initial theophany.

The various collections of laws introduced early in this chapter stretch from Exodus through Deuteronomy. Three of them display significant parallels between them: the book of the covenant (Ex 21–23), the holiness regulations (Lev 17–27), and the Deuteronomic regulations (Deut 12–26). Moreover, there are several chapters of Mosaic law strewn through narratives of the wilderness wanderings in Numbers 10–36. Clearly, the law kept expanding all the way from Sinai to Moab.

As they traveled through and camped in the wilderness with the tabernacle in their midst, for example, they could not eat meat unless they brought the animal to the tabernacle as a sacrifice. The priests would see that they offered it there as a peace offering to the Lord and would put the fat and blood on the altar in the tabernacle for them

(Lev 17:1-12; cf. Lev 3:17). This would keep them from going astray by sacrificing to goat idols or demons along the way.

At the time of the initial giving of the book of the covenant when Israel first arrived at Sinai, on the other hand, there was no tabernacle yet. Even the initial revelation and regulations for the tabernacle do not commence until Exodus 25, after the ratification of the covenant in Exodus 24. This is why the altar regulations in Exodus 20:24-26 do not mention offering only at the tabernacle altar but call for solitary altars built from earth and uncut stone "in any place where I (the Lord) cause my name to be remembered" (Ex 20:24). This is the kind of altar Moses built in Exodus 24:4 for the ratification of the covenant, and it would be the same for the ceremony on Mount Ebal after they entered the land (Deut 27:5-7; cf. Josh 8:30-35).

As noted earlier, however, after the building of the tabernacle, if they wanted to eat meat while they were traveling through the wilderness as a camp, they could only offer the animal on the tabernacle altar, as Leviticus 17:1-9 makes clear. They must not make Exodus 20:24-26 altars in the wilderness. This would change again when they conquered and spread out in the land, according to the Deuteronomy 12:15-25 regulation for "profane slaughter." The laws changed because the circumstances changed. This is important. It shows that even within the law itself, the law sometimes changed over time due to the changing realities in which the people would be living. The shift from the Old to the New Testament required changes too because the circumstances changed. Part three of this book will show how this works out according to the New Testament.

THE REDEMPTIVE SETTING OF THE LAW

As argued above, the Mosaic law draws heavily from the common customary law of the ancient Near East, locally and regionally. But biblical law is also distinctive. Scholars have observed that the so-called priestly code (Lev 1–16) lies at the center of the Pentateuch— right in the middle of it. This is distinctive in the Old Testament as compared to the ancient Near Eastern collections of law. It attends directly to the worship of God in ancient Israel, which was the first principle in the covenant then and now, from the Ten Commandments forward. Above all else, believers in ancient Israel and in the New Testament church today are worshipers of God. This has always been and continues to be our highest calling, and it is at the heart of the Mosaic law.

Furthermore, the Mosaic law is above all monotheistic. Other societies in the ancient Near East were polytheistic, and their law collections reflect that. There is only one God in Israel, Yahweh, and they were to worship him exclusively. Moreover, the Lord himself is the king in ancient Israel. It is a theocratic nation and the law corresponds to it. Human kings rule the other nations. These kings were not considered to be divine (as the Pharaoh was in Egypt). The prologue and the epilogue to the Laws of Hammurabi, for example, clearly demonstrate that the whole purpose of the composition was to show how pious and righteous he was before his gods and his people. It was a royal inscription supporting the human king's rule.[31] Some of it was simple propaganda, but it also included positive ethics of a good rule—for example, special care for the poor and the disadvantaged in society.

One other particular feature of the Mosaic law sets it apart from all others in the ancient Near East—namely, the setting of the law in the *redemptive context* of God's deliverance of Israel from slavery in Egypt. The whole narrative in Exodus 1–17 leads up to and narrates the exodus from Egypt. In addition to this, and just as important, at key points, references to this redemption frame and shape all of the law collections in Exodus through Deuteronomy. Moreover, the same theme permeates the law collections themselves.[32] It begins with the

---

[31]See the full discussion of this point in Hurowitz, *Inu Anum Ṣirum*.

[32]For a full treatment of this topic see Richard E. Averbeck, "The Egyptian Sojourn and Deliverance from Slavery in the Framing and Shaping of the Mosaic Law," in *"Did I Not Bring Israel Out of Egypt?" Biblical, Archaeological, and Egyptological Perspectives on the Exodus Narratives*, ed. James

extreme outside boundaries of the law within the Torah and moves inward: first, the whole law, from Sinai to Moab (Ex 19–Deut 26), and then the law as revealed at Sinai (Ex 19–24), and eventually to the end of Leviticus 25.

THE EXODUS FROM EXODUS 19 TO DEUTERONOMY 26

As soon as they arrive at Sinai, they camped there in the desert. After they set up camp, God called to Moses from the mountain: "This is what you are to say to the descendants of Jacob and what you are to tell the people of Israel: 'You yourselves have seen *what I did to Egypt, and how I carried you on eagles' wings and brought you to myself*'" (Ex 19:3-4). The Sinai theophany began with this: God's deliverance from Egypt. The very last chapter of legal regulations in the Torah comes back in expanded form to the importance of remembering this deliverance. Consider Deuteronomy 26:5-10, often referred to as the "small credo," which was to be recited at a first fruits festival celebration after the conquest and occupation of the Promised Land:

> My father was a wandering [or "perishing," or "ailing," or "refugee"] Aramean, and he went down into Egypt with a few people and lived there (as a *resident alien*) and became a great nation, powerful and numerous. *But the Egyptians mistreated us and made us suffer, subjecting us to harsh labor.* Then we cried out to the LORD, the God of our ancestors, and the LORD heard our voice and saw our misery, toil and oppression. *So the LORD brought us out of Egypt with a mighty hand and an outstretched arm*, with great terror and with signs and wonders. He brought us to this place and gave us this land, a land flowing with milk and honey; and now I bring the firstfruits of the soil that you, LORD, have given me.

The credo begins with a reference to Jacob as a "wandering Aramean." The following clauses speak of him and his family living in Egypt as resident aliens, growing from few into many, and then being enslaved. The Lord's merciful deliverance from Egypt comes next, and

---

Hoffmeier, Alan Millard, and Gary Rendsburg, BBRMS 13 (Winona Lake, IN: Eisenbrauns, 2016), 143-75.

finally the anticipated conquest of the land (Deut 26:7-9). The Israelites themselves had been the less fortunate, vulnerable, and enslaved resident aliens in Egypt (Deut 26:5), so the passage goes on to the concern for "the Levite, the foreigner, the fatherless and the widow" in Israel (Deut 26:11-12).

THE EXODUS IN THE FIRST COMMANDMENT

The law as given at Sinai extends from the introduction of the Ten Commandments in Exodus 20:1 to the colophon in Leviticus 26:46, "These are the decrees, the judgments, and the instructions that the LORD established between himself and the Israelites at Mount Sinai by the hand of Moses" (cf. Lev 27:34; Num 1-9). The blessings and curses of the covenant in Leviticus 26 are the natural end to the covenant law at Sinai (see also the curses and blessings in Moab in Deut 27-28).

Exodus 20:2 stands at the head of the Ten Commandments (cf. also Deut 5:6): "I am the Lord your God who brought you out from the land of Egypt, from the house of slavery." As in Deuteronomy 26 at the end of the law, the fundamental principle with which the law begins is the redemptive history that made the covenant possible.

FROM THE BOOK OF THE COVENANT TO THE CONCLUSION OF THE LAW AT SINAI

It is common for the units of law in the Torah to begin and end with cultic worship regulations. The laws of the book of the covenant actually begin with the idol prohibition and altar regulations in Exodus 20:22-26 and end with three annual feasts in Exodus 23:14-19.[33] Right after the cultic introduction, Exodus 21:1 introduces the regulations that follow in Exodus 21-23, "Now, these are the regulations which you shall set before them." What is of special interest to us here is that

---

[33]See, e.g., Joe M. Sprinkle, "'The Book of the Covenant'": A Literary Approach, JSOTSup 174 (Sheffield, 1994), 36-39. See also Lev 17 with Lev 27 for the holiness laws and Deut 12 with Deut 26 for the core legal section of the book of Deuteronomy.

the debt slave release laws for fellow Israelites follow immediately in Exodus 21:2-11. They begin in Exodus 21:2 with the release of the male slave, "When you acquire a *Hebrew slave*, he shall serve you six years and in the seventh year he shall go out as a free man, without payment," and they end with the release of the female slave in Exodus 21:11, "But if he does not do these three things for her, then she shall go out without payment; there is no money (involved)" (my translations).

As noted above, none of the extrabiblical ancient Near Eastern law collections begin with any kind of slave law. The reason for starting the casuistic laws in the Pentateuch with this topic is most likely the same reason that the Ten Commandments begin the way they do. God had just delivered them from slavery in Egypt. They must not now turn around and enslave one another in Israel (see also Deut 15:15). Yes, some people may fall into terrible financial constraints, even to the point where they would submit themselves to the service of someone else for a time, but this is limited to six years. They must go out from their bondage to such service in the seventh year, set free from any further obligations for their debt.

Not only does the book of the covenant begin with debt slave law, but the whole of the law given at Sinai also ends with debt slave regulations in Leviticus 25:39-55, just before the blessings and curses of the covenant in Leviticus 26. The main historical and theological rationale comes to full expression in the last verse of Leviticus 25: "the children of Israel are *my* slaves; they are *my* slaves whom *I* brought out from the land of Egypt. *I* am the Lord your God" (Lev 25:55, my translation; cf. Lev 26:13). The double appearance of both *my* and *I* in this verse is conspicuous and emphatic.

Furthermore, Leviticus 25 flows immediately into Leviticus 26 with no break between them, where the first verse says, "You must not make for yourselves useless images, and you must not set up for yourselves idols and standing stones, and you must not allow a carved stone in your land to bow down to it, for *I* am the LORD your God" (Lev 26:1, my translation). This yields, of course, a sequence that echoes the beginning of the covenant law at Sinai. The emphatic statement of the Lord's deliverance from slavery in Egypt in Leviticus 25:55 (see Ex 20:2, the first word) leads directly to the forceful prohibition against idol images, standing stones, or carved stones in Leviticus 26:1 (cf. Ex 20:3-6). Thus, we have here at the end of the law as given at Sinai the same sequence as at the beginning.

Finally, as noted above, the same ethos of redemption permeates the law internally. It occurs often in regulations against mistreatment and injustice against foreigners in Israel (Ex 22:21; 23:9; Lev 19:34; Deut 10:18-19; 24:17-18), in support of living holy, obedient, and faithful before the Lord (Lev 11:45; 22:31-33; Num 15:37-41; Deut 4:15-20, 32-40; 6:20-22; 8:10-14; 13:5) and treating each other justly and generously (Lev 19:35-36; 25:35-38).

Conclusion

The narrative context into which the law fits is significant. God gave the law to the ancient Israelites after having already delivered them from their slavery in Egypt. This is the whole premise of the law. The reason God brought them out of their slavery in Egypt was his previous covenant commitment to the patriarchs. While they were in Egypt, "The Israelites groaned in their slavery and cried out, and their cry for help because of their slavery went up to God. God heard their groaning and he *remembered his covenant with Abraham, with Isaac and with Jacob.* So God looked on the Israelites and was concerned about them" (Ex 2:23-25; cf. Ex 3:6 with Lev 26:45; Deut 7:7-8). There would have been no Mosaic covenant without the Abrahamic covenant. The covenant made at Sinai was a natural and necessary extension of the Lord's commitment to the patriarchs, which included a commitment to their descendants. In Egypt, God called them to put their trust in him to deliver them from their slavery. The Mosaic covenant and its law would come later.

In other words, from the beginning God gave the law to ancient Israel based on his covenant grace to them in having already delivered them from their slavery in Egypt. He did not command them to keep the law *in order for* him to deliver them, but *in response to* the fact that he had already delivered them. The sequence is essential for understanding how God works his relationship with us as fallen sinful people.[34] It corresponds to the gospel in the New Testament. His call to us to live faithfully in Christ follows salvation by faith alone in Jesus Christ alone; it doesn't come before it (see, e.g., Eph 2:8-10). This is a core principle running through the entire Bible. It is in the very nature of the way God works his covenant grace in us, among us, and through us.

---

[34]See also the emphasis on this point in Carmen Joy Imes, *Bearing God's Name: Why Sinai Still Matters* (Downers Grove, IL: IVP Academic, 2019), 12, 35, and other places.

Four

THE SINAI NARRATIVE AND
THE TEN COMMANDMENTS

THE COVENANT MAKING NARRATIVE in Exodus 19–24 provides the immediate setting for the first two major sets of regulations in the Mosaic law: the Ten Commandments (Ex 20:1-17) and the book of the covenant (Ex 21–23). This chapter will discuss the narrative and the Ten Commandments along with some of the related regulations.

THE EXODUS 19–24 NARRATIVE
CONTEXT OF THE LAW AT SINAI

The narrative in Exodus 19–20; 24 is one of those genuinely confusing passages in the Hebrew Bible—one of the classic cases. There is actually one place in the text where it appears that Moses himself is confused by all the going up and down the mountain. The Lord had descended to the top of Sinai and called Moses up to him (Ex 19:20), but then it seems that the Lord immediately told him to "go down" in order to warn the people not to follow him up the mountain. Moses had already set up the boundary around the mountain to keep the people back (Ex 19:12-13), so he objected: "the people cannot come up"

(Ex 19:23). This confusion on Moses' part suggests that perhaps our confusion is justified, and that the historical scene itself really was confusing to begin with.[1]

THE SINAI THEOPHANY

The purpose of the theophany in the narration of Exodus 19:9–20:21 was to so impress the ancient Israelites with their God, and Moses as his mediator, that they would take their covenant commitment to him seriously. According to Exodus 19:9, "The LORD said to Moses, 'I am going to come to you in a dense cloud, so that the people will hear me speaking with you and will always put their trust in you.'" The same rationale appears in the summary of the occasion in Deuteronomy 5:28-33 and also in more general terms, for example, in Exodus 32–34; Leviticus 10; 24:10-23; and Numbers 15:32-41.

Although the narrative is complex, based on certain literary features of the story and the parallel passages (see Deut 4:10-14, 33; 5:4-5, 22-31), it is probably best to treat it as largely sequential.[2] In fact, a key grammatical pattern unifies the passage and clarifies the movements. It is the consistent alternation of the Hebrew prepositions for going up "in/at/on" (Hebrew *b*) the mountain, used for what the people are supposed to do (Ex 19:12-13, 17, 23-24), which stands in contrast with going up "to/into/unto" (Hebrew *'el*) the mountain, for what Moses does (Ex 19:3, 20; 20:21; 24:1-2).

---

[1] Richard E. Averbeck, "Pentateuchal Criticism and the Priestly Torah," in *Do Historical Matters Matter for Faith: A Critical Appraisal of Modern and Postmodern Approaches to the Bible*, ed. James K. Hoffmeier and Dennis R. Magary (Wheaton, IL: Crossway, 2012), 151-79, summarizes and critiques the history of the historical critical approach and suggests a reading that is the basis for the discussion that follows here. See the helpful discussions in G. C. Chirichigno, "The Narrative Structure of Ex 19–24," *Biblica* 68 (1987): 457-79; Joe M. Sprinkle, *"The Book of the Covenant": A Literary Approach*, JSOTSup 174 (Sheffield: JSOT Press, 1994), 16-34. For the best and most recent summary of the analysis of the passage from a historical critical point of view in combination with rabbinic interpretation, see Benjamin D. Sommer, *Revelation and Authority: Sinai in Jewish Scripture in Tradition*, ABRL (New Haven, CT: Yale University Press, 2015). Consider also the careful summary, analysis, and critique of the many historical critical proposals in T. D. Alexander, *From Paradise to Promised Land: An Introduction to the Pentateuch*, 3rd ed. (Grand Rapids, MI: Baker Academic, 2012), 64-81.

[2] See, e.g., the simple outline in Shalom M. Paul, *Studies in the Book of the Covenant in the Light of Cuneiform and Biblical Law*, VTSup 18 (Leiden: Brill, 1970), 29.

Even though on the surface the storyline is confusing, if we follow the lead of these grammatical features, it actually makes good sense. A close reading of the text suggests the following. Although they trembled at the sound and appearance of the divine theophany on the ominous third day (Ex 19:16), Moses brought the people out to meet God "at the foot of the mountain" (Ex 19:17; i.e., at the lowest edge of the mountain outside the boundary referred to in Ex 19:12-13). In the meantime, the top of the mountain was ablaze and resounding with God's theophany (Ex 19:18, 20; cf. Ex 3:1-12).

As the people stood there at the foot of the mountain, "Moses was speaking and God was answering him in thunder" (Ex 19:19). Then Moses *ascended* to the *top* of the mountain (Ex 19:20) only to be told by God that he should *descend* (Ex 19:21) once more to make sure that the people obey his boundary restrictions (cf. Ex 19:12-13) and, in addition, to fetch Aaron up with him (Ex 19:21-24). It seems that the reason for the Lord's concern was that he himself was going to *descend* further down the mountain in a cloud of thick darkness (Ex 20:21; cf. Ex 19:16) in order to speak "face to face" not only with Moses but also with the people (Deut 5:4). If the people were too far up the mountain (i.e., beyond the designated border; see again Ex 19:12-13), the Lord would "break out against them" as he descended (Ex 19:22).

As Moses descended to the people at the foot of the mountain to follow the Lord's most recent instructions (Ex 19:25), the Lord God descended toward the people in the cloud to meet with Moses and the people and pronounce the Ten Commandments to them "face to face" (Ex 20:1-17; cf. Ex 19:25 with Ex 20:1; Deut 4:10-13; 5:22; 9:10). After speaking the Ten Commandments, God paused (Deut 5:22). As he had been speaking, the fear of the people grew so overwhelming that they moved back away from Moses, who was at the foot of the mountain with them, and "stayed at a distance" (Ex 20:18), thus putting Moses in a position of standing between the people and the Lord (see Deut 5:4-5).[3]

---

[3]Deuteronomy 5:5 implies that, amid all the thunder and trumpets and so on, when the people moved to stand at a distance away from the foot of the mountain (Ex 20:18-19) they also lost the

When the Lord paused the people approached Moses, who was therefore apparently within the reach of the people and standing outside the boundary, to request that he be their mediator (Ex 20:19-20; cf. Deut 5:23-27). God responded positively to their request (cf. Deut 5:28-29 with Ex 20:20) and told Moses to have them return to their tents (Deut 5:30). Meanwhile, Moses himself was to approach and stand there by the Lord (i.e., "draw near to" the cloud of "thick darkness where God was"; Ex 20:21) to hear the remainder of the revelation. Consequently, as their mediator, Moses received from the Lord "all the commands, decrees and laws" (i.e., those in Ex 20:22–23:33), which he would then be responsible to "teach" them to live by in the land (Ex 21:1; cf. Deut 5:31 with Deut 4:14).

According to Exodus 19:24, the Lord intended that Moses bring only Aaron back up with him on the mountain the next time he came up. The next reference to Aaron, however, is not until Exodus 24:1, where the Lord commanded Moses to bring "Aaron, Nadab and Abihu, and seventy of the elders of Israel" up with him. Even in this instance, however, only Moses was to "approach the Lord," while "the others must not come near" (Ex 24:2), including Aaron.

By the request of the people, Moses became the mediator (Ex 19:21), as was the Lord's intention from the beginning of the theophany: "I am going to come to you in a dense cloud, so that the people will hear me speaking with you and will always *put their trust in you*" (Ex 19:9). When Moses "approached the thick darkness where God was" (Ex 20:21), the Lord met him at the place where he had left off with the Ten Commandments, just up the slope at some distance from the people. It was there that God declared to Moses the set of regulations that came to be known as the book of the covenant (Ex 20:22–23:33;

---

ability to understand what the Lord was saying when he pronounced the Ten Commandments (Ex 20:1-17; Deut 5:6-21). Moses, therefore, had to "declare" to them even "the word of the Lord" (Deut 5:5) in the Ten Commandments, which follow immediately in Deuteronomy 5:6-21. See Sprinkle, *Book of the Covenant*, 23-24, and Chirichigno, "Narrative Structure," 470. For a good summary of the problems scholars have had with Deut 5:5, see also M. Weinfeld, *Deuteronomy 1-11*, AB (New York: Doubleday, 1991), 240-41.

cf. Ex 24:4, 7). Moses did not go up into the theophany on top of the mountain again until Exodus 24:12-18.[4]

THE THEOPHANY AND THE TEN COMMANDMENTS

Later, after the theophany, when he wrote the record of the account (i.e., the narrative of Ex 19–24), Moses fit God's proclamation of the Ten Commandments into it at the most natural place. This placement was not easy because the proclamation took place in the process of the Lord's descent down the mount, as he came closer to the people and the people backed away. Moses may have said something to the people as he reached them (Ex 19:25), but it seems that this was lost in the turn to God's theophanic proclamation of the Ten Commandments (Ex 20:1).

The purpose of the awesome and terrifying theophany at Sinai, therefore, was to establish Moses as the mediator and to do it in such a way that the people would fear the Lord and actually obey his law. The latter becomes especially clear in Deuteronomy 5:29, "Oh, that their hearts would be inclined to fear me and keep all my commands always." This would be for their own good, "so that it might go well with them and their children forever!" The law was a good thing, and God's intentions were good toward them when he gave it. The writer of Hebrews drew on this and related incidents at Sinai (and other passages), when he referred to the shaking of heaven and earth that is still to come. He refers back to Exodus 19–20, "At that time his voice shook the earth" (Heb 12:26), and then cites Haggai 2:6 (cf. Hag 2:21), looking forward to a time when God will shake not only earth but heaven too. Thus, there is coming a day when there will be "the removing of what can be shaken—that is, created things—so that what cannot be shaken may remain" (Heb 12:27).

---

[4]For further discussion of this scene, see now Richard E. Averbeck, "Reading the Torah in a Better Way: Unity and Diversity in Text, Genre, and Compositional History," in *Paradigm Change in Pentateuchal Research*, ed. Matthias Armgardt, Benjamin Kilchör, and Markus Zehnder, BZABR 22 (Wiesbaden: Harrassowitz, 2019), 24-25 and the lit. cited there. This was also the origin of the regular practice described in Ex 33:7-11.

The point Hebrews makes is that, "since we are receiving a kingdom that cannot be shaken, let us be thankful, and so worship God acceptably with reverence and awe" (Heb 12:28). As at the establishment of the Mosaic covenant at Sinai, it is still true for us today under the new covenant that "our God is a consuming fire" (Heb 12:29; cf. Deut 4:24). Note the new covenant mentioned in Hebrews 12:24 and the whole argument in Hebrews 12:18-29. There is no difference between the God of the Old Testament and the one of the New Testament. He is no one to trifle with.

There was no awe and fear inducing theophany in Moab like at Sinai. Instead, there was Moses "preaching" the law (Deut 1:5). If one wants to learn how to preach the law, this is probably one of the best places to start. At the core of Moses' preaching was the link between keeping the Lord's commandments and prosperity in the land (Deut 6:1-3; recall Deut 5:29). The call was to love the Lord by means of keeping those commands, as we see in the Great Shema that follows: "Hear [Hebrew *šəma* '], O Israel: The LORD our God, the LORD is one. Love the LORD your God with all your heart and with all your soul and with all your strength" (Deut 6:4-5). The next verse says: "These commandments that I give you today are to be upon your hearts" (Deut 6:6), and the following two expand on this: "Impress them on your children. Talk about them when you sit at home and when you walk along the road, when you lie down and when you get up" (Deut 6:7).

THE TEN COMMANDMENTS

When people think of the Old Testament law, the first laws that usually come to mind are, of course, the so-called Ten Commandments as recorded in Exodus 20:1-17 (see also Deut 5:6-21). This is good and natural. After all, these are the only commands God spoke directly to all Israel and wrote on stone tablets with his finger (Ex 31:18; cf. Ex 32:15-16; 34:1, 28; Deut 4:13; 5:22; 9:10). God gave the laws of the book of the covenant later (Ex 20:22–23:33) through the mediation of Moses (Ex 24:4, 7; cf. Heb 9:18-20). It is unclear whether the book of the covenant reading in

Exodus 24:7 included the Ten Commandments also written on a scroll for that occasion, but Exodus 24:12 anticipates God giving them to Moses on the tablets of stone high up on Mount Sinai.[5]

The relationship between the Ten Commandments and the book of the covenant is also complicated in other ways. As some have put it, the Ten Commandments are "more moral than legal,"[6] or perhaps "semi-legal . . . more of a covenant document, which defines the borders of affiliation between the Israelite people and their God."[7] As discussed in chapter three above, all ten are apodictic in nature—straight commands without sanctions or punishments given for their violation. Moreover, the tenth commandment turns attention directly to issues that law cannot regulate in any kind of direct way: "You shall not covet" (Ex 20:17; but see also, e.g., Lev 19:17). The other law collections in the Bible are a combination of casuistic and apodictic commands. The Ten Commandments told Israel what they simply must do or not do in ancient Israel, depending on whether the particular command is positive or negative. They are the essence of their covenant commitment to God. In fact, a few passages seem to equate them with "the covenant" (Ex 34:28; Deut 4:13; 9:11). Later Jewish tradition associates them with the covenant renewal at the Feast of Weeks grain harvest festival (late May–early June; later referred to as Pentecost) in the third month (Sivan), matching the chronology of Exodus 19:1.[8]

In general, the Ten Commandments are the foundational principles of the covenant and law for ancient Israel as the theocratic kingdom of God. They identify Israel as the people of the Lord. He set the rules. The rest of the law develops "the basic guidelines in the

---

[5]Dalit Rom-Shiloni, "The Decalogue," in *The Oxford Handbook of Biblical Law*, ed. Pamela Barmash (Oxford: Oxford University Press, 2019), 144; and Edward L. Greenstein, "Decalogue," in *The Oxford Handbook of Bible and Law*, ed. Brent A. Strawn (Oxford: Oxford University Press, 2015), 168.

[6]Greenstein, "Decalogue," 171.

[7]Rom-Shiloni, "The Decalogue," 149.

[8]See Jubilees 6:17 in the Old Testament pseudepigrapha (second century BC) and the helpful discussion in Greenstein, "Decalogue," 170-71.

Decalogue."[9] In fact, some scholars argue for the arrangement of the regulations in Deuteronomy 12–25 in the order of the Ten Commandments as given in Deuteronomy 5:6-21.[10] The other laws in the book of the covenant and other law collections in the Torah work out how these principle commands were to apply to ancient Israel in its ancient Near Eastern social, economic, civil, political, and religious context.[11] As Moses put it forty years later, "These are the commandments the LORD proclaimed in a loud voice to your whole assembly there on the mountain from out of the fire, the cloud and the deep darkness; *and he added nothing more.* Then he wrote them on two stone tablets and gave them to me" (Deut 5:22; cf. Deut 4:13-14).

The Decalogue starts with the vertical relationship between Israel and their God and then shifts to their horizontal relationships with one another.[12] The fact that there is a shift is clear, but scholars vary as to where they place it. The first five all mention the Lord, the second five do not, so some put the division between the fifth and sixth commandments. From this point of view, a tradition developed that envisions the writing of the first five on one of the tablets and the second five on the other (just writing on one side of each tablet).[13] Based on more recent analogies to the Hittite suzerain vassal treaties, however, it seems likely that the whole set of the Ten Commandments was written on both tablets, and on both sides of each, as the Bible itself

---

[9]Patrick D. Miller, "The Ten Commandments," in *The New Interpreter's Dictionary of the Bible* (Nashville: Abingdon, 2006-2009), 5:517; and many other scholars.

[10]Stephen A. Kaufman, "The Structure of the Deuteronomic Law," *Maarav* 1.2 (1978–1979): 105-58, followed by Walter C. Kaiser Jr., *Toward an Old Testament Ethics* (Grand Rapids, MI: Zondervan, 1983); and Roy E. Gane, *Old Testament Law for Christians: Original Context and Enduring Application* (Grand Rapids, MI: Baker Academic, 2017), 240, 260, 268. There are questionable points, but the overall observation has merit.

[11]A number of good studies have shown how this works out. Gane, *Old Testament Law for Christians*, 239-80 offers quite a good and relatively brief review of the details. See also Patrick D. Miller, *The Ten Commandments* (Louisville: Westminster John Knox, 2009) and Mark F. Rooker, *The Ten Commandments: Ethics for the Twenty-First Century*, NACSBT (Nashville: B&H Academic, 2010).

[12]See, e.g., Pamela Barmash, "Introduction," in *The Oxford Handbook of Biblical Law*, 2; Greenstein, "Decalogue," 166-67; and Rom-Shiloni, "The Decalogue," 136-37.

[13]Greenstein, "Decalogue," 166-67.

states (Ex 32:15). In the ancient Near Eastern context, each party to the treaty would have retained a copy and placed it before their god(s).[14] Of course, in Israel they placed both tablets inside the ark of the covenant as a testimony to God and the people (Ex 25:16; 40:20).

Others place the division of the Ten Commandments between the first four and the last six, since the focus of the fifth is on the relationship between children and their parents. In any case, the main point is that God's concerns include both: their loyalty and exclusive commitment to him as their God, and their loyalty and fair treatment of one another in their regular daily lives. This corresponds to Jesus' statement of the two great commandments of the law drawn from Deuteronomy 6:5 and Leviticus 19:18: "'Love the Lord your God with all your heart and with all your soul and with all your mind.' This is the first and greatest commandment. And the second is like it: 'Love your neighbor as yourself.' All the Law and the Prophets hang on these two commandments" (Mt 22:37-40 and par.).

Two other passages in the Pentateuch put together sets of laws that are reminiscent of the Ten Commandments. The first of these comes in the wake of the golden calf debacle in Exodus 32, which led to the need to reestablish the covenant in Exodus 34. Moses broke the first set of tablets in reaction to the making and worshiping of the golden calf (Ex 32:19). Because of the nature of this infidelity, the commandments highlighted in Exodus 34:12-26 emphasize the exclusive loyalty to the Lord as their God found in the first four of the Ten Commandments (esp. 1, 2, and 4). This passage does not just reiterate them, however, but elaborates on them by stressing that they must never make a treaty with the people who live in Canaan, lest they lead them astray from the Lord (Ex 34:12-16). They must also be sure to worship only the Lord their God and do it regularly according to the festival pattern and regulations in Israel (Ex 34:18-26). The second passage is Leviticus 19, which in one way or another refers to and

---

[14]See, e.g., Kenneth A. Kitchen and Paul J. N. Lawrence, eds., *Treaty, Law and Covenant in the Ancient Near East*, 3 vols. (Wiesbaden: Harrasowitz, 2012), 1:391.

sometimes expands on the fourth (Lev 19:3, 30), fifth (Lev 19:3), first and second (Lev 19:4), eighth and ninth (Lev 19:11), third (Lev 19:12), sixth (Lev 19:16), and seventh (Lev 19:20) commandments.[15]

THE ENUMERATION OF THE TEN COMMANDMENTS

The scholarly and popular literature on the Ten Commandments is voluminous. It is not my purpose here to review all the literature or even take all of it into account. Instead, the goal is to lay the Ten Commandments out before us and explain the significance of each individual command as well as the whole unit together. The term *Ten Commandments* never actually occurs in the Pentateuch, nor anywhere else in the Bible. The actual terminology in the Torah is "Ten Words" (see Ex 34:28; Deut 4:13; 10:4). This becomes important in the history of the tradition of their enumeration.[16] Table 1 summarizes these various traditions.

Table 1. Enumeration of the Ten Commandments

Most Protestants and the Greek Orthodox Church (Josephus)	Lutherans and Roman Catholics (Augustine)
1. Foreign gods, 20:2-3	1. Foreign gods and images, 20:2-6
NOTE: The *Jewish* view is that 20:2 ("I am the Lord . . .") is the first commandment and 20:3-6 (no idolatry) is the second (i.e., between the Protestant and Catholic views).	
2. Images, 20:4-6	2. Name of God, 20:7
3. Name of God, 20:7	3. Sabbath, 20:8-11
4. Sabbath, 20:8-11 (but note contrast with Deut 5:12-15)	4. Honor parents, 20:12
5. Honor parents, 20:12	5. Do not murder, 20:13
6. Do not murder, 20:13	6. Do not commit adultery, 20:14
7. Do not commit adultery, 20:14	7. Do not steal, 20:15
8. Do not steal, 20:15	8. No false witnessing, 20:16
9. No false witnessing, 20:16	9. Do not covet neighbor's house, 20:17a
10. Do not covet, 20:17	10. Do not covet neighbor's property or wife, 20:17b

---

[15]Greenstein, "Decalogue," 169.

[16]See the discussion on the enumeration of the Ten Words in Miller, "The Ten Commandments," 518; Greenstein, "Decalogue," 165-66; and Rom-Shiloni, "The Decalogue," 149.

The discussion here will follow the first column, but the second column also has good support, as well as the Jewish interpretation (see the insert between the first and second commandments in table 1).[17] The first column separates the command for worship of no other gods than Yahweh from the command to make no graven images of Yahweh. The second column combines these into one command so that the enumeration backs up by one, until you come to nine and ten. If one looks closely, it is clear that Exodus 20:17 actually does have two imperatives commanding them not to covet. Moreover, the parallel passage in Deuteronomy 5:21 divides these two clauses by placing "and" (Hebrew *waw*) between them like the previous four commandments. Also, the verb changes between the first ("covet") and second ("set your desire on") part of Deuteronomy 5:21.

The Jewish view handles all this differently. It treats Exodus 20:2 as the first commandment: "I am the LORD [*Yahweh*] your God [*'ĕlōhîm*], who brought you out of Egypt, out of the land of slavery." There is no command in this verse, but remember that the expression in Hebrew is the Ten *Words*, not Ten *Commandments*. A *word* in Hebrew can designate an imperative command, but not necessarily so. Thus, this pronouncement in Exodus 20:2 strictly speaking could be considered the first word. Of course, whether it is the first word/commandment or not, this declaration is foundational to everything else. We discussed this briefly in chapter three in the treatment of the exodus from slavery in Egypt as the theme that frames, shapes, and permeates the Mosaic narrative and the law.

In the end, aside from the question of the enumeration of the Ten Words, the structure of Exodus 20:2-6 suggests that these verses form a single unit. The expression rendered "I am the Lord your God," with which the unit begins (Ex 20:2), is the same in Hebrew as "I, the Lord

---

[17]For those who work with the Hebrew text, it is worth noting that this variation is actually reflected in the double accent system of the Ten Words in the Hebrew Bible. See the multiple accents around certain words in the Masoretic manuscript Leningrad B19a printed in the *Biblia Hebraica Stuttgartensia*, and even the lack of *soph pasuq* at the end of vv. 3-4 and 8-10.

your God" in Exodus 20:5, followed by subordinate explanatory clauses to the end of Exodus 20:6.[18] This expression, therefore, serves as the warrant for two prohibitions, one against worshiping any other god(s) (Ex 20:3) and the other against making idols (Ex 20:4-5), creating a chiastic structure: warrant > prohibition <> prohibition > warrant.

The reader will notice below that my translation of the negative commands (1–3 and 6–10) is a bit different from that given in most English translations. This is my attempt to capture the difference between the common negative imperative in Hebrew, sometimes called the "immediate prohibition" by grammarians, and the kind used here. The prohibitions in the Ten Commandments use what some grammarians refer to as a "permanent" or "emphatic" prohibition. To illustrate, there is a difference between "do not go into the house" (immediate prohibition; you may go into the house later but not now) versus "never go into the house" (a permanent prohibition against going into the house—for example, a condemned and dangerous one). In other words, these are very strong prohibitions stated in an absolute and uncompromising way. There is no excuse for anyone ever doing anything that is anything like this in any way. It stands to reason, therefore, that one should regard the positive commandments to keep the Sabbath and to honor father and mother as absolutely positive as the prohibitions are negative.

WORD ONE

You must never have other gods before me. (Ex 20:3, my translation)

This first prohibition against having any other gods before the Lord is a natural follow-up to the previous line. Yahweh had delivered them out of slavery in Egypt (Ex 20:2). Thus, they owed him absolute and exclusive loyalty (Ex 20:3). This is what they must do in response. The Sinaitic covenant and law was meant, first of all and above all, to establish and implement a reciprocal relationship between Israel and

---

[18]See Greenstein, "Decalogue," 166 and the lit. cited there.

the Lord. Reciprocity is essential to any real relationship. There has been some discussion of what it means to have no other gods "before" the Lord.[19] The Hebrew phrase is literally that they should have no other gods "upon my faces." This could mean (1) "in front of me," meaning that no other deity was to be given priority over Yahweh, (2) "in addition to me," meaning there was to be no other alongside Yahweh, or (3) "over against me," referring to other gods who would stand in opposition to Yahweh. All three were out of bounds for ancient Israel.

The first word recalls the initiation of the covenant back in Exodus 19:4-5, "You yourselves have seen what I did to Egypt, and how I carried you on eagles' wings and brought you to myself. Now if you obey me fully and keep my covenant. . . ." The Lord is going back to this starting point to articulate the stipulations of the covenant that were anticipated there. He is their God, the one and only God for them. Even if one believed that other gods did in fact exist, and most ancient Israelites probably believed this, it was an absolute imperative that they never worship and serve any of the others. The term for this is *henotheism*, the worship of only one god even if people also believe that other gods exist too. *Monotheism* is the belief that only one God exists. This is not to say, however, that there are no indications of monotheism in the Pentateuch. Consider, for example, Deuteronomy 4:35, "You were shown these things so that you might know that the LORD is God; besides him there is no other."

The ancient Israelites were ancient Near Eastern people, and they would have thought accordingly. Amid all the polytheisms of that day, the real issue was that the Israelites devote themselves completely and exclusively to this one God whose name is Yahweh, and to no other god in any way at any time for any reason. This is the anchor point of the covenant and the law. Many other passages in the Torah and throughout the Bible emphasize the key importance of this

---

[19]See, e.g., the remarks in Miller, "The Ten Commandments," 520.

commandment (see, e.g., Ex 22:20; 34:13-14; Deut 13; 2 Kings 17:35; Ps 44:20; 81:9; Jer 1:16; 7:6, 9; 11:13; 19:4; 25:6; 35:15).[20]

WORD TWO

> You must never make for yourself an idol in the form of anything in heaven above or on the earth beneath or in the waters below. You must never bow down to them or worship them; for I, the LORD your God, am a jealous God, punishing the children for the sin of the fathers to the third and fourth generation of those who hate me, but showing love to a thousand generations of those who love me and keep my commandments. (Ex 20:4-6, my translation)

The Lord keeps emphasizing this prohibition against idols in pivotal places throughout the Mosaic law (see, most immediately, Ex 20:22-23; see also, e.g., Ex 23:24; 32:4, 8, 31; 34:17; Deut 12:1-3; 29:17-18).

Several points are worthy of special notice here. First, this command applies to making or worshiping images of Yahweh or other gods. In recounting what happened here at Sinai, Moses wrote forty years later in Moab, "Then the LORD spoke to you out of the fire. You heard the sound of words but saw no form; there was only a voice" (Deut 4:12). God wanted them to know who he was. This included knowing that one cannot make an image of anything in heaven or earth that could legitimately represent him. He stands outside of this creation, so by the nature of things no form that could be recognized or fabricated within this world is acceptable. All such representation would be a violation of who he is. To worship such an image or use it in worship would be to worship something other than him, and this is idolatry. It would violate both this prohibition and the first one because it would amount to worshiping something or someone other than Yahweh.

Second, the translation of Exodus 20:5 can be confusing. The NIV has, "You shall not bow down to them or worship them," but the NRSV reads, "You shall not bow down to them or serve them." The

---

[20]For the many implications and applications of this commandment, see Gane, *Old Testament Law for Christians*, 242-43 and so on throughout his treatment of the Ten Commandments.

first verb, *bow down*, means to bow in obeisance as a worshiper. The second verb, *serve*, means in this context to serve by worshiping through some particular means, whether prayer or sacrifice, or whatever. It refers to the ways and means of worship activity. There is a noun from the same root word that actually means "service of worship." See, for example, Exodus 30:16, which refers to the atonement money designated for "the service of the Tent of Meeting." In the New Testament Paul urges us "to offer" our "bodies as living sacrifices, holy and pleasing to God" and describes this as a "spiritual [lit. 'reasonable'] act of worship" (Rom 12:1). The point is that the Israelites were not to bow down to any idols or participate in any of the worship activities that had anything to do with them.

Third, Yahweh is a "jealous" God (Ex 20:5), so to worship any other god in any way would enrage his jealousy. It is God's natural reaction. This must be an exclusive relationship. The Lord is loyal to them and he expects them to be likewise loyal to him. If they are not, he will be enraged with jealousy and attack, as he did in the golden calf catastrophe (Ex 32–34; note esp. Ex 32:34-35). In the recovery from that debacle, in fact, he remakes the covenant with an expanded reference back to the principle of this second prohibition, including another warning about his "jealousy" (Ex 34:11-17).

Fourth, as a jealous God, violating their relationship with him would lead to "punishing the children for the sin of the fathers to the third and fourth generation of those who hate me" (Ex 20:5). This stands in contrast to the fifth point, and we need to treat them together: "but showing love to a thousand generations of those who love me and keep my commandments" (Ex 20:6). The contrast is important. Within the covenant, the duration of God's love for those who love and obey him far outreaches the duration of his jealous rage against those who hate him. It reaches to "a thousand generations" as opposed to only three or four.[21]

---

[21]See the helpful discussion in Kaiser, *Toward an Old Testament Ethics*, 86-87.

There have been a number of interpretations offered for the three or four generations. One must keep in mind that, according to Deuteronomy 24:16, "Fathers shall not be put to death for their children, nor children put to death for their fathers; each is to die for his own sin" (cf. 2 Kings 14:6). It is tempting, therefore, to follow the interpretation that takes this to mean that the sinful influence of a father is no excuse for his descendant(s) to follow in his footsteps. God will punish generation after generation if they continue in the same sins as their fathers.[22] The problem, of course, is why would this be limited to only three or four generations in succession? Would God excuse the fifth rebellious generation for practicing the same sins as their fathers?

It is better to maintain a closer connection between the three to four generations in Exodus 20:5 and the thousand generations in Exodus 20:6. When the Lord brings judgment for sin on the Israelites, his judgment will endure only for a relatively short time as compared to his permanent commitment to the covenant. There are blessings and curses in the covenant statements both at Sinai (Lev 26; note esp. Lev 26:32-45) and in Moab (Deut 28–29; note esp. Deut 29:22–30:10). The curses in both places anticipate that the Lord will take the people of Israel into exile for their sinful rebellion against the Lord, but these passages also anticipate the Lord bringing them back to the land when they repent. He would remain faithful to them even though they have not been faithful to him. Recall the discussion of the permanent promises and ongoing obligations of the covenants in chapter two above.

The prime example of this in the history of ancient Israel is the Babylonian exile, which lasted seventy years (Jer 25:11-12; 29:10; Dan 9:2). The effect of the generation(s) whose sin caused the exile extended past their generation to three or four generations of their children who lived in exile not due to their own sin (a generation is

---

[22]See, e.g., Douglas K. Stuart, *Exodus*, NAC (Nashville: Broadman & Holman, 2006), 454 and some similar remarks in Kaiser, *Toward an Old Testament Ethics*, 87.

usually about twenty to twenty-five years long). Yes, there is chastisement for sin and rebellion within the covenant, but the reward for loving faithfulness will far outreach the chastisement for sin—a thousand generations as opposed to three or four. There is permanent promise. The three or four generations and the thousand generations are not intended to be precise numbers, of course, but stand in relation to each other as a way of emphasizing both the ongoing obligations and permanent promises of the covenant, respectively. God's anger against his covenant people can last for a while, but not nearly as long as his covenant commitment to them, not even close.

WORD THREE

> You must never lift up the name of the LORD your God frivolously, for the LORD will not hold anyone guiltless who lifts up his name frivolously. (Ex 20:7, my translation)

The name referred to here is "Yahweh." This was a special name from the beginning, so they must make sure that they treat it as such. On a popular level in the church, most people take this to mean that one must not use the divine name in verbal profanities—cursing. The key expression translated here "lift up the name frivolously" is rendered in various ways in the English versions. The last word comes from a combination of the Hebrew noun *šāw'* (lit. "emptiness, frivolousness, falsehood, vanity, uselessness") with the preposition "to" plus the definite article attached (*laššāw'*).[23] This yields an adverbial translation meaning "emptily, falsely, frivolously."

Some scholars have noted that the expression is ambiguous and may refer to any kind of "frivolous use of the divine Name."[24] The JPS translates it "swear falsely by the name," suggesting that it refers to

---

[23]For helpful discussions of this term see *HALOT* 1425-26, *NIDOTTE* 4:53-55, and *TDOT* 14: 447-60, esp. 452, 458. See also the careful examination in Carmen Joy Imes, *Bearing YHWH's Name at Sinai: A Reexamination of the Name Command of the Decalogue*, BBRSup 19 (University Park, PA: Pennsylvania State University Press, 2018), 100-105.

[24]Nahum M. Sarna, *Exodus*, JPS Torah Commentary (Philadelphia: Jewish Publication Society, 1991), 111.

using the name in false oaths with deceptive purposes. It assumes that "lifting up" or "taking up" here means to take the name on one's lips. Compare Psalm 16:4, "I will not take up their names [i.e., the names of other gods] upon my lips" (cf. Ps 50:16 "you take up my covenant upon your lips"). The prohibition, therefore, would require making sure that one uses the name only in oaths that proclaim and support the truth. This has been a very common interpretation of the third commandment in the scholarly literature.

The ninth commandment may also support it. In Exodus 20:16, it reads: "You must never give false [Hebrew *šāqer*] testimony against your neighbor." The parallel in Deuteronomy 5:20, however, says "You shall not give false [Hebrew *šāw'*] testimony against your neighbor," using the same term as in the third commandment in place of "false" (Hebrew *šāqer*). In this case, Hebrew *šāw'* clearly has the meaning "false" as in the common interpretation of Exodus 20:7 discussed above.

The fact that they should use the name in swearing oaths in ancient Israel is clear from other passages. See, for example, "Fear the LORD your God, serve him only and take your oaths in his name" (Deut 6:13). The problem was with making false oaths using the name. As Leviticus 19:12 puts it, "Do not swear falsely by my name and so profane the name of your God. I am the LORD" (cf., e.g., Ps 24:4). To use the name in this way would be to treat it as unholy—to profane it. The context in Leviticus 19 is about stealing, lying, and oppressing or abusing one's neighbor by such means. To swear a false oath is a way to steal or cheat someone. It is unjust and abusive. Using the Lord's name in such an oath is to bring the Lord into participation with it. This is against the very nature and character of the Lord. It profanes his name.

There is also another interpretation of the third commandment. It has been around a long time but has not been so prominent in the literature. Recently, it has received special attention and vigorous affirmation.[25] The verb meaning "lift up" or "take up" (Hebrew *nāsā'*)

---

[25]See Daniel I. Block, *Deuteronomy*, NIVAC (Grand Rapids, MI: Zondervan, 2012), 163; see also the work of Carmen Imes, who did her dissertation under Daniel Block, working out all the

can also mean "bear" or "carry," suggesting that Exodus 20:7 may mean to say, "You must never bear the name of the Lord your God frivolously." Thus, basically, one who "bears the name" is one who has God's name on them; that is, he or she is a member of the covenant God made with Israel at Sinai. What they do, therefore, represents God, and to do so frivolously in any part of their life is to dishonor rather than honor God.

Support for this reading begins with the analogy of the priest bearing (Hebrew *nāsā*) the names of the tribes of Israel in his breast piece when he represents the people before the Lord (Ex 28:29). Similarly, for the high priest they were to "make a plate of pure gold and engrave on it as on a seal: HOLY TO THE LORD" (Ex 28:36-38). He is to wear this as the representative of the people when he stands before the Lord. It was common to use seals in the Old Testament and the ancient Near East for identification of ownership.[26] Similarly, although the verb meaning "bear, carry" is not used, the high priestly blessing had the effect of putting "my name [i.e., the name of the Lord] on the Israelites" (Num 6:27). If one accepts this interpretation, the third commandment is metaphorical for the bearing of God's name by the way they lived in ancient Israel. It applies to us in the same way. The word *name* can also mean "reputation." We can give the Lord a good or a bad reputation by the way we represent him in the world.

This is certainly a fascinating and meaningful understanding and application of the command. One should keep in mind, however, that the text does not actually use the expression "bear the name" for bearing God's name in Exodus 28:29, just for the priest bearing the

---

details. I had the privilege of serving as the external examiner for this dissertation at Wheaton College. More recently, she has written a delightful popular book based on her dissertation research, *Bearing God's Name: Why Sinai Still Matters*, with a forward by Christopher J. H. Wright, who enthusiastically supports her interpretation.

[26]See Carmen Joy Imes, "Belonging to YHWH: Real and Imagined Inscribed Seals in Biblical Tradition," in *Write That They May Read: Studies in Literacy and Textualization in the Ancient Near East and in the Hebrew Scriptures*, ed. Daniel I. Block (Eugene, OR: Pickwick, 2020), 349-65.

names of the Israelites. Moreover, the verb *bear/carry* (Hebrew *nāśā*)
in Exodus 28:36-38 is used for the high priest as the one who "bears
the culpability" for the Israelites as they bring their offerings and sacrifices to him for atonement (Ex 28:37), not for "bearing" the name of
the Lord.

Whether this interpretation of the third word is correct or not, it is
true that Israel was to represent God well among the nations in the
ancient Near East. Those of us who know the Lord through faith in
Jesus Christ also have a call to do so in the world today. As noted above,
the command is ambiguous. In my view, there may be good reason for
this. I am not convinced that the two views discussed here are mutually
exclusive. Whatever ways one "lifts up" or "carries" the name in oaths,
words, actions, attitudes, motivations, and so on must show that the
person takes the Lord and their covenant commitment to him seriously. One must not do this "frivolously." Thus, this prohibition
probably also applies to other misuses of the name, including, for example, the incident in Leviticus 24:10-23, where the son of an Israelite
woman "blasphemed the Name by cursing" (Lev 24:11). This brings us
back to the mention of "cursing" at the beginning of this section.

Jesus entered into a related discussion of oaths and vows in his
sermon on a different mountain (Mt 5:33-37). He was not referring
specifically to the use of God's name in false oaths but to the manipu-
lative use of oaths and vows in all various kinds of contexts. The main
point Jesus made was that one should not need to swear oaths because
he or she always spoke truth in a straightforward way to begin with.
Others could rely on his or her word without an oath. This avoids the
vicious cycle of making oaths by one thing or the other, often with the
intent to confuse and obfuscate (cf. Mt 23:16-22).

WORD FOUR

> Remember the Sabbath day by keeping it holy. Six days you shall labor and do
> all your work, but the seventh day is a Sabbath to the LORD your God. On it
> you shall not do any work, neither you, nor your son or daughter, nor your

manservant or maidservant, nor your animals, nor the alien within your gates. For in six days the LORD made the heavens and the earth, the sea, and all that is in them, but he rested on the seventh day. Therefore the LORD blessed the Sabbath day and made it holy. (Ex 20:8-11, NIV1986)

As noted above, Moses recounted the Ten Commandments again forty years later in Moab (Deut 5:6-21) as part of his recitation of the previous history of the Lord's covenant bond with Israel. The actual command as given there is essentially the same as in Exodus 20, but the rationale is different. In Exodus the rationale is based on the Lord creating the world in six days and resting on the seventh (Ex 20:11; cf. Gen 1:1–2:3). The rationale as stated in Deuteronomy 5:15, however, is concerned with their deliverance from slavery in Egypt, not the creation pattern: "Remember that you were slaves in Egypt and that the LORD your God brought you out of there with a mighty hand and an outstretched arm. Therefore the LORD your God has commanded you to observe the Sabbath day." Why the difference?

There are probably at least two parts to the answer. One is that in Exodus the rationale emphasizes creation and in Deuteronomy the focus is redemption. These are not contrary rationales but complementary. They emphasize the two major sides of God's engagement with and commitment to the world.[27] Another part of the answer probably lies in the purpose for the recounting of the law in Deuteronomy as opposed to its original revelation in Exodus. Again, the command itself is largely the same in both places, although the statement of it is somewhat expanded in Deuteronomy. The difference is that in Exodus God was giving the initial command, while in Deuteronomy Moses was reporting the command in the context of preaching the law. In doing so, he drew special attention to their deliverance from slavery in Egypt, where they had no rest. This must not be how family, slaves, and even animals experience life in Israel. Slavery did exist in ancient Israel, but there were special protections

---

[27]See the helpful remarks in Hendrik L. Bosman, "Sabbath," in *NIDOTTE* 4:1158-59.

and provisions for slaves that did not exist in the world around them. Even servants or slaves had human rights.[28] It was not the kind of slavery known to us in the history of America. There was nothing in ancient Israel or in the ancient Near Eastern world like the early American slavery of Africans.[29]

God designated the Sabbath as the sign of the Mosaic covenant: "You must observe my Sabbaths. This will be a sign between me and you for the generations to come, so you may know that I am the LORD, who makes you holy" (Ex 31:13; cf. Ex 31:17). Keeping the Sabbath would be a natural mark of distinction between Israel and the other nations. All efforts to find the origin of this institution in the surrounding ancient Near Eastern world have failed. There may be an etymological connection between the Hebrew term and Akkadian *šap/battu*, but functionally they do not refer to the same practice since the Akkadian term relates to the phases of the moon.[30] Yes, there were festival days and various sequences of days off work through the month(s) in the world of the ancient Near East, but nothing like the Israelite Sabbath. The latter arose from within their own historical experience (deliverance from slavery) and as a pattern based on the story of the Lord's work at creation according to Genesis 1:1–2:3. Their Lord was both the creator and the redeemer, and keeping the Sabbath was to keep both remembered and highlighted in the life of ancient Israel week by week.

Some argue that the Sabbath was more than just a day of rest; it is also a day of special activity and devotion to the Lord.[31] The problem

---

[28]See Daisy Yulin Tsai, *Human Rights in Deuteronomy: With Special Focus on Slave Laws*, BZAW 464 (Berlin: De Gruyter, 2014). Even more recently, see the new dissertation by Caleb Afulike, "The Mosaic Vision of a Benevolent Society: A Study of Deuteronomy 10:12-22 and Its Implications for Deuteronomic Concern for the Most Vulnerable," PhD dissertation, Trinity Evangelical Divinity School, 2020.

[29]See Richard E. Averbeck, "Slavery in the World of the Bible," in *Behind the Scenes of the Old Testament*, ed. Jonathan S. Greer, John W. Hilber, and John H. Walton (Grand Rapids, MI: Baker Academic, 2018), 423-30 and the further discussion of this topic in chap. 5 below.

[30]Bosman, "Sabbath," 1157. See also the extensive bibliography and history of the discussion in *HALOT* 1410.

[31]Stuart, *Exodus*, 460-61, writes, for example, "The Sabbath . . . is designed to help people become spiritually stronger and closer to God; whatever it does by way of helping people recuperate from being physically tired (and it certainly can do this) is an incidental, rather than a primary,

is that there is virtually no indication of this in the text. In my view, the confusion arises from trying to make the Sabbath the same as the Christian Sunday, and *vice versa*. They are two different things. According to Ezekiel 46:1-10, the Sabbath and the new moon were to be special times of worship for the prince and the people in the temple envisioned there, whatever temple that may be referring to, whether historical, future, ideal, or visionary only. God issues no such regulation, however, in the period of the tabernacle, or the first or second temples.

The passages themselves associate keeping the Sabbath "holy" directly and only with ceasing from work (see, e.g., Ex 20:8-10; 31:14-16). This alone would set the Sabbath day apart from the regular workdays as a special holy day. The term *sacred assembly* in Leviticus 23:3 means literally "a proclamation [or 'summons'] of holiness." It does not call for an actual assembly, but for setting the day aside to sanctify it to the Lord by not doing any (regular) work on that day. All Israelites were to consider themselves summoned to do no regular work on the seventh day. The term is sometimes used within the context of a larger festival. For example, the first occurrence in the Old Testament canon is in the regulations for the first and last days of the Passover festival: "On the first day hold a sacred assembly, and another one on the seventh day. Do no work at all on these days" (Ex 12:16; cf. also Lev 23:2-3, 4, 7-8, 27, 35-36; Num 28:18-25; 29:1, 7, 12).[32]

The verb *šābat* means, "to cease, stop." Exodus 20:8 says, "Remember the Sabbath day by keeping it holy [lit. 'to keep it holy']." Again, the point is that the Lord did this on the seventh day. He did not continue his work of creation but simply stopped. This was not because he was tired and worn out, of course, but because the work was done. The seventh day rest signaled that all the work was "completed" (Gen 2:1)

---

benefit. . . . To love God is not to have a lazy day one day a week; rather it is to focus on doing his will specially on one day a week—to worship, learn, study, care, and strengthen the spirit."

[32]See Jacob Milgrom, *Leviticus 1–16*, AB 3 (New York: Doubleday, 1991), for a helpful discussion of this matter.

and, in fact, it was all "very good" (Gen 1:31). Similarly, the ancient Israelites were to work for six days and at the end of the sixth day they were to consider all their work to be done with nothing left to do (that is, until the first day of the week came around again). This was no incidental or insignificant matter for those who worked hard all week, whether owners or slaves, humans or animals.

To keep the Sabbath as a day of ceasing from work is to sanctify it (i.e., set it apart) as a day just for that, not for work and business, as if life amounts only to making worldly gain for oneself or one's family. God intended them to work hard all week. He reserved the last day of the week for them to rest and enjoy the fruits of their labor. They must do what they need to do to prepare themselves, their family, their workers, and even their animals to enjoy the Sabbath day rest. This is the point of the extended exhortation in Jeremiah 17:19-27 not to bring any loads into Jerusalem on the Sabbath day to "keep the Sabbath day holy by not doing any work on it" (Jer 17:24). It is ceasing from work, not other activities, on the Sabbath day that keeps it holy.

As Jesus himself put it amid controversy with the Pharisees, "The Sabbath was made for man, not man for the Sabbath" (Mk 2:27). The last thing the Lord had in mind when he instituted the Sabbath was to make this day a burden to people. If people are hungry, they should be allowed to take food along the way and eat it even in special circumstances (Mt 12:3-4; Mk 2:25-26; Lk 6:3-4; cf. 1 Sam 21:1-6). If people or even animals are hurting or injured, in some kind of trouble or danger, one should help them (Mt 12:10-12; Mk 3:2-4; Lk 6:7-10).

On the one hand, no one should take the Sabbath command lightly. One must not violate the Sabbath rest at their whim (see, e.g., Num 15:32-36). On the other hand, if things are so strict that one cannot even do good on the Sabbath, then how is it that priests are allowed to break the Sabbath when they do what the law calls for them to do in the tabernacle on the Sabbath? (Mt 12:5; cf. Num 28:9-10). The Sabbath was not to be a day of deprivation or imposition, making it a burden. It was a day that should bring relief from the daily grind of work. With regard to what the disciples did as they walked through the fields and picked some grain because they were hungry, even the law explicitly allows this: "If you enter your neighbor's vineyard, you may eat all the grapes you want, but do not put any in your basket. If you enter your neighbor's grainfield, you may pick kernels with your hands, but you must not put a sickle to their standing grain" (Deut 23:24-25). Matthew 12:1 was not a case of "harvesting" on the Sabbath; the disciples were not doing work.

WORD FIVE

> Honor your father and your mother, so that you may live long in the land the
> LORD your God is giving you. (Ex 20:12)

The word for "honor" (Hebrew *kabbēd*) is the active form of the verb "to be heavy" (*kābēd*). It means to treat them as important—as a "heavyweight," so to speak. Something of the converse of this command is found in Exodus 21:17, "Anyone who curses his father or mother must be put to death" (cf. also Lev 20:9; Deut 27:16). The word for "curse" here is a participle, but it is the active form of the verbal root (*qll*), which means to be light, insignificant. It means to treat someone as unimportant—as a "lightweight."[33] Similarly, "Anyone who attacks his father or his mother must be put to death" (Ex 21:15). In other words, one must treat their parents as important people in their life, worthy of serious attention, devotion, and care. The opposite of this would be to actually "curse" them, attack them physically, or neglect them. Such a crime is worthy of execution in ancient Israel.

One could misunderstand and misapply this command today. Some readers may get the idea that, under the law, they would execute any child who ever disobeyed their parents in ancient Israel. If this were true, no one would have survived their early years, and the

---

[33]The meaning "to designate as too lightweight" for the latter verb "to curse" is found even in *HALOT* 1104.

concept of discipline of a child would be of no use. This is not the intent. We know this, for example, from Deuteronomy 21:18-23. "If a man has a stubborn and rebellious son who does not obey his father and mother and will not listen to them when they discipline him, his father and mother shall take hold of him and bring him to the elders at the gate of his town" (Deut 21:18-19). Then they report to the elders, "This son of ours is stubborn and rebellious. He will not obey us. He is a glutton and a drunkard" (Deut 21:19). In other words, he has no moral standards and is completely out of control. He is a juvenile delinquent—and a dangerous one. Even his parents have seen it and have been unable to do anything about it.

We are talking here about someone who is caught up and headed for destruction and will do a lot of damage getting there; someone like the son in Proverbs 1:8-19 if he falls in with the wrong crowd. In such cases the only answer is execution, lest this kind of behavior ruin the whole society (Deut 21:21). We need to keep in mind that incarceration does not appear to have been a regular institution in ancient Israel. None of the penalties in the law call for it. No one was put in prison for anything according to the Old Testament law. Having that option available might have changed a number of rulings, including this one.

Honoring one's parents included caring for their needs in their old age. Because of her care for Naomi, her mother-in-law, the women of Bethlehem praised Ruth for being a "daughter-in-law, who loves you and who is better to you than seven sons" (Ruth 4:15). Parents depended on their children for this, and Naomi had lost both her husband and her two sons. Ruth took over. As Boaz put it to Ruth at the threshing floor, "All my fellow townsmen know that you are a woman of noble character" (Ruth 3:11; cf. Prov 31:10).

In the so-called corban passage, Jesus criticized the Pharisees and teachers of the law of his day for using one of their traditions to undermine obedience to this command (Mk 7:9-13). If a man designates as an "offering, gift" (Hebrew *qorbān*) to the Lord whatever he would have given to his parents to help them in fulfillment of the fifth commandment, "then you no longer let him do anything for his father or mother" (Mk 7:12). He concludes, "Thus you nullify the word of God by your tradition that you have handed down. And you do many things like that" (Mk 7:13). There is never any excuse for violating the Lord's commands and, in this case, to make excuses for it is to fall into a trap set by one's religion.

Finally, in Ephesians 6:1-3 the apostle Paul cites this commandment as an instruction to children in the context of submission to one another in the body of Christ (Eph 5:21–6:9). The quote is from the Septuagint (the Greek translation of the OT) and reads, "Honor your father and mother—which is the first commandment with a promise— that it may go well with you and that you may enjoy long life on the earth" (Eph 6:2-3). The promise in the Hebrew Bible is that by keeping this commandment the nation would stay long in the land of promise and prosper there (cf. Deut 5:16) rather than be expelled from it. Since that does not apply to the church, it seems that there is a shift to a promise of long life on the earth in Ephesians. In any case, the point is that there is practical benefit here.

WORD SIX

You must never commit murder. (Exodus 20:13, my translation).

This and the following two commandments each consist of only two words in Hebrew: the negative "not, never" (Hebrew lō') and the verb. They form a series of short statements that come straight to the point: don't do this, don't do this, don't do this! It is important to note that this sixth commandment does not say, "You must never kill." To kill another person and to murder another person are two different words and two different things. Sometimes killing a person is legitimate because of war, personal defense, legal sanction, or other such conditions. If one intentionally, illegally, and unjustly takes the life of another person who has done and is doing nothing that calls for it, he has committed murder.

Jesus used this as his first example in the Sermon on the Mount for how to understand and apply the Old Testament law in a way that goes beyond what the scribes and Pharisees were teaching (Mt 5:20 with Mt 5:21-26 and following). His point was that in the kingdom of heaven it is not good enough just to avoid murdering someone. One must also avoid being angry with one's brother or speaking insults against him. Notably, it is these kinds of feelings and words that, if they go unchecked, can ultimately lead to murder. One should make sure that nothing like this stands between himself and his brother. He should even interrupt bringing an offering to the Lord to pursue the brother for reconciliation.

This concern about such inner feelings and attitudes toward others appears in the Old Testament law too. Note, for example, the similar thought in Leviticus 19:17-18, "Do not hate your brother in your heart. Rebuke your neighbor frankly so you will not share in his guilt. Do not seek revenge or bear a grudge against one of your people, but love your neighbor as yourself. I am the LORD." Thus, in the immediate context of the verse that is the source of Jesus' second great commandment, the emphasis is to love one's neighbor by avoiding hateful thoughts and bearing grudges against them. One would not want another person to harbor such thoughts and intentions against them, so one should not do so against others. This is what it means to "love your neighbor as yourself." It is essentially the same as the so-called golden rule in Matthew 7:12, "So in everything, do to others what you would have them do to you, for this sums up the Law and the Prophets." Similarly, Jesus' pronouncement of the two great commandments ends this way, "All the Law and the Prophets hang on these two commandments" (Mt 22:40; cf. Mk 7:12).

The Old Testament law treats the subject of murder in various details elsewhere. One major issue of concern was, what if the murder was unintentional—an accident? The answer was to designate cities of refuge in order to manage the culturally imbedded vengeance practices of families (Num 35:6-29). This is an instance of common customary law in the culture based on principles of family, clan, and tribal justice. When one person murdered another, someone from the family or clan of the victim took on the responsibility of the "avenger [or 'redeemer'; Hebrew *gô'ēl*] of the blood." He had the right and responsibility to avenge the killing of his relative by killing the accused (see the example list of murderous acts in Num 35:16-21). God did not create this cultural institution, but he did give it the force of law (Num 35:29). He was concerned, however, to manage it by taking into consideration the difference between intentional murder and accidental homicide.

On the one hand, the avenger of the blood did indeed have the right to pursue a murderer and kill him, and no one could accuse him of murder for doing so (Num 35:16-21, 27). From God's point of view, murder is an attack not only on the victim but also on the core of his good plan for the world. He made humanity in his own image and as his likeness on the earth (Gen 1:26-28; 9:6). We are here to represent him and manage his creation according to his design. Murder is an attack on that design. Therefore, "Whoever sheds human blood, by humans shall their blood be shed; for in the image of God has God made mankind" (Gen 9:6).

On the other hand, if the murder was an accident, the one who committed the accidental deed could flee to one of the six designated cities of refuge in order to escape the avenger of the bloodshed (see the example list of such accidents in Num 35:22-23). God instructed Israel to give the Levites forty-eight cities with their surrounding pasturelands located throughout the tribal allotments (Num 35:1-5). Six of these would also be cities of refuge—three on each side of the Jordan River (Num 35:13-15). The accused could flee there for protection until the judicial assembly could meet and judge whether the death was an accident or not. If they determined it was indeed an accident, the assembly must protect him from the avenger and send him back to the city of refuge for ongoing protection. He must reside there until the death of the high priest (Num 35:24-25). If he went outside the city of refuge before that time, the avenger had the right to kill him (Num 35:26-28). At least two witnesses were required to judge a case of murder (Num 35:30; cf. also Deut 17:6-7; 19:15).

WORD SEVEN

You must never commit adultery. (Ex 20:14, my translation)

As noted above, here again we have an absolute prohibition in two words. It is simple: just do not ever do such a thing. It is important to distinguish between adultery and other kinds of illicit sexual congress. In the Old Testament law, adultery occurs when a married woman has sex with a man other than her husband.[34] For a man to get a wife in the culture of ancient Israel involved an exchange between the families. It was part of common customary law. He had to pay a bride price to her family. Consider, for example, Exodus 22:16-17, "If a man seduces a virgin who is not pledged to be married and sleeps with her, he must pay the bride-price, and she shall be his wife. If her father absolutely refuses to give her to him, he must still pay the bride-price for virgins" (cf. Deut 22:28-29; see also Deut 22:13-21, 25-27).

In a sense, the woman belonged to the man, although it was much more than that, of course. The transaction demonstrated that both families had invested in the success of the relationship. It sounds degrading to people in our modern Western culture, but people in the ancient Near East did not see it that way. In fact, they might look at our culture and think the same thing about us: As parents, how could you not see it as your responsibility to find and arrange spouses for your children? You put them at risk of finding a bad one, or none at all. You really must not love your children if you ignore such a basic responsibility. From their point of view, their way did not hinder love

---

[34]James Brooks, *Mark*, NAC (Nashville: Broadman & Holman, 1991), 158, notes that in the Old Testament law a married man was not considered to have committed adultery if he had sex with an unmarried woman who was not engaged. Adultery, strictly speaking, was limited to a married woman with a man other than her husband. Jesus changes this in Mk 10:11-12 so that a man's unfaithfulness to his wife is also considered adultery. It goes both ways.

between spouses but promoted it. There are some cultures in which this is still true today.

The study of this commandment, therefore, offers another good opportunity to observe that God did not necessarily change the social and cultural customs of the people in giving the law. Sometimes he did make radical changes, as for example in the first and second commandments, but often he just regulated their customs to make them as equitable as possible within their world. The ancient Israelites were ancient Near Easterners, with all the historical, cultural, social, and legal baggage that came with that. They were not a blank tablet on which the Lord wrote new customs without any consideration of their cultural context.

To put it another way, the Old Testament makes it clear that a good man would go to great lengths to find and marry a good woman that he loved. A prime example is found in the book of Ruth. Boaz was "a powerful noble [Hebrew *ḥayil*] man" (Ruth 2:1) and Ruth was "a noble [Hebrew *ḥayil*] woman" (3:11). It was in her character. Only two other verses in the Bible refer to a woman in this way (Prov 12:4; 31:10). It is fitting that in the Hebrew Bible the book of Ruth follows immediately after Proverbs and therefore immediately after the description of "a noble woman" that concludes the book (Prov 31:10-31). Ruth is the immediate illustration of the description in Proverbs 31, which the text presents as the words of King Lemuel's mother to her son (Prov 31:1-9). A good mother would want this kind of wife for her son.

Coming back now to the prohibition against adultery, because of the customs in the culture, for a man to commit adultery with the wife of another man was to violate the husband's relationship with her and the fact that he had paid a bride price to her family so she could become his wife. This made the marital relationship legally binding. Violating it was a criminal act perpetrated against the husband. In the case in Exodus 22:16-17 referred to above, the woman was not committed (i.e., engaged) to another man, so there was no adultery. However, because he had sex with her without paying the bride price, he now had to pay the bride price for a virgin even if the father was not willing to give her to him as his wife (cf. Deut 22:25-27). The bride price for a virgin was more than for a nonvirgin, so the violator must pay the virgin bride price lest the family lose out on the value of the daughter as a virgin. They could not now give her to another man as a virgin wife. To do so would be fraud (Deut 22:13-21).

If the woman, however, was already committed (i.e., engaged) to another man before the illicit sexual intercourse had taken place, it was then a case of adultery and both the man and the woman were to be executed for it (Deut 22:23-24; cf. Lev 20:10). On the other hand, if there were extenuating circumstances that suggested the man had taken her by force, only the man would suffer execution (Deut 22:25-27).

With all this in mind, one can see the quandary in which Mary's pregnancy put Joseph. He was a man "faithful to the law." He found out about her pregnancy after they were already committed to marry, but he loved her and did not want to "expose her to public disgrace" (Mt 1:18-21; cf. Deut 22:13-21). It took the appearance of an angel in a dream to help him through his dilemma.

After treating the sixth commandment against murder in Matthew 5:21-26, Jesus moved on immediately to the seventh commandment against adultery. Once again, he goes beyond prohibition of the act itself to the lustful thoughts and ideation behind it: "You have heard that it was said, 'Do not commit adultery.' But I tell you that anyone who looks at a woman lustfully has already committed adultery with her in his heart" (Mt 5:27-28). He carried this forward to the question of divorce in Matthew 5:31-32. We will come back to this in chapter eight below in the discussion of Jesus and the law.

In the Sermon on the Mount, the king of the kingdom of heaven (Mt 2:2; 4:23) was proclaiming the law of that kingdom (see esp. Mt 5:3, 10, 19-20, and all of Mt 5–7). His was a new kind of kingdom. Their placement at the beginning of the sermon suggests that the beatitudes of the kingdom of heaven (Mt 5:3-12) correspond to the Ten Commandments of the Israelite kingdom in the Old Testament law.

They are the first principles of the kingdom of heaven, principles of the heart. To have the law "written on the heart" (Jer 31:33) is to live it from the heart. This is the point Jesus was making all through his teaching. We can also see it in the way he lived it out in his own life as our example. He is both our teacher and our example. If one wants to know how to live out the teachings of Jesus in the Sermon on the Mount today, they need only pay close attention to how he did so himself in his own life, as testified to in the New Testament Gospels.

WORD EIGHT

You must never steal. (Ex 20:15, my translation)

This is the third and final of the blunt two-word prohibitions. Of course, there are numerous ways to steal. This prohibition proclaims the general principle, but the law deals with many possible ways of stealing. Consider, for example, Leviticus 19:11-13, which begins with the same prohibition, "Do not steal," but then develops it in the following list: lying and deceiving when one makes a deal, making a false oath, fraud, simple robbery, and holding back overnight the wages of someone you have hired for the day. One can also see this in the various kinds of "false dealing." For example, one could take what another person had given them for safe keeping and then claim that someone else had stolen it. This would be cause for going to court to find out the truth (Ex 22:7-9).

Another whole set of stealing laws deals with catching a thief and what to do about it (Ex 22:1-4), and another with stealing by negligence. This includes, for example, allowing one's livestock to eat the forage of another man's field or vineyard (Ex 22:5), or setting a fire that spreads to another man's property (Ex 22:6). The list goes on. The point is that the Ten Commandments are the larger categories into which one can fit the various stipulations of the law found elsewhere in the book of the covenant (Ex 21–23), the holiness code (Lev 17–26), and the Deuteronomic code (Deut 12–26), as well as other regulations spread throughout the Torah.

Among a litany of instructions for living the Christian life, the apostle Paul wrote, "Anyone who has been stealing must steal no longer, but must work, doing something useful with their own hands, that they may have something to share with those in need" (Eph 4:28). It is interesting and helpful that in this verse Paul instructs Christians not to steal from others but to do the opposite: not take from other people but work so that they can give to others. It is amazing how some people will work harder at stealing than they would need to if they took on some kind of work that would be useful to others. Paul puts stealing in the same basic category of other vices such as sensuality, greed, deceptive dealings, and rage. None of these do any good for anyone.

WORD NINE

> You must never give false testimony against your neighbor. (Ex 20:16, my translation)

This prohibition was essential to maintaining the integrity of the judicial system. False testimony compromises everything. It hinders the court from implementing justice. Of course, maintaining the integrity of the judicial system is of primary importance in any society. False testimony could come in various forms (see Lev 19:11-16 and the discussion of the third commandment above).

Giving false testimony was an extremely serious matter, so there were stringent rules. Deuteronomy 19:16-21 is one of the key passages. First, the witness and the accused came and stood in the presence of the Lord before the priests and judges at the central sanctuary (Deut 19:16-17; cf. Deut 17:8-9). If the judges investigated and found that the witness had been giving false testimony, "then do to him as he intended to do to his brother" (Deut 19:19). So whatever his false testimony would have brought as punishment, that was the punishment meted out to the false witness. The goal of this sanction, of course, was to make sure that no one would even consider giving false witness in ancient Israel: "The rest of the people will hear of this and be afraid, and never again will such an evil thing be done among you" (Deut 19:20; cf. Deut 19:19).

The passage ends with, "Show no pity: life for life, eye for eye, tooth for tooth, hand for hand, foot for foot" (Deut 19:21), the so-called *lex talionis* (*lex* means "law" and *talionis* means "tooth" in Latin, a shorthand way of referring to "eye for eye, tooth for tooth"). This is a common legal principle known from other ancient Near Eastern law collections as well.[35] The punishment must have the same nature and severity as the crime (cf. also Ex 21:23-25; Lev 24:19-20). Some have taken this to be a rather harsh and barbaric form of legal punishment, retaliation, and revenge, but it is really about making the law equitable. One cannot exact a heavier recompense than the violation calls for. Equitable recompense continues to be an important principle of law in legal proceedings today.[36]

WORD TEN

> You must never *covet* your neighbor's *house*. You must never *covet* your neighbor's *wife*, or his manservant or maidservant, his ox or donkey, or anything that belongs to your neighbor. (Ex 20:17, my translation)

The verb *covet* is the same in both parts. The first part is the more general prohibition and the second lends it more detail (there is no conjunction between the two clauses). As Moses recounted it in Deuteronomy 5:21, however, this commandment begins with the prohibition: "You must never covet your neighbor's wife." It then continues with a different verb and a conjunction connects the two clauses: "and you must never set your desire on your neighbor's house or land, his male or female servant, his ox or donkey, or anything that belongs to your neighbor." Some scholars have suggested that Deuteronomy 5:21 seems to highlight the coveting of a man's wife by putting her first, suggesting that she is more important than anyone

---

[35]See, e.g., the Laws of Hammurabi §§196-201 in *COS* 2:131.
[36]See the full discussion and extensive lit. cited in Herbert B. Huffmon, "'An Eye for an Eye' and Capital Punishment," in *The Oxford Handbook of Biblical Law*, 119-31.

or anything else in his household (see the discussion on adultery above). As Exodus 20:17 puts it, the wife is first in the second part where the details of the household are unpacked, yielding a similar emphasis on the prime importance of the man's wife. She comes first.

What stands out here is that this command goes to a person's intentions and heart desires, not just external actions. Of course, part of the point is that coveting and misplaced desires do tend by nature to lead to actions that are not of the best sort—and often to the kinds of violations that some of the other Ten Commandments explicitly forbid (see our discussion of the sixth and seventh commandments above). One wonders if the point of ending the Ten Words with this one is to emphasize that the Lord is concerned about all the human passions that would lead to violating these basic ideals, not just the actions themselves. It is of special interest that the commandment Paul used as his example to argue for both the goodness and the weakness of the law in Romans 7–8 is this one (see Rom 7:7). It gets to the heart of human corruption because the core of our corruption resides in our heart. We will deal with this extensively in chapter ten in the discussion of the combined goodness and weakness of the law.

CONCLUSION

As noted earlier, the Decalogue starts with the vertical relationship between Israel and their God and then shifts to their horizontal relationships with one another. Both were essential to God's covenantal concerns for their way of life in ancient Israel. This is also why Jesus gave two great commandments when the Jewish legal expert asked him for only one (Mt 22:34-40; Mk 12:28-34; and in a different way, Lk 10:25-37; cf. also 1 Jn 4:19-21, and many other passages).

The Ten Commandments are the only laws that God spoke directly in the hearing of the people as a whole at Sinai: "These are the commandments the LORD proclaimed in a loud voice to your whole assembly there on the mountain from out of the fire, the cloud and the deep darkness; and he added nothing more" (Deut 5:22). When

Moses went back up to God as the mediator of all the other laws, God began again with their worship of him, the first two commandments and the altar law (Ex 20:21-26). As far as God was concerned, the ancient Israelites were first of all and above all his worshipers.

These worship regulations in Exodus 20:22-26 stand at the head of the book of the covenant, even before the introduction to the regulations given in Exodus 21:1, "These are the laws you are to set before them." We turn now to the book of the covenant and the parallel law collections in the Torah.

Five

THE BOOK OF THE COVENANT
AND PARALLEL COLLECTIONS
OF LAW IN THE TORAH

THERE ARE IDEALS IN ANCIENT ISRAELITE LAW, but it is not an idealistic system of law. Some scholars will argue that the laws in the Bible do not correspond in any significant way to everyday law in ancient Israel. Raymond Westbrook and Bruce Wells argue convincingly, however, and show throughout their work, that this is not the case.[1] The Ten Commandments treated in the previous chapter constitute the main ideals or principles of the covenant, and the collections of judicial regulations developed in Exodus 21– Deuteronomy 26 are realistic to life in ancient Israel. Even though there is a scarcity of extrabiblical documents of Israelite law from the biblical period, we have a wealth of evidence documenting everyday legal proceedings among Israel's neighbors, especially from Mesopotamia. The substantial degree of overlap between these extant judicial documents and what we find in the Torah clearly

---

[1]Raymond Westbrook and Bruce Wells, *Everyday Law in Biblical Israel: An Introduction* (Louisville: Westminster John Knox, 2009).

suggests that we have in the Bible a set of legal regulations that largely reflect everyday life and law in ancient Israel.[2]

THE THREE PARALLEL LAW COLLECTIONS

As discussed in chapter three, the three main parallel collections of judicial law in the Torah are the book of the covenant (or covenant code; Ex 21–23), the holiness collection (or code; Lev 17–27), and the Deuteronomic collection (or code; Deut 12–26). There are many parallels between these three units of law. This is perplexing to many readers of the Torah, but it is a reality of how the law grew progressively in the forty-year history from Sinai in Exodus and Leviticus to Moab in Deuteronomy. In the study of the law, therefore, it is essential that the reader compare the parallel treatments of the various topics of law across the three collections to get a full picture of how they handled them.

DEBT SLAVERY IN THE THREE LAW COLLECTIONS

As one might imagine, there is much scholarly debate about the historical and judicial relationships between these three law collections. The parallel sections of debt slave regulations in Exodus 21:2-11, Leviticus 25:39-43 (but see also Lev 25:44-55), and Deuteronomy 15:12-18 are an especially important example of this. One scholar has noted, "Alongside the history of sacrifice and the festival calendar, the question of the sequence and relation of the laws concerning manumission of slaves has been essential to any larger attempt to construct a history of Israelite religion and a compositional history of the Pentateuch."[3]

---

[2]Westbrook and Wells, *Everyday Law in Biblical Israel*, 3-4, and, most recently F. Rachel Magdalene, Cornelia Wunsch, and Bruce Wells, *Fault, Responsibility, and Administrative Law in Late Babylonian Legal Texts*, MC 23 (University Park, PA: Eisenbrauns, 2019).

[3]Bernard M. Levinson, "The Manumission of Hermeneutics: The Slave Laws of the Pentateuch as a Challenge to Contemporary Pentateuchal Theory," in *Congress Volume Leiden 2004*, ed. André Lemaire, VTSup 109 (Leiden: Brill, 2006), 281. As is my regular practice in this volume, I will not go into the details of this historical critical debate. In regard to these debt slavery regulations, see Richard E. Averbeck, "The Exodus, Debt Slavery, and the Composition of the Pentateuch," in

There is another reason the debt slave regulations are a good topic to treat here. This is one of the most difficult topics to deal with in our modern world. Other topics are generally easier to deal with and, as noted previously, we cannot treat all the topics the law covers in this book. Some of the other challenging regulations will come under consideration later in this chapter as well. The goal of the discussion here is to show how the three sets of debt slave regulations work together to offer a realistic picture of the familial, social, economic, and judicial issues for this particular institution in ancient Israel.

The reality was that the exigencies of life for some people and the way they would most naturally be handled in the historical, social, legal, and cultural context of that day required the practice of debt slavery. One of the problems for us today, especially in the United States, is that when we read about the existence rather than elimination of "slavery" in the Bible, we think of the kind of slavery that existed earlier in the history of our continent and our country. We immediately have visions of the slave trade and the many tragic abuses that came with it. The fact of the matter is that "New World" slavery, in which peoples were captured and taken *en masse* from their homeland specifically to supply and breed for labor in another country (or on another continent), is unknown in the ancient Near East (including the Bible). In Israel and the ancient Near East, foreign chattel labor derived from warfare refugees, or from the trade carried on by merchants of various kinds, who were also the main creditors in the society and had the most access to foreign slaves.[4]

According to our legal sources, most of the principles and practices that applied to slavery were essentially the same across the ancient Near East. One of the problems, however, is that they do not usually

---

Exploring the Composition of the Pentateuch, BBRsup, ed. L. S. Baker Jr. et al. (University Park, PA: Eisenbrauns, 2020), 26-48 and the extensive lit. cited there. See also Richard E. Averbeck, "Slavery in the World of the Bible," in *Behind the Scenes of the Old Testament*, ed. Jonathan S. Greer, John W. Hilber, and John H. Walton (Grand Rapids, MI: Baker Academic, 2018), 423-30, for a discussion of slavery in the ancient Near Eastern world and the Bible.

[4]Averbeck, "Slavery in the World of the Bible," 423 and the lit. cited there.

provide the larger view of the household context of slavery. We learn more about this from administrative texts. Workers had differing status among and between them whether they were slaves or non-slaves. The status of slaves was situational and interactional. Overall, the study of slaves in household contexts in the ancient Near East suggests that slave labor filled only a negligible role in these societies.[5]

Yes, there was chattel slavery in the Bible too (Lev 25:44-46). There were some protections even for them. The master must be careful not to abuse his slaves. For example, Exodus 21:20-21, 26-27 protects slaves, whether debt or chattel slaves, from injuries caused by abuse from the master, leading to their release under such circumstances (see also, e.g., Deut 21:10-14). In fact, if a slave took refuge in another community because he or she had been mistreated, they must allow such a slave to live among them wherever he chose (Deut 23:15-16). There was plenty of room for abuse, of course, but the judicial regulations show real concerns for the humanity of both debt and chattel slaves.[6] In general, debt slavery honored the link that remained between the slave and their natal family. In chattel slavery, however, the slave actually belonged to the master and his household, whether that be a family household or the extended temple or palace household.

Exodus 22:3 requires that a thief who cannot make restitution for their theft be sold into slavery to make repayment (cf. Mt 18:25). The primary concern of debt slavery, however, was to provide an economic safety net for individuals and families. If a man's situation became so dire that he fell under a heavy load of debt that he could not pay off in any other way, he could sell himself or someone in his family into debt slavery to his creditor for a limited time. Sometimes it could even get so bad that he would lose the landed property that belonged to him through his family heritage. He could pay off his debt by working for the one to whom he owed the debt. In the meantime, of course, the responsibility for providing food and other necessities

---

[5] Averbeck, "Slavery in the World of the Bible," 424 and the lit. cited there.
[6] Averbeck, "Slavery in the World of the Bible," 428-29 and the lit. cited there.

for his family would fall on the master. The master, in turn, needed the labor and received it as payment for the debt owed to him. Now we turn to the details of each set of debt slave regulations. Note that whatever the rendering may be in the English Bible, the word *servant* is the same as *slave* in Hebrew.

Debt Slavery in Exodus 21:2-11 Compared to Deuteronomy 15:12-18

The NIV rendering of Exodus 21:2-11 reflects the structure of the Hebrew text. There are two major sections: (A) Ex 21:2-6 and (B) Ex 21:7-11, each marked by the Hebrew particle *kî*, "if." Both sections have subpoints marked by the Hebrew particle *'im*, "if."

A. If you buy a Hebrew servant, he is to serve you for six years. But in the seventh year, he shall go free, without paying anything.

- If he comes alone, he is to go free alone;

- but if he has a wife when he comes, she is to go with him.

- If his master gives him a wife and she bears him sons or daughters, the woman and her children shall belong to her master, and only the man shall go free.

- But if the servant declares, "I love my master and my wife and children and do not want to go free," then his master must take him before the judges. He shall take him to the door or the doorpost and pierce his ear with an awl. Then he will be his servant for life.

B. If a man sells his daughter as a servant, she is not to go free as male servants do.

- If she does not please the master who has selected her for himself, he must let her be redeemed. He has no right to sell her to foreigners, because he has broken faith with her.

- If he selects her for his son, he must grant her the rights of a daughter.

- If he marries another woman, he must not deprive the first one of her food, clothing and marital rights.

- If he does not provide her with these three things, she is to go free, without any payment of money.

The parallel passage in Deuteronomy 15:12-18 is different. It has three main clauses: (A) Deuteronomy 15:12-15, (B) Deuteronomy 15:16-17, and (C) Deuteronomy 15:18. Each has explanations, which are *not* all the same as the legal subclauses in Exodus 21:2-11.

A. If any of your people—Hebrew men or women—sell themselves to you and serve you six years, in the seventh year you must let them go free. And when you release them, do not send them away empty-handed. Supply them liberally from your flock, your threshing floor and your winepress. Give to them as the LORD your God has blessed you. Remember that you were slaves in Egypt and the LORD your God redeemed you. That is why I give you this command today.

B. But if your servant says to you, "I do not want to leave you," because he loves you and your family and is well off with you, then take an awl and push it through his earlobe into the door, and he will become your servant for life. Do the same for your female servant.

C. Do not consider it a hardship to set your servant free, because their service to you these six years has been worth twice as much as that of a hired hand. And the LORD your God will bless you in everything you do.

There are important similarities between the regulations in Exodus 21:2-11 and Deuteronomy 15:12-18. In both passages the debt slave is a native Hebrew, and works for six years but goes out from slavery in the seventh year (Ex 21:2; Deut 15:12; the exception in Ex 21:7-11 is treated below). Similarly, in both cases the debt slave can elect to stay with the master as a perpetual slave because things are going well for them in the master's household (Ex 21:5-6; Deut 15:16-17). In Exodus 21 this may be due not only to the good treatment of the slave by the master, in general, but the master has also given him a wife and she has born him children. He does not want to leave them behind (Ex 21:4-5).

Debt slavery was a common practice across the ancient Near East. According to the Laws of Hammurabi, for example: "If an obligation is outstanding against a man and he sells or gives into debt service his wife, his son, or his daughter, they shall perform service in the house of their buyer or of the one who holds them in debt service for three years; their release shall be secured in the fourth year."[7] The shorter term is interesting: three years of service and fourth-year release as opposed to the six years of service and release in the seventh in Exodus 21:2 and Deuteronomy 15:12. The change is likely due to the regularity of the sabbatical pattern in Israel (see the discussion of the book of the covenant below).[8]

In Exodus 21:4, since the creditor had given him his wife while the debtor was working to pay off his debt, at that time he did not have money to pay the bride price (see the discussion of the seventh commandment in chap. 4). The woman and their children, therefore, still belonged to the creditor financially, so they could not go out with the debtor at the end of his period of debt slave service. This highlights the importance of economics in the judicial regulations. They protected everyone, including the creditor. The Laws of Ur-Namma §4 is similar: "If a slave marries a slave girl of his choice, (and) this slave is set free, (she) will not leave the household."[9] Deuteronomy 15 does not consider this particular issue, but the debt slave may nevertheless choose perpetual slavery with the master "because he loves you and your family and is well off with you" (Deut 15:16).

---

[7] LH § 117; see COS 2.343.

[8] For other slavery regulations in the Laws of Hammurabi and other ancient Near Eastern law collections, see Averbeck, "Slavery in the World of the Bible," 425-26.

[9] See Miguel Civil, "The Law Collection of Ur-Namma," in *Cuneiform Royal Inscriptions and Related Texts in the Schoyen Collection*, CUSAS 17, ed. A. R. George (Bethesda, MD: CDL Press, 2011), 246 and the commentary on 254.

One of the major differences between the debt slave regulations in Exodus 21 and Deuteronomy 15 arises in the consideration of female debt slaves as opposed to male. Exodus 21:7-11 refers specifically to a daughter of another family that is indebted to a creditor. As the master, he has "selected" her for himself (Ex 21:8) or "for his son" (Ex 21:9). Exodus 21:10 says that if the master "marries [lit. 'takes'] another woman," he must still provide well for and not neglect the daughter that he had previously taken as a wife. The adjective "another" here is important. It helps us see that he "selected" the daughter as a wife for himself or for his son. Similarly, Exodus 21:9 says that " If he selects her for his son, he must grant her the rights of a daughter." She gains the status of a daughter and is thus part of the family. However, if he is not willing to provide for her as a wife any longer, she goes out free without any payment just like the male slave in Exodus 21:2. Thus, the beginning and the end of the passage both come back to freedom for the person sold into slavery.

The regulation makes it clear that there are protections for the daughter and her family. Of course, initially she would not go out in the seventh year because she is now under the legal protection of the master's household; he has selected her as a wife for himself or his son. When he took her as a wife, the forgiving of her family's debt became the payment of the bride price for this woman to be a wife (see chap. 4 above). The family had gone into debt and could not pay it off. However, they had a daughter that the creditor presumably desired as a wife for himself or his son. In the same transaction, the father of the daughter obtained a man of means as a husband for his daughter. If all goes well, everyone wins.

If things do not go well, the creditor must let her family redeem her out of his household. He cannot sell her away from her family to foreigners (Ex 21:8). If he appoints her for his son, he must treat her as one with the rights and privileges of a daughter of his household. Even if neither the master nor his son accepts her as his wife, then he has to provide for her regular needs or else allow her to go out free, with no payment of money. The master does not get his money back from his purchase of the daughter, which he originally paid by forgiving the debt of the other family. Deuteronomy 15:12-17, on the other hand, makes it clear that if a woman debt slave was not slated to be a wife when she entered into debt slavery, then she would go out free in the seventh year just like any male debt slave. The two passages are not contradictory.[10]

Deuteronomy 15:13-15 emphasizes the dignity and agency of the debt slave. The master is to provide him (or her) with plenty of supplies to get started again when he (or she) leaves his household (Deut 15:13-14). The rationale is "Remember that you were slaves in Egypt and the LORD your God redeemed you. That is why I give you this command today" (Deut 15:15).[11] This rationale for legal regulations based on the exodus from Egypt is characteristic of Deuteronomy. See, for instance, the rationale for the Sabbath in Deuteronomy 5:14-15 as compared to that in Exodus 20:11, as well as other instances of exodus rationale in Deuteronomy.[12] The debt slave regulations in Exodus 21:2-11 do not include this concern for supply of the debt slave when the master releases him. Deuteronomy has added it. One deals with it; one does not.

The regulations in Exodus 21:2-11 and Deuteronomy 15:12-18 do not contradict. They simply highlight different situations and protections for male and female debt slaves. This brings us to the relationship between the debt slave regulations in Exodus 21 and Deuteronomy 15 as compared to Leviticus 25.

---

[10]See the helpful discussion in Jeffrey Tigay, *Deuteronomy*, JPS Torah Commentary (Philadelphia: Jewish Publication Society, 1996), 148-49, 466. See also John Sietze Bergsma, *The Jubilee from Leviticus to Qumran: A History of Interpretation*, VTSup 115 (Leiden: Brill, 2007), 136n118 and the lit. cited there.

[11]See the end of chap. 4 above for a full discussion of the exodus from Egypt as the overall rationale of the law in the Torah. See also the helpful remarks on this regarding Lev 25 and all of Lev 17–26 in Christophe Nihan, *From Priestly Torah to Pentateuch: A Study in the Composition of the Book of Leviticus*, FAT 25 2, Reihe 25 (Tübingen: Mohr Siebeck, 2007), 533-35.

[12]See Deut 6:12, 20-25; 7:8, 18; 8:14; 9:12, 25-29; 10:19; 13:11; 16:1-3, 6, 12; 20:1; 24:17-22; 25:17; 26:5-10.

Debt Slavery in Leviticus 25:39-43

Leviticus 25 comes at debt slavery from a different perspective altogether. In Leviticus 25:40 (cf. also Lev 25:54), the release comes in the Year of Jubilee (see the basic Jubilee regulations in Lev 25:8-38). Again, the background of the regulation derives from their deliverance from slavery in Egypt: "I am the LORD your God, who brought you out of Egypt to give you the land of Canaan and to be your God" (Lev 25:38). The core of the debt slave regulation reads as follows:

> If any of your fellow Israelites become poor and sell themselves to you, do not make them work as slaves. They are to be treated as hired workers or temporary residents among you; they are to work for you until the Year of Jubilee. Then they and their children are to be released, and they will go back to their own clans and to the property of their ancestors. Because the Israelites are my servants, whom I brought out of Egypt, they must not be sold as slaves. Do not rule over them ruthlessly, but fear your God. (Lev 25:39-43)

Thus, the debt slave could theoretically serve as many as forty-nine years. The destitute man would "sell himself" to his creditor (Lev 25:39), but the term *slave* is never used in the context in reference to him. It is only used of foreign slaves, whom they could press into permanent and even generational slavery (Lev 25:44-46).

As noted above, it is important to keep in mind that the main subject in this part of Leviticus 25 is the Year of Jubilee. This law, therefore, anticipates the fiftieth-year release of land back to the original families who would inherit it from their ancestors as part of the conquest and occupation of the land (see Joshua). There were to be no land barons in ancient Israel, at least not beyond the limit of fifty years.

Exodus 21 and Leviticus 25 are actually referring to two different categories of debt slavery: one who enters debt slavery single or married but without children (Ex 21:2-3), as opposed to one who enters debt slavery married and with children (Lev 25:39-43; note esp. Lev 25:41).[13] The latter is the head of a family who enters slavery at a

---

[13]See the very helpful discussion in Adrian Schenker, "The Biblical Legislation on the Release of Slaves: The Road from Exodus to Leviticus," *JSOT* 78 (1998): 23-41 (esp. pp. 32-34) reprinted in

point of destitution. His circumstances have deteriorated to the point where he has even lost his landed inheritance whether through debt foreclosure or sale to pay off debt (i.e., one step more in the progression from Lev 25:23 to Lev 25:38). Thus, he enters debt slavery, although the creditor who becomes his master must not treat him as a slave but as a "hired worker," like a "temporary resident" (Lev 25:40). The debtor's purpose is not limited to paying off his debt, however. Part of the arrangement is that the master is responsible to provide for him and his whole family until the Jubilee. At that time, his family land inheritance would revert back to him, so he could once again begin providing for his family from the produce of his own land. It would make no sense for such a person to go out from debt slavery before his land reverted back to him. That would leave him without the necessary resources with which to begin again.

On the creditor's part, there was a lot of expense in providing for a whole family along with debt forgiveness. There would be little incentive to take on such a financial burden if the time period was limited to six years. In the case of a man who is the head of a family, therefore, the period of debt slavery needs to extend beyond the regular six-year period. Of course, if the period from the point of entering the debt slavery agreement to the Year of Jubilee is longer, there is more incentive for the master to do so, and if it is shorter there is less. This was a concern elsewhere in the ancient Near East as well.[14] On the other hand, generosity toward one's fellow Israelite is part of the overall burden of Leviticus 25 to begin with.

Recht und Kult im Alten Testament: Achtzehn Studien, OBO 172 (Göttingen: Vandenhoeck & Ruprecht, 2000), 134-49. See also the earlier discussion of Schenker's proposal in Richard E. Averbeck, "The Egyptian Sojourn and Deliverance from Slavery in the Framing and Shaping of the Mosaic Law," in *"Did I Not Bring Israel Out of Egypt?" Biblical, Archaeological, and Egyptological Perspectives on the Exodus Narratives,* ed. James Hoffmeier, Alan Millard, and Gary Rendsburg, BBRSup 13 (Winona Lake, IN: Eisenbrauns, 2016), 173-75.

[14]William W. Hallo, "Slave Release in the Biblical World in Light of a New Text," in *Solving Riddles and Untying Knots: Biblical, Epigraphic, and Semitic Studies in Honor of Jonas C. Greenfield,* ed. Ziony Zevit, Seymour Gitin, and Michael Sokoloff (Winona Lake, IN: Eisenbrauns, 1995), 88-93. See also Schenker, "The Biblical Legislation on the Release of Slaves," 33, 38-39; and Mark Leuchter, "The Manumission Laws in Leviticus and Deuteronomy: The Jeremiah Connection," *JBL* 127 (2008): 638.

In light of the relationship between the debt slave regulations in the Torah as outlined above, first, the debt slave regulations in Exodus 21:2-11 attend to certain considerations for poor Israelites who are not married, or at least do not have children who would go into slavery with them. They might even enter slavery as part of a larger (landed) family's management of debt. Second, Leviticus 25:39-43 adds special considerations for a *paterfamilias*, a father with his family (wife or wives and children), who has become so destitute that there is no option left but for the *paterfamilias* to "sell himself" (and his family) as an indentured servant until the Year of Jubilee, when his landed estate would revert to him.

Third, in the context of seventh-year debt relief regulations (Deut 15:1-11), the debt slave regulations in Deuteronomy 15:12-18 follow the basic principles in Exodus 21:2-11. However, the focus here is on individual independent male and female debt slaves without regard to marital status (contra Exodus 21) and the need for the master to send them out with plenty of provisions to get a new start. This is in accordance with the ethos of the regulations in Leviticus 25:35-54. Since Deuteronomy 15:12-18 is in the context of seventh-year debt relief and not the Jubilee, however, it does not consider the matter of going back to a landed inheritance.

THE BOOK OF THE COVENANT

As noted previously, the three parallel collections of law in the Pentateuch we are dealing with here all begin and end with ritual cultic worship regulations.[15] This keeps the main concern of the Mosaic covenant always before one's eyes as they read the law. They were first of all and above all worshipers of the Lord their God, and so are we today in the new covenant.

Thus, the judicial regulations in the book of the covenant end with worship regulations in Exodus 23:14-19. It starts with the three

---

[15]For the discussion of the book of the covenant presented here, see also the earlier and more detailed treatment in Averbeck, "The Egyptian Sojourn and Deliverance from Slavery," 154-58.

required annual feasts before the Lord (Ex 23:14-17). It continues with four other regulations: the prohibition against yeast in the offerings and the eating of the sacrificial food all on one day, the requirement to offer first fruits from the soil (Ex 23:18-19), and, finally, "Do not cook [lit. 'boil'] a young goat in its mother's milk" (Ex 23:19; see also the same in Ex 34:26 and Deut 14:21).

"Do not cook a young goat in its mothers milk": Laws for animals. The prohibition not to cook a young goat in its mother's milk is apodictic, and it uses the same grammar as the prohibitions in the Ten Commandments: "*You must never* cook a young goat in its mother's milk" (Ex 23:19, my translation). The fact that this rule appears *verbatim* three times in the Torah underlines its importance, but its meaning has been the subject of much scholarly debate through the centuries.[16] In rabbinic teachings it led to the practice of not eating dairy products with meat, and even using separate sets of cooking utensils for them, among other related regulations.[17] This is not likely to be its original intention.

In my view, this regulation offers an opportunity to take a deeper look at the underlying rationale of the law as a whole. Some scholars have thought that it serves as a prohibition against some kind of Canaanite sacrificial practice (see Maimonides), but there is no known support for this interpretation. The most common understanding is that this is a humanitarian regulation. It is unseemly to cook a young goat in its own mother's milk, since the milk was flowing from the mother with the intention of nurturing the kid, not boiling it. This is true, but there is more to it than that.

Growing up on a dairy farm, I learned the importance of feeding the first milk from a cow to her calf soon after it was born because of its extra load of antibodies, which would protect the calf from

---

[16]See the helpful summary of views in Nahum M. Sarna, *Exodus*, JPS Torah Commentary (Philadelphia: The Jewish Publications Society, 1991), 147.

[17]See *Mishna Hullin* 8.1-4, esp. 4; Herbert Danby, *The Mishnah* (Oxford: Oxford University Press, 1933), 524-25.

disease. It is also especially high in protein and fat for early nutritional needs. The technical term for this new milk is *colostrum*. This natural provision applies to all mammals, including human beings. All three times the prohibition against boiling a kid in its mother's milk occurs, it is in the context of festivals (Ex 23:19; 34:26) or bringing of tithes (Deut 14:21). The feast of booths and the main tithing season were at the end of the year in the fall, at the beginning of the rainy season. This was also the regular season for goats to bear their young.[18] This regulation would, therefore, apply most naturally to the fall season festivals.

The point is that God has built this into his design of nature. To violate it is to violate the core of his design. That "Do not cook a young goat in its mother's milk" appears three times, all in the context of festival or food laws, suggests that it is not just a standard regulation. It is a motto or proverb that applies to innumerable features of nature as God created it. The motto does not appear in the holiness collection, but a more comprehensive set of regulations for what it captures is found there in Leviticus 22:26-28: "The LORD said to Moses, 'When a calf, a lamb or a goat is born, it is to remain with its mother for seven days. From the eighth day on, it will be acceptable as a food offering presented to the LORD. Do not slaughter a cow or a sheep and its young on the same day.'" It is all about how to handle animals that were grown for sacrifice or eating meat in such a way as to not violate basic principles of nurture. The Israelite world was filled with pastoral animals and the law was concerned with good basic management of them. This began with the mother and its newborn offspring.

In my view, these regulations belong to the category of what some refer to as "the laws of nature," which also includes the laws of physics and other hard sciences. From the first mention of humanity in the Bible, God made it our specific responsibility to rule over and manage the animal world in his image as his likeness (Gen 1:26-28). Those

---

[18]Sarna, *Exodus*, 147.

who have lived close to nature, as ancient Israel did, realize the primary importance of this.

Other similar regulations support this interpretation. Consider, for example, the law of firstborn animals in Exodus 22:30. The firstborn of an animal of the herd or flock belonged to the Lord, and the owner must give it to him. The verse ends, "Let them stay with their mothers for seven days, but give them to me on the eighth day." To offer it in sacrifice before that would be cruel. It would not even have enough time to fulfill the basic sabbatical cycle of life. Growing up on the farm, we did not even try to ship calves to market for veal before they had gained strength enough to endure the trip.

See also the ruling in Deuteronomy 22:6-7: "If you come across a bird's nest beside the road, either in a tree or on the ground, and the mother is sitting on the young or on the eggs, do not take the mother with the young. You may take the young, but be sure to let the mother go, so that it may go well with you and you may have a long life." You can eat the eggs but must let the mother go free to produce more. This only makes sense in the cycle of life. From another perspective, "Do not plow with an ox and a donkey yoked together" (Deut 22:10). The donkey cannot match the power of an ox, so to yoke them is abusive to the donkey, and perhaps also to the ox. See also, "Do not muzzle an ox while it is treading out the grain" (Deut 25:4; cf. also 1 Cor 9:9; 1 Tim 5:18).[19] On analogy to this, there are regulations against, for example, crossbreeding, interseeding, and weaving different fabrics together (Lev 19:19; Deut 22:9-12). All these kinds of regulations are patterned on the way God designed the world to begin with, and his determination that his people should live according to his patterns and the distinctions between his created categories. It taught and illustrated his ways in all categories of life and nature so that the creation design would become integral to the way they lived in ancient Israel.

---

[19]Sarna, *Exodus*, 141 on Ex 22:29 in Hebrew (ET Ex 29:30).

These principles of nature as God designed it emerge from time to time through the law because they underlie it throughout. Where they really come through in a carefully patterned way is in the clean and unclean regulations in Leviticus 11–15. For our discussion here, it is only important to introduce the basic fact that uncleanness is about things in nature and in our lives that do not correspond to God's original design in creation. In one way or another, they are part of the groaning of the natural world and our groaning as we live in the midst of it, as Paul put it in Romans 8:18-26.

The animal laws discussed above make good sense if one understands the world of animals. Similar concerns appear in the regulations for the nurture of fruit trees in Leviticus 19:23-25. The first three years of fruit are left untouched. It takes years for a tree to get to full fruit-bearing capacity. During those years, one should not pick the fruit. This helps the tree continue to grow and mature. The fourth-year fruit is like the first fruits of the soil offered to the Lord (cf. Ex 23:19). Finally, in the fifth year, one can pick and eat the fruit, and this continues for many prosperous years.

Laws for human sexual identity and relationships. The reader may have noticed that the laws of nature discussed above are virtually all apodictic. They are basic principles of life. Living according to them makes us decent people and enables us to contribute to the tendency toward prosperity that God built into his creation design. God created the world so that it could prosper by perpetuating itself, and we are part of that design as those whom he created in his image as his likeness (Gen 1:26-28). The focus there is on how we manage the animal world under our care. The plants supply the nurturing world for the animals and humanity (Gen 1:29-30). This is all very good (Gen 1:31).

Other regulations point to similar concerns in the relations between people. One particular area of contention today is sexual identity. According to one passage, for example, "A woman must not wear men's clothing, nor a man wear women's clothing, for the LORD

your God detests anyone who does this" (Deut 22:5). There were appropriate ways to live out one's identity as male or female. Levirate
marriage was another show of concern for the family line (Deut 25:5-10;
cf. the similar kinsman culture reflected in Ruth 4:1-12). The sexual
relationship directives in Leviticus 18 define what is unfitting or incongruous, in one way or another, in the light of God's creation
design. Parallels in Leviticus 20 turn them into case laws with defined
legal consequences.

Leviticus 18:6-18 limits marital and sexual partners to those not
closely related within the family. This would go a long way to avoiding
intense family rivalries and other undesirable or abusive relationships.
The prohibition against sexual relations with one's wife during her
period has the purpose of preventing the unnecessary spread of
physical impurities among the people (see the discussion of purity
and impurity in chaps. 6–7 below). Of course, the regulations prohibit
adultery (Lev 18:20; cf. the seventh commandment) and offering
children to Molech (Lev 18:21; cf. Lev 20:1-5), which also seems to
have sexual associations.

The list concludes with prohibitions against same-sex sexual relations and bestiality (Lev 18:22-23; cf. Lev 20:13, 15-16; see also
Rom 1:26-27). Few would dispute the question of bestiality, but many
today push back against the laws regarding homosexuality. In the logic
of the text, bestiality is incongruous because interbreeding between
people and animals is a perversion and does not produce offspring
anyway. Same-sex intercourse is incongruous since one of God's main
purposes in his design for human sexuality was reproduction
(Gen 1:27-28). This does not deny, however, the importance of the
relational bond of love between a man and a woman (Gen 2:18-25).

In my view, same-sex attraction is part of our corrupt condition
due to the fall into sin in Genesis 3. In no way should we deny the
reality and powerful nature of same-sex attraction. In counseling
people who identify as LGBTQ+, my experience has been that many
of them are managing desires they do not want. Still, although many

today are offering new readings of Scripture in efforts to normalize same-sex intimacy, I do not find these arguments convincing. Personally and pastorally, I believe that those who give in to any kind of illegitimate sexual desires need to repent, but they also stand in need of careful pastoral ministry (see 1 Thess 4:3-8). There is no room for homophobia.[20]

The judicial regulations. The judicial regulations in the rest of the book of the covenant, and the law as a whole, extend the basic principles of God's design to relationship between God and people, and between people. These are a combination of apodictic and casuistic regulations. Casuistic statements of law are particularly suited to the judicial management of God's design in the world of humanity. Apodictic regulations lay out the design. Casuistic regulations manage the design in light of the fact that both humanity and our conditions within the world have become corrupt. This is a good place to discuss the internal structure and content of the book of the covenant.

Within the cultic frame surrounding the Book of the Covenant discussed above (Ex 20:22-26 <—> 23:14-19), there is an inner sabbatical frame manifested in the correspondence between the sabbatical release of the debt slave in Exodus 21:2-11 and the Sabbath for the land and the regular weekly Sabbath in Exodus 23:10-13 (i.e., Ex 21:2-11 <—> Ex 23:10-13).[21] This sabbatical correspondence between the beginning and end of the laws in the book of the covenant once again highlights the importance of their deliverance from slavery. Accordingly, they must not reenslave one another in Israel. Furthermore, and to the

---

[20]As a licensed professional counselor, I have worked with a number of Christians struggling with same-sex attraction. For careful discussion of the issues involved and a caring, positive approach, I suggest the works of Mark A. Yarhouse, starting with *Understanding Sexual Identity: A Resource for Youth Ministry* (Grand Rapids, MI: Zondervan, 2013) and continuing with his more recent works.

[21]For this discussion, see the details in Averbeck, "The Egyptian Sojourn and Deliverance from Slavery," 155-58. See also the very helpful work done on the sabbatical framework of the book of the covenant in Igor Swiderski, "Sabbatical Patterns in the Book of the Covenant," master's thesis, Trinity Evangelical Divinity School (Ann Arbor: University Microfilms International, 2013). This is truly a masterful master's thesis, written at the level of a PhD dissertation. It is worthy of serious scholarly attention.

same point, one should add the correspondence between Exodus 22:21 and Exodus 23:9:

> You must not afflict a resident alien and oppress him, for you were resident aliens in the land of Egypt. (Ex 22:21)

> You must not oppress a resident alien, since you yourselves know the life of the resident alien, for you were resident aliens in the land of Egypt. (Ex 23:9)

The close correspondence between these two verses stands out. Structurally, if we keep the cultic and sabbatical framing of the law in mind, Exodus 23:9 concludes the unit that begins with Exodus 22:21. Thus, Exodus 22:21–23:9 constitutes a discreet unit of largely apodictic laws surrounded and framed by these two verses about the treatment of resident aliens in light of their own resident alien experience in Egypt. Here again, therefore, we have the same thematic emphasis that appears elsewhere in the framing of the law. The enclosing structures within the book of the covenant, therefore, look something like figure 2.

In figure 2, units (1) and (2) set the cultic and sabbatical frame. Unit (3) sets the largely casuistic first major section of regulations in the main body of the book of the covenant off from the largely apodictic laws. Unit (4) actually initiates the apodictic unit—it highlights three major capital crimes in Israel: sorcery, bestiality, and idolatry. It is the pivot point between the larger casuistic and apodictic regulations of unit (3).

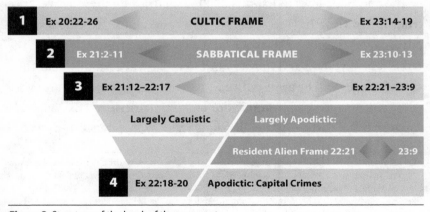

1 Ex 20:22-26 — **CULTIC FRAME** — Ex 23:14-19

2 Ex 21:2-11 — **SABBATICAL FRAME** — Ex 23:10-13

3 Ex 21:12–22:17 — Ex 22:21–23:9

Largely Casuistic — Largely Apodictic:

Resident Alien Frame 22:21 — 23:9

4 Ex 22:18-20 — Apodictic: Capital Crimes

Figure 2. Structure of the book of the covenant

Exodus 23:9 not only echoes Exodus 22:21 but also leads suitably into the sabbatical year rest for the land (Ex 23:10-11) and the regular weekly Sabbath (Ex 23:12-13). These latter laws once again emphasize the need to make special provision for the poor, the enslaved, and the resident alien. They also correspond to the seventh-year release of debt slaves in Exodus 21:2-6 at the beginning of the casuistic section (see unit 2 in figure 2). The beginning of the casuistic laws corresponds to the end of the apodictic laws in this way. This is all part of the literary framing of the book of the covenant. Virtually at every turn the rationale of the law depends on their deliverance from slavery in Egypt and its implications for how they must treat the poor and disadvantaged in Israel, including the resident alien.

In the previous section, the emphasis was on the way of nature or "natural law." Here in the judicial regulations we are dealing more with what theologians refer to as "natural theology." Paul calls it the "law of the conscience" (Rom 2:14-15). People know better, but because they are corrupt, they violate it anyway. One does not need to know the Mosaic law to know these things, but the judicial regulations of the law work out their implications for what life should look like and how they should manage it judicially in ancient Israel. Natural law is native to all people in all cultures, but the way they express it differs to some degree or another, depending on the culture.[22]

The apodictic laws in Exodus 22:21–23:9 draw on their deliverance from Egypt (Ex 22:21) to anchor God's concern for treatment of disadvantaged Israelites: "Do not take advantage of the widow or the fatherless. If you do and they cry out to me, I will certainly hear their cry. My anger will be aroused, and I will kill you with the sword; your wives will become widows and your children fatherless" (Ex 22:22-24). Ancient Near Eastern law collections refer to this concern as well,[23]

---

[22]Christopher J. H. Wright's approach to the Mosaic law as it comes to the church goes a long way toward taking this into account. See his *Old Testament Ethics for the People of God* (Downers Grove, IL: IVP Academic, 2004).

[23]See, e.g., the prologue to LU A iv 162-68 and the epilogue to the LH xlvii 59-61 in Martha T. Roth, *Law Collections from Mesopotamia and Asia Minor*, 2nd ed., WAW 6 (Atlanta: Scholars, 1995), 16, 133.

but here God declares that he is paying special attention to it and will handle violations of it in his own way. The next verse applies this in a special way to business dealings with native Israelites: "If you lend money to one of my people among you who is needy, do not treat it like a business deal; charge no interest" (Ex 22:25; cf. also Lev 25:35-37; Deut 15:7-11; 23:19-20). The following two verses carry this forward to the "neighbor's cloak as a pledge," which one must return before sunset: "What else can they sleep in? When they cry out to me, I will hear, for I am compassionate" (Ex 22:25-27). Again, the Lord pays special attention to such things.

The casuistic regulations in Exodus 21:1–22:17 describe legal cases and prescribe judicial solutions for economic distress, conflict, injury, crime, and neglect that could arise in ancient Israelite society. We have already treated some of these regulations in this volume, and for others the intent is quite transparent. The goal is equitable justice according to Israelite standards in their ancient Near Eastern context. Some cases are more complicated. For example, there is a regulation for unintended harm to a pregnant woman during a fight that causes her baby to "go out":[24]

> "If people are fighting and hit a pregnant woman and she gives birth prematurely [lit. 'and her children go out'; NRSV 'there is a miscarriage'] but there is no serious injury, the offender must be fined whatever the woman's husband demands and the court allows. But if there is serious injury, you are to take life for life, eye for eye, tooth for tooth, hand for hand, foot for foot, burn for burn, wound for wound, bruise for bruise." (Ex 21:22-25)

Numerous ancient Near Eastern law collections include regulations against injuring a pregnant woman and causing her to miscarry. They do not correspond exactly to the biblical case but fall into the same general category. According to the Laws of Ur-Namma §§ 33-34,

---

[24]See the helpful discussion in Sarna, *Exodus*, 125 and the review of scholarship with a different kind of interpretation than is offered here in Raymond Westbrook, "Lex Talionis and Exodus 21:22-25," in *Law from the Tigris to the Tiber: The Writings of Raymond Westbrook*, ed. Bruce Wells and Rachel Magdalene, 2 vols. (Winona Lake, IN: Eisenbrauns, 2009), 2.341-60.

for example, "If a [broken text] beats a gentleman's daughter and causes her to miscarry, he will pay thirty shekels of silver. If she dies, this man will be [executed (broken text restored by editor)]."[25] The assumption in all of them is that the baby dies.

There has been a good deal of discussion over this biblical regulation in the context of the abortion debate today. Some argue that "her children go out" means just that, and no more. The baby is born prematurely, but there is no injury to the baby. They still fine the offender for the distress he caused. If the baby does suffer injury, however, then the offender receives due punishment for the injury to the baby (see the discussion of *lex talionis* in chap. 4 above).

Others take "her children go out" to mean that the baby dies—it is a miscarriage, an unintentional abortion. They would fine the offender for the loss of the baby. The "serious injury" refers to any further injury to the woman who lost the baby. If this is the case, then the offender suffers due punishment for the injury to the woman. It seems to me that this would be the correct interpretation if we allow the ancient Near Eastern parallels to weigh heavily in the discussion, but no one knows for sure. In any case, the loss of a baby was a serious matter. According to the Middle Assyrian Laws § 53, they would execute any woman who intentionally aborted her baby, impale her on a stake, and not bury her.[26] The Middle Assyrian Laws are characteristically brutal, but this gives a sense of how serious abortion was in their view of things.

THE HOLINESS COLLECTION

The laws as stipulations to the covenant made at Sinai extend from Exodus 20 all the way to Leviticus 26 or Leviticus 27, with some

[25]Civil, "The Law Collection of Ur-Namma," 248, and commentary on 264-65 (see also §§ 35-36 for if this happens to a slave woman). Cf. also the Sumerian exercise tablet (*ANET* 525, Sumerian Laws §§ 1-2) and the Laws of Hammurabi §§ 209-214 (*COS* 2.348), the Middle Assyrian Laws §§ 21 and 50-52 (*COS* 2.355 and 359), and the Hittite Laws §§ 17-18 (*COS* 2.108).
[26]*COS* 2:359.

additional units in Numbers 1–9.[27] Leviticus 26 contains the blessings and curses of the covenant and ends with, "These are the decrees, the laws and the regulations that the LORD established on Mount Sinai between himself and the Israelites through Moses" (Lev 26:46). Leviticus 27, however, also ends, "These are the commands the LORD gave Moses on Mount Sinai for the Israelites" (Lev 27:34). Thus, at the end of Leviticus, two separate colophons (Lev 26:46; 27:34) seem to say that they conclude the law given at Sinai. Scholars vary on what to do with this double ending. In terms of their content, however, the regulations in Leviticus 27 seem appropriate to the book of Leviticus, especially Leviticus 17–26.

There is some debate among scholars about the extent of the so-called holiness code (labeled H) in Leviticus 17–27.[28] Some scholars limit it to Leviticus 18–26 because the standard holiness terminology does not appear in Leviticus 17 or Leviticus 27. See the holiness command in Leviticus 19:2, "You shall be holy because I, the LORD your God, am holy" (cf. Lev 20:7, 26; 21:6-8) for which this unit is named. The related formula, "I am the LORD (your God)," appears regularly throughout Leviticus 18–26.[29] Leviticus 20:7 combines elements from the two formulas: "Consecrate yourselves and be holy, because I am the LORD your God" (cf. also Lev 19:2-3).

The primary concern of the regulations in Leviticus 17 was to reinforce one of the major concerns of Leviticus 18–26: the absolute exclusivity of Yahweh worship. This would place a major unit of ritual cultic altar regulations at the beginning of the holiness code, like at the beginning of the book of the covenant (Ex 20:22-26), and at the beginning of the core legislation in Deuteronomy 12. Many scholars

---

[27]The discussion in this section is based on the notes I wrote for Leviticus in D. A. Carson, ed., *NIV Biblical Theology Study Bible* (Grand Rapids, MI: Zondervan, 2018), 172-216, also known as the second edition of the *NIV Study Bible*, ed. D. A. Carson (Grand Rapids, MI: Zondervan, 2015). In some cases, the reader can find more detail there.

[28]For this discussion, see much more detail in Averbeck, "The Egyptian Sojourn and Deliverance from Slavery," 150-51n15 and the lit. cited there.

[29]See Lev 18:2, 4, 5, 6, 21, 30; 19:3, 4, 10, 12, 14, 16, 18, 25, 28, 30, 31, 32, 34, 36, 37; 20:7, 8, 24; 21:8, 12, 15, 23; 22:2, 3, 8, 9, 16, 30, 31, 32, 33; 23:22, 43; 24:22; 25:17, 38, 55; 26:1, 2, 13, 44, 45.

take Leviticus 27 to be an appendix to the book because of the colophon at the end of Leviticus 26. As noted above, a similar colophon appears at the end of both chapters (Lev 26:46; 27:34).

The content of Leviticus 27 actually suits the pattern of cultic regulations at the beginning and end of the other law collections. Leviticus 27 contains cultic regulations for paying vows, the dedication of houses and fields, the presentation of firstborn animals, and tithes. It would seem that as Exodus 20:22-26 corresponds to Exodus 23:14-19, and as Deuteronomy 12 corresponds to Deuteronomy 26, in the same way Leviticus 17 corresponds to Leviticus 27. It belongs to the regular pattern of the cultic framing of the noncultic law collections. This may explain why Leviticus 27 is placed after Leviticus 26 in spite of the colophon in Leviticus 26:46, and why there is another colophon at the end of Leviticus 27.

In its various contexts, the "I am the LORD (your God)" formula emphasizes the importance of exclusive worship and obedience to the Lord. It is with the Lord as their only God and their lawgiver that Israel must concern itself. The Lord first gave the law in the Ten Commandments (Ex 20:1-17) and the book of the covenant (Ex 21–23). In general terms, there the law was given with legal principles, processes, and applications as their focus. The holiness code is how the kind of laws we find in the book of the covenant look when seen from the perspective of community holiness rather than legal principles and processes. The holiness code was the Lord's way of applying the law from the perspective of his personal presence as the Lord their God who dwelt in their midst in the tabernacle.

Leviticus 17 looks back to Leviticus 1–16 in the sense that it emphasizes making offerings in the tabernacle (Lev 17:1-9) along with blood "atonement" and, therefore, the prohibition against eating blood (Lev 17:10-16). By demanding that all domestic animals killed for food be brought to the tabernacle as peace offerings to the Lord (Lev 17:5), Leviticus 17 removed even the opportunity to engage in what it terms (spiritual) prostitution (Lev 17:7) while they were on their way to the

Promised Land. The same term is used elsewhere in Leviticus 18–26 for Molech worship and recourse to mediums and spiritists, which would become a potential danger, especially after they had occupied the land of Canaan where such practices were common (Lev 20:5-6; cf. Lev 18:21; 19:31; 20:27).

The internal structure of the holiness collection is more difficult to discern. On the one hand, the compliance formula in Leviticus 21:24 echoes the same terminology as Leviticus 17:2, suggesting that perhaps Leviticus 17–21 is a contained section. On the other hand, the community emphasis in Leviticus 18–20 seems to set them off as a distinct unit by the correspondence between the introduction in Leviticus 18:1-5 and the conclusion in Leviticus 20:22-27. In Leviticus 18:2-3 the Lord instructed Moses: "I am the LORD your God. You must not do as they do in Egypt, where you used to live, and you must not do as they do in the land of Canaan, where I am bringing you. Do not follow their practices." Leviticus 20:23-26 concludes in a similar vein. These chapters extend the danger of defiling the tabernacle (Lev 20:3, cf. Lev 15:31) to the danger of defiling the land (Lev 18:24-30).

Leviticus 21–22 uses variations of the holiness formula throughout (see esp. Lev 21:8, 15, 23; 22:9, 16) and concludes with, "I must be acknowledged as holy by the Israelites. I am the LORD, who makes you holy and who brought you out of Egypt to be your God. I am the LORD" (Lev 22:32-33). Other references to holiness in this unit refer to the sanctity of the priests (Lev 21:8, 15), the precincts of the tabernacle (Lev 21:23), and the sacred offerings (Lev 22:9, 16). Contact with the surrounding community and nation might defile or profane these. One particular element of holiness crosses the boundary between Leviticus 18–20 and Leviticus 21–22 and binds them together—namely, the emphasis on the sanctity of the name of the Lord God (see esp. Lev 18:21; 19:12; 20:3; 21:6; 22:32).

This concern for the name of God continues into the last major subsection of the book, Leviticus 23–26. Leviticus 24:10-23 raises the question of what to do if someone in Israel "blasphemed the Name with a curse" (Lev 24:11; i.e., Yahweh, the special name of the Lord). The term *holy* appears extensively to refer to the sabbatical regulations in Leviticus 23 and Leviticus 25. Leviticus 23 gives the regulations for the weekly Sabbath and yearly festivals. The regulations for the sabbatical and Jubilee years in Leviticus 25 conclude the sabbatical legislation. Standing in between is Leviticus 24, which emphasizes the daily (Lev 24:1-4) and weekly (Lev 24:5-9; see "Sabbath" in Lev 24:8) service for the presence of the Lord in the tabernacle and, in light of that, the importance of treating both the name of the Lord (Lev 24:10-16, 23) and his people (Lev 24:17-22) with due respect.

Leviticus 25 ends with the Lord's claim on the nation as his servants because he himself had delivered them out of their Egyptian slavery and they belong to him alone: "They are my servants [i.e., slaves], whom I brought out of Egypt. I am the LORD your God" (Lev 25:55). This flows directly into Leviticus 26, which begins with the prohibition against idols (Lev 26:1), and the command to "observe my Sabbaths and have reverence for my sanctuary" (Lev 26:2). Both verses end with the "I am the LORD (your God)" formula. At the end of Leviticus 26, the Lord once again uses the exodus motif and the "I am the LORD" formula. This provides the anchor for his ongoing future fidelity and permanent commitment to the nation even when they are in exile: "for their sake I will remember the covenant with their ancestors whom I brought out of Egypt in the sight of the nations to be their God. I am the LORD" (Lev 26:45; see chap. 2 above). The Lord had delivered Israel from Egypt to become a holy nation devoted completely to the exclusive worship and service of the only true God, the Lord, who was personally present with them in the tabernacle.

The narratives of Numbers 10–36 recount the journey from Sinai to Kadesh Barnea, the refusal to go into the land, and the thirty-eight (almost forty) years of wilderness wanderings (see Deut 2:14 with Num 14:33, 34; 32:13; Deut 2:7) until they came into Moab across the Jordan River from Canaan (Num 22:1; 36:13; Deut 1:5). Chapters of law appear strategically placed throughout this narrative of the wilderness wanderings. They consist largely of regulations that supplement those in Leviticus.

THE DEUTERONOMIC COLLECTION

We have discussed some of the specific regulations in Deuteronomy 12–26 above, where they are parallel or related to those in the book of the covenant or the holiness collection. The book of the covenant (Ex 21–23) presents the Mosaic law in terms of legal principles, processes, and applications as their focus. The holiness code views the law from the perspective of community holiness rather than legal principles and processes. It applies the law from the perspective of the Lord God's personal presence dwelling in their midst in the tabernacle.

The regulations in Deuteronomy 12–26 present Moses as the prophetic preacher of the law at the end of the wilderness wanderings forty years later on the shores of Moab. He was about to die. After this death, Joshua would lead the people into the Promised Land. As Deuteronomy 1:5 puts it, "On the other side of the Jordan in the territory of Moab, Moses undertook to expound this law [*tôrâ*, lit. 'instruction']." Deuteronomy, therefore, presents the law as a series of speeches Moses made to instruct and exhort the new generation of Israelites to faithful covenant devotion to the Lord.

Scholars generally agree that Deuteronomy consists of three speeches surrounded by a heading or preamble (Deut 1:1-5) and an epilogue about the death of Moses (Deut 31–34). The three speeches include (1) historical prologue reviewing the history of God's dealings with Israel (Deut 1:6–4:43); (2) terms of the covenant God made with them in Moab (Deut 4:44–29:1); and (3) exhortation to be faithful to the covenant (Deut 29–30).[30] The book also shows another kind of structure that overlaps with these speeches—namely, the general

---

[30]See, e.g., Tigay, *Deuteronomy*, xii, and Daniel I. Block, *Deuteronomy*, NIVAC (Grand Rapids, MI: Zondervan, 2012), 43-48.

arrangement of the Hittite suzerain vassal treaties from the Late
Bronze Age (ca. 1550–1200 BC).[31] Although scholars vary in the de-
tails here, according to this pattern, one could see the structure of
Deuteronomy this way:

> Preamble (Deut 1:1-5)
>
> Historical Prologue (Deut 1:6–4:43)
>
> Statement of Relationships (Deut 4:44–11:32)
>
> Stipulations (Deut 12–26)
>
> Curses and Blessings (Deut 27–28)[32]

In my view, both of these structures are valid, but the speeches are
primary. This is important because it connects to some of the most
important rhetorical features of the book.

For example, most people are aware of the Great Shema in
Deuteronomy 6:4-5: "Hear, O Israel: The LORD our God, the LORD is
one. Love the LORD your God with all your heart and with all your
soul and with all your strength." Jesus cited the first great commandment from it (Mt 22:37-38; Mark 12:29-30). The term *shema* is
the first word of the verse in Hebrew: "Hear." Actually, there are four
shemas in Deuteronomy 4–11:

> "Now, Israel, *hear* the decrees and laws I am about to teach you." (Deut 4:1)
>
> "*Hear*, Israel, the decrees and laws I declare in your hearing today." (Deut 5:1)
>
> "*Hear*, O Israel: The LORD our God, the LORD is one." (Deut 6:4)
>
> "*Hear*, Israel: You are now about to cross the Jordan." (Deut 9:1)

This is what lends structure and rhetorical effect to Deuteronomy 4–11.
In the midst of his speech, this expression functions similarly to when

---

[31]See examples of such treaty texts in *COS* 2.93-106 and *ANET* 199-206 and 529-30. The compre-
hensive standard source for this now is Kenneth A. Kitchen and Paul J. N. Lawrence, eds., *Treaty,
Law and Covenant in the Ancient Near East*, 3 vols. (Wiesbaden: Harrasowitz, 2012). For evalua-
tions and further developments, see Neal A. Huddleston, "Ancient Near Eastern Treaty
Traditions and their Implications for Interpreting Deuteronomy," in *Sepher Torath Mosheh:
Studies in the Composition and Interpretation of Deuteronomy*, ed. Daniel I. Block and Richard L.
Schultz (Peabody, MA: Hendrickson, 2017), 30-77. In that same volume, see also K. Lawson
Younger Jr. and Neal A. Huddleston, "Challenges to the Use of Ancient Near Eastern Treaty
Forms and Features for Dating and Interpreting Deuteronomy," 78-109.

[32]No list of gods as witnesses appears in Deuteronomy because there is only one God; perhaps the
special stones in Deut 27:1-8 replace the list of gods.

a speaker says something like, "now, listen to this," to recapture the attention of the audience or congregation. He is now going to highlight something especially important.

In his temptations, Jesus responded to the devil three times (Mt 4:1-11). He cited Scripture all three times, and all three citations were specifically from this section of Scripture (Deut 8:3; 6:16; 6:13, respectively). For this and other reasons, some say Deuteronomy is the heart of the Old Testament. The New Testament cites Deuteronomy more than any other book in the Pentateuch, and almost as much as Psalms and Isaiah. It focuses on the core importance of faithfulness to the Lord and one another in all areas of life, including how we think, feel, talk, and act. It pulls all of the core parts of the regulations in the book of the covenant and the holiness collection together for its application to the nation as they enter, conquer, occupy, and settle the Promised Land. In one place, for example, it even specifically refers back to the regulations for skin-diseased persons in Leviticus 13–14. "In cases of *defiling skin diseases*, be very careful to do exactly as the Levitical priests instruct you. You must follow carefully *what I have commanded them*. Remember what the LORD your God did to Miriam along the way after you came out of Egypt" (Deut 24:8-9). There are no specific regulations for defiling skin diseases in Deuteronomy, and the Miriam incident occurred in Numbers 12, before they refused to go into the land in Numbers 13–14.

The law collection in Deuteronomy 12–26 is one of the three main parallel law collections in the Pentateuch that have been the focus of our attention in this chapter. Deuteronomy 5–11 is part of the Mosaic law too. The purpose of these chapters was to secure the people's devotion to the Lord so that they would live accordingly. This comes to its climax in Deuteronomy 11. The first verse makes the point directly: "Love the LORD your God and keep his requirements [lit., 'keep his keepings'], his decrees, his laws and his commands always" (Deut 11:1). The last verse in this chapter reduces the terms for law down to two: "Be sure that you obey all the decrees [Hebrew *ḥuqqîm*] and laws

[Hebrew *mišpāṭîm*; lit. 'judgments'] I am setting before you today" (Deut 11:32).

The first verse in Deuteronomy 12 picks up immediately with the same two terms: "These are the decrees [*ḥuqqîm*] and laws [*mišpāṭîm*] you must be careful to follow in the land that the LORD, the God of your ancestors, has given you to possess—as long as you live in the land" (Deut 12:1). The first word means to "inscribe, carve, engrave." Its first occurrence in the Hebrew Bible is in Genesis 47:22, referring to "a regular allotment" of land to the priests of Egypt from the Pharaoh. In Genesis 47:26 it refers to the "law" Joseph established in Egypt "that a fifth of the produce belongs to Pharaoh." Exodus 5:14 uses it for the "quota" of bricks the Israelite slaves were supposed to make each day in Egypt.

This word often occurs paired with *mišpāṭîm* "judgments."[33] In some cases this combination quite clearly refers to all the combined regulations in the Mosaic law, as it does here in Deuteronomy 11:32; 12:1. Deuteronomy 12–26, therefore, contains the Mosaic regulations as he proclaimed them in Deuteronomy. Perhaps this pair of terms is used because "decrees" (*ḥuqqîm*) suggests the regulations themselves, and "laws" or "judgments" (*mišpāṭîm*) emphasizes how they are (intended to be) applied in particular legal situations.

As with the book of the covenant and the holiness collection, Deuteronomy 12–26 begins and ends with ritual cultic worship regulations. Again, the Israelites were first of all and above all called to be loyal worshipers of the Lord their one and only God. Deuteronomy 12 begins with a strong emphasis on destroying the places, ways, and means of worship of the people they would be conquering (Deut 12:1-4).[34] It then turns to the call for centralized worship at only one place—where the Lord "put his Name there for his dwelling"

---

[33]See, e.g., Lev 18:4, 5, 26; 19:37; 20:22; 25:18; 26:15, 43; Deut 4:1, 5, 8, 14, 45; 5:1; 11:32; 12:1; 26:16.

[34]For a full study of this chapter see Richard E. Averbeck, "The Cult in Deuteronomy and Its Relationship to the Book of the Covenant and the Holiness Code," in Block and Schultz, *Sepher Torath Mosheh*, 232-60.

(Deut 12:5). This would be after they settle in the Promised Land and have "rest" from all their enemies so they "will live in safety" (Deut 12:10).

At the other end of Deuteronomy 12–26 there is the call for the firstfruits ritual after they settle in the land (Deut 26:1-11) and the recollection of the third-year tithe regulations (Deut 26:12-15; cf. Deut 14:28-29). Thus, Deuteronomy 12 and Deuteronomy 26 set the cultic ritual worship frame for the Deuteronomic collection in Deuteronomy 12–26.

Deuteronomy 13 goes on to once again reinforce and repeatedly set out in detail the prohibition against worshiping any other god(s).[35] Some scholars have argued that the regulations in Deuteronomy 12–25 reflect the order of the Ten Commandments as given in Deuteronomy 5:6-21.[36] In my view, there is a general correspondence, but too many ad hoc rationalizations are required to make it fit the textual arrangement in detail. Instead, it is better to follow the connections from one unit to the next as expressed in the text. We cannot go into the details here. The regulations in Deuteronomy 14–25 show a good deal of concern for the disadvantaged in Israel, including them in consideration for all kinds of religious, social, legal, and economic instructions. Deuteronomy 16:18–18:22 focus on the basic regulations for the four major institutions in ancient Israel: the judicial, royal, priestly, and prophetic institutions.

Conclusion

The main goal of this chapter has been to overview the three major collections of the law in the Pentateuch and show how they relate to

---

[35]See the full discussion in Richard E. Averbeck, "The Tests of Prophecy and the Prophets," in *"An Excellent Fortress for His Armies, a Refuge for the People": Egyptological, Archaeological and Biblical Studies in Honor of James K. Hoffmeier*, ed. Richard E. Averbeck and K. Lawson Younger Jr. (University Park: Pennsylvania State University Press, 2020), 1-17.

[36]Stephen A. Kaufman, "The Structure of the Deuteronomic Law," *Maarav* 1:2 (1978–1979): 105-58, followed by Walter C. Kaiser Jr., *Toward Old Testament Ethics* (Grand Rapids, MI: Zondervan, 1983); and Roy E. Gane, *Old Testament Law for Christians: Original Context and Enduring Application* (Grand Rapids, MI: Baker Academic 2017), 240, 260, 268, passim.

one another. All three collections contain a unit on debt slave regulations, which makes the analysis and comparison of the debt slavery laws a helpful way to show how the collections vary but also fit together in complementary ways. This led to a look at the shape and content of each of the three collections and their regulations for how the Israelites should live in the world as God's covenant people: regulations about his designs in nature and for relationships between people. This brings us to a more detailed look at the fabrication of the tabernacle and the regulations for worship in Exodus 25–Leviticus 16, the so-called priestly laws.

Six

ISRAEL AS A KINGDOM OF PRIESTS AND THE PRESENCE OF GOD

THIS CHAPTER ANTICIPATES THE NEXT by laying necessary background for understanding the nature and purpose of the sacrificial system in Leviticus. Leviticus is where the ritual regulations and practices that constitute a large part of the Mosaic law take center stage, at the center of the Pentateuch. It is important to remember, however, that ritual and cultic regulations are not limited to Leviticus. They appear throughout the Mosaic law. In fact, as discussed in the previous chapter, they surround and set the framework for each of the three major parallel law collections in the Torah.

Many believers today find it difficult to understand and relate to these kinds of regulations. We do not sacrifice a lamb on the altar in front of the church each Sunday. God has already sacrificed the Lamb for us, once for all and for all time. Our faith depends on this overwhelming truth. For believers it is at the center of all history and at the core of our walk with God today and forever. The biblical foundations for a deep and powerful understanding of this all-consuming reality are in Leviticus.

The priests and people of ancient Israel performed these ritual procedures before the Lord God, who was present with them in the tent. We have no such tent out in our church parking lot these days, and our church buildings are no substitute. The burden of this chapter is to take a serious look at this foundation of our faith. It requires that we consider the details of who the ancient Israelites were to God in that day, how he was present with them, and how they needed to live with his divine presence in their midst.

The particulars are foreign to us in our culture, so this will require that we learn new things, some of which at times may seem to be pedantic, unnecessary, and unrelated to us in our life with God. They are not. A serious study of the ritual regulations is essential to our understanding not only of the law itself but also to our comprehension of what Jesus Christ did for us and who we are as his followers. Leviticus is one of the most theologically rich books in the Bible. Jesus is our high priest and we are his believer priests, his "chosen people, a royal priesthood, a holy nation" (1 Pet 2:9 with all of 1 Pet 2:4-10 and many other passages). Israel as a kingdom of priests (Ex 19:6) applies to the church too. Yes, these ritual regulations apply to our understanding of what Jesus Christ has done for us, but for Jesus and the writers of the New Testament they also apply to how he has called us to live for him today.

THE KINGDOM OF PRIESTS AND THE PRIESTS OF THE KINGDOM

Scholars have recognized the connection between the promise of Israel becoming a "kingdom of priests" in Exodus 19:6 and the covenant ratification ritual in Exodus 24:6-8, where the blood is splashed first on the altar and then on the people, as a general ordination rite for the "kingdom of priests."[1] This is important to our understanding

---

[1]John A. Davies, *A Royal Priesthood: Literary and Intertextual Perspectives on an Image of Israel in Exodus 19:6* (London: T&T Clark, 2004), 119-24. Earlier scholars have also argued for this interpretation, although none as thoroughly as Davies. See, e.g., Ernest W. Nicholson, *God and His*

of the core rationale of the Mosaic covenant and its law as God gave it at Sinai. It requires following this pattern into the priestly regulations in Leviticus.

The Exodus 24:6-8 blood covenant ratification ritual is comparable to the ordination of the Aaronic priests in Leviticus 8:22-24, when Moses smeared the blood of the ordination offering on the right earlobe, thumb, and big toe of Aaron and his sons to ordain them as priests (cf. Ex 29:19-21).[2] The guilt offering ritual for the cleansing of the skin-diseased person in Leviticus 14:12-18 takes this a step further. The priest smeared the blood on the right earlobe, thumb, and big toe of the common person as part of their cleansing. These are the only three instances in the Hebrew Bible where anyone applied the blood of a sacrificial offering directly to the body of a person or group of persons (Ex 24; Lev 8, cf. Ex 29; Lev 14).[3]

THE ORDINATION OF THE AARONIC PRIESTS

In the ordination of Aaron and his sons to the priesthood in Leviticus 8, Moses first anointed the altar with oil and then smeared some on the right earlobe, thumb, and big toe of Aaron (Lev 8:10-12; cf. Ex 40:9-15). This anointing had the effect of "consecrating" the tabernacle and Aaron to the service of the Lord. Then Moses presented the bull of the sin offering, and Aaron and his sons laid their hands on it, indicating that this was a sin offering specifically for them (Lev 8:14). The purpose of the offering is made clear in the following verses; namely, to purify (i.e., de-sin) the altar in order to "consecrate it to make atonement upon it" (Lev 8:15). He applied the

---

People: *Covenant and Theology in the Old Testament* (Oxford: Clarendon, 1986), 172-74 and the lit. cited there.

[2]For the discussion in this section, see my earlier treatment in Richard E. Averbeck, "Pentateuchal Criticism and the Priestly Torah," in *Do Historical Matters Matter for Faith? A Critical Appraisal of Modern and Postmodern Approaches to the Bible*, ed. James K. Hoffmeier and Dennis R. Magary (Wheaton, IL: Crossway, 2012), 173-77.

[3]Gordon Wenham also briefly anticipated certain elements of this line of argument in his earlier Leviticus commentary, but, as far as I am aware, no one has worked out the details. See Gordon J. Wenham, *The Book of Leviticus*, NICOT (Grand Rapids, MI: Eerdmans, 1979), 143, 209-11.

blood by "daubing" (Lev 8:15) it on the "horns" of the altar and then disposed of the remainder by pouring it out at the base of the altar. The end goal was to make the altar suitable for making atonement.

The burnt offering came next. Then, finally, Moses presented the ram of "ordination" and the priests laid their hands on it, since they were the ones being ordained. The verbal expression occurs later in the passage as "he will ordain you" (lit. "he will fill your hands," Lev 8:33). The underlying rationale of the expression is that their ordination fills the hands of the priests with priestly obligations and prerogatives. The blood manipulation is most important for our purposes here. Moses "daubed" (Lev 8:23) the blood on the right earlobe, right thumb, and right big toe of Aaron and his sons (Lev 8:23-24). The daubing of the blood here matches the daubing of the blood of the sin offering on the horns of the altar earlier in the procedure (Lev 8:15). The earlobe, thumb, and big toe are the "horns" of the man that stick out like the horns of the altar.[4] In other words, the ordination offering blood consecrated the priests in a way that matches the consecration of the altar. The priests thereby become fit to function in making atonement for the children of Israel at the altar. *Aaron and his sons have now become the priests for the kingdom of priests.*

The remainder of the ordination offering blood was "splashed" around on the altar (Lev 8:24) like that of the burnt offering blood (Lev 8:19). These were the normal procedures for the blood in the performance of burnt and peace offerings. The ordination offering belonged to the main category of peace offerings. The same action with the blood was used in Exodus 24:6-8, where the blood was splashed on the altar and then on the people, making them the kingdom of priests. Combine that with the "daubing" of the blood on the horns of the altar and the "horns" of the priests, one can see a correspondence between the Exodus 24 and Leviticus 8 procedures. Moses' final action was to take some of the blood and oil from the

---

[4]See the remarks in Jacob Milgrom, *Leviticus 1–16*, AB 3 (New York: Doubleday, 1991), 528-29.

altar itself and "sprinkle" it on the priests and their garments (Lev 8:30). This corresponds to the sprinkling of the oil on the tabernacle and the priests to anoint and consecrate them earlier in the chapter (Lev 8:10-13) and provides a ritual inclusion for the ordination procedures overall.[5] The important point here is that this action binds the priests and their garments directly to the altar by oil and blood.

The blood manipulation in Exodus 24:6-8 was not only an oath ritual for ratifying the covenant but also an ordination ritual for the nation to become a "kingdom of priests and holy nation." The priests and elders had a meal representing the whole people on the mountain in the presence of God himself in Exodus 24:1-2, 9-11. This shows that, as a nation, they drew close to the very presence of God, as only priests could do.[6] The meal enacted and celebrated the covenant. It was the blood manipulation and oath ceremony in Exodus 24:6-8 that came before the meal, however, that actually accomplished the ratification of the covenant, as Moses' words at the end of Exodus 24:8 declare, "See here the blood of the covenant which the LORD has made with you according to all these words." The manipulation of blood both before and after the oath made it a blood oath commitment by the people to live according to the covenant stipulations in the book of the covenant, which Moses recited to them there.

This carries substantial implications for our understanding of the Mosaic covenant and the law. The passages in Exodus 19 and Exodus 24 look at Israel's covenant relationship with the Lord from the larger perspective of the nation overall as a "kingdom of priests," seeing things from the point of view of the community looking in at the tabernacle that would be constructed (see Ex 25–40). Leviticus 8

---

[5]See the discussion of the difference between the placement of this part of the rite in Ex 29 (Ex 29:21 before the presenting of the wave offering in Ex 29:22-28) as opposed to Lev 8 (Lev 8:30, after the intervening wave offering rite in Lev 8:25-29) in Milgrom, *Leviticus 1–16*, 532-34. In either order, this is the last blood (and oil) manipulation procedure in the ordination process as a whole.

[6]For a very fine overall analysis of Ex 24:1-11 see John W. Hilber, "Theology of Worship in Exodus 24," *JETS* 39 (1996): 177-89.

looks at the Aaronic priests as the designated priests for this kingdom of priests.

THE COMMON ISRAELITE AS ONE WHO
BELONGS TO THE KINGDOM OF PRIESTS

Leviticus 14 confirms the organic connection between the two. A whole set of ritual procedures are involved in the ritual cleansing of the skin-diseased person who had become healthy again, but our focus here is specifically on the guilt offering ritual in Leviticus 14:12-18. The manipulation of the guilt offering blood corresponds closely to that of the ordination offering blood in Leviticus 8:22-24, 30.

A guilt offering rather than an ordination/peace offering was required in Leviticus 14 because the skin-diseased person, who belonged to the "kingdom of priests," had become desecrated, so he needed to stay away from the "holy nation" (cf. Ex 19:6) and from the tabernacle. He or she had to live outside the camp as required in Leviticus 13:46: "As long as he has the infection he remains unclean. He must live alone; he must live outside the camp." This interruption of community solidarity, purity, and holiness in ancient Israel was a major concern. This is why two long chapters are devoted to the diagnosis (Lev 13) and ritual purification (Lev 14) from skin diseases. It takes up most of the section on impurities in Leviticus 11–15. This continued to be a major issue in New Testament Judaism (see, e.g., Mt 8).

The general purpose of the guilt offering was to make atonement for desecration of sancta; that is, treating a holy person, place, thing, or time as if it were not holy but common. The skin-diseased person was sancta, since he was a member of the kingdom of priests and a *holy* nation. Therefore, restoring him back into the community (Lev 14:4-9) was necessary, but it was not enough. It was also necessary to restore him or her back to the tabernacle and its altar, since having been alienated from the community would have also involved alienation from the tabernacle presence of God in the midst of the community.

The application of the guilt offering blood to the body of the skin-diseased person in essentially the same manner as the priestly ordination ritual enacted and achieved her or his reconsecrated status as a member of the "kingdom of priests." Again, the three-part ritual in Exodus 24:6-8 of splashing of the sacrificial blood on the altar, the people swearing an oath to be obedient to the book of the covenant, and splashing the blood on the people was a covenant making oath ritual, which by nature also ordained them as the kingdom of priests. On that occasion, however, the blood-manipulation ritual could not match precisely that in Leviticus 8 and Leviticus 14. There were simply too many people involved—a whole nation—and it was a collective oath commitment rite in any case, so the ritual action needed to be collective. Here in Leviticus 14, however, the ritual shows that the consecration of the people corresponds closely to the consecration of the priests. The blood of the guilt offering was daubed on the right earlobe, thumb, and big toe of the healed person (Lev 14:14).

Anointing oil was also used here in Leviticus 14 as in Leviticus 8. The priest sprinkled it "seven times before the LORD" (Lev 14:16), and then daubed some of it on the right earlobe, thumb, and big toe of the healed person for his ritual cleansing. He daubed the oil right on top of the blood of the guilt offering that was already there (Lev 14:17), and then daubed the remainder of the oil on the person's head. The result obtained by this combination of blood and oil rituals is that the priest "made atonement for him before the LORD" (Lev 14:18). There is no way the priest himself would not have noticed the many correspondences between his own ordination and consecration and the rituals he performed for the healed common person. It would be hard for the priest and the person healed to miss the fact that the people were priests too—a kingdom of priests. The people were holy too—a holy nation. They were sacred.

The priest would also have noticed, however, that there were certain differences between these rites and those performed at his consecration as a priest. One of the main differences was that no blood or oil was taken off the altar and sprinkled on the healed person, as was done in the consecration of the priests (Lev 8:30). The ritual in Leviticus 14, therefore, did not consecrate the healed commoner for functioning as a priest at the altar. The ordained Aaronic priest did that for him or her. Moreover, there was no eating of the guilt offering meat by the healed person that corresponded to how the priests ate the meat of the ordination offering (Lev 8:31-32). No common person would eat the meat of a guilt offering. Since they brought the guilt offering for their atonement, the priests who made the atonement ate the meat (see Lev 7:6). The priest would have understood that he was functioning as a priest for the person who belonged to the kingdom of priests.

In effect, therefore, the Mosaic covenant and the law within it viewed ancient Israel as a nation of worshipers of their God, Yahweh their Lord. They were a people that was special to the Lord. Everything else flowed out of that. The argument here does *not* preclude the common notion found in many commentaries and articles that Israel became a "kingdom of priests and holy nation" in the sense of becoming mediators between the Lord and the other nations. This is still true (see, e.g., Is 61:6), but the main concern at Sinai was the profound emphasis on the people as holy priests in the sense of their priestly access to the presence of God at Sinai and then in the tabernacle.

The Lord brought them close to himself through the covenant bond made in Exodus 24. It was a holy priestly calling. They were called to be holy, as the Lord himself was holy, in all that they did in their homes and relationships, both within Israel (Lev 11:44-45; 19:1-2) and in maintaining their separation from the corrupting influences of the nations roundabout them (e.g., Lev 20:7-8, 26; Deut 14:1-2). He made them a "kingdom of priests" (Ex 19:6).

THE TABERNACLE PRESENCE OF THE LORD

The tabernacle sanctuary was the Lord's tented dwelling place in the midst of Israel as they traveled from Sinai to Canaan. It endured until

Solomon dedicated the temple in Jerusalem (1 Kings 8:3-4, 9; 2 Chron 5:4-5), although the ark of the covenant was removed from the tabernacle in the days of Eli (1 Sam 4–6) and never returned there.[7] In the exodus from Egypt the Lord guided and protected them on their journey from Egypt through the wilderness to Sinai by means of the pillar of cloud by day and pillar of fire by night (Ex 13:21-22). As a continuing part of the Sinai theophany, the Lord gave Moses instructions for the building of the tabernacle at the same time he gave him the two tablets of the law (Exodus 25–31).

While they continued to camp at Sinai for almost one year (cf. Ex 19:1 with Num 10:11), they fabricated the tabernacle (Ex 35–39) and finally erected it (Ex 40). At that time, the Lord promptly occupied the tabernacle in the form of his glory cloud (Ex 40:34-35). From that point forward he continuously manifested his guiding and protecting presence to all the people in the form of a cloud by day with fire in it by night over the tabernacle (Ex 40:36-38; Num 9:15-23; 10:11-12, 33-34). The whole point of the tabernacle and the sacrificial procedures that took place within it (Lev 1–16) was to provide a place to practice his presence among them (Ex 33:14-16). Sinai was the "mountain of God" (Ex 3:1; 4:27; 18:5; 24:13; Deut 4:11, 15). The tabernacle was a moveable Sinai, so to speak. In this tent, the Lord would leave Sinai, his mountain (Ex 3:1), and travel with them to the Promised Land.

THE DESIGN AND PURPOSE OF THE TABERNACLE

The tabernacle complex as a whole was about fifty yards long (half the length of an American football field) and about twenty-five yards wide (almost half as wide as an American football field). Based on the dimensions of the curtains and the frames, and depending on the way

---

[7]This discussion of the tabernacle draws from Richard E. Averbeck, "Tabernacle," in *Dictionary of the Old Testament: Pentateuch*, ed. T. Desmond Alexander and David W. Baker (Downers Grove, IL: IVP Academic, 2003), 807-27. The reader will find much more detail and extensive bibliography there.

they were assembled together, the tented structure within the complex was perhaps about fifteen yards (45 ft) long, five yards (15 ft) wide, and five yards (15 ft) high. The inside of the tent was divided into two parts: the holy place was ten yards (30 ft) long and the most holy place in the back was half that, five yards (15 ft) long (see figure 3).

Within the tabernacle complex there was, from west to east, the actual tented building itself, then the "basin" (or "laver"; Ex 30:18) and then "the altar of burnt offering" (Ex 30:28) out near the entrance on the east (see figure 3). Within the tented building there were two main areas: I "the most holy place" (Ex 26:33; Num 4:4, 19) and II "the holy place" (Ex 26:33; 29:30; Lev 6:30; Num 3:28). Within the most holy place was "the ark of the testimony" (Ex 25:22; or "the ark of the

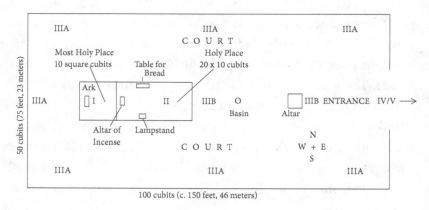

100 cubits (c. 150 feet, 46 meters)

Zone	Description	References
INSIDE the tabernacle complex:		
I	The most holy (place) (*qōdeš haqqŏdāšim*)	Ex 26:33; Num 4:4, 19
II	The holy (place) (*haqqŏdeš*)	Ex 26:33; 29:30; Lev 6:30; Num 3:28
I-II	The tabernacle (*miškān*)	Ex 25:9; 26:1, 7, 15, 26
III	The court(yard) (*ḥāṣēr*)	Ex 27:9-19; Num 4:26, 32
A	A holy place (*māqôm qādōš*)	Ex 29:31; Lev 6:16, 26-27; 7:6; 10:13
B	Entrance (doorway) of the tent of meeting (*petaḥ ʾōhel môʿēd*)	Ex 29:4, 32, 42; Lev 1:3; 3:2; 12:6; 16:7
I-III	The sanctuary (*miqdāš*)	Ex 25:8; Lev 12:4; 19:30; 20:3; Num 3:28
OUTSIDE the tabernacle complex:		
IV	A clean place (*māqôm ṭāhôr*)	Lev 4:12; 6:11; 10:14; Num 19:9
V	An unclean place (*māqôm ṭāmēʾ*)	Lev 14:40, 41, 45

Figure 3. The tabernacle (Exodus 25–31; 35–40)

covenant of the Lord"; e.g., Num 10:33). Within the holy place was "the altar of incense" (Ex 30:27), "the table of (the bread of) the presence" (Lev 24:5-9; Num 4:7), and the "lampstand" (Ex 25:31; Lev 24:1-4). IIIA designates "holy places" within the courtyard (Ex 29:31; Lev 6:16, 26-27; 7:6; 10:13) and IIIB is the area known as the entrance (doorway) of the tabernacle complex (Ex 29:4, 32, 42; Lev 1:3; 3:2; 12:6; 16:7). IV/V refers to areas outside the tabernacle that were clean and unclean, respectively.

There are three major terms used for what we commonly refer to as the tabernacle: "sanctuary" (*miqdāš*), "tabernacle" (*miškān*), and "tent of meeting" (*'ōhel mô 'ēd*). The term *sanctuary* is the most common way to refer to the tabernacle complex as a whole (see, e.g., Ex 25:8 with Lev 12:4 and Num 3:28). It derives from the root *qdš*, which in the Bible is used in various forms to identify a person, place, thing, or time as "holy" (or "sacred"; cf. "sanctuary" as a sacred place, Latin *sanctuarium*) as opposed to "common" (or "profane," *ḥll*). Note especially the Lord's statement of principle in Leviticus 10, when he commands Aaron "to distinguish between the holy [*qōdeš*] and the common [*ḥōl*]" (Lev 10:10) and in Leviticus 11:45, "you shall be holy because I am holy" (cf. Lev 11:44 and the virtual repetitions of this formulaic statement in Lev 19:2; 20:7, 26; similarly Lev 21:8). One of the core concerns and responsibilities of the priests, especially the high priest, was to maintain the holiness of the sanctuary and not "profane" it (i.e., not treat it as just any old common place; Lev 21:12).

The effect of the holiness of the tabernacle and the specific holy places within the tabernacle was to impress the ancient Israelites (and the modern reader) with both the holiness of God and his concerns and intentions for the holiness of his people. Except for the sanctification of the seventh day referred to in Genesis 2:3, the first occurrence of any form of the root *qdš* in the Hebrew canon is the reference to the "holy ground" at the burning bush on Mount Sinai (Ex 3:5). Later, again at Sinai, the Lord promised that if they commit themselves to a covenant with him, the Israelites would become his "treasured possession out of all the nations"—they would become his "kingdom of priests" and "holy nation" (Ex 19:5-6; cf. also the very end of the legal stipulations of the Pentateuch in Deut 26:16-19).

The term *tabernacle* (i.e., "dwelling place") shifts our attention from the holiness and transcendence of God expressed by the term *sanctuary* to the presence and immanence of the Lord. Exodus 25:9 is the first occurrence of this term in the Bible. Moses constructed it according to the "pattern" the Lord showed him on the mountain (Ex 25:9; 26:30; cf. also Acts 7:44; Heb 8:5; 9:23). This tells us that he saw what it was supposed to look like when it was finished (Ex 40). The Lord gives him the detailed instructions in Exodus 26, but, like when putting a child's toy together, it is always helpful to have a picture of it all assembled on the box.

Within two verses (Ex 25:8-9), the text binds the transcendence of God together with his immanence. They belong together. A meaningful understanding of one is essential to grasping the other. The Lord's transcendence is only understandable to us when held in relationship to his immanence, and *vice versa*. It is the holy God of heaven, creator and sustainer of the universe, who took up a tented abode in the midst of a nation that he himself called and delivered out of slavery into his blessed light (Num 6:24-26; cf. the sovereign creator and the incarnate savior in John 1). Each side of this duality sets the other in relief. Like any other tent, it could move about, and that was specifically the reason for its construction. It was a moveable dwelling place for the Lord in his travels with Israel through the wilderness to the Promised Land. It was the Lord's tent in the midst of the tents of the Israelites.

This brings us to the term *tent of meeting*. The difference between "tabernacle" and "tent of meeting" is that the latter emphasizes the "tent" nature of the dwelling and especially its function as a place of "meeting" between God and his people. It is most important to take note of the combination of the daily lighting of the lampstand (Ex 25:31-40 with Lev 24:1-4) and associated burning of incense

(Ex 30:7-8), plus the bread constantly on the table (Lev 24:5-9). If a tent has lamps burning inside, incense giving off its fragrance, and bread on the table, then someone is "home." The Lord took up residential presence in the tabernacle. This is what the tabernacle was all about for God and the people.[8]

THE TABERNACLE PRESENCE OF GOD

We constantly face a tension in Scripture between God's transcendence and immanence, both of which are important to a correct and meaningful understanding of God, his revelation of himself, and how he relates to us. Starting at the beginning, God is transcendent in Genesis 1:1–2:3 but fully active in the creation of the world by fiat, whereas in Genesis 2:4–4:26 the Lord presents himself in intimate earthly relationship with people. Scholars have pointed to the correspondences between the creation accounts in Genesis 1–4 and the tabernacle construction account in Exodus. There is, for example, the pattern of seven divine speeches in Exodus 25–31, like the seven days of the creation, and ending with the Sabbath command (cf. Gen 2:1-3 with Ex 31:12-17; 35:2-3). Other verbal and literary patterns are also important.[9] Similarly, there are numerous parallels between the Garden of Eden account in Genesis 2–3 and the tabernacle. For instance, the garden was the ideal "sanctuary" within which the Lord would be present with his people and walk with them (see Gen 3:8 with Lev 26:12).[10]

---

[8]For divine presence in the tabernacle/temple in Israel and the ancient Near East, see Michael B. Hundley, *Keeping Heaven on Earth: Safeguarding the Divine Presence in the Priestly Tabernacle*, FAT II/50 (Tübingen: Mohr Siebeck, 2011); and *God in Dwellings: Temple and Divine Presence in the Ancient Near East*, WAWSup 3 (Atlanta: SBL Press, 2013).

There was also another "tent of meeting" that was pitched outside the camp other than the tabernacle in the midst of the camp. The one outside the camp was a place for Moses to consult with the Lord (see, e.g., Ex 33:7-11; Num 11:16-17, 24-26).

[9]S. E. Balentine, *The Torah's Vision of Worship* (Minneapolis: Fortress, 1999), 138-41; and J. D. Levenson, *Creation and the Persistence of Evil*, 2nd ed. (Princeton, NJ: Princeton University Press, 1994), 78-90, and the lit. cited in both.

[10]G. J. Wenham, "Sanctuary Symbolism in the Garden of Eden Story," in *Proceedings of the Ninth World Congress of Jewish Studies* (Jerusalem: World Union of Jewish Studies, 1986), 19-24.

Essentially, to build a sanctuary was to create a microcosm, a small properly ordered world within the larger cosmos. A sanctuary is the cosmos in miniature, and the cosmos is a sanctuary, depending on which way you look at it. By building the tabernacle and performing the ritual functions within it, people participate in the ordering of the world.[11] In the New Testament book of Revelation, Jesus "walks" in the midst of the churches (Rev 2:1; 3:4), and eventually in the new heaven and earth the presence of God will be unmediated once again (Rev 21:3: "the tabernacle of God is with men").

According to the Mosaic covenant blessings, if the Israelites would make no idols, observe the Lord's sabbaths, reverence his sanctuary, and keep his covenant statutes and commandments (Lev 26:1-3), the Lord promised, "I will put my dwelling place [or 'tabernacle'] in your midst. . . . I will *walk in your midst*" (Lev 26:11-12, my translation). This passage explicitly links the tabernacle dwelling of God to his walking in the midst of Israel (see also Deut 23:14; and 2 Sam 7:6-7: "I have been walking about from place to place with a tent as my dwelling. I have been *walking about* in a tent, a tabernacle"; my translation). His active presence with them and their obedience to his revealed will along the way was essential to the covenant nature of the relationship between God and Israel.

The correspondences between the creation account and the tabernacle are important, but the near context in Exodus is even more significant. It begins with the burning bush through which the Lord appeared to Moses at "the mountain of God" (Ex 3:1-2). This was "holy ground" (Ex 3:5), and it was there that the Lord promised not only to be "with" Moses as he brought Israel out of Egypt but also to bring him back there to worship God "on this mountain" (Ex 3:12). From there God would lead them "to a good and spacious land, to a land flowing with milk and honey" (Ex 3:8 ESV). In other words, the Lord would be present with Moses and the Israelites all the way from Egypt to Mount Sinai, and from Sinai to the Promised Land.

---

[11]Levenson, *Creation and the Persistence of Evil*, 53-127.

From the exodus until they arrived at Sinai, "The LORD was traveling before them *by day in a pillar of cloud* to lead them on the way and *by night in a pillar of fire*" (Ex 13:21-22 ESV; cf. Ex 14:19-20, 24). In the aftermath of the golden calf catastrophe (Ex 32:27-28, 34-35), the absolute necessity of the divine presence with Israel from Moses' point of view becomes clear (Ex 33). Because the people were so "stiff-necked," the Lord had proclaimed: "I will not go up [to the Promised Land] in your midst . . . lest I destroy you on the way" (Ex 33:3). Instead, "I will send an angel before you" (Ex 33:2, my translation; cf. Ex 14:19; 23:20-23; 32:34). To both Moses and the people this was an even more severe calamity (Ex 33:4-6, 12-16).

Moses objected and the Lord responded, "My *presence* [lit., 'my faces'] will go with you and I will give you rest" (Ex 33:14). Then Moses said, "If your *presence* does not go with us, do not send us up from here" (Ex 33:15). In the following scene Moses asked to see God's glory (Ex 33:18), perhaps meaning that he wanted to see the manifestation of the glory of his "presence" (cf. "face to face" in Ex 33:11). The Lord agreed but insisted, "You cannot see my *faces* [Hebrew *pānāy*]" (Ex 33:20), which is exactly the same term rendered "my *presence*" in Exodus 33:14. The Lord explained, "No one may see me and live" (Ex 33:20). This tells us that we should consider the "presence" (i.e., "faces") of the Lord to be identified with the Lord himself.

The Lord God, therefore, showed his glory to Moses in a special way, face to face, but he also made his glory known to Israel. After the erection of the tabernacle in Exodus 40:17-33, "the cloud covered the tent of meeting, and the glory of the LORD filled the tabernacle. Moses could not enter the tent of meeting because the cloud had settled on it, and the glory of the LORD filled the tabernacle" (Ex 40:35, my translation). Since Moses could not enter the tabernacle, according to Leviticus 1:1, "The LORD called to Moses and spoke to him from the tent of meeting." In the meantime, the last three verses of Exodus highlight the ongoing presence and guidance of the Lord in the tabernacle: "Whenever the cloud lifted from above the tabernacle, they would set out; but if the cloud did not lift, they did not set out—until the day it lifted. So the cloud of the LORD was over the tabernacle by day, and fire was in the cloud by night" (Ex 40:36-38). Numbers 9:15-23 elaborates on this repeatedly just before their departure from Sinai in Numbers 10:11-12, 33-34. All of this, of course, recalls the original pillar of cloud and with fire in it by night that led them out of Egypt to begin with (see the remarks on Ex 13:21-22 above).

Leviticus 1–Numbers 9:14, therefore, is encased between these two tabernacle presence and guidance passages (Ex 40:34-38 and Num 9:15-23). The regulations contained therein focus especially on the need to "practice" that presence. They needed to do that on various levels, in the tabernacle as well as in the community at large, and in multiple ways: in worship, through maintaining the purity and holiness of God's presence, in relationships within the community, and through separation from corrupting influences of the surrounding nations. The same glory of the Lord "appeared to all the people" on the inauguration day in a fire display that consumed the inaugural sacrifices on the altar (Lev 9:23-24) and then regularly "in the cloud over the atonement seat" on top of the ark of the covenant in the most holy place of the tabernacle (Lev 16:2).

CONCLUSION

Centuries later, this glory cloud presence of the Lord occupied the temple of Solomon on the day of its dedication. The priests had to withdraw from the temple, like Moses in Exodus 40:35. They could not enter the temple (1 Kings 8:10-11; 2 Chron 5:13-14). The Lord also consumed the temple dedication sacrifices on the altar, like in Leviticus 9:23-24 (see 2 Chron 7:1-3). When Solomon referred to God's dwelling in the temple in his prayer for the dedication of the temple, he went to great pains to emphasize that God was not "contained" therein: "But will God truly dwell on the earth? Even the heavens and the highest heavens cannot contain you, much less this house which I have built" (1 Kings 8:27 and its parallel in 2 Chron 6:18;

cf. also God's dwelling in heaven in, e.g., 1 Kings 8:30, 39, 43, 49). Both the tabernacle and later the temple were places of access to God's continuous manifest presence in the midst of his people, but neither suggests that God limited his presence to them exclusively.

Unfortunately, by the time of the Babylonian captivity the Israelites had so desecrated and defiled the temple that the glory cloud presence of the Lord actually departed from it, discontinuing his presence there and abandoning it to destruction (Ezek 8:4; 10:3-4, 18-19; 11:22-25). Even then, however, there was the promise of the Lord's return to a new and permanent temple (Ezek 43:1-9). This does not appear to have happened at the dedication of the second temple (Ezra 6:13-18).

Seven

OFFERINGS AND SACRIFICES, HOLINESS AND PURITY

WE CANNOT DEAL with every detail of the sacrificial system in this chapter. Understanding how it functioned, however, requires more than a superficial treatment. The following discussion, therefore, offers a relatively complete (but not comprehensive) walk through the various offerings and sacrifices, showing what they were, how they worked as a system, and how they related to principles of holiness and purity. This part of the Old Testament is seldom studied and poorly understood by most Christians. The old quip is true: many start reading through the Bible in a year but stop at Leviticus—or skip over it. This is a big problem because Leviticus comes through extensively in the New Testament and, as noted above, theologically, it is one of the most important books in the Bible.

OFFERINGS AND SACRIFICES, WORSHIP AND ATONEMENT

The five offerings in Leviticus 1:1–6:8 divide into two units. The first three chapters are one unit with no introductory formulas intervening between them (cf. Lev 1:2 with Lev 2:1; 3:1). These chapters contain the regulations for the burnt offering, the grain offering, and the peace (or fellowship, or communion) offering, respectively. These kinds of offerings were previously presented to the Lord at solitary altars before there ever was a tabernacle (see, e.g., Gen 8:20; 22:14; Ex 20:24-26; 24:4-5; cf. Gen 4:3-5). Leviticus 4:1 gives a separate introduction for the sin (purification) offering unit, which extends from Leviticus 4:1 to Leviticus 5:13. Two units of guilt (reparation) offering regulations follow in Leviticus 5:14–6:8, with brief introductions in Leviticus 5:14 and Leviticus 6:1. The sin and guilt offerings, especially the sin offering, only made sense in the tabernacle, not at solitary altars. Altars were not places of divine occupation, but the tabernacle was. The sin and guilt offerings focused on maintaining the holiness and purity of the divine presence in the midst of the ancient Israelite community.[1] Leviticus 6:8–7:36 consists of regulations for the priests' handling and disposition of the five kinds of offerings and their various parts, including the priestly prebends (i.e., their stipend, or allotment, for services rendered).[2]

The burnt offering and its accompanying grain and libation constituted the regular morning and evening offerings that the priests offered as a daily maintenance of the tabernacle presence of God (see, e.g., Ex 29:38-46; Num 28:1-8). This was part of their regular way to meet with the Lord and worship him at the tabernacle: "There I will meet you and speak to you; there also I will meet with the Israelites, and the place will be consecrated by my glory" (Ex 29:42-43). When a specific worshiper brought a burnt offering to the Lord, the

---

[1]For a detailed chart of the five kinds of offerings, see the *NIV Biblical Theology Study Bible*, ed. D. A. Carson (Grand Rapids, MI: Zondervan, 2018), 178; also known as the second edition of the *NIV Study Bible* (Grand Rapids, MI: Zondervan, 2015), 197.

[2]For those readers who want detailed treatments of all the procedures for each of the five offerings, they can find them in Richard E. Averbeck, "Sacrifices and Offerings," in *Dictionary of the Old Testament: Pentateuch*, ed. T. Desmond Alexander and David W. Baker (Downers Grove, IL: IVP Academic, 2003), 706-33. See also earlier and even more detailed treatments in Richard E. Averbeck, "Clean and Unclean," "Leviticus, Theology of," and "Offerings and Sacrifices" in *NIDOTTE* 4:477-486, 907-923, and 996-1022, respectively. One can also find articles on most of the Hebrew sacrificial terminology in volumes 1-4 of *NIDOTTE*. Most recently, see also Richard E. Averbeck, "Reading the Ritual Law in Leviticus Theologically," in *Interpreting the Old Testament Theologically: Essays in Honor of Willem A. VanGemeren*, ed. Andrew T. Abernethy (Grand Rapids, MI: Zondervan, 2018), 135-49.

instruction was, "You are to lay your hand on the head of the burnt offering, and it will be accepted on your behalf to make atonement for you" (Lev 1:4). Whatever the situation might have been, the burnt offering would at least participate in making atonement, even if other offerings were involved as well. It did so as "a food offering, an aroma pleasing to the LORD" (Lev 1:9).

The English word *atonement* is a combination of "at" and Middle English "one(ment)," meaning "to be or make one." It is, therefore, a word for reconciliation—rectifying something that stood between the offerer(s) and God. In some ways, this is a good way to understand the end result of the Hebrew word *kipper*, "to make atonement," and its derivatives, but it is not adequate to capture all the features of it. Moreover, the peace offering, for instance, was not offered to make atonement, but to celebrate fellowship between God and his covenant people, and one another.

The Hebrew verb *kipper* has two interrelated meanings and usages. First, the basic meaning of the verb is "to purge, wipe clean." It is related to the Akkadian cognate verb *kuppuru* "to wipe clean," which appears extensively in ritual purification contexts. This meaning comes through especially in the sin offering ritual procedure and corresponds to the way the priests handled the blood of the sin offering in the tabernacle.

Second, the verb also shows a correspondence to the noun *kōper* in Hebrew, which means "ransom, bribe."[3] This usage of the verb comes to the surface in contexts where the priest splashes the blood all around on the burnt offering altar as part of the offering gift to the Lord. This is the case with the burnt, peace, and guilt offerings. One can see the connection between the verb and the noun, for example, in Exodus 30:11-16:

---

[3]See *HALOT* 493-95 (the verb *kpr* I and the noun *kpr* IV). See also Richard E. Averbeck, "*kpr*, to make atonement," in *NIDOTTE* 2:689-710, for extensive discussion and bibliography, and the brief summary by Jay Sklar, *Leviticus: An Introduction and Commentary*, TOTC (Downers Grove, IL: IVP Academic, 2014), 50-54.

Then the LORD said to Moses, "When you take a census of the Israelites to count them, each one must pay the LORD a ransom (Hebrew *kōper*) for his life at the time he is counted. Then no plague will come on them when you number them. Each one who crosses over to those already counted is to give a half shekel. . . . Receive the atonement [Hebrew *kippurîm*] money from the Israelites and use it for the service of the tent of meeting. It will be a memorial for the Israelites before the LORD, making atonement [*kipper*] for your lives."

BURNT AND PEACE OFFERINGS

They would burn the whole carcass of the burnt offering on the altar to create a "pleasing aroma," with the exception of the hide (they skinned the animal; Lev 1:6), which belonged to the officiating priests as his prebend (Lev 7:8). If one burns a carcass without skinning it, it gives off a terrible stench, but the carcass of a skinned animal smells like a barbeque. The grain offering usually accompanied the burnt or peace offering and did not normally make atonement in itself (see Lev 2 with Num 15:1-9). One exception is the grain used as a sin offering for the poor in Leviticus 5:11-13 (without the regular oil and incense on it). If the person was extremely poor, they could bring a much less expensive grain offering rather than an animal to make sin offering atonement.

The one who brought the burnt offering would press his hand on the head of the animal to identify himself as the one who was bringing it, and to dedicate it to the purpose(s) of the particular offering. Many think this act indicated the transfer of the sin of the person to the animal, but there are good reasons to question this. The most important reason is that the goal was to present the animal holy and pure to the Lord. To put sin on it would transfer the sin or impurity to the animal and therefore to the altar and the tabernacle. This was the last thing a person should be doing. One should keep anything loaded with sin away from the tabernacle so as not to defile the Lord's presence (see, e.g., Lev 15:31, just before the Day of Atonement regulations in Lev 16).

In Leviticus 16:21-22, the priest pressed both his hands on the head of the scapegoat and confessed all the sins of the people over it, placing them on the goat. This is how they showed the transfer of sin to the goat. However, in this case, they did not offer this goat on the altar but instead sent it as far as possible away from the altar, the tabernacle, and the community. Moreover, they also pressed the hand on the head of peace offerings, from which they would eat the meat as a celebratory banquet (Lev 3:2). Would God want them ingesting meat that was loaded with their sin? No.

The handling of the blood of sacrificial animals was a key element of the sacrificial system. The one who brought the burnt offering would slaughter the animal, and the priest(s) would take all the blood drained from the animal and splash it around on all sides of the altar (Lev 1:5). The peace and the guilt offering blood rituals were the same as the burnt offering (e.g., Lev 3:2; 7:2), but the meat of the peace of-fering animal supplied a banquet for the one who offered it and his family (Lev 7:11-18; 19:5-8). They burned the fat of a peace offering on the altar as a pleasant aroma to the Lord (like the whole carcass of the burnt offering, Lev 1:9), and they splashed the blood all around on the sides of the altar (Lev 3:2, 8, 13). The chapter ends, "This is a lasting ordinance for the generations to come, wherever you live: You must not eat any fat or any blood" (Lev 3:17). This regulation does not appear in the burnt or guilt offering regulations because the common people did not eat anything from them anyway.

The prohibition against eating blood has its origin in the Noahic prohibition in Genesis 9:4, "you must not eat meat that has its lifeblood still in it." Life always belongs to God. The blood represents the life of the animal, so the blood always goes back to God. One must not make it part of the peace offering meal. Leviticus 17:10-11 explains and force-fully emphasizes this concern: "I will set my face against any Israelite or any foreigner residing among them who eats blood, and I will cut them off from the people. For the life of a creature is in the blood, and I have given it to you to make atonement for yourselves on the altar; it is the blood that makes atonement for one's life." A better rendering of the last clause would be, "for the blood, it makes atonement by the soul life [it contains or represents]."[4] The word for life is the Hebrew word *nepeš*, which is a notoriously difficult word to translate. We often gloss it as "soul." All animate creatures are "souls" (see, e.g., "soul of life" in all birds, fish, land animals, and humans in Gen 1:20, 24; 2:7).

In sum, the handling of the blood in the burnt, peace, and guilt offerings made the blood part of the offering on the altar—all of it was splashed around on the sides of the altar. For the burnt offering, the offering on the altar included the whole carcass of the animal (less the hide), including all its blood. For the peace and guilt offerings, it included all the fat and all the blood of the animal. The meat of the peace offering supplied a banquet for the one who offered it and his family, as they celebrated good relations with the Lord together.

Sin Offerings

As for the meat of the guilt offering and the sin offering, "Any male in a priest's family may eat it, but it must be eaten in the sanctuary area; it is most holy" (Lev 6:29; 7:6). The priests would eat the meat of these offerings because they offered them as mediators to make atonement for the one(s) who brought the particular offering. The meat was the prebend for the priests, but they had to eat it in the sanctuary because it was "most holy"; that is, set apart for holy sacred purposes only. If the priest, however, had brought the sin offering into the holy place for his own atonement from sin, they must burn the carcass outside the camp on the ash heap (Lev 6:30; cf. Lev 4:11-12 and the discussion below). The priests could not gain the benefit of prebends from offerings they made for their own atonement from sins they themselves had committed.

The handling of the blood of the sin offering, however, was completely different from the other offerings. The priests did not splash it

---

[4]For detailed discussion of this key passage, see Averbeck, "*kpr*," *NIDOTTE* 2:693-95, 697-98.

all around on the sides of the burnt offering altar. Instead, if the anointed high priest sinned, he needed to bring a sin offering and present it to Lord for himself by pressing his hand on it, and then slaughter it (Lev 4:3-4). Then he took some of the blood, dipped his finger into it and sprinkled it (not "splashed"; a different verb) seven times inside the tent of meeting on the ground in front of the curtain that separated the holy place from the most holy place. He then rubbed some of the blood on the horns of the incense altar that stood in front of the curtain. He poured the rest of the blood out at the base of the burnt offering altar near the entrance to the tabernacle complex (Lev 4:5-7). Here some of the blood serves as a cleansing agent to purify the tabernacle. The rest of blood was simply disposed of by pouring it out on the ground at the base of the burnt offering altar. It did not become part of the offering on the altar.

The next step was to take all the fat of the animal and burn it on the burnt offering altar, like the fat of the peace offering (Lev 4:8-10). Later in the chapter, in the regulations for the sin offering of the common Israelite, the text tells us that this burning of the fat produced "an aroma pleasing to the LORD" (Lev 4:31; as in the peace offering in Lev 3:5). This is not stated explicitly anywhere else in the chapter, but it seems to apply in all instances of burning the fat. Essentially, this part of the sin offering functioned as a burnt offering following the sin offering blood manipulation. This finds support in the Leviticus 5:7-10 regulation for the less expensive sin offering of two birds as a concession to the poor. The first bird serves as a sin offering, but the second is a burnt offering (Lev 5:10). As noted above, the burnt offering made atonement as a gift of "an aroma pleasing to the LORD" (Lev 1:9).

The point is that the sin offering combined the two different meanings of *kipper* in its ritual. The blood manipulation procedure purified the tabernacle. The burning of the fat was a pleasing aroma that served as a gift to the Lord to gain his grace toward the sinner. The combination of the two made the one who brought the offering right with God once again. When they offered the sin offering in combination with the burnt and peace offerings, the order was first the sin offering, then the burnt offering, and finally the peace offering (see, e.g., the ritual for the fulfillment of a Nazirite vow in Num 6:16-17). The sin offering and burnt offering made the atonement. The worshipers ate the meat of the peace offering in a banquet as a celebration of the good relations with the Lord they had attained through the other combined offerings.

The ritual for the sin offering of the whole congregation (Lev 4:13-21) is the same as that for the high priest (Lev 4:2-12), but there are some important differences in the sin offering for tribal and clan leaders (Lev 4:22-26) and for the common Israelites (Lev 4:27-36). In these cases, the mediating priest rubbed some of the blood on the horns of the altar of burnt offering out near the doorway to the tabernacle complex, not the horns of the incense altar inside the tent itself (Lev 4:25, 30, 34). This is only a small detail in the written text but was visibly very distinct in the actual performance of the ritual. It would have stood out to the priest doing it and anyone looking on.

The reason for this difference arises from the rationale of the sin offering, which included the purging of impurities from the tabernacle that had accrued to it from the original sinful act (see, e.g., 4:2, 13, 22, 27).[5] This is why the priest applied the blood as a cleansing or purifying agent in the sin offering ritual. The anointed priest could enter into the holy place in the tabernacle tent, so when he sinned, the impurity from it penetrated that far too. A nonpriestly leader or a common Israelite could only enter into the gate of the tabernacle complex, not beyond the burnt offering altar, so the impurity of their sin would only penetrate as far as the burnt offering altar. Thus, the priest applied the blood of the sin offering only as far as the impurity of the sinner and their sin had penetrated into the tabernacle complex.

---

[5]For a detailed study of the rationale of the sin offering, see Richard E. Averbeck, "Crucial Features of Sin Offering Atonement in Leviticus 4–5 and 16," (forthcoming) and the discussion that follows here.

Hebrews 9–10 applies this background in Leviticus to how we should understand the sacrifice of Christ in comparison to the Old Testament sacrifices. There are four main steps in the comparison. First, the Old Testament high priest applied the blood of the animal sacrifices to the tabernacle (and later the temple) on earth (Heb 9:6-10), but Jesus Christ the high priest (cf. Hebrews 7–8) applied his own sacrificial blood to the tabernacle in heaven, in the throne room of God (Heb 9:11-12; cf. Heb 4:14-16). Second, the Old Testament sacrificial blood of the animals cleansed outwardly (lit. "cleansed the flesh"; Heb 9:13), but the blood of Jesus cleanses the conscience of the believer (Heb 9:14). Both cleanse; the difference is in *what* they cleanse—the flesh or the conscience.

Third, the blood of the animal sacrifices in the Old Testament cleansed the physical tabernacle on earth (Heb 9:21), whereas the blood of Jesus cleansed the heavenly tabernacle, the very presence of God (Heb 9:23-24). This corresponds to the application of the blood to the tabernacle and its altar in the sin offering, as discussed above. Fourth and finally, the Old Testament high priest had to perform the Day of Atonement sacrifices every year (Heb 9:25; 10:1-4; cf. Heb 10:11), but our high priest Jesus offered his blood once for all, with no need to offer it again (Heb 9:25-28; 10:5-10, 12-13). The Old Testament sacrifices could not permanently "take away" the problem of sin and corruption. The Old Testament priests had to keep on doing sacrifice for more sins later. In Christ, our conscience is cleansed permanently and forever. He does not have to keep on doing his work over and over. It is finished (Jn 19:30)!

There is one final point that bears special attention here. It gets to the heart of the ministry of the high priest in Israel. One particular feature of the first unit of sin offering regulations stands out from the other units in this chapter. All the other units say something to the effect that the priest shall make atonement through the sin offering procedure and the offender(s) will be forgiven (see Lev 4:20, 26, 31, 35; 5:6, 10, 13, though forgiveness is not explicitly mentioned in

Lev 5:6). Its absence is conspicuous in the case of the high priest. The sin offering unit for the anointed priest in Leviticus 4:2-12 includes no such conclusion.

Some commentators ignore or do not attend directly to this issue.[6] Other scholars give varying explanations for the exclusion.[7] A careful look at this matter suggests that it is actually crucial for understanding the ritual and conceptual mechanism of sin offering atonement. One of the most important functions of the priest(s) was to "bear the culpability" (Hebrew *'āwōn*) for the peoples' sin by "making atonement" (*kipper*) for them before the Lord (see, e.g., Ex 28:38; Lev 10:17; Num 18:1).[8] The rendering "culpability" seeks to capture the overall variations in the meaning of the term, which can include the violation itself, the objective guilt of having committed the violation, and the punishment for it as well as the overall responsibility for it. When a person committed a sin, their culpability for doing so became a load or burden they bore. By making atonement for the person, the priest took the burden of that culpability off the person and took it on himself. The high priest bore all of these burdens on himself until the Day of Atonement.

Within the sin offering unit, Leviticus 5:1 brings this into consideration: "If a person sins when he hears a call of cursing [to testify] and he himself is a witness or saw or knew [about the matter], if he does not make it known, he shall *bear his own culpability*" (my translation). In other words, a person who sinned in this way remained culpable

---

[6]See, e.g., Sklar, *Leviticus*, 112; Baruch A. Levine, *Leviticus*, JPS Torah Commentary (Philadelphia: Jewish Publication Society, 1989), 22; John Hartley, *Leviticus*, WBC (Dallas: Word, 1992), 61.

[7]See, e.g., Martin Noth, *Leviticus: A Commentary* (Philadelphia: Westminster, 1965), 41; Roy Gane, *Leviticus, Numbers*, NIVAC (Grand Rapids, MI: Zondervan, 2004), 102; and Jacob Milgrom, *Leviticus 1–16*, AB 3 (New York: Doubleday, 1991), 241.

[8]For helpful remarks on the expression "bearing culpability," see the brief summary in K. Koch, " 'āwōn" in *TDOT* 10:559-61 and *HALOT* 800. See also Gane, *Leviticus, Numbers*, 280-83; and esp. the more complete study by Baruch J. Schwartz, "The Bearing of Sin in the Priestly Literature," in *Pomegranates and Golden Bells: Studies in Biblical, Jewish, and Near Eastern Ritual, Law, and Literature in Honor of Jacob Milgrom*, ed. David P. Wright, David Noel Freedman, and Avi Hurvitz (Winona Lake, IN: Eisenbrauns, 1995), 3-21.

for what he had done.[9] The only way to change this was to confess his sin and offer a sin offering so the priest could make atonement for him and therefore bear his culpability for him as his mediator before the Lord (Lev 5:5-6).

Ezekiel 4:4 helps in an illustrative way. The Lord charged the prophet Ezekiel, who was also a priest, to perform a symbolic prophetic act: "As for you, lie on your left side and put the *culpability* of the house of Israel upon it. The number of days you lie on your side, you shall *bear* their *culpability*" (my translation; see also Ezek 4:5-6). In the context, the culpability referred to is the sins of the people that resulted in the final stage of the Babylonian captivity of Judah.

Returning to Leviticus 4:3-12, if the priest himself committed the sin, he was not acting as a mediator. He bore the weight of his own culpability, so there was no mediation. This is why there is no statement of atonement and forgiveness in Leviticus 4:10-12. Every year on the Day of Atonement the high priest unloaded all the culpabilities of Israel for the year onto the scapegoat: "Aaron shall lay both hands on the head of the live goat and confess over it all the *culpabilities* and rebellion of the Israelites—all their sins—and put them on the goat's head. He shall send the goat away into the wilderness in the care of someone appointed for the task. The goat will carry on itself all their *culpabilities* to a remote place; and the man shall release it in the wilderness" (Lev 16:21-22, my translation).

The high priest could do this because he had been bearing all the culpabilities for sin on himself the whole year until this day. He was the mediator for them all as the one who wore the gold plate on his forehead (Ex 28:36-38). The scapegoat, therefore, bore them away from the community into the far reaches of the wilderness, never to return again (Lev 16:21-22).

The implications of this understanding of bearing culpabilities by the high priest are wide ranging. Among other things, for example, it

---

[9]See the helpful discussion of this verse in Bruce Wells, *The Law of Testimony in the Pentateuchal Codes*, BZABR 4 (Wiesbaden: Harrassowitz, 2004), 56-82.

may explain why the unintentional manslayer had to stay in the city of refuge until the high priest died (Num 35:25; Josh 20:6). The culpability for this accidental homicide remained until the high priest himself died so that the culpability died with him.[10] No other ransom for the accidental murder would be adequate, because even accidental murder polluted the land (Num 35:31-34).

GUILT OFFERINGS

The primary unit of guilt offering regulations in Leviticus 5:14-16 refers to the one who "commits sacrilege by sinning unintentionally with regard to *any of the holy things of the LORD*," as opposed to Leviticus 6:2 where a person "sins and commits sacrilege against the LORD, and commits fraud against his fellow [Israelite]" (my translation). Much of the terminology is the same, but the first text is about unintentionally violating what is referred to as the Lord's holy things, and the other is about intentionally violating the property of a fellow Israelite. The Lord's holy things are those devoted to him for use in the sanctuary, whether it be an offering or a utensil or a vessel, or whatever it may be that is designated for use in the tabernacle worship. To use it in a common way would be to violate it as sancta. It would be to commit an act of desecration or "sacrilege." For example, the meat of a sin offering for a common person was to be eaten by the priests (Lev 6:24-29; 7:7). If a commoner ate it, he would desecrate it—he would be violating (i.e., trespassing on) sancta (cf. Lev 22:10-16).[11]

Leviticus 6:3, 5 makes it clear that the offender supported his intentional and deceitful trespass violation of the fellow's property with a false oath that denied the charge.[12] He would have taken the false oath in the name of the Lord in violation of, for example, Leviticus 19:12, "You must not swear in my name falsely and (so) profane the name of

---

[10]See this suggestion by William H. C. Propp, *Exodus 19–40*, AB 2A (New York: Doubleday, 2006), 449-50.

[11]See a more complete review in Richard E. Averbeck, "*ʾāšām*, nom. guilt offering," in *NIDOTTE* 1:557-61.

[12]See the discussion in Wells, *The Law of Testimony*, 138-41.

your God. I am the Lord." Swearing falsely in the name of the Lord is
to "profane the name"—it is to commit sacrilege. According to one
interpretation, if it were not for the swearing of the false oath, there
would have been no guilt offering required.[13]

In my view, yes, to swear falsely using the Lord's name is indeed
to violate the sanctity of his holy name, but it is another matter altogether to *limit* the violation of sancta here to the misuse of the Lord's
name.[14] Other sancta is violated here too—namely, the fellow
Israelite, who is a member of the kingdom of priests, the holy nation.
He or she is also part of the Lord's sancta. According to Leviticus 6:7,
the concluding clause of this regulation, the atonement and forgiveness made through the guilt offering was "for anything he does
by which he incurs guilt," referring primarily to the list of violations
in Leviticus 6:2-3.

The applications of the guilt offering are extensive. Any desecration
of the Lord's holy things and fraud against his holy people called for
it too, since they were part of the Lord's sancta. It functions on a wide
spectrum. For example, if a man sleeps with a slave woman who is
promised to become the wife of another man, he has violated what
belongs to the other man. He must bring a guilt offering to obtain
atonement so that he can be forgiven by the Lord (Lev 19:20-23).
Another example is Isaiah 53:10, where the suffering servant is designated a guilt offering because he would deliver the holy people from
their captivity. To take the holy people into captivity was to desecrate
the Lord's sancta. This called for a guilt offering.[15]

---

[13]Proposed by Milgrom, *Leviticus 1-16*, 365-73, followed by Levine, *Leviticus*, 32. See also Sklar,
Leviticus, 123-25; Gane, *Leviticus, Numbers*, 134-35; and James W. Watts, *Leviticus 1-10*, HCOT
(Leuven: Peeters, 2013), 372-73; Rolf Rendtorff, *Leviticus*, BKAT 3/3 (Neukirchen-Vluyn:
Neukirchener Verlag, 1992), 207-8.

[14]Averbeck "*ʾāšām*," 560-61. See also, e.g., Erhard Blum, "Issues and Problems in the Contemporary
Debate Regarding the Priestly Writings," in *The Strata of the Priestly Writings: Contemporary
Debate and Future Directions*, ed. Sarah Shectman and Joel S. Baden (Zürich: Theologischer
Verlag Zürich, 2009), 35n18. He refers there to the work of Baruch Schwartz, "The Holiness
Legislation," in *Studies in the Priestly Code* (Hebrew) (Jerusalem, 1999).

[15]See the full discussion in Richard E. Averbeck, "Christian Interpretations of Isaiah 53," in *The
Gospel According to Isaiah: Exploring a Deeper Understanding of Isaiah Chapter 53*, ed. Darrell

HOLINESS AND PURITY

Leviticus 1–7 gives the primary regulations for the five main kinds of offerings treated above. Leviticus 8 narrates the consecration of the tabernacle and the priests, and Leviticus 9–10 recounts the first day of the inauguration of their priestly ministry in the tabernacle. Leviticus 11–15 follows with detailed regulations for holiness and purity.[16] These holiness and purity regulations became a key point of contention between Jesus and the Jewish leaders in the Gospels.

The death on the inauguration day of Aaron's two oldest sons, Nadab and Abihu, was of course an overwhelming catastrophe for Aaron (Lev 10:1-2). They had violated some regulation having to do with presentation of fire (and incense) before the Lord, so the Lord consumed them with fire. They violated the holiness of the Lord (Lev 10:3). In the follow through from this incident, the Lord declared: "*Distinguish* between *the holy and the common*, between *the unclean and the clean*" (Lev 10:10). The two polarities, holy versus common and unclean versus clean, are core issues in the theology of Leviticus. The holy Lord was present, dwelling with them in his tabernacle tent amid all their tents. On the one hand, living according to the distinction between holy versus common (Lev 10:10), highlights the importance of the status of a person, place, time, or thing. Some translations render this holy versus "profane," but this term can have a negative connotation in English, so it is better to translate it as "common." There was nothing wrong with a person or thing being common or profane in ancient Israel. It was just a matter of its relative status as compared to holy.

For instance, one must distinguish between holy priests and common people within Israel (e.g., Lev 8:30), but this does not change the fact that all Israel was a holy people in contrast to the other

---

Bock and Mitch Glaser (Grand Rapids, MI: Kregel, 2012), 33-60.

[16]This discussion draws from the more detailed analysis in Richard E. Averbeck, "Clean and Unclean," in *NIDOTTE* 4:477-486, and my notes on Leviticus in Carson, *NIV Biblical Theology Study Bible*, 209-18.

non-Israelite peoples who lived round about them. Moreover, a common Israelite could also consecrate various kinds of "common" property (animals, fields, etc.) to the Lord as "holy" (see, e.g., Lev 27:9, 14, 16, 23, 28, 30, 32, 33). They must also distinguish between holy and common places (e.g., holy tabernacle versus common camp; Lev 8:10), holy and common things (e.g., holy firstborn animals versus common non-firstborn animals; Ex 13:2), and holy and common times (e.g., holy festival times versus common days and weeks; Lev 23).

On the other hand, making the distinction between the unclean (impure) versus the clean (pure) was a matter of the condition of the person, place, or thing, no matter what their status (holy or common) might have been. Like a "common" Israelite, a "holy" priest could become unclean, for instance, through sexual intercourse (Lev 15:16-18). He would not be able to go into the tabernacle to function as a priest on the day(s) of his uncleanness, lest he defile the tabernacle (see Lev 15:31). He would first need to cleanse himself (i.e., make himself clean, pure; see, e.g., Lev 22:1-9). This did not affect his status, however. He would not need to reconsecrate himself as holy again. They needed to keep holiness and uncleanness apart, but uncleanness was not the opposite of holiness. According to Leviticus 10:10, "holy" is opposite "common," and "unclean" is opposite "clean."

For this pair of distinctions, and the terminology associated with them, see figure 4.[17] If someone or something holy ("sacred") is "desecrated" ("profaned"), he, she, or it becomes common ("profane"). If the same someone or something is common and is "consecrated" ("sanctified"), they become holy. If someone or something clean ("pure") is "defiled," he, she, or it becomes "unclean" ("impure"). If the unclean someone or something is made clean, they are "purified" ("cleansed"). These are the basic categories of status and condition, according to which the tabernacle system functioned. Again, it all had to do with the fact that God was actually present in their midst.

---

[17]For a more detailed chart and explanation, see Carson, *NIV Biblical Theology Study Bible*, 173.

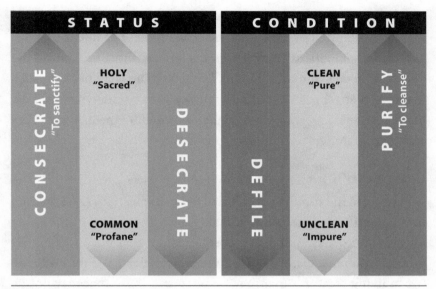

Figure 4. Status and condition terminology

As for holiness (i.e., holy versus common in Lev 10:10), since God is most holy, the core of holiness in Israel was the tabernacle in which he dwelt in the center of the camp, and the priests who officiated there (see esp. Lev 8:10-15, 30; 10:3, 12-13, 17-18; 16:19, 24). In regard to purity, people could not avoid becoming unclean during the regular course of life. However, they must avoid coming into contact with people, places, or things that were holy while they were unclean, especially the tabernacle presence of God: "You must keep the Israelites separate from things that make them unclean, so they will not die in their uncleanness for defiling my dwelling place, which is among them" (Lev 15:31). Moreover, they must do the procedures necessary to become clean in a timely manner. During the time when they were unclean, other people must avoid physical contact with them lest they too contract their uncleanness by contagion (see, e.g., Lev 15:19).

The holiness and purity regulations are very detailed, but there are summary statements strewn throughout the section (Lev 11:46-47;

13:45-46, 59; 14:54-57; 15:31-33; 16:29-34). These brief passages summarize virtually all of the textual material in these chapters. The one exception is Leviticus 12, which is a relatively short section on the purification of a woman after childbirth, so there is no need for such a summary statement. It seems that these summary statements served to help the ancients grasp the essential substance of the material. They also help us understand these regulations today.

CLEAN AND UNCLEAN ANIMALS

According to the summary statement in Leviticus 11:46-47, "These are the regulations concerning animals, birds, every living thing that moves about in the water and every creature that moves along the ground. You must distinguish between the unclean and the clean, between living creatures that may be eaten and those that may not be eaten." The details are too many and diverse to handle here, but everyone recognizes that the categories of animals and terminology in Leviticus 11 are, in most essentials, the same as those in Genesis 1. There are four main categories in Leviticus 11:46: animals, birds, swarming water creatures, and creeping land creatures. As Leviticus 11:47 puts it, the primary issue is distinguishing between edible and inedible "living creatures" (a term that applies to all the animate beings). The term *animals* in Leviticus 11:46 is the same as that in Leviticus 11:2-8. In Genesis 1:24-25 it is normally translated "cattle" or "livestock." Here it refers to four-footed land creatures.

The edibility of "birds" (including "flying insects") and water creatures comes next (Lev 11:9-23). According to Genesis 1, God created the birds and fish on the fifth day, but he created the land animals and humanity on the sixth day. The birds and especially the fish do not share exactly the same natural domain as the land animals and humans. This distinction comes through in a particular way in Leviticus 11. The inedible land animals are "unclean" while inedible fish and birds are termed "detestable," as are the creeping land creatures, all of which are inedible and detestable (Lev 11:41-43).

Unfortunately, the NIV does not make this distinction, but the NRSV, ESV, NLT, and others do.

God wanted his chosen people to live within the world in a way that corresponds to how he originally designed it. Some of the recent work done on these animal laws has come from the anthropological discipline. Anthropologists are fond of saying that people shape their own world by the way they select and deselect things in their world. I grew up on a farm in Wisconsin. As such, there are certain kinds of food that I have "selected," but there are others I have "deselected"— squid, for example.

From a biblical-theological point of view, God was shaping their world *for* them. From the beginning his basic design was for people and animals to live off the vegetation, not off one another (see Gen 1:29-30). In my view, this does not mean that God did not create any carnivorous animals in Genesis 1. Psalm 104 is a creation psalm. It tells us that God's good creation included graciously providing prey for the wild beasts, even the lions (Ps 104:19-22). The point in Genesis 1:29-30 is that humanity and the animal world depended on the plants growing on the ground as their natural and nurturing environment. Without this, there would be no place and no prey for the beasts to hunt.

These regulations are not about what is healthy to eat. There are poisonous plants too, but there is no such thing as an "unclean" plant. The struggle that came into the realm of humanity and all animate life due to the fall into sin in Genesis 3 created a chaotic corruption, the extremes of which the ancient Israelites were to avoid even in their diet. According to Genesis 6:5-7, 11-12, the Lord brought the flood on the earth due to the level of violence that had engulfed the earth in the wake of the fall. Human depravity led to the groaning of all creation (Rom 8:18-25). He designed us to be those who would maintain his good will on the earth (Gen 1:26-28), but our rebellion turned it all into one big catastrophe. The flood wiped it clean, but afterward it remained true that "every inclination of the human heart is evil from childhood." Nevertheless, God determined then and there that "never again will I destroy all living creatures, as I have done" (Gen 8:21).

After the flood the Lord instituted the regulations in Genesis 9:1-7 along with the Noahic covenant (Gen 9:8-17). He designed both of these as means of stabilizing the creation in spite of the continuing effects of the fallen and corrupt condition of humanity that caused the groaning of the whole creation. God made the Noahic creation covenant that included the animals, the first of its kind (Gen 9:9-10). The regulations at the beginning of the chapter include a special emphasis on the sanctity of life and, accordingly, the prohibition against eating the blood of animals (Gen 9:4-5). The blood represented the life of animals. Life belongs to no one but God because he is the one who created it. People must not eat the blood.

This is the underlying core rationale of the clean and unclean animal regulations in Leviticus 11. *We must not eat the blood of animals, so we must not eat animals that eat blood either.* Land animals that chew the cud are by nature vegetarian. The divided hoof is also a natural feature of pastoral animals because it is more suitable for walking on grassy turf (Lev 11:2). Cattle, for example, chew the cud for the mastication and digestion of fodder like grass and grain. Their four stomachs regurgitate the fodder they have swallowed so that they can chew it up stage by stage. This makes such animals vegetarian because they cannot eat and digest meat. There are some animals—for example, the pig—that divide the hoof to walk on turf but do not chew the cud (Lev 11:7). This makes them unclean.

The camel, hyrax, and rabbit are unclean for the opposite reason (Lev 11:4-7)—they chew the cud but do not divide the hoof; in fact, rabbits and hyraxes do not even have hooves. It is true that the latter three are also herbivores, not carnivores, but the chapter bases its rationale on the observable taxonomy of the bodies of animals. Both factors were important for determining whether a four-footed land animal was clean or unclean because no animal that both divides the hoof and chews the cud eats other animals. The regulations eliminate scavenger birds based on the same rationale. They eat meat with the blood in it (Lev 11:13-19).

Our understanding of the underlying rationale of the clean and unclean animal laws must begin here. It does not explain every detail of the regulations, and we cannot touch on every point here, but it gives us the right start. The first occurrence of the holiness motto in the Hebrew Bible and in Leviticus connects directly to keeping the clean and unclean animal food regulations: "I am the LORD your God; consecrate yourselves and be holy, because I am holy. Do not make yourselves unclean by any creature that moves along the ground. I am the LORD, who brought you up out of Egypt to be your God; therefore be holy, because I am holy" (Lev 11:44-45). Leviticus 11, therefore, binds Israel to holiness amid the corruption of creation itself. It draws on the Lord's original design of creation to shape the world of ancient Israel.

In terms of the animal world, the Israelites were to be pastoralists, raising plant-eating animals for food and other kinds of provisions (e.g., wool, milk, leather). This would naturally put them in opposition to predatory animals. They would need to "subdue" them: "Be fruitful and increase in number; fill the earth and *subdue* it" (Gen 1:28). As a shepherd boy, David fought and killed the lion and the bear when they attacked the flock—he subdued them (1 Sam 17:34-37). For those who live close to nature, this distinction is a major issue. In fact, even we can become prey. It is a matter of survival in more than one way.

Later, in Leviticus 20:25-26, these food regulations from Leviticus 11 are connected to holiness amid the corruption of the foreign peoples roundabout ancient Israel. This was another very important effect of these regulations and was one of the main reasons they are so important in the New Testament. These verses come as the conclusion to the regulations against Molech worship, mediums and spiritists, and prohibited sexual relationships rampant among the surrounding peoples. With these in mind, the Lord said,

You must not live according to the customs of the nations I am going to drive out before you. Because they did all these things, I abhorred them. . . . You must therefore *make a distinction between clean and unclean animals* and between unclean and clean birds. Do not defile yourselves by any animal or bird or anything that moves along the ground—*those that I have set apart as unclean for you.* You are to *be holy to me because I, the* LORD, *am holy*, and I have set you apart from the nations to be my own. (Lev 20:23, 25-26)

The Lord arranged their world, including what they could eat, so that they would stay separate from the corrupting influences of the non-Israelite people around them. Having different dietary regulations would hinder any kind of social or religious associations with them. It is amazing how many relationships happened around food in ancient Israel. This is true in our world today too (marriages, funerals, etc.). If they could not eat with other people, they could not carry on relationships with them to any significant degree. This would keep the Israelites separate from their corrupting influences.

HUMAN BODY UNCLEANNESS

The purity regulations apply this same principle of logic to the condition of the human body more directly. Our bodies show the effects of the fall into corruption too. The ultimate end of this is death: "for dust you are and to dust you will return" (Gen 3:19). The dead human corpse, therefore, was the most defiling object in ancient Israel (see Num 19). Anyone who touched it was unclean for seven days and must purify their body with the water mixed with the ashes of a red heifer. If he or she did not do this, they contaminate the tabernacle of the Lord's presence with uncleanness.

In such a case, the person would be "cut off" from his people (Num 19:11-13), which probably means that he and his offspring were under the hand of God's judgment in this life and the next. The technical term for this is *extirpation*. It may have also included execution by stoning (see, e.g., Lev 20:2-3).[18] Alternatively, some suggest that it involves exclusion from participation in family gatherings and community assemblies. In any case, this was a very serious matter. The preparation of this purification water made it a "sin [or 'purification'] offering" (Num 19:9). In our age, sin is normally associated with a moral violation of some kind, such as the sin offering regulations in Leviticus 4:1–5:13. The priest made atonement for the violator(s) so that they would be "forgiven" (e.g., Lev 4:20, 26, 31).

The purity regulations in Leviticus 12–15, however, have to do with flows from the genitals (Leviticus 12; 15) and diseases that manifested on the skin (Leviticus 13–14). The latter became an issue in the New Testament when Jesus healed the skin-diseased person (Mt 8:1-4; Mk 1:40-45; Lk 5:12-16). We cannot go into all the details here. The important point for our discussion is that priests were in charge of both the diagnosis and treatment of the unclean person (Lev 13) and the examination and purification procedures after he became healthy again (Lev 14). Thus, Jesus ordered the person that he had healed to show himself to the priest and go through the ritual cleansing procedures under his supervision. We will return to this issue in the discussion of Jesus and the law in the next chapter.

Leviticus 12 focuses on the impurity of a woman's flow of blood during and after childbirth. In this case, the priest made atonement for the woman so that she would become "clean," not so that she would be "forgiven" (Lev 12:7-8 and all the way through Leviticus 15; contrast Lev 4:1–5:13). There was no violation of the Mosaic law in becoming unclean, but such flows from the body are part of our natural condition and connected to death. If the body loses all its blood, the person dies. This was a very real possibility when a woman bore a child. It was inherently dangerous and still is today.

---

[18]Jacob Milgrom, *Numbers*, JPS Torah Commentary (Philadelphia: Jewish Publication Society, 1990), 405-8, 457-60; and the more complete discussion in Donald J. Wold, "The Meaning of the Biblical Penalty Kareth" (PhD diss., University of California, Berkeley, 1978).

No woman sinned by bearing a child. Even in the New Testament before the initiation of the new covenant and the pouring out of the Spirit on the Day of Pentecost, Mary brought a "sin offering" for bearing Jesus because of the laws regarding the blood flow after bearing a child (Lk 2:24; cf. Lev 12). Mary certainly did not sin morally by giving birth to Jesus. There was no violation in becoming unclean unless the person did not follow the regulations for their purification. For example, Leviticus 5:2-3 refers to a person who was not aware that they had become unclean. When and if they discovered it (some days later perhaps), it would have been too late to follow the standard regulations. He or she would need to confess their sin and bring a sin offering to make atonement for their sinful oversight (Lev 5:5-6).

The regular regulations for purification depended on the kind of uncleanness contracted. If a person contracted their uncleanness by contact with someone or something else that was unclean, they must wash their clothes, bathe in water, and remain unclean until the evening (see, e.g., Lev 15:4-11). After that, the person was clean again. Sexual relations made a person unclean for the day because it involved emissions from the genitalia (Lev 15:16-18). If a man had an unclean genital discharge in his own body for a period of time, when it stopped he remained unclean for seven days, after which he washed his clothes, bathed in water, and brought two birds for a sin offering and a burnt offering. After all this, he was clean from his diseased discharge (Lev 15:13-15; cf. for the woman in Lev 15:25-30). For her menstrual period, a woman was unclean for seven days. The text is not clear on this, but it seems that she would wash her clothes, bathe her body, and remain unclean until the evening of the seventh day, after which she was clean.

This brings us back to Leviticus 12.[19] Why is uncleanness twice as long for giving birth to a female baby (initially 14 days) as compared to a male baby (initially 7 days)? Some scholars have proposed, for

---

[19]For a more thorough discussion of Leviticus 12, see Richard E. Averbeck, "*ṭmʾ*, be unclean," *NIDOTTE* 2:368-70.

example, that it reflects the relative status of the sexes in ancient Israel. In my view, the answer lies in the fact that the blood flow associated with childbirth was much more severe and dangerous than that of the menstrual period. As noted, the impurity period from the blood flow for menstruation was seven days. One would expect the blood flow impurity for bearing a baby would last longer than the seven days— more like the fourteen days for the female baby. This would make sense. The reason for shortening this time to seven days for the male baby was because the mother needed to be past the required initial time before the baby boy was circumcised on the eighth day (cf. Gen 17:12), which is specifically mentioned in the passage (Lev 12:3).

These bodily impurity regulations frequently mention the need to avoid defiling the tabernacle. The conclusion to the regulations in Leviticus 15 summarizes the concern this way: "You must keep the Israelites separate from things that make them unclean, so they will not die in their uncleanness for defiling my dwelling place, which is among them" (Lev 15:31). It is inherently dangerous to have a defiled people dwelling in close proximity to a holy God. Human uncleanness made this a precarious proposition, but the Lord remained committed to dwelling in the presence of his people and walking with them.

Jesus our high priest fulfilled the sacrificial requirements to maintain the ongoing presence of God with us in the new covenant. In the Old Testament, these purity regulations kept this issue constantly before the people. The ritual procedures on the annual Day of Atonement purged the tabernacle from all such impurities once a year. It was the fall cleaning day for the tabernacle. This is why the Day of Atonement regulations in Leviticus 16 follow immediately after the impurity regulations in Leviticus 12–15.

THE DAY OF ATONEMENT

The high priest made five offerings on the Day of Atonement. First, he offered the slain sin offering for the priests (Lev 16:11-14) and for the

people (Lev 16:15-19). Second, he performed the scapegoat sin offering ritual for the whole congregation (Lev 16:20-22; see Lev 16:5,
9-10 for the scapegoat as a sin offering that made atonement even though
the priest did not slay it). Third and finally, the high priest offered the
burnt offering for the priests and then for the people (Lev 16:24).

The purpose of the slain sin offerings for the priests and the people
was to purge the tabernacle from the impurities that had accrued to
it during the previous year. Of course, this was the purpose of the sin
offering blood manipulation procedures when they offered sin offerings through the year as well, as noted above. On the Day of
Atonement, however, the blood ritual penetrated even into the most
holy place and the ark of the covenant, something that occurred only
on this day. The purification from impurities started in the most holy
place and worked its way step by step all the way out to the burnt offering altar, progressively purging the entire tabernacle from the
inside out. The Day of Atonement sin offerings were not redundant
because during the year the goal was to maintain the purity of the
sanctuary, while the Day of Atonement included a whole new purification and consecration of the sanctuary for the upcoming year. It did
not just look back but also forward. This is not the place to go into all
the details, but the purification and consecration of the altar in
Leviticus 16:18-19 corresponds to the same in Leviticus 8:15 at the time
of the original erection and initiation of the tabernacle.

After recounting the manipulation of the blood in the most holy
place (Lev 16:11-15), the text says: "So he shall make atonement upon
the holy place from the *impurities* [Hebrew *ṭumʾâ*] of the Israelites and
from their *transgressions* with regard to all their *sins*, and thus he shall
do (also) for the tent of meeting which dwells with them in the midst
of their *impurities*" (Lev 16:16, my translation). In applying this to the
altar of burnt offering, Leviticus 16:18-19 says, "And he shall go out to
the altar which is before the Lord and make atonement upon it, and
take some of the blood of the bull (for the priests) and blood of the
goat (for the people) and rub it all around on the horns of the altar.

Then he shall sprinkle upon it some of the blood with his finger seven times and so purify and consecrate it from the *impurities* of the Israelites" (my translation).

Finally, Leviticus 16:20 summarizes the outcome of all this and makes the transition to the scapegoat offering that follows: "When he [the priest] finishes purging the [most] holy place and the tent of meeting and the altar, he shall present the live goat" (my translation). In this verse the holy place, tent of meeting, and the altar are all direct objects of the verb *kipper* "to make atonement, purge," as is also the case in the summary at the end of the chapter (Lev 16:33). The blood manipulation atoned (i.e., purged) the whole tabernacle directly so it was now purified and (re)consecrated once again for the next year (Lev 16:19; cf. Lev 8:15). Transgressions and sins are mentioned only once in the unit (Lev 16:16) in subordinate relation to impurities. This is apparent from the fact that *impurities* is the operative term elsewhere in the passage, without sins and transgressions added (twice in Lev 16:16 and again in Lev 16:19). The transgressions and sins caused impurities that had accrued to the tabernacle through the year, from which these offerings purged it.

The scapegoat ritual that follows in Leviticus 16:21 substitutes "culpabilities" (Hebrew *ʿāvōn*) for "impurities" (Hebrew *ṭumʾâ*), and once again transgressions and sins are in subordinate relation to the primary term, which is *culpabilities* in this case. The previous purification rituals purged the sanctuary from all impurities, but it remained necessary to rid the high priest and community as a whole of all the culpabilities for their sins that he had been bearing for the people through the year.

The scapegoat ritual procedure was as follows: "Aaron shall lay his two hands on the head of the live goat and confess over it all the *culpabilities* of the Israelites and all their *transgressions* with regard to all their *sins*, and he shall put them on the head of the goat and send it away by the hand of an appointed man into the wilderness. So the goat will *bear* upon itself all their *culpabilities* into a solitary land, and

he [the appointed man] shall send the goat away into the wilderness"
(my translation). The purpose of the scapegoat ritual was for the high
priest to unload on the head of the scapegoat all the culpabilities he
had been bearing as the mediator for the people through the year. He
then sent the goat into the wilderness as far as possible away from the
tabernacle and the community. The goat would "bear [*nāśā'*] on itself
all their culpabilities [*'āwōnōt*] to a remote place" (Lev 22).

Up until this point in the year the high priest carried all the culpabilities of the people for which they made atonement through the year
so that they could be forgiven (Lev 4:20, 26, 31, 35; 5:6, 10, 13).[20] If he
or she did not make atonement for their sin, or if they committed a
sin for which atonement could not be made, they would continue to
bear the load of culpability for their sin on their own.[21] In this case,
the person would be excluded from the benefits of the mediatorial
protection of the priestly system and, therefore, vulnerable to retri-
bution from God.

Finally, the priest made atonement on behalf of himself and the
people with the two burnt offerings (Lev 16:24) and burned the fat of
the sin offering(s) on the altar. These burnt offerings and the burning
of the fat of the slain sin offerings finished off the atonement procedures of the Day of Atonement. Because the blood of the two slain
offerings had been brought into the holy place to make atonement,
their carcasses were taken outside the camp to be burned up
(Lev 16:27), as was the normal practice (Lev 4:11-12, 21; 6:30 [= Hebrew
v. 23]). The priests could not eat them as prebends.

CONCLUSION

The priestly conception of things embraces all of creation and Israel's
relationship to it as a nation with the Lord dwelling in their midst.
Both Leviticus 11 and Leviticus 20 connect the clean and unclean
animal laws with the holiness formula (e.g., "be holy, because I am

---

[20]Koch, " 'āwōn," 559.
[21]See Lev 5:1, 17; 7:18; 17:16; 19:8; 20:17, 19; Num 5:31; 14:34; 30:15; Ezek 14:10, 12.

holy," see Lev 11:45; 20:26), but they make the connection in two different ways. Leviticus 11 simply prohibits the eating of unclean animals, while Leviticus 20:22-26 connects the same laws to setting
Israel "apart from the nations" around them. This setting apart of
Israel from the other nations was God's intention from the very start
of their national existence as "a kingdom of priests, a holy nation"
(Ex 19:6). This is why these particular holiness and purity laws needed
to be set aside in the New Testament lest they have the effect of upholding the "the barrier, the dividing wall of hostility" between Jews
and Gentiles in the church (Eph 2:14; cf. Acts 10:9-16; Gal 2:11-14).

As for the other purity laws (i.e., unclean versus clean in Lev 10:10),
even in the New Testament before the pouring out of the Spirit on the
Day of Pentecost, Mary brought a "sin offering" for bearing Jesus because of the laws regarding the impure blood flow after bearing a child
(Lk 2:24; cf. Lev 12). We also see other examples of adherence to the
Old Testament purity laws elsewhere in the Gospels (e.g., Mt 8:4 with
Lev 14:1-20). In fact, the baptism of John the Baptist was a Jewish
washing purification procedure that prepared the people for the
coming of the Messiah, Jesus (Mt 3:1-12). This baptism remains as a
remnant of these old purifying washings, but now in the name of Jesus
(Jn 4:1-2; cf. Mt 28:19; Acts 2:38). As was already anticipated by both
John the Baptist and Jesus, in the church, baptism provides background
for the "baptism of the Holy Spirit" (Jn 3:4-8 with Jn 1:33; Acts 1:5-8; 2:38).

Probably the best way to understand the physical ritual purification
laws is to recall the manifest visible physical presence of God in the
Old Testament tabernacle by cloud and fire, and later the temple. This
place of visible physical presence was precisely the focus of the priestly
worldview and the theology with which the book of Leviticus is concerned. The *physical* purity laws correspond to the *physical* presence
of the Lord in the tabernacle. Since God was visibly physically present,
the people needed to be physically ritually pure in his presence.

In the New Testament church the focus shifts to God's presence
with his people in a different way, by the indwelling of the Holy Spirit.

We will return to this discussion in chapter eleven below. Here it is worth noting, however, that we have no tent or building over which the cloud of God's presence appears in a pillar of cloud by day with fire in it by night. The concern for purity shifts to the spiritual level since that is the level of the presence.

In the Old Testament there were physical purifications, but the concern for spiritual purity was no less real. Where God is present in a visible, physical way, he is also present spiritually. This comes through even in the Old Testament, for example, when the physical cleansing terminology is used for spiritual purity and cleansing (see, e.g., Ps 51:2, 6-7, 10, 12, 16-17). This brings us to further discussion of the New Testament use of the Old Testament law for the church and the Christian life.

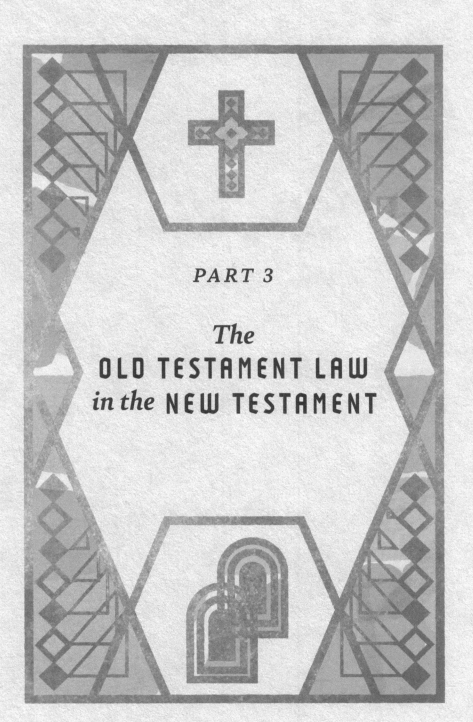

PART 3

The
OLD TESTAMENT LAW
in the NEW TESTAMENT

Eight

JESUS AND THE MOSAIC LAW

THIS CHAPTER MAKES THE SHIFT from the Old Testament focus in part two to the teachings about the Old Testament law in the New Testament in part three. In the Old Testament discussion we looked in some depth at the law in the Old Testament: its background in the ancient Near East, the various collections within the Mosaic law, and how each contributes to our understanding of how God intended the law to function in ancient Israel. We also took a few specific opportunities to look forward into the New Testament from the perspective of the Old Testament law.

The discussion that starts in this chapter will look directly at the major passages in the New Testament that contribute to our understanding of how the Old Testament law comes through into the life of the church and the believer. Admittedly, as an Old Testament scholar, I come at the reading of the New Testament teachings about the Old Testament law through the eyes of the Old Testament. I submit that this is a good way to come at the topic. Jesus came at it this way, and so did the earliest church. Jesus was Jewish and the earliest church was Jewish through and through. Moreover, Jesus' Bible was the Hebrew Old Testament, and the same was true for the church, although largely in the form of its Greek translation because of the Hellenization of the Near East and Mediterranean world during the intertestamental period (the four hundred years before Christ).

When we start with the New Testament we come at it all backward. The church is largely Gentile today, and it has been for almost two thousand years. We naturally come to the New Testament and the Bible as a whole from that perspective. Yes, there has always been a Jewish remnant in the church (Rom 11:1-7), but by and large the Jewish people rejected their Messiah (Rom 9:1-5). This was a painful reality for Jesus and for Paul, Peter, John, James the half-brother of Jesus, and all the writers of the New Testament.

The point is that looking at the New Testament with the Old Testament as its foundation is historically and theologically cogent. The apostles preached the gospel of Jesus Christ from the Old Testament. These were the only Scriptures they had. Peter started with Joel 2:28-32 on the Day of Pentecost. Even at the end of his life, the apostle Paul had not let go of the Old Testament as Scripture for the church (2 Tim 3:15-17). These were the Scriptures Timothy had been learning since he was an infant. Since then they had been growing gradually to include what we now know as the New Testament. Actually, the term *Old Testament* is anachronistic. Jesus never called it that, and neither did the apostles. *First Testament* is hardly better. It was simply the *Scriptures*, or the *Hebrew Bible*, or its translation in the Septuagint (LXX), the Greek Bible.

THE HISTORICAL CONTEXT AND SOURCES

The relationship between the law of Moses and the life and teachings of Jesus has been a topic of much debate since the first century.[1]

---

[1] I have a written a more detailed and technical discussion of Jesus and the law in Richard E. Averbeck, "The Law and the Gospels, with Attention to the Relationship Between the Decalogue and the Sermon on the Mount/Plain," in *The Oxford Handbook of Biblical Law*, ed. Pamela Barmash (Oxford: Oxford University Press, 2019), 409-23. In the present chapter I have cut down or cut out some of the more technical discussions, added new material to suit our purposes here, and done a good deal of rearranging and rewriting. One should also add the following to the bibliography cited in my earlier essay: David C. Sim, "Sermon on the Mount," and especially

From many passages in the Gospels, it is clear that Jesus distinguished between the law compiled in major sections of the Jewish Torah and the developing rabbinic interpretations and traditions that were important to many of the Jewish leaders and teachers of his day. It is not always clear when and where these rabbinic traditions arose. The official codification of many of them dates to the Mishnah in the early third century AD, and some of them even later in the Talmud in the fifth century AD. We know, however, that there were conflicts even between the various Jewish sects in the first century and earlier. This is evident from the well-known Qumran sectarian documents (second century BC to AD 68), Josephus (ca. AD 37–100), and other sources.

The most important primary sources for the study of Jesus and the Mosaic law, of course, are the four New Testament Gospels (Matthew, Mark, Luke, and John), all of which were written with different early Christian communities in mind. It is important to take this early church context into consideration when we read them. Both the Gospels and the book of Acts tell us a good deal about some of the tensions that were rampant in those early days—for example, between the Pharisees and the Sadducees (see, e.g., Mt 22:23-40 with Acts 23:6-10).

According to Acts, the church started out Jewish (Acts 2), and those who accepted Jesus as the Christ, the Messiah, saw themselves as continuing to be properly Jewish (Greek *christos*, "the anointed one" = Hebrew *māšîaḥ*, "Messiah"). From the Day of Pentecost onward, "every day they continued to meet together in the temple courts" (Acts 2:46; 3:1). This apparently continued until the destruction of the temple by the Roman general Titus in AD 70, if we can take our cue from Paul's worship there in AD 57 (Acts 21:20-26). The Jewish church in Jerusalem remained "zealous for the law" (Acts 21:20).

Thomas Kazen, "Theology of Law: New Testament," in *The Oxford Encyclopedia of the Bible and Law*, 2 vols., ed. Brent A. Strawn (Oxford: Oxford University Press, 2015), 2:285-89 and 2:384-400, respectively.

Beginning in Acts 10, however, Gentiles coming to faith in the Jewish Messiah became one of the primary issues of concern in the church. Tensions arose among the Jewish believers and even the leaders themselves over the Gentile believers (see, e.g., Gal 2:11-18). Eventually, this led to the first church council in Jerusalem in AD 48 (see Acts 15). The Jewish leaders and the Jewish church as a whole eventually accepted the Gentiles as legitimate followers of Jesus who would practice their faith as Gentiles. The writing of the four Gospels took place during the time when these controversies were alive and well in the church.

Most of the complications in the discussion of Jesus and the law arise from two complementary historical problems: the distinction between the Mosaic law and the developing rabbinic traditions of Jesus' day, and the early church setting of the writing of the Gospels. These historical problems are an ongoing point of contention among scholars of Jesus and the law. There are some difficulties in the dating of the Gospels, but Mark was probably the earliest Gospel written. He probably wrote it sometime during the 60s, which was at least thirty years after the death of Jesus. This is after most of what is described in the book of Acts had already taken place. How did this historical context influence the way he wrote the story about Jesus' life and teachings?

In the Bible, as in all historical writing, the human authors wrote from different perspectives. This is why we have four different Gospel accounts. Authors can tell the same story in different ways and still do so accurately just by selecting what they include and how they word things. Yes, there are many parallels between Gospels, especially the Synoptic Gospels (Matthew, Mark, and Luke), but they are arranged in different ways and focus on different themes in the life of Jesus.

JESUS, THE LAW, AND HIS FOLLOWERS

Scholars today fall into two major camps in their view of how Jesus saw the law. One camp consists of those who believe that Jesus fulfilled the law for us and transformed its teachings for their application in the kingdom of heaven. He passed certain laws on to his followers directly, abrogated others, and transformed the law as a whole for the new covenant people of God (see Jer 31:31-37). Jesus taught this law from the perspective of the future coming of the kingdom of heaven. Then his people would obey it as he lived and taught it. The church, therefore, obeys the "law of Christ," not the Mosaic law directly.[2] The other camp argues that Jesus lived and taught as a pious Jew with no intention of undermining the law of Moses, although he disputed some of the "traditions of the elders" that sometimes took precedence in some interpretations and applications of the law.[3]

Two of the major articles just referred to come from the *Dictionary of Jesus and the Gospels*, the first one from the first edition and the second from the second edition published twenty years later. The shift in those twenty years is largely due to the further development of the "third quest" for the historical Jesus.[4] Previously many argued that Jesus was contending with a very "legalistic" Judaism, but this new historical work showed that the Judaism of New Testament times was characterized by an emphasis on the covenant relationship between God and his people, not a rigid legalism. Obedience to the stipulations of the Mosaic law was expected, but they understood that the purpose of such obedience was to show covenant faithfulness. This understanding requires some nuancing, but the basic point has been generally well received among New Testament scholars.[5] Before this shift, there was a pronounced tendency to read Jesus as if he were the apostle Paul, which in turn also involved a misunderstanding of Paul.

---

[2]See, e.g., R. Banks, "Matthew's Understanding of the Law: Authenticity and Interpretation in Matthew 5:17-20," *JBL* 93 (1974): 226-42; and Douglas J. Moo, "Law," in *Dictionary of Jesus and the Gospels*, ed. Joel B. Green and Scott McKnight (Downers Grove, IL.: IVP Academic, 1992), 450-61.

[3]James D. G. Dunn, "Law," in *Dictionary of Jesus and the Gospels*, 2nd ed., ed. J. B. Green, J. K. Brown, and N. Perrin (Downers Grove, IL: IVP Academic, 2013), 505-15.

[4]See the work of N. T. Wright, *The New Testament and the People of God*, COQG 1 (Minneapolis: Fortress, 1992), and *Jesus and the Victory of God*, COQG 2 (Minneapolis, MN: Fortress Press, 1996). Wright's work was stimulated by the previous groundbreaking work of E. P. Sanders, *Jesus and Judaism* (Philadelphia: Fortress, 1985).

[5]D. A. Carson, Peter T. O'Brien, and Mark A. Seifrid, eds., *Justification and Variegated Nomism: A Fresh Appraisal of Paul and Second Temple Judaism*, vol. 1, WUNT 2.140 (Tübingen: Mohr Siebeck, 2001).

Both Matthew and Luke present Jesus as one who kept the law but was not concerned to maintain the Jewish expansionist "traditions of the elders" that so many of the teachers of the law were devoted to in his day. Some take Mark to be more critical of the law, but this depends on how one interprets certain passages in his Gospel. John wrote his Gospel later. He seems to regard Jesus as a keeper of the law but, more than that, as the embodiment and fullest expression of the law.[6] The earlier Gospels also seem to point in this direction, but John developed it more fully and theologically. In the discussion below, we use Matthew as a guide but bring the others into play as necessary.

The Sermon on the Mount/Plain

The Sermon on the Mount (Mt 5–7) and the Sermon on the Plain (Lk 6:17-49) are somehow related. Perhaps the latter should be considered a relatively brief extract from the former. Matthew 5:18-20 is the first and most well-known text for the study of the Mosaic law in the Gospels. Jesus said:

> Do not think that I have come to abolish the Law or the Prophets; I have not come to abolish them but to fulfill them. For truly I tell you, until heaven and earth disappear, not the smallest letter, not the least stroke of a pen, will by any means disappear from the law until everything is accomplished. Therefore anyone who sets aside one of the least of these commands and teaches others accordingly will be called least in the kingdom of heaven, but whoever practices and teaches these commands will be called great in the kingdom of heaven. For I tell you that unless your righteousness surpasses that of the Pharisees and the teachers of the law, you will certainly not enter the kingdom of heaven.

This passage and the "golden rule" (Mt 7:12) form a structural inclusion for the teachings that stand between the two: "So in everything, do to others what you would have them do to you, for this sums up the Law and the Prophets." The internal unit extends from

---

[6]D. Lioy, *Jesus as Torah in John 1–12* (Eugene, OR: Wipf & Stock, 2007).

Matthew 5:21 to Matthew 7:11. It begins with six antitheses (Mt 5:21-48) to illustrate what Jesus meant by his statement in Matthew 5:17-20.

The Sermon on the Plain does not repeat Matthew 5:17-20, but a form of Matthew 5:18 appears again in Luke 16:16-17, where Jesus says, "The Law and the Prophets were proclaimed until John. Since that time, the good news of the kingdom of God is being preached, and everyone is forcing their way into it. It is easier for heaven and earth to disappear than for the least stroke of a pen to drop out of the law." The main point Jesus was making was that his proclamation of the good news of the kingdom of God was never intended to eliminate the fact that everything in the law of Moses is still in effect until heaven and earth pass away. We need to look at the details here.

The Gospel of Matthew gives special attention to Jesus as the Davidic king of Israel (see, e.g., Mt 1:1; 2:2). He proclaimed the coming of the "kingdom of heaven" (Mt 4:17; cf., e.g., Mt 3:2; 5:3, 10, 19-20). In the Sermon on the Mount, Jesus essentially proclaimed the "law" of that kingdom. It begins with the beatitudes, which stand in the position of the Decalogue in the Mosaic law (Mt 5:3-12; cf. the variations on these in the Sermon on the Plain in Lk 6:20-22). In these beatitudes, Jesus was calling for his followers to become the salt of the earth and the light of the world (Mt 5:13-16). With that foundation laid, Jesus turned directly to the subject of the law in the Hebrew Bible.

JESUS DID NOT COME TO ABOLISH THE LAW

Jesus started with this: "Do not think that I have come to abolish the Law or the Prophets; I have not come to abolish them but to fulfill them" (Mt 5:17). The last thing Jesus would want his hearers and followers to think was that he wanted to abolish or destroy the Law or the Prophets. That would have been the mark of a heretic. If he were teaching that, he would have deserved complete and consummate rejection, if not stoning. The Old Testament law was part of the Word of God to him and to all who were there.

Some interpret "fulfill" here to mean that he intended to fulfill the law for his followers so that they would not need to fulfill it themselves.[7] On this view, Jesus fulfilled the law in the same sense as he fulfilled prophetic predictions (e.g., his virgin birth in Mt 1:22), so now his followers need to fulfill it only as he himself brings it through to them in the "law of Christ" (see, e.g., 1 Cor 9:19-23). They argue that his teachings in Matthew 5:21-48 supersede and sometimes even contradict the law of Moses. There are many problems with this approach to the passage, one of which is "until heaven and earth pass away" (Mt 5:18). Another is the further explanation in Matthew 5:19 that breaking the law and teaching others to do the same would make one the least in the kingdom of heaven.

Others who maintain the view that Matthew 5:17-20 has the effect of Jesus bringing the Law and Prophets to their intended fulfillment, as in the fulfillment formula, suggest that this does not imply that he fulfills the law in the sense that there are no other fulfillments to come, as with the fulfillments of prophecy. In their view, Jesus brings the Law and Prophets to their fullest expression.[8] Those who follow Christ should fulfill the law the way he taught it because he was the one who filled it up to its full intent and potential. This is a better way to look at it, but there are other factors that one should also take into consideration.

One of them is the fact that the verb *fulfill* here is active (as in Mt 3:15; 23:32), not passive as in the regular prophetic fulfillment formula that occurs throughout the book. The prophetic fulfillment formula is literally, "that it might be fulfilled" (Mt 1:22; 2:15, 17). Some scholars brush this aside as an insignificant detail,[9] but the other two active uses of the verb in Matthew suggest otherwise. According to Matthew 3:15, John was to baptize Jesus "to fulfill all righteousness"—that is, as a part of

---

[7]See, e.g., Banks, "Matthew's Understanding," 226-42, and Moo, "Law," 450-61.

[8]See, e.g., R. T. France, *The Gospel of Matthew* (Grand Rapids, MI: Eerdmans, 2007), 182-83.

[9]See, e.g., D. A. Carson, "Matthew," in *The Expositor's Bible Commentary*, rev. ed., ed. T. Longman III and D. E. Garland (Grand Rapids, MI: Zondervan, 2005), 175-77.

living a life that filled up all righteousness. John's baptism was meant to call people to this kind of life. The teachings and actions of Jesus were to bring righteousness to its fullest expression. It is the same for the righteousness that the Law and Prophets had been calling for according to Jesus in Matthew 5:17. In Matthew 23:32, Jesus recalled the ancestors of the Jews who had killed all the prophets and said, "Fill up, then, the measure of your ancestors." That is, go ahead and follow in their footsteps. Other similar uses of this verb appear elsewhere in the New Testament (e.g., Rom 13:8; Gal 5:14).

This suggests that *fulfill* here means that Jesus will teach and live it fully so the people see and learn what it looks like to teach and live the law the way God intended.[10] Some scholars have rightly emphasized the importance of the combination "the Law and the Prophets" in Matthew 5:17 and other passages (cf. Mt 7:12; 11:13; 22:40).[11] Jesus taught the law from a prophetic point of view, the way the prophets in the Hebrew Bible understood and proclaimed it. This often comes through in his controversies with the Jewish leaders, as, for example, his references to Hosea 6:6 ("I desire mercy and not sacrifice") in Matthew 9:13 and 12:7 suggest.

According to Matthew 5:18, absolutely no part of the Old Testament law has passed away, not even today, nor will it until heaven and earth pass away. Jesus uses hyperbole here, which is an exaggerated way of saying something to emphasize its importance. The NIV translates this as "not the smallest letter, not the least stroke of a pen, will by any means disappear from the law until everything is accomplished." The ESV is more literal: "not an iota, not a dot." Greek *iōta* refers to the Hebrew letter *yod*, the smallest letter in the Hebrew consonantal alphabet. The "dot" actually means "little horn," which probably refers

---

[10]See the full discussions in Craig C. Evans, *Matthew* (Cambridge: Cambridge University Press, 2012), 114-19; and J. Daryl Charles, "Garnishing with the 'Greater Righteousness': The Disciple's Relationship to the Law (Matthew 5:17-20)," *BBR* 12 (2002): 1-15.

[11]Klyne Snodgrass, "Matthew and the Law," in *Treasures New and Old: Recent Contributions to Matthean Studies*, ed. D. R. Bauer and M. A. Powell (Atlanta: Scholars, 1996), 99-127, and Charles, "Garnishing with the 'Greater Righteousness,'" 6.

to just a very short extension of a stroke in the writing of a consonant. One must remember that Jesus was speaking to Jewish people who took the Law and the Prophets very seriously. He was concerned that they not take him to be one who would deny them in any way.

Therefore, the law as understood, lived, and taught by Jesus (see the "antitheses" in Mt 5:21-48) remains valid even today since heaven and earth have not disappeared and everything is not yet accomplished. Moreover, one's status in the "kingdom of heaven" depends on whether one breaks the law as explained and lived by Jesus and as he teaches others to do so (Mt 5:19). If a teacher "sets aside one of the least of these commandments," he will be the least in the kingdom of heaven.

Matthew presents Jesus not only as the authoritative teacher of the law (Mt 7:28-29) but also their example of how to live it. If one wants to know how to live properly according to a full and filled up understanding of the law, they need only hear his teaching and observe his way of life as narrated in this Gospel. One could not say this of the other teachers of the law: "For I tell you that unless your righteousness surpasses that of the Pharisees and the teachers of the law, you will certainly not enter the kingdom of heaven" (Mt 5:20). This must have shocked the crowd. The scribes and Pharisees, who were the teachers of the law, sat in the seat of Moses (Mt 23:2), and were highly regarded as keepers of the law. The point is that Jesus is not critical of the law itself but the way the Jewish leaders were teaching it.[12] His attitude toward the law is not in question. He was fully in support of its ongoing significance and application in the kingdom of heaven.

THE ANTITHESES

Jesus explains and illustrates his meaning and intention with the antitheses that follow (Mt 5:21-48).[13] They are not just simple antitheses,

---

[12]W. Loader, "Jesus and the Law," in *Handbook for the Study of the Historical Jesus*, ed. T. Holmén and S. E. Porter (Leiden: Brill, 2011), 3:2745-72.

[13]See the helpful discussions of the antitheses in Evans, *Matthew*, 120-37; Snodgrass, "Matthew and the Law"; and G. H. Stassen, "The Fourteen Triads of the Sermon on the Mount (Matthew 5:21–7:12)," *JBL* 122 (2003): 267-308.

however. They are triadic in structure: first, a statement of traditional righteousness introduced with some version of "You have heard that it was said"; second, an explanation of the vicious cycle the traditional righteousness produces; and third, a transforming initiative that breaks the vicious cycle. The third element of the triadic structure points the way forward to righteousness that goes beyond that of the scribes and Pharisees.[14]

Rabbinic discussions sometimes took the form of antitheses similar to but not exactly the same as the ones Jesus uses here. For example, an early rabbinic exposition of the fifth commandment goes like this: "'Honor your father and your mother.' I might understand, honor them with words only. But there is a teaching in what another verse says (Prov 3:9), 'Honor the Lord with your substance.' So honoring means honoring with food, drink, and clean garments" (Mekhilta on Ex 20:12).

Not all of them refer to somewhere else in Scripture but may use logical deduction. Similarly, on a narrative rather than a law in particular, Rabbi Judah the Prince says regarding Exodus 19:20,

"And the Lord came down upon mount Sinai." I might hear this as it is heard, I might understand this according to its literal meaning. But you [the exhortation is to another teacher of the law] must say: "If the sun, one of the many servants of God, may remain in its place and nevertheless be effective beyond it, how much more He by whose word the world came into being."

That is, the Lord actually stayed in his place, though his activity was especially manifest on Mount Sinai.[15]

The similarities to the antitheses of Jesus in Matthew 5:21-48 are clear, but there are also some differences. Jesus changes the formula from "I might understand . . . but there is a teaching" or "but you must say" to "You have heard that it was said . . . but I tell you." The

---

[14]Stassen, "Fourteen Triads."
[15]See also Mekhilta on Ex 19:20, where Rabbi Akiva held to a more literal interpretation. This and the previous rabbinic citation on Ex 20:12 are quoted in David Daube, *The New Testament and Rabbinic Judaism* (Peabody, MA: Hendrickson, 1990), 55-62.

rabbis give supportive reasoning. Jesus simply says, "But I tell you." There is no debate here. Jesus is *the* rabbi, not just *a* rabbi (see Mt 7:28-29; Jn 1:38; cf. Mt 23:7-8; Jn 1:49; 3:2, 26; 6:25). Also, the rabbinic discussion was limited to the realm of the rabbis, an academic debate between teachers. Jesus was talking to the common people about their understanding of the teachings and stating that they must go beyond the rabbis (remember Mt 5:20).

Jesus begins his antitheses in Matthew 5:21-48 with references to two of the Ten Commandments: the prohibitions against murder (Mt 5:21-26) and adultery (Mt 5:27-30, 31-32). The first antithesis begins, "You have heard that it was said to the people long ago, 'You shall not murder, and anyone who murders will be subject to judgment'" (Mt 5:21-22). He combines the sixth commandment with its judicial response (Ex 21:12; Lev 24:17; Num 35:12; Deut 17:8-13). The next verse describes the vicious cycle of anger and interpersonal conflict that leads to murder (Mt 5:22). Jesus concludes by calling for a different way to handle such conflicts—a way that brings reconciliation rather than judicial action (Mt 5:23-26). The righteous person will learn to disarm the conflicts that would lead to murder. This compares well with Leviticus 19:17-18, "You shall not hate in your heart anyone of your kin. . . . You shall not take vengeance or bear a grudge against any of your people, but you shall love your neighbor as yourself: I am the LORD." One can see that this approach to such conflicts comes through in the Old Testament law as well as in the New Testament teachings of Jesus.

In his second antithesis (Mt 5:27-30), he turns to the next command in the Decalogue, "You shall not commit adultery" (Ex 20:14). Once again, Jesus highlights the vicious cycle: lust leads to adultery. As far as Jesus is concerned, such lust amounts to committing adultery in one's heart. The way forward and away from such temptation is to take radical action against any source of temptation to lust. Again, he uses hyperbole—plucking out an eye or cutting off a hand (Mt 5:29-30). This emphasizes how seriously people need to take this issue. What Jesus is doing here is applying the tenth commandment to the command against adultery: "you shall not covet your neighbor's wife" (Ex 20:17). He is going beyond what the command against adultery actually says, but he is not going beyond the law as a whole.

There are probably only five antitheses rather than six. The third is actually part of the second, having an abbreviated introduction and once again referring to adultery.[16] The passage reads, "It has been said, 'Anyone who divorces his wife must give her a certificate of divorce.' But I tell you that anyone who divorces his wife, except for sexual immorality, makes her the victim of adultery, and anyone who marries a divorced woman commits adultery" (Mt 5:31-32). This extends Jesus' remarks on the adultery in the previous unit, and so becomes part of his teachings on this point of the Decalogue. Divorce was a major issue back then, as it is today, but the main point is to reinforce his teaching about not lusting after another woman (Mt 5:29-30). Such lust could lead to a man wanting to divorce his wife for another woman, but, according to Jesus, sufficient grounds for divorce arises only if his wife commits some kind of "unchastity" (Greek *porneia*; cf. also Mt 19:9).

Jesus draws on Deuteronomy 24:1, which refers to "something indecent" (NIV), which is literally in Hebrew, "nakedness of a matter." It occurs only one other time in the Hebrew Bible in Deuteronomy 23:14, where it refers to covering up excrement so that the Lord "will not see among you anything indecent and turn away from you." It refers, therefore, to some sexually inappropriate behavior that involved nudity, perhaps anywhere from lewd behavior to adultery. She has somehow broken faith with her husband sexually. The whole passage reads,

> *If* a man marries a woman who becomes displeasing to him because he finds
> something indecent about her, and he writes her a certificate of divorce, gives
> it to her and sends her from his house, and if after she leaves his house she
> becomes the wife of another man, and her second husband dislikes her and

---

[16]Evans, *Matthew*, 123.

writes her a certificate of divorce, gives it to her and sends her from his house, or if he dies, *then* her first husband, who divorced her, is not allowed to marry her again after she has been defiled. That would be detestable in the eyes of the LORD. Do not bring sin upon the land the LORD your God is giving you as an inheritance. (Deut 24:1-4)

The point of this passage comes down to the issue of a man remarrying a woman whom he had divorced previously. This is forbidden. Similarly, in Jeremiah 3:1: "If a man divorces his wife and she leaves him and marries another man, should he return to her again? Would not the land be completely defiled?" In other words, the woman has already had sexual relations with another man, so for the first husband to remarry her would be virtually the same as adultery. It would be like "wife swapping" today. There is no legal "loophole" for such behavior in ancient Israel.

We must also consider here Matthew 19:3-12 (par. Mk 10:1-12), where the subject of the certificate of divorce comes up again. The Pharisees asked, "Is it lawful for a man to divorce his wife for any cause?" (Mt 19:3). If we can rely on the tradition in the Mishnah for information on the days of Jesus, there was a well-known rabbinic debate about this very issue. Shammai took a very strict view, as Jesus does here, versus Hillel, who allowed divorce for something as trivial as burning dinner (*m. Git.* 9:10). According to the same tractate, Akiva joined later with the view allowing divorce even if the other woman was more beautiful in the husband's eyes. Jesus responded with God's intention from creation that a husband and wife never separate. They responded to Jesus by calling attention to the "certificate of divorce" Moses referred to in Deuteronomy 24:1. Jesus answered, "It was because you were so hard-hearted that Moses allowed you to divorce your wives, but from the beginning it was not so" (Mt 19:8). Thus, he maintained his point, which was that God made clear from the beginning that divorce was not part of the plan. That said, he reiterated the substance of what he had already proclaimed in Matthew 5:32.

The last clause of Matthew 5:32 says, "anyone who marries a divorced woman commits adultery." The focus here is on the problem caused by a man who divorces his wife without her having committed sexual indecency. In doing so he "makes her commit adultery" (not NIV, "makes her the victim of adultery") when she goes to marry another man. If she has not committed adultery in her first marriage, she will when she has sexual relations with the second man she marries because the divorce was not legitimate in the first place. Moreover, the other man commits adultery by marrying her. This would not be perpetual adultery, since once the bond has been broken through adultery, no such bond any longer exists. The relationship has been broken.

The last three antitheses do not treat the Decalogue directly. Jesus was concerned about the abuse and misuse of the law that he saw in some of the shortsighted teachings of his day, but he would never disregard the law itself. The fourth antithesis is about swearing oaths (Mt 5:33-37). His main point was that one should always speak truth in a straightforward way to begin with, so that he would have no occasion to swear an oath anyway. Anyone could rely on his word without an oath. This avoids the vicious cycle of making oaths by one thing or the other, often with the intent to confuse and manipulate the situation (cf. Mt 23:16-22).[17] This is about relationships with other people in private life. It does not forbid taking oaths in legal court cases, which the law sometimes required them to do in ancient Israel (see, e.g., Deut 6:13).

Numbers 30 distinguishes between making an oath and taking a vow, but the point is that one must fulfill what he or she vows or swears on oath to do. A man, as a husband or father, may retract an oath or vow made by a woman under his authority (Num 30:3-16) since his own household resources were likely to be at stake. Other than that, however, he must be sure to fulfill what has been vowed.

---

[17]Evans, *Matthew*, 126-30.

Deuteronomy 23:21-23 emphasizes the importance of fulfilling one's vows. Amid this concern, however, it says, "if you refrain from vowing, you will not incur guilt" (Deut 23:22). This may underlie the conclusion Jesus draws, "All you need to say is simply 'Yes' or 'No'; anything beyond this comes from the evil one" (Mt 5:37).

The fifth antithesis draws on a very ancient legal tradition that even goes back before Moses—in the Laws of Hammurabi, for example. The same tradition appears in each of the three major sections of law in the Hebrew Bible (Ex 21:24; Lev 24:20; Deut 19:21): "Eye for eye, and tooth for tooth" (Mt 5:38). Scholars often refer to it in Latin as the *lex talionis*. It is most important to take note of the fact that it always occurs in law court contexts, not personal relationships outside of court. In this sermon, Jesus is talking about how one should handle personal relationships in such a way as to disarm those who are unfair and demanding: "Do not resist an evildoer. But if anyone strikes you on the right cheek, turn the other also" (Mt 5:39-42). As an earlier beatitude says, "Blessed are the peacemakers, for they will be called children of God" (Mt 5:9). When Jesus denied the application of *lex talionis* he was not contradicting the law. It never applied in personal relationships in the first place. His point is that personal vengeance has no place in the kingdom of heaven. This is nothing new to the law either: "You shall not take vengeance or bear a grudge against any of your people, but you shall love your neighbor as yourself: I am the Lord" (Lev 19:18).

The sixth antithesis is closely related to the fifth. Luke actually combines them together into one in the Sermon on the Plain in Luke 6:27-31:

> But to you who are listening I say: Love your enemies, do good to those who hate you, bless those who curse you, pray for those who mistreat you. If someone slaps you on one cheek, turn to them the other also. If someone takes your coat, do not withhold your shirt from them. Give to everyone who asks you, and if anyone takes what belongs to you, do not demand it back. Do to others as you would have them do to you.

The principle of Matthew's sixth antithesis, therefore, becomes the background for Luke's parallel selections from Matthew's fifth antithesis. He binds them together as one teaching but has no statement of the traditional teaching that Jesus is disputing according to Matthew.

The traditional teaching in Matthew's form of the sixth antithesis is "You shall love your neighbor and hate your enemy" (Mt 5:43). The Hebrew Bible has no command that one should hate his or her enemy. Here it is important to remember that Jesus is not disputing the Law or the Prophets, but rather the way the scribes and Pharisees taught them in his day (Mt 5:20).[18] Apparently, they were at least implying from Leviticus 19:18 that they could hate their enemy just as long as they loved their neighbor. Jesus went the opposite direction: they must love their enemies too. Leviticus 19:34 calls for the same love toward foreigners: "You shall love the alien as yourself, for you were aliens in the land of Egypt." The Egyptians treated them as enemies and enslaved them. In Israel they were forbidden to treat foreigners that way. In fact, quite the opposite: they were to love them. Since their heavenly Father showed love to both good and evil people, they should do the same. In this regard, therefore, they could become "perfect" as their heavenly Father was perfect.

Jesus had three main goals in Matthew 5:17-48. First, he wanted to assure his hearers that he was not in any way intending to undermine the law (Mt 5:17-19). Second, he wanted them to understand that the way the Pharisees and teachers of the law were teaching the law did not produce the kind of righteousness called for in the kingdom of heaven (Mt 5:20). Third, he wanted to declare his own reading of the law and his authority as a teacher of it (Mt 5:21-48). As Matthew 7:29 says, "He taught as one who had authority, and not as their teachers of the law."

---

[18]Evans, *Matthew*, 133.

PRIORITIES WITHIN THE LAW

Jesus declares one of his most severe criticisms of the honored teachers of the law in one of his eight "woes" against them in Matthew 23:23-24. Here he puts special emphasis on "the more important matters of the law—justice, mercy and faithfulness" (Mt 23:23; cf. Lk 11:42): "Woe to you, teachers of the law and Pharisees, you hypocrites! You give a tenth of your spices—mint, dill and cumin. But you have neglected the more important matters of the law—justice, mercy and faithfulness. You should have practiced the latter, without neglecting the former. You blind guides! You strain out a gnat but swallow a camel." Jesus is alluding here to Micah 6:6-8, "With what shall I come before the LORD, and bow myself before God on high? Shall I come before him with burnt offerings, with calves a year old? . . . He has told you, O mortal, what is good; and what does the LORD require of you but to do justice, and to love kindness, and to walk humbly with your God?" As in Matthew 5:18, he does not deny the need to observe even the smallest details of the law, but there are certain emphases in the law that must take priority. This woe illustrates how easy it is to focus on religious zeal for the details of the law in a way that loses track of what the Law and the Prophets are all about to begin with. So again, Jesus guarded against denying the importance of keeping the law even while he criticized the way it was being taught.

Similarly, in Matthew 22:34-40 Jesus responded to an expert in the Mosaic law who asked him, "Teacher, which is the greatest commandment in the law?" (Mt 22:36). Jesus answered, "'Love the Lord your God with all your heart and with all your soul and with all your mind.' This is the first and greatest commandment. And the second is like it: 'Love your neighbor as yourself.' All the Law and the Prophets hang on these two commandments." These two great commandments appear also in Mark 12:28-31 and Luke 10:25-37 in somewhat different form and with contextual variation. The problem today is that so many people do not read the law this way. If we do not read it this way, we are reading it wrongly, missing what it is all about. Jesus said so!

These two commandments make up the core substance of what is referred to as "the law of Christ" later in the apostle Paul's letters to the churches (see, e.g., 1 Cor 9:21; Gal 6:2; cf. also Jas 2:8). The fact that "all the Law and the Prophets hang on these two commandments," suggests that "the law of Christ" is the way that Jesus mediated the Old Testament law to us for our lives as his followers. The law of Christ does not leave the Old Testament law behind but gets to the matter of having the law written on the heart. In new covenant terms, God writes the law on the very heart of the follower of Jesus (Jer 31:33) by the Spirit of God (Ezek 36:26-27; cf. Lk 22:20 with 2 Cor 3:2-6). We observed earlier that the so-called golden rule forms a structural inclusion with Matthew 5:17-19, providing a frame for all that stands between: "In everything do to others as you would have them do to you; for this is the Law and the Prophets" (Mt 7:12). In the Sermon on the Plain, Luke not only combines the last two antitheses into one argument but also works the golden rule into the same unit (Lk 6:31).

There is reason to believe that Jesus gave an answer to the lawyer's question that would have been in accord with good rabbinic teaching in his day.[19] The lawyer asked for one commandment, but Jesus gave two. Many have argued that the first great commandment corresponds to the so-called "first table" of the Decalogue; that is, the first five commandments, all of which mention the Lord (Ex 20:2-12). The second corresponds to the "second table" of the Decalogue, which has commandments devoted to how we treat one another and make no mention of the Lord (Ex 20:13-17). First, he cited from the Great Shema Deuteronomy 6:5, but he refused to stop there. He added Leviticus 19:18.

---

[19]See D. C. Allison, "Jesus and the Torah," in *The Law in Holy Scripture: Essays from the Concordia Theological Seminary Symposium on Exegetical Theology*, ed. Charles A Gieschen (St. Louis: Concordia, 2004), 75-95; and K. H. Tan, "Jesus and the Shema," in *Handbook for the Study of the Historical Jesus*, 3:2677-2707.

The parallel passage in Mark 12:29-31 starts the first great commandment with Deuteronomy 6:4 and runs through the next verse. In that instance, the scribe who asked the question affirmed his answer, so Jesus affirmed him. Luke has Jesus asking the question of the lawyer, who responded with the two great commandments (Lk 10:25-28). Jesus then affirmed the lawyer's response, but the lawyer still wanted to trap him and asked, "And who is my neighbor?" Jesus answered with the well-known parable of the Good Samaritan (Lk 10:29-37). The point is that here, once again, Jesus affirmed the Decalogue and did so without even citing it directly. Moreover, by this means, he also brought his way of reading and applying the law to the forefront. Jesus himself is the chief rabbi. He was and is the full expression of the Law and the Prophets and all that they anticipated.[20]

THE PURITY REGULATIONS

According to Matthew, immediately following the Sermon on Mount in Matthew 5–7, a "leper" (i.e., a person with skin disease) came to Jesus for healing (Mt 8:1-4; par. Mk 1:40-44; Lk 5:12-14). The leper said to Jesus, "Lord, if you choose, you can make me clean." In response, Jesus "stretched out his hand and touched him, saying, 'I do choose. Be made clean!' Immediately his leprosy was cleansed" (Mt 8:3).

Some argue that Jesus violated the purity laws by touching the leper, thereby contracting impurity. According to the Levitical regulations, the unclean person must keep their distance so that no one would touch them, causing the spread of their uncleanness to others in the community: "Anyone with such a defiling disease must wear torn clothes, let their hair be unkempt, cover the lower part of their face and cry out, 'Unclean! Unclean!' As long as they have the disease they remain unclean. They must live alone; they must live outside the camp" (Lev 13:45-46). The trouble with this understanding is that, according to the account, Jesus is not just touching but healing. This

---

[20]Joshua W. Jipp, *Christ Is King: Paul's Royal Ideology* (Minneapolis: Fortress, 2015), 43-76.

puts the whole incident into a realm beyond purity considerations, where the concern was not healing but separation from the community to avoid spreading such impurities, and the purification procedures after the person had already been healed (Lev 14).[21] Jesus immediately complied with those regulations when he instructed the leper to "go, show yourself to the priest, and offer the gift that Moses commanded, as a testimony to them" (Mt 8:4).

Probably the most important passage on the issue of Jesus and the purity laws is the dispute between Jesus and the scribes and Pharisees in Mark 7:1-23 (par. Mt 15:1-20). In that story, a conflict emerged over hand washing and other "tradition of the elders" (Mk 7:3). The Jewish leaders asked Jesus why his disciples were "eating their food with defiled hands" (Mk 7:5). The tradition of the elders was to wash one's hands before eating. Jesus rebuked them for their "hypocrisy" with a quote from Isaiah and then cited a ruling in their traditions that allowed children to avoid taking care of their elderly parents (Mk 7:6-13). At the end he added, "And you do many things like that."

With that rebuke issued, he turned to the crowd and said, "Nothing outside a person can defile them by going into them. Rather, it is what comes out of a person that defiles them" (Mk 7:15). Later, he was alone with his disciples and they questioned him about his teaching. Jesus said to them, "Are you so dull? Don't you see that nothing that enters a person from the outside can defile them? For it doesn't go into their heart but into their stomach, and then out of the body" (Mk 7:18-19). Mark immediately inserted a brief parenthetical remark, which he does not attribute to Jesus but presents as Jesus' intention, "In saying this, Jesus declared all foods clean" (Mk 7:19). In the parallel passage, Matthew does not draw out this implication of Jesus' teaching on this occasion (see Mt 15:15-20).[22]

---

[21]T. Holmén, "Jesus and the Purity Paradigm," in *Handbook for the Study of the Historical Jesus*, 3:2709-44.

[22]See the masterful discussion of Mark 7 as a whole and this passage in particular in R. T. France, *The Gospel of Mark: A Commentary on the Greek Text*, NIGTC (Grand Rapids, MI: Eerdmans, 2002).

Some have argued that Mark's insertion refers to Jesus' rejection or demotion of the expansionist Jewish traditions of his day, wherein they extended the defilement by physical contact regulations beyond what one finds in the Hebrew Bible. In this view, Jesus was not rejecting the clean and unclean animal distinction in the law (Lev 11).[23] Part of the argument is that if Mark intended to say that Jesus eliminated the distinction between clean and unclean animals, this should have settled the dispute in the early church without further ado. The problem, of course, is that Mark wrote his Gospel after the dispute had already picked up momentum in the church.

Mark's insertion reflects the concern in the early church to break down the divide between Jewish and Gentile believers caused by the Jewish food laws (see Lev 11 with Acts 10; Gal 2). Of course, this was not a concern that Jesus had before the church even began on the Day of Pentecost (Acts 2). According to the law in the Old Testament, one of the main purposes of the food regulations had always been to keep the Israelites separate from the Gentile peoples around them and their corrupting influences (Lev 20:22-26). These laws came to have the effect of dividing the church and disrupting its unity once it came to include both Jewish and Gentile believers.[24]

Neither Jesus nor Mark was denying the importance of purity and holiness regulations in the law. God never intended that such regulations should produce divisions between the people of God. On the contrary, the food laws bound the ancient Israelites together and separated them from the corrupt peoples around them. Recall that, even in the Torah, the law itself changed when the Israelites moved from wandering in the wilderness to occupying the land. In the wilderness, since they were traveling as a camp surrounding the tabernacle, if they wanted to eat meat, they were to sacrifice their animals

---

[23]See, e.g., David H. Stern, *Jewish New Testament Commentary*, 5th ed. (Clarkesville, MD: Jewish New Testament Publications, 1996), 93-94; and the full discussion in Thomas Kazen, *Jesus and the Purity Halakhah: Was Jesus Indifferent to Purity?* CBNTS 38 (Winona Lake, IN: Eisenbrauns, 2010), 228-31.

[24]P. Fredriksen, "Did Jesus Oppose the Purity Laws?" *BRev* 11, no. 3 (1995): 19-25, 42-47.

only at the doorway of the tabernacle (Lev 17:1-9). Later, after they conquered and occupied the land, they could kill animals and eat meat anywhere in the land as long as they did not eat the blood (Deut 12:15-25).[25]

When the church became a mix of Jews and Gentiles, the food laws became an obstacle to the unity of the church (see, e.g., the conflict between Peter and Paul regarding this issue in Gal 2:11-21). Not being able to eat together would drive a wedge between Jewish and Gentile believers, rather than break down the "dividing wall" between them, as Paul put it in Ephesians 2:14. As he wrote his Gospel, therefore, Mark simply pointed out the readily apparent application of Jesus' teaching to the concerns for the unity of the church.

Other passages raise essentially the same concerns about the purity laws.[26] It seems that Jesus did indeed take these regulations seriously, but he did not accept what he considered to be overly pedantic and burdensome extensions of the biblical purity laws in the form of "the tradition of the elders." The same basic principle applies to Jesus and the Sabbath.

The Sabbath

The Sabbath controversy between Jesus and the Pharisees appears in similar form in three passages in the Synoptic Gospels (Mt 12:1-14; Mk 2:23-3:6; Lk 6:1-11). All three have two sequential narratives: one controversy over plucking grain to eat it on the Sabbath and another over healing on the Sabbath. In all three Gospels, the first ends with some variation of "the Son of Man is lord of the Sabbath." Jesus proclaimed his lordship over the Sabbath but did not set it aside or resist the basic principle of rest on the Sabbath. The questions raised are

---

[25]See the full discussion in Richard E. Averbeck, "The Cult in Deuteronomy and Its Relationship to the Book of the Covenant and the Holiness Code," in *Sepher Torath Mosheh: Studies in the Composition and Interpretation of Deuteronomy*, ed. Daniel I. Block and Richard L. Schultz (Peabody, MA: Hendrickson, 2017), 235-41.

[26]See the summary in D. A. deSilva, "Clean and Unclean," in *Dictionary of Jesus and the Gospels*, 2nd ed., 142-49; and, again, the full discussion in Kazen, *Jesus and the Purity Halakhah*.

trivial, not of any substance.[27] The second narrative ends with a remark about the Pharisees and other Jewish leaders going away to plot against Jesus in all three Gospels.

In Mark and Luke the Sabbath controversy is preceded by Jesus teaching about putting new wine into new wine skins, not old ones (Mk 2:22; Lk 6:37-39). The point was that one could not hold Jesus within the confines of the current Jewish interpretations and applications of the law. They will burst. His Sabbath teachings do just that, but they do not violate the command to keep the Sabbath and its importance. Jesus was rejecting their overly restrictive application of Sabbath law. According to Mark, Jesus said, "The Sabbath was made for man, not man for the Sabbath. So the Son of Man is Lord even of the Sabbath" (Mk 2:27-28).

Matthew is different. He arranges his Gospel so that the invitation to rest that Jesus gives in Matthew 11:28-30 precedes and leads directly into the Sabbath controversy in Matthew 12. This is a turning point in the Gospel of Matthew. Jesus began his invitation with this: "Come to me, all you who are weary and burdened, and I will give you rest" (Mt 11:28).[28] He was inviting them to a "rest" for their "souls" (Mt 11:29), citing, or at least alluding to, Jeremiah 6:16. In the historical context of Jeremiah, the Israelites had refused to return to the "ancient paths" of the Mosaic law, where they would find rest for their souls, rather than Babylonian captivity. Jesus turned it against the rejection he himself was experiencing from his people (Mt 11:20-24). He prayed to the Father (Mt 11:25-26), made a pronouncement about the Father's commitment to him (Mt 11:27), and then turned to the crowd with his invitation. It was an invitation to those who felt their desperate need of deliverance from the burdens that were crushing them (Mt 11:28-30).

---

[27]Loader, "Jesus and the Law."

[28]See now the full discussion of this passage and the Sabbath controversy in Matthew 12, in Richard E. Averbeck, "A Rest for the Soul," *Journal of Spiritual Formation and Soul Care* 11:1 (2018): 5-22.

Jesus was not trying to load his followers down but lighten them up with an easier yoke and a lighter load. One would not normally think of putting "rest" and "yoke" together. A yoke was a means of harnessing animals for work. Here Jesus was calling those who would come to him as Savior and Lord to take on his yoke so they could learn from him, in contrast to the yoke they were currently bearing and the load they were carrying. His followers have only one to please, so his yoke would not be tiresome or heavy, since Jesus is "gentle and humble in heart" toward those who come to him. He does not want to load us down. Quite the opposite, he wants to lighten us up. He wants us to have "rest" for our "souls" no matter what our circumstances may be in life. This rest for the soul would make the yoke of turning to Jesus and following him easy—it would lighten the load of their lives (Mt 11:30).

For Matthew this invitation to rest for the soul is the foil for the Sabbath controversy that follows immediately in Matthew 12. The Sabbath was a good thing, but the teachers of the law had loaded it down with a heavy burden of regulations that were not native to it and its purposes. The disciples were not violating anything in the Old Testament law when they "began to pick some heads of grain and eat them" (Mt 12:1). They were not doing regular daily labor, such as harvesting the crop or anything of the sort. They were simply picking and eating as they went along because they were hungry.

According to Deuteronomy 23:24-25, they were doing nothing wrong: "If you enter your neighbor's vineyard, you may eat all the grapes you want, but do not put any in your basket. If you enter your neighbor's grainfield, you may pick kernels with your hands, but you must not put a sickle to their standing grain" (Deut 23:24-25). They were not working. This was not harvesting on the Sabbath. The Pharisees were not accusing them of theft, since that would be illegal on any day of the week, and this activity was not theft according to the law anyway. Their accusation was "Look! Your disciples are doing what is unlawful on the Sabbath" (Mt 12:2).

Jesus responded with two examples from the Old Testament, and added to them certain pertinent pronouncements about himself and his work: (1) David and his men eating the priestly bread because they were hungry (Mt 12:3-4; cf. 1 Sam 21:3-6), and (2) the practice of priests doing laborious work in the tabernacle (and later in the temple) on the Sabbath when they performed the regular Sabbath day rituals (Mt 12:5; cf. Num 28:9-10; also note Jn 7:22-23). The former speaks to the issue of hunger, and the second to doing the work of the Lord on the Sabbath. Jesus responded to the latter by stating, "I tell you that something greater than the temple is here" (Mt 12:6), so why would it be wrong for his servants to take handfuls of grain and eat as they were serving him on the Sabbath day?

He responded to the former with the rebuke, "If you had known what these words mean, 'I desire mercy, not sacrifice,' you would not have condemned the innocent" for eating as they were walking along (Mt 12:7, citing Hos 6:6). After all, "the Son of Man is Lord of the Sabbath" (Mt 12:8). As servants of the Lord of the Sabbath, the disciples of Jesus certainly could not be condemned for what they were doing.

Jesus was not denying the importance of the Sabbath and, in fact, he did not violate it, but neither did he bow to the casuistry that the Pharisees had added to its regulations. As he put it in Matthew 23:4, "They tie up heavy, cumbersome loads and put them on other people's shoulders, but they themselves are not willing to lift a finger to move them" (cf. Lk 11:46; Acts 15:10; Gal 6:13). They liked to make things difficult for people. Jesus did not. He is "gentle and humble in heart" (Mt 11:29).

The reality, of course, is that sometimes and in some ways the lives even of those who have heard the invitation and come to Jesus are not so restful. Jesus did *not* say that life as a whole would be easy but that bearing his yoke would be easy compared to bearing the yoke they were currently bearing and the load that the so-called wise and learned of the day had loaded on them (see Mt 11:25). Life is full of difficulties of various kinds. This has been true since Genesis 3. We live as fallen people in a fallen world with others who are fallen. All of us are both agents of corruption and victims of the corruption of others and the groaning of all creation. As Paul put it in Romans 8:18-30, we groan deeply in the midst of the groaning of the whole creation, looking forward to the day of relief when we are glorified and the whole creation is released from its bondage to corruption. In the meantime, there is rest to be found in the Holy Spirit's groaning for us to the Father, whose purpose and plan in all that we experience, both the good and the bad, is to "conform" us to "the image of his Son" (Rom 8:27-29). This, in fact, is what spiritual formation is all about.[29]

The "rest for the soul" that Jesus offered in Matthew 11:28-30 is the kind of rest we can have right in the middle of all the "groaning." Jesus is saying he has a yoke for us to bear, but it is easy and light because he is "gentle and humble in heart" toward those who would come to him. The problem with the other yoke was that those masters were harsh and difficult to please. At the first church council in Jerusalem there were those who wanted to make it a rule that Gentiles who came to faith in Christ "must be circumcised and required to obey the law of Moses" (Acts 15:5). The Gentiles who had come to Christ as their savior would need to convert to Judaism. Peter's response was: "why do you try to test God by putting on the necks of the disciples a *yoke* that neither we nor our fathers have been able to bear?" (Acts 15:10; cf. Gal 5:1 with Gal 2:4; also 1 Tim 6:1, which refers to literal slavery as a "yoke"). None of us are redeemed through keeping the law, neither Jew nor Gentile, so why add the requirement to keep the law to the believing Gentiles, who were never under the law in the first place?[30]

The yoke that Jesus wanted to replace in Matthew 11:28-30 was not so much the Mosaic law itself but the burdensome way the leaders of

---

[29]See the discussion of this in Richard E. Averbeck, "Spirit, Community, and Mission: A Biblical Theology for Spiritual Formation," in *Journal of Spiritual Formation and Soul Care* 1 (2008): 27-53.
[30]See the helpful discussion in Darrell L. Bock, *Acts*, BECNT (Grand Rapids, MI: Baker Academic, 2007), 500-501.

the Jews in the days of Jesus taught the law, as illustrated by the Sabbath controversy in Matthew 12. It was the law as it was understood, taught, and enforced by the Pharisees. The people who resisted Jesus the most were the self-righteous—the ones who thought they were "wise and learned" (Mt 11:25). Self-righteous people are always judgmental and hard on others. They cannot hear the invitation to rest that Jesus issued because of the din of their own protestations. This is what Jesus wanted to deliver the weary and heavy-loaded ones from, and it applies to us today too.[31] The irony is that it is hard work to get people to rest. One of the great tragedies in the lives of so many Christians today is that they are anything but restful.

Some theological and ecclesiastical traditions maintain that a day of rest is an ongoing requirement for godly obedience to the will of God. Some of them would say it must be the seventh day (i.e., Saturday). This sometimes gets confused with the day of worship, so that Saturday, not Sunday, is a day of corporate worship rather than a day of rest as it was in the Old Testament. It seems that in the New Testament the first day of the week, the day of resurrection, became the day on which the earliest church came together for worship (see Acts 20:7; 1 Cor 16:2; Rev 1:10).[32] Saturday was the synagogue day. Others say that it is the principle of the one day out of seven that is the proper application of the fourth commandment in the Christian's life, so "Sabbath" applies to Sunday.

There is good reason to question this. According to Colossians 2:16-19, "Do not let anyone judge you by what you eat or drink, or with regard to a religious festival, a New Moon celebration or a Sabbath day. These are a shadow of the things that were to come; the reality, however, is found in Christ." Similarly, but with less specificity, Paul writes in Galatians 4:9-11, "How is it that you are turning back to those weak and miserable forces? Do you wish to be enslaved by

---

[31]See France, *The Gospel of Matthew*, 448-49n30 and the lit. cited there.

[32]See the full discussion in D. A. Carson, ed., *From Sabbath to Lord's Day: A Biblical, Historical, and Theological Investigation* (Grand Rapids, MI: Zondervan, 1982).

them all over again? You are observing special days and months and seasons and years! I fear for you, that somehow I have wasted my efforts on you."

Then we also have Romans 14:5-6, "One person considers one day more sacred than another; another considers every day alike. Each of them should be fully convinced in their own mind. Whoever regards one day as special does so to the Lord." This passage goes on to suggest that even if I myself do not believe the Sabbath commandment to be binding in a literal sense on us today, nevertheless I must show love to others by not causing them to violate their conscience and thereby sin against God (Rom 14:15, 19-23; 15:1-3). I need to be sensitive to those for whom violating the Sabbath would have the effect of damaging their life of faith (Rom 14:20–15:6).

It is important to recognize the significance of rest in the theology of the Bible and in living the Christian life. In my view, what Jesus invited us to in Matthew 11:28-30 is the "Sabbath" written on the heart, in the new covenant sense of the law written on the heart. This does not mean that physical rest is not important to us, but the concern that Jesus had in mind in Matthew 11–12 is about our experience of the Sabbath every day of our lives.

CONCLUSION

Along with his close attention to the Mosaic law itself, we need to keep in mind that Jesus came to establish the new covenant. He died to do it, but he also rose again to give us new covenant life (Jer 31:31-37; Lk 22:20). As we have frequently noted, one of the main features of the new covenant was to have the Mosaic law written on the hearts of the covenant people (Jer 31:33). The Sabbath was a key feature of the Mosaic law since it was the "sign" of the Mosaic covenant (Ex 31:12-17; cf. Ex 20:8-11). It marked them as the people God delivered from slavery and gave them rest on the seventh day of every week (Deut 5:12-15). Jesus was very concerned, therefore, that his followers have the Sabbath written on their hearts and fully experience it every day in their walk with him. This is not limited to one day a week! This is what Jesus offered all of us in Matthew 11:28-30.

It is the same law, but in accordance with the new covenant, Jesus was concerned about its application to the hearts of the people so that they lived it from the heart. His emphasis was on the transformation of people by the change of heart that the law itself calls for when properly understood. He taught it that way. When Jesus proclaimed the coming of the kingdom of heaven, this was the kind of kingdom community he had in mind.

With the inauguration of the church in Acts came some discontinuity as well as continuity with the law in the new covenant redemptive community. The makeup of the community of faith gradually shifted from Jews to a mix of Jews and Gentiles. This called for some transformation of the law to accommodate the needs and concerns of the new covenant community of faith, much like the transformation that came with the change from travel through the wilderness to the occupation of the Promised Land in ancient Israel. Such transformations in the law are not new in the New Testament.

The Gospels support the ongoing application of the law for followers of Jesus. He had disputes with the Jewish leaders of his day over the intent and proper reading and application of the law of Moses, but he never intended that anyone undermine its key importance for guidance in the lives of his followers. This brings us to the book of Acts.

Nine

THE MOSAIC LAW IN ACTS AND
THE EARLIEST CHURCH

WITH THE BOOK OF ACTS we enter into the earliest stages of the new covenant era in which we now live as followers of Jesus. Jesus himself lived and died under the Mosaic covenant and the law. He rose again to inaugurate the new covenant and give birth to the church, his kingdom of heaven on earth today. The introduction to chapter eight highlighted the fact that Jesus was thoroughly Jewish—and so was the earliest church from its beginning on the Day of Pentecost (Acts 2). This began to change with the Petrine vision in Acts 10.

Once the Gentiles began to turn to Christ, one of the most significant and recalcitrant problems became the question of what to do with them as it relates to the Mosaic law. The law was given by God to the Jews, not the Gentiles, but now Gentiles were joining them. The believing Jews saw themselves and the church as a movement within Judaism, not separate from it. This is clear from their ongoing gatherings and even sacrificial worship in the temple (see, e.g., Acts 2:46; 3:1; 21:26). It was, therefore, natural for those followers of Jesus who were zealous for the law to expect the Gentiles to fall in line with obligations to the law along with them (Acts 15:5). In this chapter we will look closely at the major chapters in Acts that relate to the question of the Mosaic law in the church, especially Acts 10–11, 15, 21. Before that, however, we need to consider some of the common misconceptions about the Old Testament law that have arisen and become popular since the first century.

COMMON MISCONCEPTIONS ABOUT THE OLD TESTAMENT LAW IN THE EARLY CHURCH AND TODAY

Three main theses help to carry and organize the discussion of the law in the New Testament, and its application to the life of the church and the believer: the law is good, the law is weak, and the law is a unified whole. The first of these has been a regular theme throughout the discussion of the law in part two of this book. The second thesis is just as essential. The law is weak. The apostle Paul developed this point in Romans 7–8, which we will discuss extensively in the next chapter. Ultimately, the law is weak not because it is not good but because of our own fleshly corruption: "We know that the law is spiritual; but I am unspiritual, sold as a slave to sin" (Rom 7:14). The problem is in us, not the law. No law can change a person's heart, not even God's law.

The first church council in Jerusalem in Acts 15 met to deal with the first great doctrinal controversy of the church age: the Gentiles and the law. We will look closely at this controversy and the council later in this chapter. For now it is important to anticipate the conclusion they reached and understand why. In brief, they concluded that Gentiles do *not* need to "be circumcised and required to keep the law of Moses" (Acts 15:5). Part of the rationale was, as Peter put it, why would we want to put "on the necks of Gentiles a yoke that neither we nor our ancestors have been able to bear?" (Acts 15:10). Peter saw the law as a good thing, like Paul did, and Paul was there at the council too. Peter also grasped the fact that, in their whole history, the Jews had not been able to live up to the standards of the law. God regularly chastised them for this, and this was a continuing reality in Peter's day under Roman rule. Again, since Genesis 3, the problem has always been human corruption, not God's law. The law is good, holy, and spiritual, even if it is also weak in the sense that it cannot change the human heart. That takes the work of the Holy Spirit in the human spirit (Rom 8).

The Jerusalem council took place long before the Roman church ecumenical councils that focused on doctrinal controversies such as the deity of Christ and the doctrine of the Trinity (see the first council of Nicaea in AD 325). By that time, the issue of Gentiles and the law was no longer center stage because, in the meantime, the church had become largely Gentile rather than Jewish—in fact, unfortunately and predominantly anti-Jewish. According to the early church father Tertullian (ca. AD 155–240), the earlier church leader, Marcion of Sinope (ca. AD 85–160), for example, was anti-Jewish and even promoted a limited canon that avoided any positive reference to the Mosaic law as he saw it.[1] The early church fathers rejected Marcion as a heretic, but the Marcionite "antinomian" ("against the law") tendency has remained alive and well in the church nonetheless.

This has contributed to the ongoing confusion over the application of the Mosaic law to the life of the church and the believer. It has brought controversy and even division especially in the Protestant churches since the sixteenth-century Reformation. Many misconceptions about the law have become rampant. It is common to find those in the church today who think of the Old Testament as old and worn out, and largely without relevance to the church, except perhaps the Psalms and Proverbs. Whether or not believers hold these misunderstandings depends to some degree on the particular kind of church they belong to and its theology. In any case, these attitudes are certainly common in many circles, so it is important to face them directly.

When you think about the Mosaic law, what comes to mind? How do you feel and think about the Old Testament and especially the Old

---

[1]See the brief summary and bibliography in Ronald V. Huggins, "Marcion," in *Eerdmans Dictionary of the Bible*, ed. David Noel Freedman (Grand Rapids, MI: Eerdmans, 2000), 855-56.

Testament law? As regularly stated in this volume, the first step toward a good understanding of the relationship between the Old Testament law, the church, and the Christian is to gain a realistic view of how the law was intended to work as it was originally given to ancient Israel. With that in view, what are these common misconceptions?

COMMON ANTINOMIAN MISCONCEPTIONS

The first and one of the most common antinomian misconceptions is that God never really expected that ancient Israel should or would be able to keep the law. This is often based on a certain kind of misunderstanding of passages like Romans 3:19-20, "Now we know that whatever the law says, it says to those who are under the law, so that every mouth may be silenced and the whole world held accountable to God. Therefore no one will be declared righteous in his sight by observing the law; rather, through the law we become conscious of sin." Many take this to mean that the law was then, and is still today, only a means God uses to show people that they are sinful and need salvation by grace through faith, not by the works of the law. So God purposely set up a standard that they could not meet.

The problem with this notion is that God says quite the opposite in Deuteronomy 30:11, 14, "What I am commanding you today is not too difficult for you or beyond your reach. . . . No, the word is very near you; it is in your mouth and in your heart so you may obey it." As far as God himself was concerned, the law was not beyond their reach or ability to obey.[2] Nevertheless, it is true that one of the uses of the law

---

[2]See the remarks, e.g., in Daniel I. Block, *Deuteronomy*, NIVAC (Grand Rapids, MI: Zondervan, 2012), 707-8; and Christopher J. H. Wright, *Deuteronomy*, NIBC (Peabody, MA: Hendrickson, 1996), 290. The attempt to transfer this to the times of the new covenant rather than the Mosaic covenant, in order to suggest that this keeping of the law is possible under the new covenant during the millennial kingdom but not in ancient Israel, is rather bizarre; Wayne G. Strickland, "The Inauguration of the Law of Christ with the Gospel of Christ: A Dispensational View," in *The Law, the Gospel, and the Modern Christian*, ed. Wayne Strickland (Grand Rapids, MI: Zondervan, 1993), 251. Among other things, it completely ignores the shift in grammar between Deut 30:1-10 and Deut 30:11-14.

was then as now to show people that they are sinners and need God's grace, but it is not the *only* use of the law.

This brings us to the second misconception, which is closely related to the first. It is sometimes thought that no one was ever successful at being "blameless in the law." The problem is that, once again, the text says quite the opposite. For example, according to Luke 1:5-6: "There was a priest named Zechariah, who belonged to the priestly division of Abijah; his wife Elizabeth was also a descendant of Aaron. Both of them were upright in the sight of God, observing all the Lord's commandments and regulations blamelessly."[3]

Paul himself also said of his own life as a Jew before he came to know Jesus, "If anyone else thinks he has reasons to put confidence in the flesh, I have more: circumcised on the eighth day, of the people of Israel, of the tribe of Benjamin, a Hebrew of Hebrews; in regard to the law, a Pharisee; as for zeal, persecuting the church; as for legalistic righteousness, faultless" (Phil 3:4-6; *faultless* here is the same Greek word as *blameless* in Lk 1:6). These passages are hard to square with this misconception. They tell us that this notion is in fact just that—a misconception. If God never intended that they be able to keep the law, then how can these passages be explained? The problem here is resolved when we come to the next misconception.

The third common misconception is that the Mosaic covenant in which the law is imbedded is all about works. There is no grace in the law. Again, at least in some circles, this is common thinking, and it is often based on misreading passages like John 1:17, "For the law was given through Moses; grace and truth came through Jesus Christ."[4] One problem with misreading this passage in this way is that if there is no *grace* in the law, then there is no *truth* in the law either. Few would argue that the Ten Commandments, for example, are falsehoods.

---

[3]See the remarks in Darrell L. Bock, *Luke 1:2–9:50*, BECNT (Grand Rapids, MI: Baker, 1994), 77-78; Joel B. Green, *The Gospel of Luke*, NICNT (Grand Rapids, MI: Eerdmans, 1997), 65.

[4]See the very helpful review of scholarship and the exegetical remarks on this verse in D. A. Carson, *The Gospel According to John* (Grand Rapids, MI: Eerdmans, 1991), 132-34.

Another problem is that the Old Testament law, in fact, was actually a manifestation and a means of God's grace to ancient Israel. For example, God's choice of Israel to be his special people amid all the peoples of the earth and his deliverance of them from slavery in Egypt (Ex 19:4-6) was not based on them being a great and righteous people (see, e.g., Deut 9:4-6). On the contrary, it was based on his previous commitments to the patriarchs (see, e.g., Ex 2:23-25; Deut 7:6-8).

Moreover, the law was key to their worship of God and walk with him in his tabernacle presence. It even had within it the means of seeking forgiveness from God as part of the grace that is in the law. This was what the sacrificial law was about. As Leviticus 4:20 puts it, for example, "In this way the priest will make atonement for them, and they will be forgiven" (see also, e.g., Lev 4:26, 31). So, by God's grace forgiveness was available in the law. This was what made it possible to be "blameless" in the law. A person could deal with their need for forgiveness or cleansing from God according to the regulations and provisions that were actually part of the law itself.

Even today one can get right with the law of their society, for example, by paying the fine stipulated for violating some part of it. Similarly, many of the stipulations in the law provide within them this or that means to rectify whatever problem had arisen. For example, according to Exodus 21:33-34, "If a man uncovers a pit or digs one and fails to cover it and an ox or a donkey falls into it, the owner of the pit must pay for the loss; he must pay its owner, and the dead animal will be his." Or consider Exodus 22:1, "If a man steals an ox or a sheep and slaughters it or sells it, he must pay back five head of cattle for the ox and four sheep for the sheep." The point of John 1:17 is that the grace and truth of God came through in the Mosaic law (this was the grace of the old covenant), but the grace and truth that came through Jesus Christ was a more "full expression of God's unfailing love and faithfulness."[5] This is the grace and truth of the new covenant.

---

[5]Grant R. Osborne, *John Verse by Verse* (Bellingham, WA: Lexham, 2018), 35.

A fourth misconception is that the law is only a set of rules and does not call for genuine heart devotion to the Lord. The problem with this notion is obvious, but it is often voiced in the church today anyway. The answer begins with Jesus' two great commandments (Mt 22:34-40; par. Mk 12:28-31; Lk 10:25-37). Where did Jesus draw them from? The answer, of course, is the Old Testament law—specifically, Deuteronomy 6:4-5, "Hear, O Israel: The LORD our God, the LORD is one. Love the LORD your God with all your heart and with all your soul and with all your strength," and Leviticus 19:18, "Do not seek revenge or bear a grudge against one of your people, but love your neighbor as yourself. I am the LORD." Note also the extension of the latter to the alien in the land later in the same chapter: "The alien living with you must be treated as one of your native-born. Love him as yourself, for you were aliens in Egypt. I am the LORD your God" (Lev 19:34). No wonder Luke has Jesus turning the question back on the questioner and then illustrating the second great commandment with the story of the Good Samaritan (Lk 10:30-37). The Lord has always wanted the same thing from everyone in all times and all places, and under any and all conditions.

There are also many other closely related passages in the Old Testament law and throughout the Old Testament. Consider, for example, Deuteronomy 11:22-23, "If you carefully observe all these commands I am giving you to follow—to love the LORD your God, to walk in all his ways and to hold fast to him—then the LORD will drive out all these nations before you, and you will dispossess nations larger and stronger than you" (see also Deut 10:15-17). There are other ways of saying the same thing too. Circumcision of the heart is one example. Compare Leviticus 26:41, "when their uncircumcised hearts are humbled," with Deuteronomy 30:6, "The LORD your God will circumcise your hearts and the hearts of your descendants, so that you may love him with all your heart and with all your soul, and live" (cf. also Jer 4:3-4). Circumcision of the heart was not a new concept when Paul used it in the New Testament (Rom 2:28-29).

The fifth and final misconception, which we can only touch on here, is that we are free from the law (e.g., Rom 7:6, Gal 5:13). This would be fine as it stands, but to say therefore that we have no good reason to pay any attention to it today is another matter. This faulty conclusion arises from two misunderstandings: (1) that it was not a good standard by which to live in the first place, and (2) that we are under no obligation to fulfill the standards of the law.

It is true that we are free from any condemnation under the law because we are not under the law but under grace if we are in Christ Jesus. As Romans 8:1 says, for example, "Therefore, there is now no condemnation for those who are in Christ Jesus." Nevertheless, to connect this to the notion that the law was not a good standard to live by in the first place is to deny what Paul wrote just a few verses earlier in Romans 7:12, 14: "So then, the law is holy, and the commandment is holy, righteous and good. . . . We know that the law is spiritual; but I am unspiritual, sold as a slave to sin." Actually, the law is good and holy, and even spiritual according to Paul. The real problem is with us, not the law (i.e., we are what is fleshly and unspiritual, not the law).

Furthermore, to say that we are under no obligation to fulfill the standards of the law is to miss the point of passages like Romans 8:4, which states "that the righteous requirements of the law might be fully met in us, who do not live according to the sinful nature but according to the Spirit." More can be seen in that context as well. For example, "The sinful mind is hostile to God. It does not submit to God's law, nor can it do so" (Rom 8:7; cf. also Rom 13:8-10; Gal 5:13-15, 22-26). The point is that the person who walks according to the person and power of the Holy Spirit actually can follow the law in a written-on-the-heart, new covenant way. The whole point is that, even though we are not under the law, we fulfill it when we live by the power of the Spirit. The same Spirit, who inspired the writing of the Old Testament law in the first place, works within us and among us to bring our hearts and therefore our lives into conformity to the law he inspired.

COMMON LEGALISTIC MISCONCEPTIONS OF THE
LAW AND THE THREE USES OF THE LAW

Unfortunately, other kinds of misuses and misunderstandings of the law that existed among the Jewish teachers of the law in Jesus' day have continued into the church. The antinomian tendencies discussed above have an opposite—"legalism." In this tendency, people seek to establish themselves as righteous by the works they do. A colleague of mine once said, "We are all innate legalists." We like to think that we measure up to the standard, and that if we do, we can compare ourselves positively with other people who do not, as we see it. Legalists do not see themselves needing grace from God or anyone else. This is one of the reasons legalistic Jewish leaders had such a hard time with Jesus. Even when they came to be baptized by John the Baptist, they did so to show how righteous they were. John reacted strongly:

> But when he saw many of the Pharisees and Sadducees coming to where he was baptizing, he said to them: "You brood of vipers! Who warned you to flee from the coming wrath? Produce fruit in keeping with repentance. And do not think you can say to yourselves, 'We have Abraham as our father.' I tell you that out of these stones God can raise up children for Abraham. The ax is already at the root of the trees, and every tree that does not produce good fruit will be cut down and thrown into the fire." (Mt 3:7-10)

In the earliest church, since it was thoroughly Jewish, legalism would take on Jewish forms. These were the "Judaizers," who wanted not only the Jews but also the Gentiles in the church to take on the law (Acts 15). They thought of the law as having power to motivate godly living. The law was a good guide for those who lived by faith in Jesus Christ by the power of the Holy Spirit, but it never had the power to change a human heart.

Today there are "gentilized" forms of legalism in the church, in which people set up a certain set of cultural or political standards, live up to them, and therefore consider themselves to be righteous. The church that supported the group of students that the Lord used to bring me to faith in Jesus were very dear believers who loved me very well. They were also very conservative culturally. Those were the days of the Vietnam War, hippies, and the Jesus Movement. I was part of that. Although I did not look like a hippie, I had some of the same views and attitudes, and could not accept—and sometimes could not even understand—why these good people took some issues so seriously. In part, they were trying to influence me and others like me away from the bad tendencies in the hippie world, such as drugs and free sex. This was good. Yet, it still had the effect of setting up a standard to which one could adhere and thereby feel like a righteous person. They would also measure others by it to see if they were "righteous" or "mature." I recall them thinking that when I did not conform to the standard, I must have been "backsliding."

For example, those were also the days when bell-bottom pants were becoming popular around campus. The good people of the church thought these pants were horrible because, in their view, boys wearing them were dressing like girls (see Deut 22:4). This shocked me. Such clothing was not suggesting that at all. There are still certain churches like this today. I hasten to add that the same kind of self-righteous logic is alive and well on the other end of our culture too—the liberal end, the political left.

Paul highlights Jewish legalism as a serious problem even in the teaching and preaching of the first-century church. He wrote to Timothy, the pastor and bishop of the church in Asia Minor, that some "want to be teachers of the law, but they do not know what they are talking about or what they so confidently affirm" (1 Tim 1:7). It must be understood "that the law is good *if one uses it properly*. We also know that law is made not for the righteous but for lawbreakers and rebels, the ungodly and sinful, the unholy and irreligious" (1 Tim 1:8-9). No one should seek their own righteousness by means of the law. Early in the twentieth century, one scholar put this very well and concisely: "Law with its penalties is needed to control sinners, but when once the true love of God is created in a man's heart, there is no longer need to appeal to its sanctions; love fulfills it. . . . Law is put on a firmer basis, not as a penalizing force, but as the guidance of a loving God."[6]

As Paul put it earlier in 1 Timothy 1:5, "The goal of this command is love, which comes from a pure heart and a good conscience and a sincere faith." He was calling for a better way of teaching—better than the way things were being done by too many of the teachers in the church at Ephesus. The purpose of the law was to promote love, which corresponds to the two great commandments of Jesus.

This brings us to the three legitimate uses of the law according to the Scriptures. The first use of the law focuses on its effectiveness for showing that God is holy and righteous, but we as people are sinners, corrupt and in need of God's grace. This is a good thing, not a bad thing! It is one of the ways the law is still "good" (see, e.g., Rom 3:19-20; 7:7). The Holy Spirit, in fact, uses the law to drive people to repentance and faith in Christ.

The second use of the law corresponds to God's original intention to regulate his covenant relationship with Israel as a nation. It can have some of the same kind of effect in the church and in the world today. People can fear the disfavor that comes with violating basic standards of decency and justice in the world and in the church. Romans 13:1-7 highlights this even for the civil authorities who have the power of law to implement judicial punishments. This was one of the purposes of the law in the Old Testament too. Ancient Israel was a nation that needed governmental regulation from its theocratic king, the Lord. This brings us to the third use of the law in the church.

The third use of the law takes it to be a useful scriptural guide for the Christian life. As noted above, the purpose of teaching and preaching the Word of God in the church, including the Old Testament

---

[6]Walter Lock, *The Pastoral Epistles*, ICC (Edinburgh: T&T Clark, 1924), 11. See also the helpful discussion of these verses in Linda Belleville, Jon C. Laansma, J Ramsey Michaels, and Philip W. Comfort, *1 and 2 Timothy, Titus, Hebrews*, CBCS 17 (Carol Stream, IL: Tyndale, 2009).

law, "is love, which comes from a pure heart and a good conscience and a sincere faith" (1 Tim 1:5). This corresponds to Jesus' two great commandments (Mt 22:34-40) as well as Paul's explanations in Romans 13:8-10 and Galatians 5:13-14, 22-23 (see esp. Gal 5:23; cf. also James 2:8). This is the positive point in 1 Timothy 1:3-11.

The Old Testament law was then and is still today good. Paul emphasized this in Romans 7:12-14 in the midst of his focus on the weakness of the law as compared to the power of the Holy Spirit in the life of the believer. In fact, it is not only good but it is also *useful* for the Christian: "All Scripture is God-breathed and is useful for teaching, rebuking, correcting and training in righteousness, so that the man of God may be thoroughly equipped for every good work" (2 Tim 3:16-17). It applies to the life of the Christian today in a new covenant, written-on-the-heart sense so that we live it from a transformed heart by the power of the Sprit and therefore manifest it in the way we live (Jer 31:31-33; Rom 8:4, 6; 2 Cor 3:3, 6-8).

PETER'S VISION IN ACTS 10

The Acts 10 Petrine vision of a sheet coming down from heaven shows that, as far as God was concerned, the Jewish church of the day must make room for Gentiles in the church. This was a surprise to Peter and to the church as a whole. Perhaps it should not have come as such a complete surprise in light of the conversion of the Ethiopian eunuch in Acts 8:26-40, but it did. The Ethiopian was probably a God-fearing Gentile, or perhaps, but less likely, a convert to Judaism.[7] In any case, the purpose of this vision was to prepare Peter for preaching the gospel to the Gentile centurion Cornelius, who would receive the Lord and the gift of the Holy Spirit a few days later. Again, this was a complete surprise to all the Jews there (Acts 10:44-48). To complicate matters even further, Peter had to explain all this to leaders back in Jerusalem (Acts 11).

---

[7]F. F. Bruce, *Commentary on the Book of Acts*, NICNT (Grand Rapids, MI: Eerdmans, 1954), 186-87.

As the story goes, Peter was hungry. While they were preparing food for him, he "fell into a trance" (Acts 10:10). In this state, "he saw heaven opened and something like a large sheet being let down to earth by its four corners. It contained all kinds of four-footed animals, as well as reptiles and birds. Then a voice told him, 'Get up, Peter. Kill and eat'" (Acts 10:11-13). Peter responded, "Surely not, Lord! I have never eaten anything impure or unclean" (Acts 10:14). His response is similar to that of Ezekiel the prophet after the Lord instructed him to eat defiled, unclean food: "Not so, Sovereign LORD! I have never defiled myself. From my youth until now I have never eaten anything found dead or torn by wild animals. No impure meat has ever entered my mouth" (Ezek 4:14). The Lord responded to Peter, "Do not call anything impure that God has made clean" (Acts 10:15). This happened three times. Peter awoke and was puzzled by the vision.

Peter was in Joppa. In the meantime, in Caesarea (about 25 miles north of Joppa), a God-fearing Roman centurion named Cornelius had seen a vision of an angel who told him to send messengers to Peter in Joppa to bring him back to Caesarea. These messengers arrived right after Peter had seen the vision of the sheet coming down out of heaven, and while he was still thinking about it. The Holy Spirit told him to go with them (Acts 10:1-7, 19-23).

The next day he left with the messengers. Some believers from Joppa went with them and they arrived the following day. In the meantime, Cornelius had gathered his family and friends for the occasion. They were waiting for Peter to arrive. Peter began with saying, "You are well aware that it is against our law for a Jew to associate with or visit a Gentile. But God has shown me that I should not call anyone impure or unclean" (Acts 10:28), referring to the vision of the sheet from heaven. Cornelius explained his own vision, so Peter promptly preached the gospel to him (Acts 10:30-43).

Even before they knew what was happening, "While Peter was still speaking these words, the Holy Spirit came on all who heard the message. The circumcised believers who had come with Peter were astonished that the gift of the Holy Spirit had been poured out even on Gentiles. For they heard them speaking in tongues and praising God" (Acts 10:44-46). Peter immediately concluded, "Surely no one can stand in the way of their being baptized with water. They have received the Holy Spirit just as we have" (Acts 10:47). Peter, therefore, gave orders to baptize them. Afterward, they asked Peter to stay with them a few days (Acts 10:48). This, of course, implies that he ate with them—and ate what they would normally eat as Gentiles. He did not deny this when he went back to Jerusalem and the Jewish believers accused him: "You went into the house of uncircumcised men and ate with them" (Acts 11:3).[8] Jewish Messianic believers today sometimes try to avoid this conclusion, arguing that this is about people, not food, citing Acts 10:28, "God has shown me that I should not call anyone impure or unclean."[9] Yes, of course, it is about people, but the Jewish food laws were one of the main ways to keep the Jews separate from the Gentiles. Moreover, this interpretation ignores the point of including Acts 10:48 with Acts 11:3 in the account.

For a full discussion of the clean and unclean animal regulations in Leviticus 11 and Deuteronomy 14, see chapter seven. In sum, God intended these regulations to effect Israel in two major ways. First, they worked the prohibition against eating blood into the warp and woof of their daily existence in Israel (see, e.g., Gen 9:4-5; Lev 3:17; 17:11). The rationale was that they must not even eat animals that eat blood. For people to eat blood would be for them to become predatory animals that do not drain the blood from animals before eating them. God did not design us for that. The fall into corruption in Genesis 3, however, broke all the boundaries to the point where violence of all kinds took over and moved the world far away from God's design. This was deeply painful to him: "his heart was deeply troubled"

---

[8]See the comments in Bruce, Acts, 218-19, 233-34, and the more extended explanation in Bock, Acts, 388-91.

[9]See, e.g., David H. Stern, Jewish New Testament Commentary, 5th ed. (Clarkesville, MD: Jewish New Testament Publications, 1996), 257-59.

(lit. "he was in pain in his heart"; Gen 6:5-7). The clean and unclean regulations moved Israel one step further away from the corruption that resulted from the fall into sin, as compared to all the other cultures and nations around them. It fulfilled God's call to "be holy, because I am holy" (Lev 11:45).

Second, the book of Leviticus later refers to Israel's separation from the corrupting influence of the Gentile foreign people around them. These verses come as the conclusion to the regulations against Molech worship, mediums and spiritists, and prohibited sexual relationships rampant among the surrounding peoples. With these in mind, the Lord said,

> You must not live according to the customs of the nations I am going to drive out before you. Because they did all these things, I abhorred them. . . . You must therefore *make a distinction between clean and unclean animals* and between unclean and clean birds. Do not defile yourselves by any animal or bird or anything that moves along the ground—*those that I have set apart as unclean for you.* You are to *be holy to me because I, the* LORD, *am holy*, and I have set you apart from the nations to be my own. (Lev 20:23, 25-26)

In this way, the Lord arranged their diet so that they would stay separate from the corrupting influences of the non-Israelite people around them, who were not committed to the same diet limitations. This would hinder any kind of social or religious associations with them. If they could not eat with other people, they could not carry on relationships with them to any significant degree. This was the point of bringing the clean and unclean animal regulations into the conclusion to Leviticus 20.

For the same reason, these regulations could not continue in the mixed Jewish and Gentile church community envisioned in Acts 10 and following. To maintain them would have the effect of creating two churches, one Jew and one Gentile. This was already evident to Peter in Acts 10-11, but his fuller understanding and the details of how to manage it had to be worked out in the following chapters. Note also the conflict over this between Peter and Paul in Galatians 2:11-18. Paul "blew up" right in Peter's face over this very matter! Of course, Paul was the Jewish missionary to the Gentiles and Peter to the Jews (Gal 2:6-10), so he was more attuned to the overall seriousness of this matter (see, e.g., his comments on the breaking down of the wall between Jews and Gentiles in Eph 2:11-22).

This reality, therefore, was alive and well in the New Testament division between Jews and Gentiles. Peter's vision and its aftermath shows that, as far as God was concerned, they could not maintain these Jewish diet restrictions in the church. In order to fulfill God's call to join Jews and Gentiles together in one faith in Jesus Christ, they had to set these regulations aside. There are a couple of additional points that must be kept in mind.

First, there is no less interest in holiness and purity in the church than in ancient Israel. This concern, however, had to find expression in a different way if the church was to become a unified body of Jews and Gentiles together in Christ. Second, recall that even within the law there were adjustments for new circumstances. We have already given one particular example. Leviticus 17 required that while they were traveling through the wilderness with their tents in close proximity to the tabernacle, they must bring all the animals they ate to the tabernacle to present them there as peace offering sacrifices. When Israel conquered and occupied the Promised Land, however, they would not be able to bring the animal to the sanctuary every time they wanted to eat meat. Deuteronomy 12 anticipates this shift with a regulation for profane slaughter once they occupied the Promised Land. They could slaughter animals for meat anywhere in the land if they drained the blood from the animal and poured it out on the ground (see the full discussion in chap. 3 above).

As noted previously, the shift from the Mosaic covenant to the new covenant caused an even greater shift in God's kingdom program. The inclusion of the Gentiles was part of the plan since God's original commission to Abraham: "all peoples on earth will be blessed through you" (Gen 12:3), and this is fulfilled in the church today in a very special way. The church, however, is not a nation but consists of communities spread out amid all the nations of the earth made up of Jews and Gentiles (Acts 1:8). God has called us all to function together as one unified community of faith under all conditions and in all circumstances.

Coming back now to Acts 10–11, when Peter returned to the church in Jerusalem, he reported the whole story about the vision of the sheet, the trip to Joppa, their acceptance of the gospel, the Holy Spirit coming on them, and their baptism (Acts 11:4-16). He concluded his report with this: "So if God gave them the same gift he gave us who believed in the Lord Jesus Christ, who was I to think that I could stand in God's way?" (Acts 11:17). The account ends with this: "When they heard this, they had no further objections and praised God, saying, 'So then, even to Gentiles God has granted repentance that leads to life'" (Acts 11:18). They accepted this surprising advance of the gospel to the Gentiles, and the story moves on to the ministry in Antioch, where they went to the Jews first, while the gospel continued to spread to the Gentiles as well. Acts 10–11, therefore, recounts the beginning of the Gentile inclusion in the church that continued to grow and eventually dominated the church.

Someone may ask, Why did they not go the other way and have the Gentiles adopt the Jewish (Old Testament) food regulations? The Pharisees who had come to faith in Christ were arguing for this very thing at the first church council. This brings us to a fuller discussion of Acts 15 and the decisions made at the Jerusalem council.

THE JERUSALEM COUNCIL IN ACTS 15

The church council in Jerusalem in Acts 15 follows naturally from Peter's vision and his report to the church in Jerusalem in Acts 10–11. The Jewish church just did not know what to do with the Gentile believers. They had to bring together all the major "players" to consult over this matter. There was naturally a very strong push from some of the Jewish Messianic believers (especially Pharisees who had come to faith in Christ) to remain zealous for the law by requiring that "the Gentiles must be circumcised and required to keep the law of Moses" (Acts 15:5). We will find later in Acts 21 that there was no problem with their zeal for the law as Jews, but by that time, the decision had already been made (in Acts 15) that they could not impose this on Gentile believers. They had come to accept that decision as long as the Gentiles believers did not live in such a way as to become an obstacle to acceptance of the gospel among the Jews (see Acts 21:25 with the letter in Acts 15:19-32).

Peter himself recalled the story of the Acts 10–11 incident and its implication for the issue at hand. No, the Gentile believers had come to Christ without keeping the law and they must be allowed to live their Christian life as Gentiles. They must not "test God by putting on the necks of Gentiles a yoke that neither we nor our ancestors have been able to bear" (Acts 15:10). At that point, Paul and Barnabas gave their report of what God had been doing in drawing the Gentiles to faith in Christ.

James, the half-brother of Jesus, picked up the discussion at this point. After all, they were in Jerusalem and he was the leader of the largely Jewish church there. James began by making reference to Peter's report of the event in Acts 10–11. They all knew about this, and they had also just heard the account of God's awe-inspiring work among the Gentiles from Paul and Barnabas. So he drew attention to the Old Testament anticipation of the Gentiles coming to the Lord from Amos 9:11-12 (recall Gen 12:3). He drew the profound conclusion that they must not put the Gentiles under the law. This would impose unnecessary difficulties on them (Acts 15:19). This settled the matter for the church that day.

There was, however, another related concern—namely, the need to continue reaching the Jews with the gospel. The law of Moses was regularly recited and preached in the synagogues every week. They would be regularly hearing the kinds of regulations that Peter had been concerned about during his vision of the sheet from heaven. To

James this did not mean the Gentiles needed to live according to the clean and unclean animal regulations. Instead, he drew out certain violations of the law that would be especially offensive to the Jews. The Gentiles should stay away from these things to avoid offending the Jews and driving them away from Christ. So James sent a letter to the Gentile believers in the churches urging them "to abstain from food polluted by idols, from sexual immorality, from the meat of strangled animals and from blood" (Acts 15:20; cf. Acts 15:29). As they put it in the letter, "It seemed good to the Holy Spirit and to us not to burden you with anything beyond the following requirements" (Acts 15:28). The Gentile believers were elated about the decision of the council and raised no objections to the special requirements listed in the letter (Acts 15:30-32).

What was so special about these four particular prohibitions? Some say they would be especially important in mixed company and would go a long way toward preventing strained relationships between Jewish and Gentile believers. A Jew who remained convinced in their conscience of the diet regulations, for example, would be the weaker brother that they should be careful not to offend or cause to sin by violating their conscience (cf. Rom 14).[10]

This concern for relationships between Jews and Gentiles in the church was certainly part of the concern. There may, however, be more to it than that. Some have argued that these requirements reflect the early stages in the growth of what the rabbis later referred to as the "Noahide laws."[11] It seems that this tradition was not fully developed this early, which is why only parts of it are included here. The seven Noahide laws found in later rabbinic literature include the following: prohibition of idolatry, blasphemy, bloodshed by murder, sexual sins (especially adultery), theft, eating from a living animal

---

[10]See the remarks in Bruce, *Acts*, 311-12, and the more extensive discussion in Bock, *Acts*, 505-8.
[11]See, e.g., Stern, *Jewish New Testament Commentary*, 278 and the rabbinic sources cited there. David G. Peterson considers this interpretation in his treatment of Acts 15:20 in *The Acts of the Apostles*, PNTC (Grand Rapids, MI: Eerdmans, 2009), but he rejects it outright.

with the blood still in the meat, and an injunction to establish a legal system for social laws (see the Babylonian Talmud tractate *Sanhedrin* 56-60). The four requirements in Acts 15:20, 29 would be included in these. Some of them are found in the commands to Noah after the flood in Genesis 9:1-7. For this reason they are referred to as the "Noahide laws," but Leviticus 17–18 also contributes to the set.

According to the Jews, the Mosaic law was given to them, not the Gentiles. However, non-Jews who observed the Noahide laws were considered "sons of the covenant of Noah." They would consider Gentiles who observed them to be resident strangers or semi-converts. Maimonides, the medieval Jewish sage (ca. AD 1000), said that the "righteous of the [Gentile] nations" who had a share in the world to come without being a Jew was the Gentile who kept these laws.

The covenant kingdom of the Old Testament included Gentiles who attached themselves to Israel and their covenant(s), as for instance the mixed multitude that left Egypt with them (e.g., Ex 12:38; Num 9:14; 11:4; Josh 8:35). The covenant kingdom in the New Testament is a continuation of this kingdom with Jewish roots (see Rom 9:4-5) but is now largely made up of Gentiles (Rom 11:7-32) with only a Jewish remnant (Rom 11:1-6). We are still looking forward to the salvation of "all Israel" (Rom 11:26) according to their "irrevocable" gifts and calling from God (Rom 11:29). In the meantime, the largely Gentile church is to make sure they do not hinder or abandon the preaching of the gospel to the Jews.

Although we cannot be certain about this understanding of the letter sent in Acts 15:19-21, 23-31 because of the problem of dating the sources and the traditions that underlie them, it would make sense to be concerned that the Gentile believers in Jesus not violate these regulations. James and the others at the council would be concerned that they live as decent Gentiles in the presence of the Jews. They would not want the Jews to be able to accuse the Gentile believers of not even being *decent* Gentiles. These four requirements in the letter to the churches would not have settled issues of kosher food for Jews zealous for the law, but it could very well make the Gentile witness to the Jews more palatable and effective.

PAUL AND TEMPLE SACRIFICE IN ACTS 21

Acts 15 is about the Gentiles who came to faith in Christ and their following Christ in a Gentile way. Acts 21 concerns Jews who accepted Jesus as their Messiah and their walking with Christ in a Jewish way. The backstory begins with Acts 18:18, "Paul stayed on in Corinth for some time. Then he left the brothers and sisters and sailed for Syria, accompanied by Priscilla and Aquila. Before he sailed, he had his *hair cut off at Cenchreae because of a vow* he had taken." Cutting the hair corresponds to the Nazirite vow as set forth in Numbers 6, and this is almost certainly the kind of vow Paul made.[12] The Mishnah and other later rabbinic teachings would not allow such a vow to be made outside of Jerusalem.[13] No such limitation appears in Numbers 6 or anywhere else in the Old Testament. It is doubtful, therefore, that Paul would have considered it binding. Jesus regularly pushed back against regulations the rabbis added to the law. It is important to note, however, that this vow was apparently meaningful and helpful to him in his walk with Jesus as a Jew.

The Nazirite vow was voluntary. Its length was at the discretion of the one who engaged in it. During the period of the vow the Nazirite must abstain from drinking or eating anything that came from the grapevine and avoid any contact with a dead corpse, lest they contract severe uncleanness. If they contracted such uncleanness by chance, it would void the vow and they would have to start it all over again, beginning with the seven-day period of uncleanness for corpse contamination and the reshaving of their head. They would also need to bring sin, burnt, and guilt offerings to

---

[12]See the explanation in Bock, *Acts*, 585-86.
[13]Stern, *Jewish New Testament Commentary*, 290-91.

make atonement for their violation of the Nazirite vow (Num 6:1-12; cf. Num 19:14-16).

The regulations required that the person allow his hair to grow during the whole period of the vow. He would then shave it off as part of the ritual procedures for successfully fulfilling the vow in the sanctuary of the Lord (Num 6:13-21). His hair that grew during the period of Nazirite dedication to the Lord was holy to the Lord. The person would, therefore, place it in the fire on the burnt offering altar as part of his sacrifice to the Lord. Other sacrificial procedures for fulfilling the vow included a sin offering, a burnt offering, and a peace offering, including all the grain and drink offerings that would go with them. We do not know when Paul fulfilled the ritual procedures for completing the Nazirite vow in Acts 18:18. Perhaps it was the next time he was in Jerusalem (see Acts 18:22).

Eventually, when Paul came back to Jerusalem in Acts 21, he went directly to the Jewish church there—specifically, to James and the elders. He made his report to them of his ministry to the Gentiles. "When they heard this, they praised God" (Acts 21:20), but they immediately raised a major concern. All the Jews who had come to Jesus as the Messiah were "zealous for the law," and they had heard that he was telling the Jewish believers in Jesus who lived in dispersion among the Gentiles "to turn away from Moses, telling them not to circumcise their children or live according to our customs" (Acts 21:21). This was going to be a serious problem between Paul and the church in Jerusalem. James's solution was for him to show that he was not preventing the Jews in dispersion from following the Mosaic law. He could do this by taking four others among them who were under a "vow" (Acts 21:23; the same word as in Acts 18:18) and do the required procedures in the temple, including the shaving of their heads. He should even pay all their expenses (Acts 21:24). The next day he did this very thing, preparing for the seven days of their purification, after which he would also pay for the sacrifices that he and all four of his companions needed to bring (Acts 21:26-27).

What are the seven days of purification about? There is confusion here and scholars have made various proposals.[14] Perhaps the best explanation is that the four others under Nazarite vows had become defiled, so they needed to undergo the required seven-day purification period and, after that, bring offerings for atonement.[15] It is less certain how Paul had become defiled that he needed to perform purification rites for himself as well (Acts 21:26; cf. Acts 24:17-18). Some have thought it had to do with defilements from his ministry among the Gentiles, or perhaps he was engaged in a Nazirite vow himself and was defiled in the same way as the other four. The text does not give us this detail.

In this very context, the leaders of the Jewish church made it clear that they had no problem with the Gentiles living their Christian faith in a Gentile way. They recalled the letter they had sent to the churches in Acts 15 (see Acts 21:25). What they were concerned to affirm was that Jews could live their life as believers in Jesus in a Jewish way. Neither Paul nor anyone else should compromise this. They wanted to make sure Paul and everyone else knew that.

In any case, it is clear that Paul did not feel any compulsion against participating in the temple procedures, even making burnt, sin, and guilt offerings for atonement. Some have thought that perhaps what he did was a mistake or even a contradiction to his faith in Christ. This misunderstands the relationship between the sacrifice of Christ and the Old Testament sacrifices (see discussion of Heb 9–10 in chap. 7 above). The Old Testament sacrifices brought atonement, forgiveness, and cleansing on the level of the earthly tabernacle. They cleansed the flesh (Heb 9:13) and had to be offered repeatedly (Heb 9:25; 10:3). The sacrifice of Christ made atonement to cleanse our conscience and did so permanently, once and for all (Heb 9:2–10:10).

The sacrifice of Christ was on a completely different level than the Old Testament sacrifices. Continuing in the temple for Paul and the

---

[14]See the helpful summary in Bock, *Acts*, 647-49.
[15]Bruce, *Acts*, 430-31. Contra Bruce, these would be the offerings of Num 6:11-12, not Num 6:14.

earliest Christian church was just a natural part of being Jewish. To think that Paul made a mistake here is to come at the church backward. It was Jewish first. It did not become a mix of Jews and Gentiles until later. Before that the Jewish believers in Jesus as the Messiah thought of themselves as a movement within Judaism, not a reaction against it or separation from it.

Paul sheds important light on Acts 21 and his ministry as a whole in 1 Corinthians 9:19-23:

> Though I am free and belong to no one, I have made myself a slave to everyone, to win as many as possible. To the Jews I became like a Jew, to win the Jews. To those under the law I became like one under the law (though I myself am not under the law), so as to win those under the law. To those not having the law I became like one not having the law (though I am not free from God's law but am under Christ's law), so as to win those not having the law.

> To the weak I became weak, to win the weak. I have become all things to all people so that by all possible means I might save some. I do all this for the sake of the gospel, that I may share in its blessings.

Personally, on the one hand, he had no problem with living as a Jew (1 Cor 9:20). After all, he was a Jew—and a well-trained one at that (Acts 22:2-3; Phil 3:4-6). He found it spiritually fulfilling to live his Christian faith as a Jew, even to the point of engaging in Nazirite vows, doing temple sacrifice, and so on.

On the other hand, he was not bound to living as a Jew. He could give it up in a flash. God had called him to preach the gospel not only to the Jews but also and especially to Gentiles. He was the apostle to the Gentiles (Gal 2:6-10), so he met the Gentiles on their own ground, except that he was very much bound to "Christ's law" (1 Cor 9:21). He would not do anything to compromise his commitment to the teachings of Christ. They were God's law for the church and the believer—and actually for everyone else too, whether they know it or not, and whether they like it or not. For Paul this was not just a Jewish versus Gentile issue either. It stretched across the issues of life economically, socially, ethnically, politically, and in every other way (1 Cor 9:22-23).

If someone challenged Paul on this, suggesting, for example, that he was being duplicitous and speaking out of both sides of his mouth—Jewish one time and Gentile the other—his response would have been something like: "I just do not give a rip!" I simply do not care what you or anyone else says about this. I will not allow any such boundaries between people groups stop me from preaching the gospel openly and freely to any and all of them. That is God's call on my life.

Finally, what is "Christ's law," sometimes rendered "the law of Christ" (1 Cor 9:21)? In the discussion of priorities within the law we gave special attention to Jesus' two great commandments (Mt 22:34-40 and par.; see chap. 8 above). The argument there was that these two commandments make up the core substance of what Paul refers to as "the law of Christ" in his letters to the churches (see, e.g., 1 Cor 9:21; Gal 6:2; and similarly Jas 2:8). The fact that "all the Law and the Prophets hang on these two commandments" suggests that the law of Christ is the way Jesus mediated the Old Testament law to us for our lives as his followers.

The law of Christ does not leave the Old Testament law behind. In new covenant terms, God writes the law on the heart of the follower of Jesus (Jer 31:33) by the Spirit of God (Ezek 36:26-27; cf. Lk 22:20 with 2 Cor 3:2-6). Jesus' pronouncement that he did not come to abolish the law but uphold it (Mt 5:17-19) along with the "golden rule" (Mt 7:12) provide a frame for all that stands between: "In everything do to others as you would have them do to you; for this is the Law and the Prophets" (Mt 7:12 NRSV). The Sermon on the Mount provides the core of the law of Christ along with the two great commandments and his other teachings.

CONCLUSION

Scholars often refer to the history of the church in the book of Acts as a transitional period from the time of the old, Mosaic covenant to the new covenant in Christ. Jesus the Christ died and rose again to establish the new covenant and initiate the age of the church. He ascended to the Father in Acts 1, leaving us his commission, "You will receive power when the Holy Spirit comes on you; and you will be my witnesses in Jerusalem, and in all Judea and Samaria, and to the ends of the earth" (Acts 1:8). At that time the Jewish apostles of Jesus and leaders of the church had no idea of all that would be involved in fulfilling this commission. They remained fixed on their question: "Lord, are you at this time going to restore the kingdom to Israel?" (Acts 1:6). Jesus refused to give an answer (Acts 1:7).

This all began to change in Acts 10 with Peter's vision of a sheet coming down out of heaven and the conversion of the Gentile Cornelius and his household to Jesus Christ. This was a hard transition for them to make. It was fraught with conflict and misunderstanding that had to be worked through in order to fulfill their commission. Luke (the writer of Acts) recounts some of the details of the story for us, and some of it appears in other places later in the New Testament.

The book of Acts, however, ended before the destruction of the temple in Jerusalem in AD 70, which created another great and painful transition for the Jewish people and the earliest church. From that point in history, Judaism went one way, and the mixed Gentile and Jewish church went another. Along the way, before and after 70, the church became more and more Gentile rather than Jewish, and the Jewish connection began to weaken. This was a divine "mystery" in God's plan that no one had anticipated (Eph 3:1-13). God hardened the Jews so that the Gentiles could be grafted into the kingdom of God in a major way by coming to faith in Jesus, the Jewish Messiah (Rom 11:11-24). This was part of the divine plan already revealed in the commission to Abram (Gen 12:3), but no one understood how it would happen. It was a mystery.

However, God would never forget the Jews. After all, they and their history supplied the nourishing root of the kingdom of God (Rom 9:1-5), and they are still the natural branches (Rom 11:17-24). Since they are the natural branches, there will come a time when God will graft them back into the kingdom by bringing them to faith in their Messiah (Rom 11:25-29). This is not referring to a remnant of the Jews, which already existed in the early church (Rom 11:1-6) and still exists today. This remnant consists of the true Jews that Paul referred to in Romans 9:6-9. In the meantime, God is working still another mystery: "I do not want you to be ignorant of this *mystery*, brothers and sisters, so that you may not be conceited: Israel has experienced a hardening in part *until* the full number of the Gentiles has come in, and in this way all Israel will be saved" (Rom 11:25-26). The word *until* here is very important.[16] The passage goes on to emphasize God's ongoing commitment to his covenant promises to the Jews: "As far as the gospel is concerned, they are enemies for your sake; but as far as election is concerned, they are loved on account of the patriarchs, for God's gifts and his call are *irrevocable*" (Rom 11:28-29). Our God is faithful to his covenant commitments. He is not fickle. It is still a mystery to us how God is going to work this part of his ongoing plan, but we can depend on it.[17]

In the meantime, the wall of partition has been broken down between Jews and Gentiles in the church (Eph 2). We must be sure not to build up that wall again. We are all one in Christ. Maintaining this unity does not require that Jews give up being Jews or that Gentiles give up being Gentiles. Jews who believe in Jesus can continue to identify as Jews in how they live their faith but not in ways or in community of faith contexts that cause them to separate from their Gentile brothers and sisters in Christ (Gal 2).

Many messianic Jewish believers today follow their Jewish customs with their unsaved families and in their worship of Yeshua, the

---

[16]I thank Darrell Bock for this observation about *until*.

[17]See the discussion of this important matter, for example, in the essays in Darrell L. Bock and Mitch Glaser, eds., *Israel, the Church, and the Middle East: A Biblical Response to the Current Conflict* (Grand Rapids, MI: Kregel, 2018); Gerald R. McDermott, *Israel Matters: Why Christians Must Think Differently about the People and the Land* (Grand Rapids, MI: Brazos, 2017); and the lit. cited in these works.

Messiah. It ties their own personal and family background, their faith, and their witness together in deeply meaningful ways. Others do not follow this pattern. They simply function as good believers in the church and world at large. This is a matter of freedom in Christ (Col 2:16-17).

Gentiles have never been under the Mosaic law, unless they were foreigners who lived among the Jews and attached themselves to the Jewish nation in Old Testament days. In fact, some Jews today consider it offensive when Gentiles try to act like Jews. Gentiles are to live their faith in Jesus as faithful Gentiles. No one should get in the way of that either (Acts 15).

Ten

THE GOODNESS AND THE WEAKNESS OF THE LAW

THE MAIN ARGUMENT OF THIS BOOK begins with the need to understand the Old Testament law on its own terms. The first step toward understanding the relationship between the Old Testament law, the church, and the life of the believer is to gain a realistic view of how the Mosaic covenant, in which the law is embedded, fits into the covenantal framework within the Bible and its relationship to the other covenants. This provides the necessary background and context for understanding the purpose and content of the Old Testament law as God originally gave it to Israel.

When we come directly to the subject of the Old Testament law in the New Testament and in the church, the argument in this volume focuses on three major theses: the goodness of the law, the weakness of the law, and the unity of the law. These are essential to sorting out what Jesus and the writers of the New Testament said about the law. We will treat the third thesis in the next chapter. For now, we need to focus on the first two. They are taken directly from the apostle Paul's discussion of the law and the Spirit in Romans 7–8. This is probably the most important passage in the New Testament for understanding the relationship between the Old Testament law and the lives of believers today. Many other passages will also come under consideration, however, as we work our way through these two chapters of Romans.

The first thesis is that the Old Testament law is good. It was good in the Old Testament, it was treated as good in the New Testament, and it will always be good. As Paul put it, "The law *is* holy, and the commandment *is* holy, righteous and good. . . . The law *is* spiritual" (Rom 7:12, 14; note the present tense). Furthermore, the law as given through Moses was then, in the time of the writing of the New Testament, and still today is not only good but also *useful* for the Christian (2 Tim 3:15-17). It applies to the life of the Christian today in a new covenant, written-on-the-heart sense, and it is the Holy Spirit who writes it there (see esp. Jer 31:31-34 and Ezek 36:25-27, and their combination in 2 Cor 3:3-8). We have said a lot about the goodness of the law already in this book. The focus in this chapter is on the second thesis.

The second thesis is that as good as it is, the law is also weak. It always was weak, and it continues to be weak, in contrast to the power of the Holy Spirit in the life of the believer (Rom 8:3). In the context of emphasizing the goodness and spirituality of the law, in Romans 7:14 Paul identified the real issue: "I am unspiritual, sold as a slave to sin." This comes back with implications in the next chapter: "What the law was powerless to do in that it was *weakened* by the sinful nature, God did by sending his own Son in the likeness of sinful man to be a sin offering, in order that the righteous requirements of the law might be fully met in us, who do not live according to the sinful nature but according to the *Spirit*" (Rom 8:3-4).

In other words, the law was and still is weak in that it has never had the power in itself to push fleshly human corruption out of the human heart and motivate godly living. This strength, the power in the believer's life, comes not from the Old Testament law but from the continuing practice of *faith* through the work of the *Holy Spirit* (Rom 8:4-16; Gal 3:1-7; 1 Cor 2:10-13). There are certain things no law can do, not even God's law. The law has never had the power to change a human heart. Only the Holy Spirit can do that. The law, however, is an inerrant and wonderfully rich guide for those who have the power of the Holy Spirit working in them. The Holy Spirit inspired the writing of the Scriptures, including the Mosaic law, and is now working in us to bring it all to bear effectively in our lives. The Holy Spirit was and is the driving force on both ends of the process—in the Bible and in us.

One of the major problems and sources of confusion in the ongoing discussion and debate about the Old Testament law in the church today is that some want to hold on tightly to one or the other of these two theses, but not both. Some say with the right hand that the law is good, but they take it back with the left hand, so to speak. They really do not believe that the law is good. The same is also true the other way around. Some say with the right hand that the law is weak, but they take it back with the left. They really do not believe that the law is weak. It is my contention that we need to hold tightly to both at the same time and not let go of either of them ever, under any circumstances.

OLD AND NEW COVENANT AND THE
LAW WRITTEN ON THE HEART

Over the last forty-five years or so, what scholars refer to as the "new perspective on Paul" has raised an important challenge to what many have thought to be Paul's view of the relationship between faith and law. According to this new perspective, the church, especially the Protestant church, misreads Paul when it understands him to be arguing against Jewish legalism in favor of his own theology of grace in Christ (see the discussion of legalism in chap. 9 above). Instead, the Judaism of that day was characterized by what E. P. Sanders has dubbed "covenantal nomism" (from Greek *nomos*, "law"): one gets into covenant relationship with God through faith by God's mercy, but one stays in that relationship through obedience to God's law as the working out of that faith.[1] If this is correct, as the argument goes, Paul's reaction against the Judaism of his day was not based on salvation through God's grace versus God's law, since the Jewish view itself included, first of all and above all, covenant bond by the gracious mercy of God.

In my view, this has been a healthy discussion, but there still remains a major difference between covenantal nomism and Paul's gospel message. One way to put it would be to say that Paul's gospel is characterized by covenantal "fideism" (faith) as opposed to covenantal "nomism." According to Paul, one is not only saved by faith but also sanctified by living the life of faith through the power of the Spirit—not by moving over to a life motivated by keeping the Old Testament law. This is the main burden of passages like Galatians 3:1-14, where we read: "Are you so foolish? After beginning by means of the Spirit, are you now trying to finish by means of the flesh?" (Gal 3:3). Similarly, "For all who rely on the works of the law are under a curse, as it is written: 'Cursed is everyone who does not continue to do everything written in the Book of the Law'" (Gal 3:10). Again, "The law is not based on faith; on the contrary, it says, 'The person who does these things will live by them.' Christ redeemed us from the curse of the law by becoming a curse for us" (Gal 3:12-13).

COVENANT, LAW, AND SPIRIT

According to Galatians 3:17-18, "*The law*, introduced 430 years later, does not set aside the covenant previously established by God and thus do away with the promise. For if the inheritance depends on the law, then it no longer depends on the promise; but God in his grace gave it to *Abraham through a promise*." Chapter two in this book discusses the major biblical covenants and the relationships between

---

[1]See E. P. Sanders, *Paul and Palestinian Judaism* (Minneapolis: Fortress, 1977). For a thorough analysis of this view and the various aspects of it, see D. A. Carson, Peter T. O'Brien, and Mark A. Seifrid, eds., *Justification and Variegated Nomism: A Fresh Appraisal of Paul and Second Temple Judaism*, vol. 2, WUNT 2/140 (Tübingen: Mohr Siebeck, 2004).

them. It uses an umbrella chart to illustrate the biblical teachings about the redemptive covenants. In summary, God engages in covenant relationship with his people through a combination of permanent promise and ongoing obligation. Permanent promise assures those who know him of his covenant faithfulness to them. Ongoing obligation challenges those who know him to live in reciprocal covenant faithfulness. Both are essential to the way God enacts a covenant relationship with us in our fallen condition.

God made the Abrahamic covenant with the head of a family, so it was a family-level covenant meant to regulate and guide a family as they walked with the Lord. By the time God delivered the Israelites from Egypt, however, the family had grown into a nation, so the Mosaic covenant was a national covenant. It was designed to guide and regulate the nation in their relationship with the Lord. Similarly, the Davidic covenant fit under both the Abrahamic and Mosaic covenants. The *family* had grown into a *nation* that needed a *king*. The Davidic kings were expected to have Abrahamic faith in the Lord and rule the nation according to the law of Moses. In fact, according to Deuteronomy 17:18-20, when a new king ascended to the throne, he was to write his own copy of the law under the supervision of the Levitical priests so that he could read and study the law all the days of his life, and rule according to it (see, e.g., David's charge to Solomon on his deathbed in 1 Kings 2:1-4). None of these covenants eliminate the ones that come before them. Instead they each function under the umbrella(s) that come before them.

This redemptive covenant program comes to its full expression in the new covenant in Christ. The law of God in the Mosaic covenant is anything but left behind in the new covenant. Through the prophet Jeremiah, the Lord introduced the new covenant as one that "will not be like the covenant I made with their ancestors when I took them by the hand to lead them out of Egypt" (i.e., the Mosaic covenant; Jer 31:31-32). He goes on to say that in this new covenant, "I will put my law in their *minds* and *write it on their hearts*" (Jer 31:33).

This naturally raises a question: What does it mean to have the law written on the heart as a new covenant believer? The answer is that this is a way of talking about living the law from the heart—from a heart transformed by the application of the law to the core of our being—our "heart." It is having the law worked into how we think and feel about things. Yes, it is a metaphor. God, of course, does not literally cut open our chest surgically and inscribe the law physically on our heart with a knife or stylus. He does this by putting the Holy Spirit within us. Jesus elaborated on what the law is like when it is written on the heart, for example, in the Sermon on the Mount and in his two great commandments.

Having the law written on the heart is similar to another expression found in the Old Testament law itself and in Jeremiah: "circumcision of the heart." See, for example,

When their uncircumcised hearts are humbled . . . (Lev 26:40-41)

Circumcise your hearts, therefore, and do not be stiff-necked any longer. (Deut 10:16)

The LORD your God will circumcise your hearts and the hearts of your descendants, so that you may love him with all your heart and with all your soul, and live. (Deut 30:6; recall the first great commandment, Mt 22:37-38)

Circumcise yourselves to the LORD, circumcise your hearts. (Jer 4:4)

"The days are coming," declares the LORD, "when I will punish all who are circumcised only in the flesh—Egypt, Judah, Edom, Ammon, Moab and all who live in the wilderness in distant places. For all these nations are really uncircumcised, and even the whole house of Israel is uncircumcised in heart." (Jer 9:25-26, cf. Jer 32:39)

God has always wanted the same thing from everyone, not just in the Old Testament but in the New Testament too. Therefore, this way of talking about the transformation of the heart comes through into the New Testament as well. As Steven put it to the Jews who stoned him to death: "You stiff-necked people! Your hearts and ears are still uncircumcised. You are just like your ancestors: You always resist the

Holy Spirit!" (Acts 7:51); and as Paul writes, "A person is not a Jew who is one only outwardly, nor is circumcision merely outward and physical. No, a person is a Jew who is one inwardly; and circumcision is circumcision of the heart, by the Spirit, not by the written code. Such a person's praise is not from other people, but from God" (Rom 2:28-29). From these passages we can see that circumcision of the heart involves having a humble heart, not stubbornly resisting the Lord's work and guidance in life, and loving the Lord with one's whole heart and soul.

Romans 2:29 in particular highlights the importance of the Holy Spirit in circumcising the heart, which is something the written code of the law could never do. One could know the written law without having it written on the heart. This has been the case with many all through redemptive history, and it is, of course, also a problem in our day. The Old Testament background for understanding the work of the Spirit of God in this regard appears, for example, in Ezekiel 36:26-27, "I will give you a new heart and put a new spirit in you; I will remove from you your heart of stone and give you a heart of flesh [i.e., a soft heart rather than a hard one]. And I will put my Spirit in you and move you to follow my decrees and be careful to keep my laws." God spoke this through the prophet Ezekiel in the context of his promise to bring them back from the Babylonian exile. They were a dead and dried-up nation, like the bones in Ezekiel 37. God promised he would not allow his work with Israel to end this way.

The apostle Paul applies a combination of Jeremiah 31 and Ezekiel 36 to the new covenant ministry of the gospel in 2 Corinthians: "You are a letter from Christ, the result of our ministry, *written* not with ink but with *the Spirit of the living God*, not on tablets of stone but *on tablets of human hearts.* . . . He has made us competent as *ministers of a new covenant—not of the letter* but of the *Spirit*; for the *letter kills*, but the *Spirit gives life*" (2 Cor 3:3, 6).

The new covenant writing of the law on the heart (Jer 31:33) is something that the Holy Spirit does (Ezek 36:27). Servants of Christ are minsters of the new covenant not the old one (Jer 31:31-32). This new covenant is not based on the letter (of the law) but on the Spirit who gives life (Ezek 36:27). No law can change a heart, not even God's law. That is not what law does. It is the Spirit of God that brings the law of God to life in the church and the believer. The letter of the law without the Spirit of God has no life in it. In fact, it kills.

WE ARE NOT "UNDER" THE LAW

The Mosaic law was never designed to give anyone spiritual life: "For if a law had been given that could impart life, then righteousness would certainly have come by the law" (Gal 3:21). As discussed in detail in chapter two above, the Mosaic covenant fits under the umbrella of the Abrahamic covenant. God gave the Mosaic covenant and its law as a guide to those who already had the kind of faith Abram showed in Genesis 15:6: "Abram believed the LORD, and he credited it to him as righteousness" (cf. Gal 3; Rom 4). The law was never intended to do what only faith can do through the Spirit of God in the human heart.

This does not mean, however, that we push the Old Testament law aside in our lives as believers. No, the Holy Spirit uses it as an indispensable guide for those who follow Jesus. Even near the end of his life, the apostle Paul highlighted the importance of these Old Testament Scriptures that Timothy had been learning since he was a little child (2 Tim 3:15). There was no New Testament yet when Timothy was a little child. The apostles could expect that those who would read their inspired New Testament writings would have the inspired Old Testament Scriptures as their Bible—and that they would know it well. The situation today is different. This is why we spent so much time pursuing a meaningful understanding of the Old Testament law itself earlier in this book.

In Galatians 3:23–4:7 the apostle Paul compares the law to a "tutor" (Greek *paidagōgos*). This is a very helpful analogy. Greek and Roman families employed slaves to have charge over a boy from about six to sixteen years old. This slave was responsible for the boy's training and discipline until he came of age to take up his role as the heir to the household. As Paul put it, Israel was "held in custody under the law, locked up until the faith that was to come would be revealed" (Gal 3:23). In the old covenant era the law functioned in this way, but this only lasted "until Christ came that we might be justified by faith" (Gal 3:24). In Christ we are no longer "under the law" as a tutor. That age is past. Paul goes on to say, "As long as an heir is underage, he is no different from a slave, although he owns the whole estate. The heir is subject to guardians and trustees until the time set by his father" (Gal 4:1-2). He concludes the analogy with this: "Because you are his sons, God sent the Spirit of his Son into our hearts, the Spirit who calls out, '*Abba*, Father.' So you are no longer a slave, but God's child; and since you are his child, God has made you also an heir" (Gal 4:6-7).

So what does the apostle Paul mean when he writes that we are not "under the law" (e.g., 1 Cor 9:20; Gal 3:23, 25; 4:4-5, 21)? To begin with, it means that we are no longer under "the curse of the law" (Gal 3:13; cf. Gal 3:10). The law cannot condemn us because we have been justified by God through accepting by faith the work of Jesus Christ on the cross. Moreover, the law was never designed to give anyone spiritual life: "For if a law had been given that could impart life, then righteousness would certainly have come by the law" (Gal 3:21). The life of faith in God in the Old Testament begins with the kind of faith Abraham showed in Genesis 15:6 (cf. Rom 4:16-24). The life of faith does not, and it never did, begin with keeping the law but with a personal faith commitment to God himself. Paul teaches this always, everywhere, and in various ways.

Again, the Mosaic law came along later as a way for Abrahamic faith believers to live out their Abrahamic faith in the covenant God made with the nation of Israel. It was given as a guide to those who already had Abrahamic faith and would live according to that faith. Paul refers to it as a tutor (Gal 3:24-25) and states that we are no longer under this tutor. The curse of the law does not apply to those who are in Christ because we have been redeemed out from under it: "There is now no condemnation for those who are in Christ Jesus" (Rom 8:1).

Second, not being "under the law" means that the law does not provide the power for living the Christian life. The power for conformity to the image of Christ comes from the Holy Spirit filling the life of the person who has Abrahamic faith. Abraham kept the law as a man of faith (Gen 15:6) before it was even given: "Abraham obeyed Me and kept My charge, My commandments, My statutes and My laws" (Gen 26:5 NASB; cf., e.g., Deut 6:2; 11:1).[2] Moses wrote the law long after Abraham was dead, so he was not under the law. Since he was a righteous man before God in his own day, however, he could be labeled a keeper of the law, using terms that the later Israelite readers, who had the law in their day, would have understood.

In a similar way, as people of Abrahamic faith today (Gal 3:14), we keep the law even though we are not under the law any more than Abraham was in his day. As Paul puts it later in Galatians 5:14, "For the entire law is fulfilled in keeping this one command: 'Love your neighbor as yourself.'" Of course, this goes back to Jesus' two great commandments (see Mt 22:34-40 and par.) and is part of "the law of Christ" as Paul labels it: "To those not having the law I became like one not having the law (though I am not free from God's law but am under Christ's law)" (1 Cor 9:21). The "law of Christ" is the way the Old Testament law is mediated to us in Christ, described in Scripture as "written on the heart."

When Jesus gave the two great commandments, both of which come from the Old Testament law itself, he added at the end, "All the Law and the Prophets hang on these two commandments" (Mt 22:40). God has always desired the same from everyone: a love for God and a love for people. The Ten Commandments and the entirety of the law given in the Pentateuch are all about how to live out the two great

---

[2]See, e.g., the remarks in Tremper Longman III, *Genesis*, The Story of God Bible Commentary (Grand Rapids, MI: Zondervan, 2016), 341-42; Allen P. Ross, *Creation and Blessing: A Guide to the Study and Exposition of the Book of Genesis* (Grand Rapids, MI: Baker, 1988), 458-59.

commandments as a nation of Abrahamic believers in Israel's ancient Near Eastern context.

THE WEAKNESS OF THE OLD TESTAMENT LAW

It is the weakness of the legal stipulations by themselves, without the heart of faith, that Paul emphasizes in Romans 6–8. This weakness applies to the whole law, including the so-called moral law. I am not fond of the threefold division of the law into moral, civil, and cere-monial law. Some traditions make this distinction as a means of de-termining what from the Old Testament law applies to the church and the believer, and what does not. In any case, we know that the "moral" law is weak along with all the other parts of it because Paul begins his argument in Romans 7:7–8:17 with a quote of the tenth com-mandment: "What shall we say, then? Is the law sinful? Certainly not! Nevertheless, I would not have known what sin was had it not been for the law. For I would not have known what coveting really was if the law had not said, 'You shall not covet'" (Rom 7:7). On that basis he proceeds to argue both for the goodness of the law and its weakness (Rom 7:8–8:3). It is easy to understand the goodness of the tenth com-mandment, but what about the weakness?

The argument in Romans 6–8 begins with three images that illus-trate our status in Christ: "We are those who have died to sin; how can we live in it any longer?" (Rom 6:2). The three images are (1) our baptism as death, burial, and resurrection to a new life in Christ free from sin and death (Rom 6:3-14); (2) our deliverance from slavery to sin to serve the God who delivered us (Rom 6:15-23); and (3) our freedom from the authority of the law by our death to the law through the body of Christ, "so that we serve in the new way of the Spirit, and not in the old way of the written code" (Rom 7:1-6). The point is that the law does not set me free from sin. Instead, my "flesh" (Greek *sarx*) takes it and uses it to promote sin in my life (Rom 7:8-12).

Paul uses the word *flesh* in his argument here to refer to the cor-ruption that is within us due to the fall into sin (Gen 3). The flesh uses the body for its own purposes. Our physical body is not evil, but our flesh uses it for evil. The apostle goes to great pains here to make sure we understand that the law itself is good, holy, and even spiritual (Rom 7:7, 12-14), "but I am unspiritual, sold as a slave to sin. I do not understand what I do. For what I want to do I do not do, but what I hate I do" (Rom 7:14-15 through Rom 7:24).

Since the early centuries of the church, there has been an ongoing debate about the general background and meaning of the argument in Romans 7:7-24.[3] Some scholars have argued that Paul is referring to himself in his unsaved condition. Others think he is referring to his battle with sin as a Christian. In my view, this debate has distracted us from the point Paul is really making. He is talking here about how the dynamic of living by the law works whether you are a Christian or a non-Christian. He is treating the law generically in terms of its inherent dynamic if one attempts to live by means of it as their principle of life. The "I" that he uses here is a way of putting himself and all of us together in one group that includes all of humanity, believer or not. Anyone anywhere in any time who takes the law to be the driving force of their life is doomed to this kind of experience.

That which is good (the law; Rom 7:8-11, 13) becomes, in the depraved human heart, an occasion for the outworking of the dynamics of deception unto death. This is because, as spiritual as it is, the law cannot change the fact that each of us is "unspiritual, sold as a slave to sin" (Rom 7:14). We keep on replaying the dynamics of the original fall into sin. Romans 7:11 recalls the pattern of the fall in Genesis 3, from the command not to eat of the fruit of the tree of the knowledge of good and evil, to the deception that caused them to eat anyway, to the death that all of us will someday experience. Therefore, the law, which is completely good and spiritual (Rom 7:12, 14), is likewise completely weak and ineffective at making *us* spiritual: "For what the

---

[3]See the extensive and very helpful review of this debate in Douglas J. Moo, *The Epistle to the Romans*, NICNT (Grand Rapids, MI: Eerdmans, 1996), 442-51.

law was *powerless* to do because it was *weakened* by the flesh, God did by sending his own Son" (Rom 8:3).

The writer of Hebrews, whoever he is, uses the same root word in its adjectival form in Hebrews 7:18-19, "The former regulation is set aside because it was *weak* and useless (for the law made nothing perfect), and a better hope is introduced, by which we draw near to God." The weakness of the law here relates to the distinction between the Old Testament system of priesthood and sacrifice, which was also a good thing in its time for its purposes but does not compare to the better and eternal priesthood and sacrifice of Christ. It is not referring to the same thing as Romans 8:2, but the argument is related and complementary to what Paul is arguing in Romans 7–8.

Paul's emphasis on our struggle with sin in Romans 1–8 reaches its peak in the tangled up mess described in Romans 7:14-23. In the immediately following verses he makes an abrupt turn to God's work in Jesus Christ as the answer to the whole problem: "What a wretched man I am! Who will rescue me from this body that is subject to death? Thanks be to God, who delivers me through Jesus Christ our Lord! So then, I myself in my mind am a slave to God's law, but in my sinful nature a slave to the law of sin. Therefore, there is now no condemnation for those who are in Christ Jesus" (Rom 7:24–8:1).

It may help to recall the Greek legend of the cutting of the Gordian knot as an illustration of the point here. Briefly, as the legend goes, in the days of Alexander the Great there was a town in the hinterlands called Gordius after the name of its king. In that region, there was a widely known oracle associated with a cart that was bound to a yoke with a knot that no one could untie (there were no ends visible and it was tied very tightly). It was called the Gordian knot. The oracular tradition was that whoever could untie it would become the ruler of all Asia. When Alexander came to Gordius he learned of the traditional oracle. He responded by drawing his sword and cutting through the knot with one fell swoop. Thus, he became the conqueror and ruler of all Asia, and we have the expression "cutting the Gordian knot," referring to one drastic action that accomplishes everything that is necessary.

The point in Romans 7:25–8:4 is that this is exactly what Jesus did for us in one fell swoop through his death, burial, and resurrection. He cut right through the sin that knots us up. One can even feel the twisted knot when one reads Romans 7:14-25. Then comes the fell swoop of God's sword in 8:1. God does not try to untie it, and neither should we. There is no condemnation for those in Christ Jesus, so even though we are not rid of sin in our life, we can move on "because through Christ Jesus the law of the Spirit who gives life has set you free from the law of sin and death" (Rom 8:2). We cannot untie the knot anyway! In fact, as far as God is concerned, the knot does not exist. It has already been completely severed by Jesus Christ who became a sin offering for us to set us free from now through all eternity: "For what the law was powerless to do because it was weakened by the flesh, God did by sending his own Son in the likeness of sinful flesh to be a *sin offering*. And so he condemned sin in the flesh" (Rom 8:3).

We are called by God himself to just get on with walking by the power of the Spirit: he condemned sin in the flesh, "in order that the righteous requirement of the law might be fully met in us, who do not live according to the flesh but according to the Spirit" (Rom 8:4). There is an ongoing dispute over what it really means that the righteous requirement of the law has been met. One view takes this to mean that the meeting of the requirement has been accomplished for us by what Jesus did as a sin offering.[4] This is true, of course, but the verse goes on to talk about how we live as believers walking by the Spirit (NIV's "live . . . according to the Spirit" is not as clear about the meaning of the text here). This hardly suggests that the meeting of the law's requirements is forensic or positional in this context.

The other view is that Jesus became a sin offering for us (Rom 8:3) for the purpose of enabling our pursuit of the righteous requirements

---

[4]See, e.g., Moo, *Romans*, 481-85.

of the law in our lives as believers, by the power of the Holy Spirit working in us.[5] If we walk by the Spirit, we fulfill the law as God had always intended his people to do. This interpretation is supported by the following verses. For example, according to Romans 8:7, "The mind governed by the flesh is hostile to God; it does not submit to God's law, nor can it do so." Only the mind governed by the Spirit can submit to the law. This, of course, is in accordance with the new covenant promise that God would put the law of Moses in the minds and hearts of believers.

THE POWER OF THE HOLY SPIRIT

Romans 7:24–8:4, therefore, makes it clear that it is only through faith in Jesus Christ that "the law of the Spirit who gives life" can "set you free from the law of sin and death" (Rom 8:2). The imagery is based on the threefold metaphorical use of the term *law*. Aside from the Old Testament law of God (Rom 7:7-14, 22, 25; 8:3, 4, 7), there are at least three other "laws" Paul is concerned about in Romans 7–8. The first is "the law of sin (and death) at work within my members" (Rom 7:23; cf. Rom 7:25; 8:2), the explanation of which begins in earnest with Romans 7:21, "So I find this law at work: When I want to do good, evil is right there with me"—and all this against the experiential backdrop of Romans 7:14-20.

The existence of this law shows itself by the war it wages (Rom 7:23) with the "law of my mind" (or the inner being), which delights in God's law and wishes to do good (Rom 7:22, 23, 25). This is the second metaphorical use of the term *law*. Victory in this war between these two laws comes only by switching to another principle of law altogether, namely, the "law of the Spirit who gives life" in Christ Jesus, which is identified with the work of the Holy Spirit in the human spirit (Rom 8:2), which Paul then develops fully. The point of all this is that we are captivated by our own depravity, and the Old Testament

---

[5]For this view, see C. E. B. Cranfield, *The Epistle to the Romans*, ICC (Edinburgh: T&T Clark, 1975), 1:382-85.

law, as good as it is, cannot deliver us from that captivity—only the Spirit can (Rom 8:3-17).

There are, therefore, basically three main stages or steps in this passage overall. First, there is living under the condemnation of "the law of sin and death" (Rom 7:7-24; cf. the argument of Romans 1–2; Rom 2:14-15 even applies this to the Gentiles, who have only the law of the conscience). Second, there is no condemnation for those who are in Christ Jesus because through him "the law of the Spirit that gives life set you free from the law of sin and death" (i.e., the law can no longer condemn us; Rom 7:25–8:3; cf. the argument of Rom 3–5). Third, there is living by "the law of the Spirit who gives life . . . in order that the righteous requirements of the law might be fully met in us, who do not live according to the flesh but according to the Spirit" (Rom 8:2-4).

It is conspicuous that the term *law* does not occur in the chapter after Romans 8:7. Paul moves on to the human spirit and the Holy Spirit in the core of the discussion from this point forward. We are called to leave the "flesh" behind, which the law has no power to transform and, in fact, makes use of for its own corrupt purposes. So he leaves the term *law* behind in the discussion in favor of *spirit* or *Spirit*. This shift began in Romans 8:2 but now takes on full force. The Holy Spirit works in our human spirit so that "we cry 'Abba, Father'" because "the Spirit himself testifies with our spirit that we are God's children" (8:15-16).

The translation of the Greek word *pneuma*, referring either to the Holy "Spirit" of God or the human "spirit" of a person is disputed in a few places in Romans 8:5-17. "But if Christ is in you, then even though your body is subject to death because of sin, *the Spirit* gives life because of righteousness" (Rom 8:10) in the NIV, NRSV, and ESV. However, NASB has *spirit*, highlighting the correspondence between the human "body" and the human "spirit" in the verse (NIV and NRSV put this rendering in the margin).

Romans 8:15 is even more difficult. The NIV has "The *Spirit* you received does not make you slaves, so that you live in fear again;

rather, the *Spirit* you received brought about your adoption to sonship," capitalizing both occurrences of *Spirit*. The ESV has "For you did not receive the *spirit* of slavery to fall back into fear, but you have received the *Spirit* of adoption as sons," capitalizing the second but not the first. The NRSV rendering is "For you did not receive a *spirit* of slavery to fall back into fear, but you have received a *spirit* of adoption," putting both occurrences of *spirit* in the lower case, as the NASB does. The latter seems more likely to me because in Greek *spirit* does not have the definite article, and this verse seems to contrast one kind of human spirit over against another.

There is no debate about Romans 8:16: "The *Spirit* himself testifies with our *spirit* that we are God's children." The first clearly refers to the work of the Holy Spirit and the second says that he does this work in "our spirit," clearly referring to the human spirit. The general purpose of testifying is to convince someone of something. The core work of the Spirit of God in our human spirit is to convince us ever more deeply in our human spirit that we are the adopted children of God.

First Corinthians 2:10-13 develops the same point more fully. In that passage, Paul is referring to his ministry focus of proclaiming the gospel above any and all other concerns. "The *Spirit* searches all things, even the deep things of God. [11] For who knows a person's thoughts except their own *spirit* within them? In the same way no one knows the thoughts of God except the *Spirit* of God" (1 Cor 2:10-11). Just as the Holy Spirit knows the depths of God, so a particular person's human spirit knows the depths of that person.

The passage goes on: "We have not received *the spirit* of the world but *the Spirit* who is from God, that we may understand *what God has freely given us*" (1 Cor 2:12). The power is tied directly to what God has freely given us in Christ—the gospel. The gospel is always "good news" to everyone because there are always ways it has not come to bear in our human spirit. It is the overwhelming grace of God to us through Jesus Christ that the Holy Spirit testifies to in our human spirit (see Rom 8:16).

Not only has he delivered us from condemnation (Rom 8:1), he has gone so far as to adopt us as his children, so we are "heirs of God and co-heirs with Christ" (Rom 8:17). We will inherit the very kingdom of God. All this God has "freely given us" (1 Cor 2:12). We are no longer even under the law as a tutor (Gal 4:1-7): "For you did not receive a *spirit* of slavery to fall back into fear, but you have received a *spirit* of adoption" (Rom 8:15). The Spirit has all this to work with in testifying to our human spirit (Rom 8:16). Paul concludes in 1 Corinthians 2:13, "This is what we speak, not in words taught us by human wisdom but in words taught by *the Spirit*, explaining spiritual realities with *Spirit-taught words*." This work of the Holy Spirit in our human spirit is the essence of what the Holy Spirit has been doing in people's lives since Pentecost.[6]

The "spirit of adoption" in Romans 8:15-17 issues in the hymn at the end of the chapter (Rom 8:31-39). This is a poetic passage. It begins with this, "What, then, shall we say in response to these things? If God is for us, who can be against us? He who did not spare his own Son, but gave him up for us all—how will he not also, along with him, graciously give us all things?" God is for us, not against us, and who can stand up against God? He did not even spare his Son in his design for our redemption. He designed us in his image and likeness in creation, and he is invested in his design. He will give us anything we need to fulfill his design for us in Christ.

The passage goes on to Christ's commitment to us as our advocate in heaven before the Father (Rom 8:34-36), so "we are more than conquerors through him who loved us" (Rom 8:37). The Holy Spirit testifies in my human spirit to make me fully "convinced that neither death nor life, neither angels nor demons, neither the present nor the future, nor any powers, neither height nor depth, nor anything else in all creation, will be able to separate us from the love of God that is in Christ Jesus our Lord" (Rom 8:38-39).

---

[6]See the helpful detailed remarks on Rom 8:31-39 in Cranfield, *The Epistle to the Romans*, 1:434–44; and James D. G. Dunn, *Romans 1–8*, WBC 38 (Dallas: Word, 1988), 496–513.

This is what the Spirit/spirit of adoption sings within us. There is absolutely nothing from anywhere or on any level in this entire cosmos that can separate us from the love of God. The more deeply we are convinced of this in our human spirit by the Holy Spirit who is within us, the more there is nothing left to do but go love God and people, which is indeed the fulfillment of the whole law. Nothing else makes sense anymore! From here we can truly go into the world as the salt and light we are called to be (Mt 5:13-16). We can now participate in and contribute to God's mission of redemption in the world through Christ in ways that will thrill our creator and redeemer. This can never happen without the core reordering of our lives through the Spirit/spirit of adoption in our human spirit.

THE HOLY SPIRIT IN OUR SPIRITUAL FORMATION

The discussion above skipped over the section of Romans 8 that deals with the "groaning" we experience in life and how the Holy Spirit is with us in it (Rom 8:18-30). We now return to this important discussion to unpack further what it looks like to walk by the power of the Spirit in our lives. This is actually a very large topic deserving a whole book-length treatment. We can only touch on it here.[7]

The term that has increasingly become used in evangelical ministry contexts over the past thirty years or so is "spiritual formation," although its roots in the larger Christian tradition go back centuries earlier. The focus is on building depth, commitment, and active pursuit of God into the lives of individual Christians and their communities of faith. It requires a commitment to in-depth biblical spirituality in the lives of those who have put their trust solely in the pure gospel of salvation by grace through faith alone in Jesus Christ alone.

---

[7]For a lengthier treatment, see Richard E. Averbeck, "Spirit, Community, and Mission: A Biblical Theology for Spiritual Formation," *Journal of Spiritual Formation and Soul Care* 1, no. 1 (Spring 2008): 27-53. The current discussion offers only a brief summary of that essay with some material added since it was written.

From a biblical point of view, probably the best way to define and describe spiritual formation is to consider passages that put the Holy Spirit in the context of forming, conforming, or transforming our lives toward Christ likeness. For instance, in Galatians 4:19 Paul expresses the concern in a very straightforward way, "My children, with whom I am again in labor until Christ is *formed* in you" (the Greek verb is *morphoō*, where we get the English "metamorphosis," "morphology," etc.). Consider also 2 Corinthians 3:18, where we are described as "being *transformed* [*metamorphoō*] into his image with ever-increasing glory, which comes from the Lord, the Spirit." And again, Romans 12:2, "Do not conform any longer to the pattern of this world, but be *transformed* [*metamorphoō*] by the renewing of your mind."

Romans 8:26-29 is one of the most important passages. It gives us a whole pattern to work from in anchoring spiritual formation to Scripture:

> The Spirit helps us in our weakness. We do not know what we ought to pray for, but *the Spirit* himself intercedes for us through wordless groans. And he who searches our hearts knows the mind of the Spirit, because the Spirit intercedes for the saints *in accordance with the will of God*. And we know that in all things God works for the good of those who love him, who have been called according to his purpose. For those God foreknew he also predestined to be *conformed* [*summorphos*] *to the likeness of his Son*, that he might be the firstborn among many brothers.

Rightly understood, "spiritual formation" is first of all, above all, and throughout, the shaping (i.e., forming) work of the divine Holy Spirit, carried out according to the will of God the Father, for the purpose of conforming us to the image of his Son Jesus Christ. It is trinitarian. It begins with the Holy Spirit and moves to the Father and, finally, to the Son. The whole Godhead is directly involved.

The context of this key passage begins with Romans 8:18: "I consider that our present sufferings are not worth comparing with the glory that will be revealed in us." Note how the unit also ends with the glory to come (Rom 8:30). In fact, the whole creation "waits in eager expectation for the children of God to be revealed" (Rom 8:19). In the meantime, the reality is that the whole creation is "subjected to frustration, not by its own choice, but by the will of the one who subjected it, in hope that the creation itself will be liberated from its bondage to decay and brought into the freedom and glory of the children of God" (Rom 8:20-21). God is the one who subjected the fallen creation to this frustration in response to the rebellion in Genesis 3. His plan is to use it to drive people to repentance in order to put them on the road to glory rather than corruption. The whole creation "groans" (Rom 8:22) right up to now, and we groan in the midst of the groaning of all creation, "as we wait eagerly for our adoption to sonship, the redemption of our bodies" (Rom 8:23). In the midst of this groaning experience, "the Spirit himself intercedes for us through wordless groans" (Rom 8:26).

The point is that the Holy Spirit's work of formation takes place right in the midst of our life circumstances and struggles. This is not about an escape from the harsh realities of life. The Holy Spirit works in the midst of it all. In fact, without the groaning, we would not even see how desperately we need God to work in lives.

There are actually three dimensions of the formative work of the Holy Spirit in our lives according to Scripture (see figure 5). Each of these dimensions has connections from the Old Testament into the New Testament, and each has specific applications for the Christian life. We are talking about a whole-Bible spirituality here. Moreover, these dimensions of the work of the Holy Spirit are intimately bound together, not mutually exclusive or isolated from each other. Each has direct impact on the effective working of the others in the lives of believers. At the core of this spirituality is intimacy with God through the presence of the Holy Spirit who works in us and among us to conform us to the image of Christ

Figure 5. Prophetic spirit and Holy Spirit

(the inner circle), bind us together in community with other believers (the middle concentric circle), and empower us as servants of God in our kingdom mission to spread the gospel and live as salt and light in the world (the outer concentric circle). It is founded on a biblical theology of the Holy Spirit's work *in* us, *among* us, and *through* us. The so-called spiritual disciplines engage us in all three dimensions of the Holy Spirit's work.

THE HOLY SPIRIT AND THE HUMAN SPIRIT

The first dimension focuses on the significance and power for the Christian life derived from the Holy Spirit's work in the personal life of the believer. This dimension is often associated with solitude, devotion, and meditation. The fact of the matter, however, is that anything that stimulates, activates, or challenges us in our human spirit toward walking with God through the Holy Spirit's work in our human spirit is part of this. The empowerment for our spiritual growth comes from the Holy Spirit's work in our human spirit. This is the point of direct contact for the transformational work of God in our lives. One of the most helpful passages in this regard has been 1 Corinthians 2:10-12, which we already discussed above in connection with the "spirit of adoption" in Romans 8:16.

The terms for *spirit* and even *(Holy) Spirit* in both the Old Testament (Hebrew *rûaḥ*) and the New Testament (Greek *pneuma*) are the same words that are used for "wind" or "breath" (see, e.g., English *pneumonia*). In fact, in about 40 percent of its occurrences in the Old Testament, *rûaḥ* means "wind/breath," not "spirit" as we use the term in the church today (see, e.g., Ps 1:4, the wicked "are like chaff that the wind blows away").[8] The connection is important. If a person has breath, they are alive physically, and if they have the Spirit of God occupying their human spirit, they are alive spiritually. The Spirit of God is the person of God who makes the spirit of people alive to God.

The vision of the valley of dry bones in Ezekiel, symbolizing the death of Israel in exile, plays off this connection to communicate God's intention to revive them through restoration to the Promised Land: "Prophesy to the breath [*rûaḥ*]; prophesy, son of man, and say to it, 'This is what the Sovereign LORD says: Come, breath [*rûaḥ*], from the four winds [*rûaḥ*] and breathe into these slain, that they may live. . . . I will put my Spirit [*rûaḥ*] in you and you will live, and I will settle you in your own land. Then you will know that I the LORD have spoken, and I have done it, declares the LORD" (Ezek 37:9, 14)

This is the same play on words Jesus uses with Nicodemus in John 3:8, "The wind [*pneuma*] blows wherever it pleases. You hear its sound, but you cannot tell where it comes from or where it is going. So it is with everyone born of the Spirit [*pneuma*]." Much more could and should be said about this, of course. It has massive ramifications for our understanding what God is doing and how he is doing it.

The human spirit in the New Testament can, for example, refer to that which gives the human body life, "As the body without the spirit is dead, so faith without deeds is dead" (Jas 2:26). It is also the seat of human character as well as capacities and dispositions: the seat of intuition (Mk 2:8), a disposition of discouragement or internal despair (Mk 8:12), joy (Lk 1:47), intense affection (Jn 11:33), gentleness (1 Cor 4:21), a spirit of fear, as opposed to a spirit of power, love, and self-discipline (2 Tim 1:7). A human spirit that has a "spirit (or Spirit) of adoption," therefore, is occupied with "what God has freely given us" (see 1 Cor 2:12). The person approaches life with this as the center

---

[8]See a full treatment in Richard E. Averbeck, "Breath, Wind, Spirit, and the Holy Spirit in the Old Testament," in *Presence, Power and Promise: The Role of Spirit of God in the Old Testament*, ed. David G. Firth and Paul D. Wegner (Downers Grove, IL: IVP Academic, 2011), 25-37.

of their attention (Rom 8:31-39). This is what is most important to them and it shapes how they see everything else.

TEMPLE OF GOD AND TEMPLE OF THE HOLY SPIRIT

This dimension of the Holy Spirit's work in spiritual formation focuses on the building of the community connection between believers. The Holy Spirit is present both in us and among us. The church as a redemptive community is the temple of God the Holy Spirit today. This is an essential part of our identity in Christ. This dimension calls for us to engage together in the "practice of the presence of God" through prayer, worship, purity, relational love, and spiritual giftedness.

The Old Testament background for this is in the tabernacle presence of God considered in chapter six above. It comes through into the New Testament in ways we will develop more fully in the next chapter. This is one of the main avenues through which the tabernacle and its sacrificial system come into the church for application to the church and the believer.

THE PROPHETIC SPIRIT AND THE HOLY SPIRIT

The same Holy Spirit who indwells us and transforms us also empowers us for prophetic ministry, standing up and speaking out in the world. This is the essence of our mission in the church and in the world. Thus, he works not only in us and among us but also *through* us. This dimension of spiritual formation focuses on the Holy Spirit's work to transform and empower believers for spreading the gospel and, as part of that, to live life as salt and light in the church and in the world.

At its core, the church is by nature a prophetic institution, an organism of the work of the Holy Spirit in the world. It began as that on Day of Pentecost and has been called to it ever since. The first sermon was by Peter in Acts 2, where he quoted directly from Joel. He was responding to people who saw and heard them speaking in various tongues (languages), proclaiming the gospel of Christ, but suggested that they were just drunk. Peter responded this way:

These people are not drunk, as you suppose. It's only nine in the morning! No, this is what was spoken by the prophet Joel: "In the last days, God says, I will *pour out my Spirit on all people.* Your sons and daughters *will prophesy,* your young men will see visions, your old men will dream dreams. Even on my servants, both men and women, *I will pour out my Spirit in those days, and they will prophesy.*" (Acts 2:16-18, citing Joel 2:28-29)

The Holy Spirit inaugurated the church as a continuation of the prophetic tradition from the Old Testament. We continue in this role today. Only the prophets had this kind of work of the Holy Spirit in them in the Old Testament, but everyone who knows Jesus today has the same kind of work within them and through them. As Paul put it, "We were all baptized by one Spirit so as to form one body—whether Jews or Gentiles, slave or free—and we were all given the one Spirit to drink. Even so the body is not made up of one part but of many" (1 Cor 12:12-14).

All Christians are called to be "prophetic," although not all of us have the "gift of prophecy," and not all of us have the gift of speaking in "different kinds of tongues," like they did at Pentecost (1 Cor 12:27-30). Believers differ on their understanding of the gifts of the Holy Spirit. God has distributed these gifts among us as he sees fit, and he does not want us to forget that they are not an end in themselves. The gifts of the Holy Spirit are important, but their purpose is to serve as tools for us to love others with: "Now eagerly desire the greater gifts. And yet I will show you the most excellent way. If I speak in the tongues of men or of angels, but do not have love, I am only a resounding gong or a clanging cymbal. If I have the gift of prophecy and can fathom all mysteries and all knowledge, and if I have a faith that can move mountains, but do not have love, I am nothing" (1 Cor 12:30–13:2). First Corinthians 13 is known as the love chapter. It is very poetic, so we might even call it a love hymn. No matter what view of the spiritual gifts we hold to today, and whatever gifts we each may have, we should never forget what they are for.

Be that as it may, the church as a whole and each one of us is called to live prophetically in this world. We are one unified body in this way.

It is the will of God for each of us, not just the "elite" or especially gifted people. It is the norm for every Christian. The local church, in fact, is a collection (a fellowship) of people who are filled with the Holy Spirit and empowered by that Spirit to carry out prophetic life and ministry.

In the Sermon on the Mount, Jesus himself anticipated this prophetic nature of the church that would become the expression of his kingdom of heaven on earth. He proclaimed, "Blessed are you when people insult you, persecute you and falsely say all kinds of evil against you because of me. Rejoice and be glad, because great is your reward in heaven, *for in the same way they persecuted the prophets who were before you*" (Mt 5:11-12).

This is the final beatitude—the end result and culmination of them all. The previous ones were all in the third person plural (see, e.g., Mt 5:3: "Blessed are the poor in spirit, for theirs is the kingdom of heaven"). In Matthew 5:11-12 he shifted to the second person plural, as if to point his finger at them and look them straight in the eye. He gathers up the full effect of the whole set of beatitudes in this one. A person who lives the law of Christ as he delivered it in the Sermon on the Mount lives as a prophet today. If we live as a prophet, we may well get in trouble in this world because we will not fit in. Prophets are the kind of people that stick out. They are activists! If a prophet fits into the world well, something is terribly wrong—"fit in" is the last thing a prophet should do. This, in fact, is what makes us the "salt of the earth" and the "light of the world" (Mt 5:13-16). We live a life that makes a difference! If we try to fit into the world, we are salt that has lost its savor and light that does not shine. We become useless. Worse than useless. We become *false* prophets (Mt 7:15-27).

CONCLUSION

In my view, the human spirit has not received the attention it should in theological discussions about human nature. This is the point of direct contact between God and us in his work of forming us into the image of Jesus Christ. The power comes from the work of the Holy Spirit in our human spirit. The Old Testament law is an inspired revelation of God's will for our lives as we live by the Spirit's work in our human spirit. The Holy Spirit works *in* us.

The same Holy Spirit works *among* us in the redemptive community that is the church of Jesus Christ. We are the temple of the Holy Spirit called to live together in unity as believers who serve him together. The Holy Spirit also works *through* us as we step up and speak out for him as his prophets in this world. We are called to be light in the midst of a deep darkness, calling the lost to the light. The Holy Spirit works *in* us, *among* us, and *through* us to build the kingdom of heaven here and now right in the middle of the darkness. Just a little light makes a big difference especially as it shines into such darkness. This is the work of the Holy Spirit that no law, not even God's law, as good as it is, can ever do. This is what we are here for!

The Lord has given us the Holy Spirit to indwell and empower us toward these ends, and his Old Testament law is a guide for us to follow as the Holy Spirit does his work. The Holy Spirit inspired the writing of the whole Bible, including the Old Testament law, and the same Holy Spirit uses what he inspired to instruct and challenge us in our walk as Christians. The Old Testament was the source the apostles used in their day to write the New Testament, so they just naturally preached the gospel and instructed the church from it. They did this in light of the death, burial, and resurrection of Jesus Christ, the special pouring out of the Holy Spirit at Pentecost, and the ongoing development of the church from a movement within Judaism to one that became a mix of Jews and Gentiles together in Christ.

Eleven

THE UNITY OF THE LAW

PREVIOUSLY, WE HAVE ATTEMPTED to establish two main points essential to a good understanding of how the Old Testament law comes into the life of the church and the believer. First, the Old Testament law was then and is still today not only good (Rom 7:12-14) but also useful for the Christian (2 Tim 3:15-17). Second, although it is truly good, the law is also weak in that it has never had the power to change a human heart, provide eternal hope, or motivate godly living. This requires the empowering work of the Holy Spirit in the human spirit.

A third essential point has to do with the unity of the law in the Old Testament and in its New Testament application to the church and the believer. This does not mean that the Old Testament law applies to the church today in the same way it applied to ancient Israel. For Israel it was enculturated for them in their ancient Near Eastern setting. Nevertheless, what God was working toward in the life of ancient Israel was the same as what God is concerned about in the world of the church and believers today.

He is just as concerned that his people love him with all their heart and soul, and with all they have. He is just as concerned about us showing love to our neighbor, even including people not like our-selves and in fact even our enemies. He is just as concerned with the separation of the church and believers from the corrupting influences in our surrounding world. He is just as concerned that we shine a light on who he is by representing him and his ways well to all people with whom we come into contact. He is just as concerned that we live in our world in ways that correspond to his creation design, not in a way that fights against it or damages the world in which we live. The list goes on.

Creation, wisdom, and the law are closely related, but what is wise in one culture may not be wise in another, at least not in every detail. This is especially true with judicial regulations, as anyone familiar with crosscultural ministry will know. Wisdom sees into and through all this. We must take into consideration that Israel was an ancient Near Eastern theocratic nation when we pursue the application of the law in the church and the life of the believer today.

THE APOSTOLIC MINISTRY AND THE OLD TESTAMENT LAW

The apostles had to make shifts and transformations in how they ap-plied the Old Testament law for obvious reasons, based on the shift from the Mosaic covenant to the new covenant in Christ. God has, nevertheless, put the Mosaic law in the mind of the new covenant believer, and written it on their heart: "I will put my law in their minds and write it on their hearts. I will be their God, and they will be my people" (Jer 31:33). The implications of this are far reaching. Jesus articulated them powerfully in the Sermon on the Mount, the two great commandments, and in all his teachings. He also showed us how to live out these implications in the way he lived. So if we want to know how to live his teachings in the Sermon on the Mount, we only need to look at how he himself lived. He is our teacher and our example.

Jesus, however, lived his life faithfully under the Mosaic law, not the new covenant, so we need to take this into consideration too. It is true that he sometimes anticipated the Gentiles coming to faith in him. As he said, for example, in his good shepherd discourse, "I have other sheep that are not of this sheep pen. I must bring them also. They too will listen to my voice, and there shall be one flock and one shepherd" (Jn 10:16). Nevertheless, Jesus was a Jew and he lived as a Jew faithful to the Law and the Prophets.

After the church began in the book of Acts, the apostles still saw the importance of living according to the guidance of the Old Testament law. After all, it was the word and will of God, and it continued to be so all through the period of the writing of the New Testament (2 Tim 3:15-17). It remains so today as well. This being said, however, they saw the need to adjust for the shift from living under the Mosaic covenant to the church of the new covenant.

For example, the church is not a nation, but communities of faith spread out in all the nations around the world. This was and continues to be God's intention (Acts 1:8). The justice called for in the Old Testament law cannot be implemented in the same way in the church. For this we depend, accept, and even pray for the authority of the government under which we live (Rom 13:1-7). Our concern in this regard is only that they allow the church to function as the kingdom of God within their political and administrative realm (Rom 13:8-14). Sometimes this works well. Sometimes not. Sometimes there is even persecution. Such are the realities of living as God's prophetic people in the midst of a fallen and corrupt world.

Similarly, the nature of God's presence in the midst of his people has shifted from his physically manifest presence in the tabernacle, and later the temple, to the church as the temple of the Holy Spirit. They saw this as more than just an illustration from the Old Testament law for the church. It was how they actually applied tabernacle and sacrificial law to the life of church and the believer. The priesthood change was significant too. Jesus is now the high priest, not the descendants of Aaron (Heb 5-7), and we are the believer priests (1 Pet 2:9-10).

Another shift is in the work of the Holy Spirit. The whole church has been from the start, and continues to be today, a community with the prophetic impulse of the Holy Spirit poured out on us (Acts 2). The church is by nature a prophetic institution that God has called to stand up and step out for him in the world, spreading the gospel message through word and deed (Mt 5:11-16). The prophets in the Old Testament had the Spirit of God poured out on them too, but only select people were prophets, not the whole people, as it is in the church (see chap. 10 above). Other shifts were made too, but we now move on to the unity of the law in more detail.

THE PRINCIPLES AND RATIONALE OF THE UNITY OF THE LAW

The whole, unified Old Testament Mosaic law applies to the New Testament church and the believer in the sense that it is written on our hearts. This does not mean just one aspect of it or another, or some combination thereof. The tripartite dividing of the law into the so-called moral law (the Ten Commandments and other such laws), the "civil" law (the bulk of the book of the covenant in Ex 21–23), and the "ceremonial" law (e.g., Ex 20:22-26; 23:14-19; Lev 1–16) is unnecessary, misguided, and misleading in interpreting the Old Testament law. It is just as unnecessary, misguided, and misleading in applying it (or, alternatively, limiting its application) to the church and the Christian life.

It is true that we gain our righteousness standing before God from what Christ did in his life and in his death on the cross, fulfilling all the requirements of the law for us. We have his righteousness imputed to us by God, so we are no longer under condemnation. There is much about this in the New Testament. It is at the core of the gospel, the "good news." There is mystery in it too. According to the account of Jesus on the road to Emmaus with two disciples, "beginning with Moses and all the Prophets, he explained to them what was said in all the Scriptures concerning himself," and later "they asked each other, 'Were not our hearts burning within us while he talked with us on the road and opened the Scriptures to us?'" (Lk 24:27, 32). Undoubtedly, he talked about various aspects of the Old Testament and how he himself was the ultimate fulfillment of it all. We should not see this as a distinctive reference to every recorded law individually, although every detail of the Law would indeed fit under one category or another of Old Testament law, as would its exposition in the Prophets.

What we are concerned about here does not dispute this in any way. It is not about that but instead about how we as Christians continue to live out the Old Testament law as the church and as believers according to the New Testament. It is also important to note that this is not meant to imply that every individual law in the Old Testament is specifically applied to the Christian in the New Testament, or even cited at all in the New Testament. This is simply not the case. Moreover, it is not advisable to try to figure out some principle for bringing each individual regulation from the Old Testament into the New Testament with a distinct application.

Instead, since we are to follow Christ, and since in fact the Holy Spirit is working in us to grow us into conformity to Christ (Rom 8:27-29), we should think of ourselves as following in his footsteps in the way we also keep the Old Testament law. The main point here is that this writing of the law on the heart includes all of it, including even the badly neglected so-called ceremonial law. In effect, we need to shift our thinking about this subject to the *level* or *kind* of application, not the *limit* or *extent* of application.

In some circles the practice of dividing the law into three categories of moral, civil, and ceremonial has become the rationale for distinguishing between those parts of the law that are applicable to the Christian life and those that are not. Normally, the applicability of the so-called moral law is emphasized over the civil and especially the ceremonial law.[1] "Theonomy" or "Christian reconstructionism,"

---

[1]See the discussion in the introduction above. See also, e.g., Walter C. Kaiser Jr., "The Law as God's Gracious Guidance for the Promotion of Holiness," in *The Law, the Gospel, and the Modern Christian: Five Views*, ed. Wayne G. Strickland (Grand Rapids, MI: Zondervan, 1993), 188-99, and

however, holds to the thesis that "in the realm of human society the civil magistrate is responsible to enforce God's law against public crime."[2] Those who hold this view want to apply both the moral and the civil law today. The main problem with this is the attempt to apply the Old Testament law outside of a redemptive covenantal context. This makes no biblical sense. The Old Testament law was never intended to function outside of a redemptive relationship with God. No government today corresponds to the theocratic rule of God in ancient Israel. To argue that the law of God is universally applicable because it embodies the eternal principles of God's righteous judgment for all societies does not mean that God intended that the kingdom of light overtake the kingdom of darkness (Col 1:13; cf. Eph 2:2) by imposing God's law there.

The law is weak (see chap. 10 above). Theonomy holds to this with one hand but takes it back with the other. They believe it can be a powerful deterrent to the evil in the world. Contrary to this, God's law applies within his kingdom to those who are of that kingdom by covenant. The goal outside of that is to incorporate those who are in the kingdom of darkness into the kingdom of light so that they live according to the law of that kingdom. This includes living as salt and light in the world so, yes, we need to stand up for righteousness and justice in the world around us. The problem with theonomy is that it wastes so much time and effort on controlling the politics by imposing theocratic values on non-theocratic governments.

Bruce K. Waltke, "Theonomy in Relation to Dispensational and Covenant Theologies," in *Theonomy: A Reformed Critique*, ed. William S. Barker and W. Robert Godfrey (Grand Rapids, MI: Zondervan, 1990), 68-69. Many others follow this tradition as well. As I understand him, Vern Poythress, *The Shadow of Christ in the Law of Moses* (Phillipsburg, NJ: Presbyterian & Reformed, 1991), 99-106, wants to keep the law unified but ends up dividing it into two parts, "moral" and "ceremonial," by collapsing the "civil" and "ceremonial" categories. He limits direct application to the "moral" law, which he in turn identifies primarily with the Ten Commandments.
[2]Greg Bahnsen, *Theonomy in Christian Ethics* (Nutley, NJ: Craig, 1977), xiii. For a concise exposition of the tenets of theonomy see Greg Bahnsen, "The Theonomic Reformed Approach to the Law and Gospel," in *The Law, the Gospel, and the Modern Christian*, 93-143, and the responses by nontheonomists on the following pages.

The threefold division of the law has no place in the Old Testament or in the New Testament, at least not in the way and with the implications suggested by those who hold to it. True, some of the law collections in the Pentateuch emphasize different concerns than others, but none of them do so in a way that suggests the threefold division. In fact, a careful look at the arrangement of the parallel law collections in the Pentateuch reveals that they all begin and end with "ceremonial" regulations and have others embedded within them (see chap. 5 above).

Moreover, even if we did accept the threefold division of the law, still the New Testament cites all three "divisions" and applies them to the Christian life. The moral law is easy. No one has a problem with the prohibitions against such things as murder. Even with this, however, Jesus took it further than the teachers of the law in his day (Mt 5:20-26). The apostles have no problem with applying the civil law either, as Paul does in 1 Corinthians 9:8-14, citing the regulation against muzzling an ox while it is threshing the grain (Deut 25:4; cf. also 1 Tim 5:18 and the discussion in chap. 5 above). The same is true for what is labeled the ceremonial law, as we will see in the discussion below. The basic rationale from a New Testament perspective is that we are free from the Mosaic covenant law (Gal 5:13); therefore, it cannot be used to condemn us because we are in Christ (Rom 7:24–8:1). Moreover, it is not the principle nor does it provide the power by which we live our lives during our days on this earth.

Nevertheless, part of the essence of the new covenant in Christ is the writing of the Old Testament law on the heart. This is what the "law of Christ" is all about (Gal 6:2), under which we do indeed live (see chap. 8 above). In other words, the "law of Christ" is the means by which the Old Testament law is mediated to us in Christ (1 Cor 9:21: "I am not free from the law of God but am under the law of Christ"). This is the so-called third use of the law. All parts of the law are included here. Even the pattern of the ceremonial law extends not only from the Old Testament into and through the sacrificial life and death of Christ but also from Christ to the life of the faithful Christian.

Like Christ, we are to become "sacrifices" (Rom 12:1) and "priests" (1 Pet 2:9). We now turn to some of the New Testament details.

TABERNACLE AND LEVITICAL REGULATIONS
IN THE LIFE OF THE CHRISTIAN

The focus of application of the Old Testament law to the Christian life is to have the law written on our hearts so that we live it from the heart (i.e., in attitude as well as action). The tabernacle and Levitical regulations are all connected with the worship of the Lord in ancient Israel. They were to be worshipers first of all and above all. So are we. This is the broad framework within which we can see how these elements of the Old Testament law come into the life of the church and the believer.[3]

Earlier in this chapter and in earlier chapters we have discussed the importance of how Jesus fulfilled the ritual sacrificial requirements for our salvation. Many New Testament passages focus on this.[4] Through the sacrifice of himself Jesus fulfilled all the requirements for our atonement and therefore our acceptance by grace before God. In fact, much of our understanding of the significance of Jesus' death on the cross is dependent on how well we understand the Old Testament sacrificial system. The New Testament writers often assumed this as a foundation.

For example, Christ as our peace offering died as the new covenant ratification sacrifice (see Ex 24:5, 11 with, e.g., Lk 22:19-20; 1 Cor 11:23-25). Christ as our Passover lamb died as the lamb of God, whose blood was shed to create an unleavened community of faith; that is, a community not corrupted by sin in its midst (1 Cor 5:6-8; cf. Ex 12:1-15 with Jn 1:29, 36; 1 Pet 1:17-21; see also *Mishnah Pesahim* 1-3). Christ as our sin offering made atonement on our behalf and brought

---

[3]For this unit see also Richard E. Averbeck, "Reading the Ritual Law in Leviticus Theologically," in *Interpreting the Old Testament Theologically: Essays in Honor of Willem A. VanGemeren*, ed. Andrew T. Abernethy (Grand Rapids, MI: Zondervan, 2018), 135-49.

[4]See, e.g., Mk 10:45; Lk 22:19-20; 1 Cor 11:23-26; Acts 13:38-39; Rom 3:24-31; Eph 3:7; Heb 5–10; 1 Pet 1:18-19; Rev 5.

forgiveness to those who trust in him (see Lev 4:1-5:13, esp. 4:27-31 [50 times in Leviticus] with, e.g., Rom 8:3, and perhaps also 2 Cor 5:2 [NIV margin]; and 1 Jn 1:9). See also all the redemption and ransom terminology (e.g., Rom 3:25; Eph 1:7).

Priesthood

One of the founding principles of the Israelite covenant with God at Sinai was that the nation as a whole would become "a kingdom of priests" (Ex 19:6), but there were also the Aaronic "priests of the kingdom," so to speak (see chap. 6 above). Hebrews 5–10 devotes a great deal of attention to the matter of the royal high priesthood of Jesus based on the pattern of Melchizedek in Genesis 14 and Psalm 110.

These priesthood patterns (esp. Israel as a kingdom of priests and Jesus as a royal priest) connect to the royal priesthood of believers: "You are a chosen people, a *royal priesthood*, a holy nation, God's special possession, that you may declare the praises of him who called you out of darkness into his wonderful light. Once you were not a people, but now you are the people of God; once you had not received mercy, but now you have received mercy" (1 Pet 2:9-10; see also Rev 1:6; 5:10; 20:6). Earlier in the same chapter, Peter refers to believers as "a holy priesthood, offering spiritual sacrifices acceptable to God through Jesus Christ" (1 Pet 2:5). Similarly, we also have "the priestly duty of proclaiming the gospel of God, so that" we might present those we bring to him as "an offering acceptable to God, sanctified by the Holy Spirit," just as Paul offered the Gentiles to God (Rom 15:16). In the last chapter of Hebrews we are told to "continually offer to God a sacrifice of praise—the fruit of lips that openly profess his name. And do not forget to do good and to share with others, for with such sacrifices God is pleased" (Heb 13:15-16).

Tabernacle and Temple

In ancient Israel God was actually present with them in a physically visible way in the tabernacle and later the temple (see, e.g.,

Ex 25–Num 9; 1 Kings 8; and chap. 6 above). This theme of God's presence comes through into the New Testament but in a different way.

As far as we know, the cloud of God's glorious presence never returned to the Jerusalem temple after the Babylonian exile in the Old Testament. Instead, as John 1:14 puts it, "The Word became flesh and *made his dwelling* [Greek *skēnoō*, "tabernacled"] among us. We have seen *his glory, the glory of the One and Only*, who came from the Father, full of grace and truth" (cf. Jn 2:11; 7:18; 17:24). The LXX uses the Greek *skēnē*, "tent, booth, tabernacle," to render the Hebrew *miškān*, "tabernacle." It occurs twenty times in the New Testament, half of them in Hebrews 8–13, referring to the holy place (e.g., Heb 9:2), the most holy place (Heb 9:3), and the heavenly tabernacle made without hands (Heb 9:11). Jesus entered the most holy place of the heavenly sanctuary when he gave up his body, "the veil of his flesh," as our high priest once for all (Heb 10:19-21; "veil" is Greek *katapetasma*, the word the LXX uses to translate the Hebrew *pārōket*, the veil separating the most holy place from the holy place).

Later, in his "high priestly prayer" on behalf of those who would believe in him (Jn 17:20), Jesus said to the Father, "I have given them *the glory* that you gave me, that they may be one as we are one: I in them and you in me" (Jn 17:22-23). This glory comes from the Holy Spirit of God who indwells us (2 Cor 3:17-18; 4:4, 6; cf. Jn 14:16-17). The church is "a *holy temple* in the Lord . . . *a dwelling* in which *God lives by his Spirit*" (Eph 2:21-22; cf. 1 Cor 3:16-17; 1 Pet 2:4-5). According to 2 Corinthians 3:18, we are actually the reflection of God's glory in the world: "And we, who with unveiled faces all reflect the Lord's glory, are being transformed into his likeness with ever-increasing glory, which comes from the Lord, who is the Spirit." In fact, the glory of the new covenant is greater than that of the Mosaic covenant.

As in the Old Testament, the sanctuary presence of God is nothing to trifle with. The corporate body of believers is sacred to him, and God takes violation of that sacred domain seriously: "If anyone destroys God's temple, God will destroy him; for God's temple is *sacred*, and you are that temple" (1 Cor 3:17). Similarly, the individual believer is "a temple of the Holy Spirit," so we must not defile ourselves through immorality (1 Cor 6:18-19), but instead "honor [lit. 'glorify,' Greek *doxazō*] God" with our bodies (1 Cor 6:20).

The main point is that one can trace the theology of sacred *space* in the Old Testament into the New Testament in terms of the theology of sacred *community*. It has major implications for who we are in Christ individually and as the redemptive community of the church. We too are first of all and above all worshipers. As Jesus said, instead of worshiping God at Jerusalem, "a time is coming and has now come when the true worshipers will worship the Father in spirit and truth, for they are the kind of worshipers the Father seeks. God is spirit, and his worshipers must worship in spirit and in truth" (Jn 4:23-24 NIV).

The most important passage in the New Testament for this idea is Ephesians 2–3. Paul is talking about the breaking down of the barrier between Jews and Gentiles in the church:

> For through him [Jesus] we both [Jew and Gentile] have access to the Father by one Spirit. Consequently, you [the Gentiles] are no longer foreigners and strangers, but fellow citizens with God's people [the Jews] and also members of his *household, built* on the *foundation* of the apostles and prophets, with Christ Jesus himself as the chief *cornerstone*. In him the whole *building* is joined together and rises to become a holy *temple* in the Lord. And in him you too are being *built together* to become a *dwelling* in which God *lives by his Spirit*. (Eph 2:18-22)

Notice all the words related to building a temple to the Lord. It is a house that is built on a foundation with a cornerstone. The builder is constructing it so that all the parts fit together into one building. That building is a temple, occupied by God the Holy Spirit.

The building consists of people, the Jews and Gentiles that make up the church by their one faith in Jesus Christ. The foundation is the apostles and the prophets. They are the historical foundation of the whole church. It is built on what they did. Most importantly, it all lines up with Christ, who is the cornerstone. The whole building squares with him and the place he filled in the divine program to establish it.

The same theme continues into Ephesians 3, but with an interruption. Paul takes the occasion to insert remarks about how much the church had been a secret mystery in God's divine program of redemption (Eph 3:1-13). He begins in Ephesians 3:1 with "for this reason" and again picks up the topic of the church as a temple with a repetition of "for this reason" in Ephesians 3:14.

> For this reason I kneel before the Father, from whom every *family* in heaven and on earth derives its name. I pray that out of his glorious riches he may strengthen you with power through *his Spirit* in your inner being, so that Christ may *dwell* in your hearts through faith. And I pray that you, being *rooted and established* in love, may have power, together with all the Lord's holy people, to grasp *how wide and long and high and deep* is the love of Christ, and to know this love that surpasses knowledge—that you may be *filled* to the measure of all the fullness of God. (Eph 3:14-19)

He begins developing the temple household theme again with "family" and the Holy Spirit "in your inner being [lit. 'inner man']." The goal is that Christ will "dwell" in the hearts of the believers through faith, with roots sunk deeply in love. This is part of belonging to the holy people of God with dimensions that are beyond comprehension. The text uses the terms for the width, length, height, and depth of the foundation of an immense building, which is a temple consisting of the love of Christ. This is an immeasurable love that fills up the temple with the fullness of God, like the glory cloud of the Lord filled up the tabernacle (Ex 40:34-35) and later the temple of Solomon.

This leads, finally, in Ephesians 3:20-21 to Paul's doxology, "Now to him who is able to do immeasurably more than all we ask or imagine, according to his power that is at work within us, to him be *glory in the church and in Christ Jesus* throughout all generations, for ever and ever! Amen." The glory of the tabernacle and temple is now in the church in the form of Christ by the presence of the Holy Spirit.

Just before Jesus went to be crucified, he prayed to the Father, "I have given them *the glory* that you gave me, that they may be one as we are one: I in them and you in me" (Jn 17:22-23). Jesus passed his glory on to us with one purpose in mind, that we "may be one" as his body of believers like God the Father and the Son are one. This is so that we "may be brought to complete unity. Then the world will know that you sent me and have loved them even as you have loved me" (Jn 17:23). Recall that at the beginning of the Upper Room Discourse in John 13:34-35 Jesus issued a new command to his disciples: "A new command I give you: Love one another. As I have loved you, so you must love one another. By this everyone will know that you are my disciples, if you love one another." This was what was on Jesus' mind as he headed off toward the cross. This was his greatest concern.

The apostle Paul expressed the same primary concern in what follows from his theme of the "glory" presence of the Holy Spirit and the love of Jesus in the temple that is the church. Paul begins with it in Ephesians 2 and then picks it up again at the end of Ephesians 3. In Ephesians 4 he turns to the same concern that Jesus expressed in his high priestly prayer:

> As a prisoner for the Lord, then, I urge you to live a life worthy of the calling you have received. Be completely humble and gentle; be patient, bearing with one another in love. Make every effort to *keep the unity of the Spirit through the bond of peace.* There is *one* body and *one* Spirit, just as you were called to *one* hope when you were called; *one* Lord, *one* faith, *one* baptism; *one* God and Father of all, who is over all and through all and in all. (Eph 4:1-5)

Paul refers to the unity that comes through our love for one another because of our mutual commitment to the one Spirit, one hope, one Lord, and his whole list of "ones"—this enables the glory of God to shine forth in the world from his temple of the Holy Spirit, the church. This is how the Lord intends us to experience the church, and it is from this that our joint ministry is made effective by him.

We have plenty of divisions in the church. Some of them have arisen for good reasons, and some out of bad motives and sin. This being the case, one of the things that fills my heart with joy when I travel the world in ministry to followers of Jesus is that no matter what language and culture barrier there may be between me and another believer, there is an unbreakable bond of fellowship between us. We both know the most important thing we will ever know about each other—we both know God and love him and his people.

I have had this experience many times, but one stands out as I write this. I was in Shanghai, China, some years ago, teaching the Bible to a group of pastors and other leaders of the underground house church. One morning, as class was proceeding, the door opened and a group of people walked in. At first, I thought we were getting a new group of students, but it turned out that we were being raided by a group of Chinese officials from four different government agencies. They were shutting down the meeting. One of the officials proceeded to the front to read their pronouncement. After that they ordered me to come with them for interrogation. As we walked toward the door, one of the old pastors stood up and walked over to me to shake my hand. This was a way for him to say to me: "Now you are one of us!" I see the scene in my mind every time I think or talk about it, and it brings me almost to tears. There is a lot more to the story, but I will never forget this scene and will always feel a deep bond with the Chinese house church people because of it.

The point is that the theology of the presence of God that comes through into the New Testament for the life of the church and the believer is a very important part of apostolic teaching. These are the kinds of things that are at the core of living for Jesus. They are transformative. Peter develops the same temple theme for the church in 1 Peter 2:4-5, "As you come to him, the living Stone—rejected by humans but chosen by God and precious to him—you also, like living stones, are being built into a spiritual house to be a holy priesthood, offering spiritual sacrifices acceptable to God through Jesus Christ." So we are both the living stone used to build the temple and the priests who offer the sacrifices in the temple. This is how Peter uses the Old Testament temple and priesthood theology to teach the Christian life. This is how it applies to us today as believers. This brings us to our lives as sacrifices.

THE SACRIFICES

Jesus said, "Whoever wants to be my disciple must deny themselves and take up their cross daily and follow me" (Lk 9:23). And again, "Whoever does not carry their cross and follow me cannot be my disciple" (Lk 14:27). Matthew has Jesus saying it this way, "Whoever does not take up their cross and follow me is not worthy of me. Whoever finds their life will lose it, and whoever loses their life for my sake will find it" (Mt 10:38-39). A genuine Christian is sacrificial. This is one of the ways we are called to be like Jesus. Jesus offered himself up as a sacrifice. So must we.

One of the most well-known passages for this idea in the Epistles is Romans 12:1, where Paul writes, "Therefore, I urge you, brothers and sisters, in view of God's mercy, to offer *your bodies* as a *living sacrifice, holy and pleasing* to God—this is your true and proper worship." Old Testament sacrificial concepts ooze from this passage. God's mercy has abounded to us. Our true and meaningful worship of him requires that we offer our bodies, our lives, to him as a sacrifice, a living sacrifice. As with the Old Testament sacrifices, ours has to be holy and pleasing so that it is acceptable to him (see, e.g., Lev 1:3-4). In other words, we need to live our lives as a burnt offering, all of which goes on the altar to offer a "pleasing aroma" to him (Lev 1:9).

It has often been said when referring to this passage that the only problem with a living sacrifice is that it keeps crawling off the altar. Paul's point is that our only appropriate response to God's overwhelming mercies to us is that we completely offer ourselves back to him. This is how this part of the Old Testament sacrificial system continues to apply to the church and the believer today.

Many other passages pick up on this same theme in teaching the Christian life. In Philippians 2:17, Paul refers to his life as being "poured out as a drink offering upon the sacrificial offering of your faith" (ESV). Hebrews 13:15-16 says, "Through Jesus, therefore, let us continually offer to God a sacrifice of praise—the fruit of lips that openly profess his name. And do not forget to do good and to share with others, for with such sacrifices God is pleased." Every good thing that we do can be considered part of our sacrificial worship of the Lord, in his name.

One passage in particular is surprising and somewhat over-whelming in this regard. In Peter's instructions to Christians who are slaves, he tells them "in reverent fear of God submit yourselves to your masters, not only to those who are good and considerate, but also to those who are harsh" (1 Pet 2:18). He reasons that this is especially important when the master is unreasonable and harsh for no good reason. There is nothing special about bearing up under harsh treatment if one deserves it (1 Pet 2:19-20). He then turns to the suf-fering servant passage in Isaiah 53 and applies to the slave:

> To this you were called, because Christ suffered for you, leaving you an ex-ample, that you should follow in his steps. "He committed no sin, and no deceit was found in his mouth" [Isa 53:9]. When they hurled their insults at him, he did not retaliate; when he suffered, he made no threats [Isa 53:7]. Instead, he entrusted himself to him who judges justly. "He himself bore our sins" [Isa 53:4, 11] in his body on the cross, so that we might die to sins and live for righteousness; "by his wounds you have been healed" [Isa 53:5]. For "you were like sheep going astray," [Isa 53:4-6] but now you have returned to the Shepherd and Overseer of your souls. (1 Pet 2:21-25)[5]

Jesus was the ultimate suffering servant. If we are going to be like him, we too need to be ready, willing, and able to accept unjust treatment in service to him. As Paul puts it 2 Timothy 3:12, "Everyone who wants to live a godly life in Christ Jesus will be persecuted." This is not the Christian form of a persecution complex. It is a reality of

---

[5]I have added the references to Isaiah 53 here in brackets. For discussion of the suffering servant as a "guilt offering" and its application to Jesus, see Richard E. Averbeck, "Christian Interpretations of Isaiah 53," in *The Gospel According to Isaiah: Exploring a Deeper Understanding of Isaiah Chapter 53*, ed. Darrell Bock and Mitch Glaser (Grand Rapids, MI: Kregel, 2012), 33-60.

life if we step up and stand up for Christ in this world. It comes with the territory.

PURITY

The Old Testament pattern continues to manifest itself and even grow in its application specifically to the church after Pentecost in Peter's "sheet" of all kinds of unclean animals in his Acts 10:10-16 vision (see chap. 9 above). In that context, God said to him: "Do not call anything impure that God has made clean" (Acts 10:15). Peter correctly applies the vision to the acceptance of Gentiles into the church (Acts 10:23-48). However, at that time and for some time to come, he did not grasp the full implications of the vision, or at least the principle that underlies it. We can surmise this from Paul's confrontation with Peter in Galatians 2:11-14 (cf. Acts 15).

Eventually, Peter grasped it in full. He still applied the purity laws of the Old Testament to the church, but in a different way (1 Pet 1:13-25). He begins with the famous command in Leviticus 11:44, "But just as he who called you is holy, so be holy in all you do; for it is written: 'Be holy, because I am holy'" (1 Pet 1:15-16). He continues with the Old Testament purity and purification terminology in the following verses: "You know that it was not with perishable things such as silver or gold that you were redeemed from the empty way of life handed down to you from your ancestors, but with the precious blood of Christ, a lamb without blemish or defect" (1 Pet 1:18-19).

Then he comes to a most important point for our purposes here: "Now that you have purified yourselves [lit. 'your souls'] by obeying the truth so that you have sincere love for each other, love one another deeply, from the heart" (1 Pet 1:22). The purification terminology of the Old Testament applies to the New Testament believer too, but on the level of the presence of God in the life of the believer in the New Testament, in his or her heart and soul. In the Old Testament God was visibly and physically present in the tabernacle and later the temple.

In the New Testament church God is present with his people in a different way, by the indwelling of the Holy Spirit. There is no tent out in the church parking lot with the glory cloud of God's presence in it. Moreover, the church sanctuary is not a replacement for it. Rather, the concern for purity shifts to the level of the Holy Spirit's presence in the lives of believers.

In the Old Testament there were physical purifications, but the concern for spiritual purity was no less real. Where God is present in a visible physical way, he is also present spiritually. This comes through even in the Old Testament, for example, when the physical cleansing terminology is used for spiritual purity and cleansing (e.g., Ps 51:2, 6-7, 10, 12, 16-17).

First Peter 1:22 gets to this point. We need to purify our souls. We do this "by obeying the truth" so that we "have sincere love for each other." This way we "love one another deeply, from the heart." If our heart and soul are not pure, we cannot love well. We have alternative motives and self-interests that get in the way. Loving well fulfills the whole law. Jesus said this in more than one way (see, e.g., Mt 7:12; 22:34-40 and par.) and so did the apostolic writers of the New Testament (Gal 5:14; Rom 13:9-10; Jas 2:8; and here in 1 Pet 1:22).

Conclusion

Loving well was the whole purpose and modus operandi of the gifts of the Spirit (1 Cor 12:27–13:13), ending in, "Now these three remain: faith, hope and love. But the greatest of these is love" (1 Cor 13:13). Faith and hope are of no small importance in the life of the Christian, but love trumps them both. It is the first of the fruit of the Spirit, "the fruit of the Spirit is love, joy, peace, forbearance, kindness, goodness, faithfulness, gentleness and self-control. Against such things there is no law" (Gal 5:22-23). All these fruits contribute to loving your neighbor the way you yourself would want them to love you.

Sometimes "filling" terminology applies to the church as the "fullness" of Christ (Eph 1:22-23), and the filling of Christians and the church by the Father (Eph 3:19), the Son (Eph 4:10, 13), and especially the Holy Spirit. In Ephesians 5:18-21 Paul exhorts us all,

> Do not get drunk on wine, which leads to debauchery. Instead, *be filled* [the only imperative from here on!] *with the Spirit*. Speak [lit. "speaking"] to one another with psalms, hymns and spiritual songs. Sing [lit. "singing"] and make music [lit. "making music"; Greek *psallontes*] in your heart to the Lord, always giving thanks to *God the Father* for everything, in the name of *our Lord Jesus Christ*. Submit [lit. "submitting"] to one another out of reverence for Christ.

The husband and wife relationship is a continuation of this sequence (Eph 5:22-33).

The whole Trinity is involved here. First, the filling of the Spirit makes us thankful worshipers of God the Father. We offer this worship to him in the name of Jesus our Lord. We really are first of all and above all worshipers. This sets the tone for everything else, including our relationships with one another, "submitting to one another out of reverence for Christ" (Eph 5:21). There is no escaping the combination of the two great commandments here.

CONCLUSION

IT HAS NOT BEEN MY INTENTION in this book to treat directly
all the regulations in the Old Testament law and how they come
through into the New Testament. It would not be possible to accom-
plish that in a single volume. Instead, the goal has been to offer a solid
perspective and approach to the topic and show its validity from a
biblical, theological, and practical point of view. In my view, we
should not be thinking in terms of the *limits* of the application of the
Old Testament law in the life of the church and the believer but rather
the real issue of *how* it applies—all of it!

This means that the reader needs to understand how the law worked
in its original Old Testament context in the first place. What was it
intended to do and how did it do that? The first two parts of this book,
therefore, focused on the covenant context and the content of the Old
Testament law, respectively. With regard to the covenant context,
there was some discussion about the nature of a covenant, the historical development of God's covenant program, and how the covenants relate to one another. The Old Testament law fit originally
within the Mosaic covenant, but that covenant, in turn, fit under the
umbrella of the previous Abrahamic covenant. The later covenant did
not eliminate the previous one but depended on it. In fact, the whole
series of redemptive covenants (Abrahamic, Mosaic, Davidic, and
new) built an accumulative program of God that finds its full expression in the new covenant. This includes the Old Testament law,
which is written on the heart of new covenant believers (Jer 31:33).

The content of the Old Testament law came under consideration in part two, including the nature of the Mosaic law and its application in ancient Israel as a legal tradition and how it relates to the ancient Near Eastern context in which it was written. The ancient Israelites were ancient Near Eastern people. God revealed his law to them in a way that met them in their native world. We looked at some of the regulations in detail, comparing and contrasting some to regulations found in ancient Near Eastern law collections such as the Laws of Hammurabi.

As we worked further into the content of the Mosaic law, we discussed the Ten Commandments and probed the regulations in the book of the covenant (Ex 20–23) as compared to those in the holiness (Lev 17–27) and Deuteronomic collections (Deut 12–26). We showed how important it is to study these sets of regulations as units in themselves, but also compare them—for example, in the study of similarities and differences between the debt slave regulations found in each.

One of the emphases in this book has been the tabernacle/temple, ritual, holiness, and purity regulations in Leviticus and the surrounding chapters in Exodus and Numbers. The reason for this emphasis is threefold. First, I have spent a good deal of time and effort on understanding these regulations. It is my work in this area that has opened up the topic of Old Testament law in the New Testament to me in a special way. Second, it is true, of course, that Jesus Christ fulfilled this part of the Old Testament law for us as Christians, providing for our eternal salvation through his death on the cross and his resurrection. Third, this does *not* mean that the New Testament does not apply the tabernacle, ritual, holiness, and purity regulations to our lives as believers. On the contrary, if we allow the New Testament writings to speak for themselves, they regularly use these regulations to teach us who we are and how we should live our lives as believers in Jesus Christ.

This treatment of the law in the New Testament was the main subject of part three. The church and the believer are the temple of the Holy Spirit today. The Lord is present and working in us, among us, and through us individually and corporately. The "law of Christ" is the way Jesus applied the Old Testament law to us as his followers. We need to take seriously the new covenant line about having the Old Testament law written on our minds and hearts (Jer 31:33). The Holy Spirit does this writing on the heart and mind (Ezek 36:26-27; cf. 2 Cor 3:3-6). Jesus taught the law this way in the Sermon on the Mount and throughout the Gospels. The whole Old Testament law hangs on Jesus' two great commandments. They come from the Old Testament law too. This way of teaching the Old Testament law continues into the Acts and the Epistles. The tabernacle ritual and purity regulations are an important part of this. As noted above, we are the temple of the Holy Spirit. We are also priests and a kingdom of priests that offers sacrifices in the temple. As a temple, we are called to be holy and pure people. These are all important dimensions to thinking and living as Christians. They are practical concerns.

Yes, there are shifts and transformations in the way the Old Testament law comes through into the New Testament, the church, and the Christian life. This was already a reality in the Old Testament itself. The Old Testament law changed even within the Old Testament as the situation and circumstances of Israel changed. Adjustments were made. This happens in the move from the Old Testament to the New Testament and our new covenant relationship with the Lord. The church is not a nation like Israel was; the Messiah was anticipated in the Old Testament and has come in the New Testament; the wall of partition between Jew and Gentile has been broken down in the church; God has poured out the Holy Spirit on all who believe in the New Testament so that the church is essentially a prophetic institution. The list goes on.

Even now, however, God's program with the church continues on the basis of God's work with Israel in the Old Testament (Rom 9:4-5). This includes "the receiving of the law" and the "temple worship," not to mention the patriarchs, all the covenants, and "the Messiah, who is God overall." All of this comes into the church in new covenant ways. The New Testament does much to develop these themes and their application to us. The Old Testament law is written on our minds and hearts. Jesus taught it that way, the apostles taught it that way, and we need to live it that way.

The Old Testament law was, is, and always will be a good thing, not just theoretically but as guidance for the life of the believer. Some people and traditions say this but do not really mean it. It is clear that they have set the law aside and do not give it much sustained attention in and for the church. On one level, this is just one part of the ongoing and widely recognized neglect of the Old Testament in general in the church, but it is an especially important gap in the teaching of the church. It had no place in the earliest church when the apostles were still alive and running things. After all, the Old Testament was their source Bible for the writing of what came to be known as the New Testament.

The Old Testament law continues to be good for the believer, but it is also weak. It never had the power to change the mind and heart of any believer in any age. No law can do that, not even God's law. Law simply does not work that way. It takes the Holy Spirit in the life of the believer to transform the heart. The Spirit does that by bringing all that God has freely given us in Christ to bear down deep within us—our thoughts, motives, perspectives, purposes, and all.

The gospel is always good news to every one of us because there are always ways in which it has not come to have the effects on us that it should have. The Holy Spirit testifies in our human spirit to the fact that, in Christ, we are the adopted children of God, and, more than that, we are heirs to all the privileges of God's kingdom. In this process he uses the Old Testament law as a guide for the life of the believer and the church. He inspired the writing of the Old Testament law to begin with and now he is on the other end of it, bringing it to bear in our lives by writing it on our hearts, working it into our thinking and the way we live.

The three main collections of the law in the Torah—the book of the covenant, the holiness collection, and the Deuteronomic collection—are all surrounded by worship law, and the priestly law in Leviticus is focused on worship throughout. When Jesus encountered the Samaritan woman at the well, he was talking with her about the Holy Spirit as water that wells up within a person for eternal life. She turned the discussion to the schism between Samaritans and Jews, whether the proper place of worship was Mount Gerizim or on the temple mount in Jerusalem. Jesus responded by affirming the temple in Jerusalem but turned the discussion back again to worship in spirit and truth, which is the kind of worship the Father really seeks. True worship comes from the Holy Spirit in the human spirit. Old Testament worship law is most suited to writing on the heart. It is at the heart of the new covenant and comes from the heart of the new covenant believer. We are above all worshipers!

APPENDIX

JEWISH MESSIANIC BELIEVERS AND THE TORAH

SOME PEOPLE THINK I LOOK JEWISH, but I am not. My interest and involvement in the lives and congregations of Jewish messianic believers (JMBs) and the messianic movement arose out of my increasing interest in the Jewish foundations of my faith in Jesus, Yeshua. I became a believer and follower of Yeshua in 1969, my first semester in college. It was the time of the Vietnam War and hippies. I had grown up on a dairy farm in Wisconsin, the dairy state. As a farm boy at a state agricultural school (commonly referred to as "Moo-U"), my major was agronomy, the science of soils and plants. After coming to the Lord, however, I became part of the Jesus Movement and almost immediately lost interest in everything else. I had never read the Bible before and had never heard the gospel before this, as far as I know. Someone soon told me that the Old Testament was originally written in Hebrew (and partly in Aramaic, I found out later) and the New Testament in Greek, so I assumed Christians learn Greek and Hebrew. Actually, it was not long before I noticed that not even the leaders of faith that I knew necessarily studied Hebrew and Greek, but it still seemed obvious to me that they should.

For me this led to finding a college that taught Hebrew and Greek and going there to study. One thing led to the other. I found my beautiful wife, Melinda, there, a zealous believer who wanted to serve the Lord in her life. We have been doing that together ever since. We went on to seminary, where it occurred to me one day that perhaps the Lord wanted me to help the church with the Old Testament. That turned out to be God's call on my life and ministry. After seminary we went on to a well-known Jewish school for advanced Hebrew and cognate learning in Philadelphia, Dropsie College. This was a great environment for me to do my PhD study.

From the start of my walk with the Lord, I was passionate for learning about the biblical and historical foundations of my faith. I still am. This book is a product of the same pursuit. As I went forward in life, I kept going backward in history, until I ended up doing my dissertation in the Cylinders of Gudea, a Sumerian cuneiform ("wedges in clay") composition from around 2100 BC. Sumerian is the oldest written language in the world. The Gudea Cylinders are two large clay barrels with a temple building text inscribed on them. The text is about two-thirds as long as the book of Genesis. They are now on display in the Louvre. I still do research and publish in this field of study.

MY BACKGROUND IN THE MESSIANIC MOVEMENT

My reasons for including these reflections on the messianic movement are threefold. First, I have had the experience of teaching a good number of JMBs in my forty-year teaching career at three different seminaries on the master's and PhD levels: Grace Theological Seminary, Dallas Theological Seminary, and now for the last twenty-seven years at Trinity Evangelical Divinity School. These wonderful students, many of whom are now either pastors/rabbis or missionaries or both, kept on drawing my attention to some of the concerns that messianic believers have in life and ministry. They have often caused me to take a second look at Scripture and the church. They asked questions from a different perspective on history and experience. I have learned a lot from them. Some of them and many non-Jewish students have taken my course Old Testament Law and the Christian at Trinity Evangelical Divinity School.

Second, over the years the Lord has seen fit to draw me into the world of messianic congregations and missionary organizations. As a scholar of Hebrew, the Hebrew Bible, ancient Near Eastern history and languages, with a special focus on the Torah, I have been deeply interested in and have taught on the topic of this book many times. Around twenty years ago, the Adat Hatiqvah congregation invited me to speak on the topic of the Torah and the Jewish believer in Yeshua. I did not know at the time how historically significant this congregation has been. At the time they were located in Evanston, Illinois, a northern suburb of Chicago. Dan Juster had been one of their leaders, and after that Roy Schwartz and Jeff Feinberg, two of my good friends. One graduate of the PhD program at Trinity Evangelical Divinity School, Jacob Rosenberg, is now the rabbi in the same congregation, now located in Deerfield, Illinois. Roy Schwartz made the tape series that came from the lectures I gave there. I did not know they were going to do this but became aware of it when some messianic leaders later told me that they had listened to the tapes with appreciation. I have been told that the organization Jews for Jesus was distributing them for a while.

One of my students at Trinity Evangelical Divinity School was Michael Zinn, who is the director of Chosen People Ministries in Israel. In his master's degree program he took my course on Old Testament law and the Christian. There were about twenty-five students in the course, including an intellectual-property lawyer and others in their master's and PhD programs. We had some interesting discussions along the way, and some tension, but Michael and I have become good friends. This and my friendship with Darrell Bock, the New Testament scholar at Dallas Theological Seminary, led to meeting and developing a friendship with Mitch Glaser, president of Chosen People Ministries. Eventually, he invited me into some writing projects and then to sit on the US board of Chosen People. I have enjoyed this very much.

The following reflections begin with the biblical support for the messianic movement, which is substantial. From there we will move on to what appear to me to be some cautions that the Bible raises for the movement today, and finally to some conclusions.

BIBLICAL SUPPORT FOR THE MESSIANIC MOVEMENT

It is abundantly clear to me from the Bible that the modern messianic Jewish movement is in accord with God's good will for the church overall. This has been true from the beginning of the church on the Day of Pentecost up until today, and it will continue to be important. The church started as a Jewish movement within the Judaism of New Testament days, and neither the rejection of Yeshua as Messiah by most of the Jews (Rom 9) nor the acceptance and growing dominance of the Gentiles in the church changed that (Rom 11).[1] The church today tends to come at the whole thing backward. The question in the earliest church was not whether Jews could live their faith in Yeshua in a Jewish way, but whether or not Gentile believers must convert to Judaism. This was the point of contention in the first Jerusalem council. Some of the Jewish believers in Yeshua believed that "the Gentiles must be circumcised and required to keep the law of Moses" (Acts 15:5). But, after debate, the leaders of the church decided the Gentiles could live their faith as Gentiles (Acts 15:6-21). However, they sent a letter to the Gentile believers to make sure they did not do the kinds of things that would discredit the gospel in the eyes of the Jews (Acts 15:23-29).

PAUL'S ACTIONS IN ACTS 21

Acts 15 does not raise the question about how Jewish believers in Yeshua should live their faith. It seems to have never occurred to them to question whether Jews would or could live their faith as Jews, doing the things that Jews did in that day. In Jerusalem this included meeting

---

[1]For a brief history of the Jew/Gentile split in the early centuries and the anti-Semitic (more accurately, anti-Jewish) tendencies that came with it, see the helpful review in David Rudolph, "Messianic Judaism in Antiquity and in the Modern Era," in *Introduction to Messianic Judaism*, ed. David Rudolph and Joel Willitts (Grand Rapids, MI: Zondervan, 2013), 21-36, esp. 24-25, and the lit. cited there.

in the temple and doing ritual procedures there as regular Jews, including even animal sacrifices (see, e.g., Acts 2:46–3:1). This becomes clear also in Acts 21 when Paul comes back to Jerusalem and meets with James and the elders there. I have treated this in some detail in chapter nine of this book and will not review all the details here. The main points of significance for us here are these.

First, the church in Jerusalem rejoiced in what God was doing among the Gentiles. There was no pushback here (Acts 21:19-20, 25). Second, they were zealous for the law and concerned that Paul and others not teach the Jews who trusted in Christ in the dispersion to violate the law (Acts 21:20-21). Third, Paul had no problem with their concern about this and, in fact, regularly lived as a Jew too (Acts 21:23-27). Fourth, the apostle Paul even performed purification procedures and sacrificial procedures in the temple. He saw no conflict between this and his acceptance of the sacrifice of Jesus Christ for his eternal salvation. The Old Testament sacrifices and that of Yeshua never stood in conflict with each other. Both were efficacious, but on different levels. Paul knew this. The writer of Hebrews knew this. The people in the Jerusalem church knew this. Everyone who understood the law knew this.

Moreover, this understanding may shed light on the question of sacrifices in the millennial temple, if we are to read Ezekiel 40–48 in a relatively literal way, even making adjustments for the symbolic nature of the language there (e.g., the dimensions of the temple). If this is the case, then the sacrifices offered in that temple would have the same purpose as those in the Old Testament—on the physical and temporal level on earth. This includes the burnt, grain, drink, peace, sin, and guilt offerings for making atonement, as well as the Zadokite priesthood; the daily, weekly, and monthly regular cult; and the annual festivals (see Ezek 40:38-43; 42:13-14; 43:18-27; 44:15-16; 45:15–46:24).

The temple is no longer standing on the temple mount, at least for now, so what Paul did in Acts 21 is not possible today. However, the zeal for the law did not end there in that day and is still active and well among many within the Jewish messianic movement. Zeal for the law has strong foundations in the Old Testament (see, e.g., Josh 1:8; Ps 1:2; 119) and is a good thing even today when it is understood, taught, and preached according to God's intended purposes for the law (1 Tim 1:3-11; 2 Tim 3:16-17). I devoted this book to explaining what this should look like in the life of the church and the believer in Yeshua.

PAUL'S WAY OF LIFE AND MINISTRY RATIONALE

There is good reason to connect Paul's actions in Acts 21 with his ministry rationale in 1 Corinthians 9:19-23: "To the Jews I became like a Jew, to win the Jews. To those under the law I became like one under the law (though I myself am *not under the law*), so as to win those under the law" (1 Cor 9:20). His freedom in Christ allowed him to adjust for the context in which he was ministering. If he was with Jewish believers in Yeshua, he lived like a Jew. That is what he was doing in Acts 21. With regard to Gentile ministry contexts, however, he wrote in the next verse: "To those not having the law I became like one not having the law (though I am not free from God's law but am *under Christ's law*), so as to win those not having the law" (1 Cor 9:21). If someone would accuse him of being two-faced, his response would be something like this: "I just do not give a rip about that! My passion is for preaching the gospel in the most winning way possible without any compromise in my commitment to Yeshua." As he put it in the next few verses, "I have become all things to all people so that by all possible means I might save some. I do all this for the sake of the gospel, that I may share in its blessings" (1 Cor 9:22-23).

Paul did not see himself as "under" the Mosaic law, and neither should anyone who lives the messianic life. He was free to live as a Jew, and he did, but his life was about living for Yeshua. He did indeed live "under Christ's law" (1 Cor 9:21; see chap. 8 in this volume). Essentially, the law of Christ is the way Yeshua mediates the Mosaic law to us as believers in him. The two great commandments make up the core substance of the law of Christ (cf. Gal 6:2; Jas 2:8). "All the Law and the Prophets hang on these two commandments" (Mt 22:40). The law of Christ, therefore, does not leave the Old Testament law behind but gets to the new covenant matter of having the law written on the heart (Jer 31:33) by the Spirit of God (Ezek 36:26-27; cf. 2 Cor 3:2-6). Similarly, as Jesus put it in the "golden rule": "In everything do to others as you would have them do to you; for this is the Law and the Prophets" (Mt 7:12). This summarizes the way he taught the law in the Sermon on the Mount, which also belongs to the law of Christ.

On the one hand, as Paul put it, "Though I am free and belong to no one, I have made myself a slave to everyone, to win as many as possible" (1 Cor 9:19). He was free to give up his Jewish practices, if in his estimation the situation called for it, in order to remove obstacles to the gospel message. He once blew up at Peter over this matter when Peter separated from Gentile believers to meet the expectations of Jewish ones (Gal 2:11-21). There is one church fellowship, not two. Jews and Gentiles together in the church must have the wall broken down between them at all cost.

On the other hand, as he wrote earlier in that letter, "Each person should live as a believer in whatever situation the Lord has assigned to them, just as God has called them. This is the rule I lay down in all the churches. Was a man already circumcised when he was called? He should not become uncircumcised. Was a man uncircumcised when he was called? He should not be circumcised" (1 Cor 7:17-18). Actually, I am not sure what it could mean for someone to become physically "uncircumcised." But his point is that we should not get caught up in changing from one to the other, Jew or Gentile, but all of us should be concerned about "keeping God's commands" (1 Cor 7:19). We can do this in a Jewish way or a Gentile way, as the comparison between Acts 15 and Acts 21 shows. It is most natural, for example, that JMBs keep the annual festival cycle, whereas Gentile believers generally do not. They keep the ecclesiastical cycle. Gentiles can celebrate the Jewish cycle too, and Jews can celebrate the ecclesiastical cycle. In any case, we are all called to keep God's commands as they are mediated and taught to us in Yeshua in the new covenant.

It was never intended that Jews stop living their life in Yeshua in a Jewish way. This is one of the great tragedies of the church age. The Jew and Gentile divide and anti-Jewish polemic in the second to the fourth century—and even up to the present day—has always been wrong-headed, and its catastrophic effects for people and the faith that it generated throughout Western history have kept on multiplying. In spite of all this, God has remained faithful to his irrevocable covenant commitments to the Jewish people, including the new covenant (see Jer 31:35-37 with Rom 11:29).[2]

CAUTIONS FOR THE MESSIANIC MOVEMENT TODAY

As I move on to cautions, there is a real sense of caution in my own soul. I am not Jewish and have not lived the Jewish experience. The reflections that follow here come from a Gentile believer in Yeshua who loves the Lord, the Jewish people, the Hebrew Bible, and the teaching of it. I feel at a real disadvantage here but am concerned about certain problems within the messianic movement based on the research and writing of this book and my experience in ministry.

One major scholar in the field has argued that there are eight types of messianic Jewish theology today.[3] He arranges them on a continuum from those closest to "Protestant Evangelicalism" and those closest to "Jewish religious and theological norms." I will not review all of them here but will reflect on some additional cautions they raise for the messianic movement. Three of them stand out to me from a biblical point of view.

The danger of compromising the gospel. The first caution is the most important of all. It is the problem of compromising the gospel

---

[2]See Richard E. Averbeck, "Israel, the Jewish People, and God's Covenants," in *Israel the Church and the Middle East: A Biblical Response to the Current Conflict*, ed. Darrell L. Bock and Mitch Glaser (Grand Rapids, MI: Kregel, 2018), 21-37, and all the essays in that volume.
[3]Richard Harvey, *Mapping Messianic Jewish Theology: A Constructive Approach* (Colorado Springs, CO: Paternoster, 2009), 267-77.

of salvation by faith alone in Jesus Christ alone. This gospel really is good news, but some do not see it that way. A minority of JMBs have given in to this temptation. There is so much concern for living as a Jew within Judaism that there are those who believe that Jews today can stand justified by God without explicitly turning to Yeshua as their savior. Some have argued for a more inclusivist soteriology in which "all salvation comes through Yeshua, though all who receive that salvation may not have confessed Yeshua in this life."[4] This falls outside of what New Testament teaching will allow. It cuts the heart out of what it means to be messianic as a Jewish messianic believer.

The exclusive nature of the gospel is part of the essence of it. This is one of the reasons the evangelistic mission to reach Jews and Gentiles is so urgent. I understand the concern not to lose Jewish identity and have argued for the ongoing legitimacy of it from a biblical point of view above and elsewhere, but there is no substitute for expressing personal faith in Yeshua. It is part of the offense of the gospel, yes, and it takes the Holy Spirit to enable someone to make it a stepping stone rather than a stumbling block (Rom 9:30–10:17). The reaction against Yeshua among Jews includes arguing that one cannot become a believer in Yeshua and remain Jewish. From a biblical point of view, the reality is quite the opposite. The most natural thing for a Jew to do is accept their Messiah, Yeshua. In fact, this makes them more complete as a Jew, from a biblical point of view, in spite of the sociohistorical confusion and baggage.

From God's point of view, they become a fulfilled Jew only by turning to Yeshua. This is one of the best reasons for JMBs to live their life in a Jewish way so that other Jews do not see turning to Yeshua as turning away from their Jewish life. It never did mean that, at least it should not have. Those Jews who have come to faith in Yeshua have enough to overcome with the resistance of their own rabbis and

---

[4]Mark S. Kinzer, "Messianic Jews and the Jewish World," in *Introduction to Messianic Judaism*, ed. David Rudolph and Joel Willitts (Grand Rapids, MI: Zondervan, 2013), 133.

families, not to mention the tragic but well-earned reputation of so-called Christians and the Christian church as persecutors of Jews over the centuries and even up to the present day.

The danger of compromising Jewish freedom and the unity of the believers in Yeshua. Paul continued living his faith in Yeshua as a Jew and largely in a Jewish way all the way through the history recorded in Acts and beyond until his death (ca. AD 67). Moreover, as explained above, he saw no reason for Jews to give up their Jewish identity when they turned to Yeshua, although he was concerned that they not let this get in the way of fellowship between Jewish and Gentile believers. It went both ways. The Gentiles should not let their way of life get in the way of Jews turning to Yeshua either (see again the letter in Acts 15).

Paul was very concerned with the problem of conscience that might arise from one's Jewish background. In Romans 14 he specifically brings up the issue of abstaining from certain foods and keeping certain days sacred. His point was "Make up your mind not to put any stumbling block or obstacle in the way of a brother or sister" (Rom 14:13), and later, "Let us therefore make every effort to do what leads to peace and to mutual edification" (Rom 14:19). The bottom line is "Whoever has doubts is condemned if they eat, because their eating is not from faith; and everything that does not come from faith is sin" (Rom 14:23). Those "strong" in their conscience must not use their strength to harm those with a "weak" conscience regarding such matters. This is part of living out the gospel as a unified community of faith that shows love for one another and respects differences in a self-sacrificial way (Rom 15:1-9).

In the meantime, it is also true that Paul died before the destruction of the temple in AD 70. This has important implications for the messianic movement today. For example, JMBs can no longer do what Paul did in Acts 21. No one can keep the law in that way because there is no temple to do it in. The temple was destroyed by the Romans and has never been rebuilt. Again, the whole history of the earliest church in the book of Acts took place before the destruction of the temple.

Judaism today is a mix of biblical teaching and rabbinic tradition. This tradition is valuable and some of it is even embedded in the New Testament, but Jesus also reacted against some of the traditions of the Jewish teachers of his day (see chap. 8). Scripture, of course, is the ultimate arbiter of God's truth, but good tradition also goes beyond the destruction of the temple and the observance of temple-related *halakha*. The diaspora was also already in place in the days of Jesus and all the writers of the New Testament. Paul himself was born in Tarsus, located in what is today southern Turkey. The synagogue had already become a firmly established institution especially in the diaspora. Moreover, the rabbinic traditions were developing during the days before, during, and after the time of Yeshua's life and ministry on this earth. Thus, there is still a good deal of continuity today with the Judaism of Paul's day.

Nevertheless, up until AD 70 the source and center was the temple in Jerusalem. This is no longer true. Moreover, there was a good deal of tension between the rabbinic leadership of the Jews and Yeshua. He was not happy with how they were reading and applying the law and was quite confrontational about it: "I tell you that unless your righteousness surpasses that of the Pharisees and the teachers of the law, you will certainly not enter the kingdom of heaven" (Mt 5:20). One of the implications of this for JMBs today is that, at least theoretically, following the law of Christ may sometimes call for rejection or at least relaxation of certain halachic standards that JMBs may have grown up with. Messianic believers must not put themselves in the position of standing against Yeshua, who stood against some of the ways the Jewish legal specialists taught and applied the law in his day.

The danger of sanctification by keeping the law. Raising this caution is risky. Some might immediately take this to mean that, in my view, we should not feel the need to keep the law as believers in Yeshua. The major thesis of this book is really quite the opposite. One of the primary features of the new covenant is that the Holy Spirit writes the Mosaic law on the heart of the followers of Yeshua so that we live it from the heart, empowered by the Spirit (see chap. 10). It is important to remember, however, that this includes all believers, both Jews and Gentiles. Living as a follower of Yeshua entails understanding how good, holy, and even spiritual the law really is in the life of the believer.

The problem arises when there is no effective reckoning with the corresponding reality that the law is also weak. We need to take this point just as seriously as the goodness of the law. No law can change a person's heart, not even God's law. That is simply not what law does. It is a good, holy, and spiritual standard and guide for a person whose heart God has already changed through faith and the baptism of the Holy Spirit, but it cannot change the reality that I am of flesh, sold into bondage to sin (Rom 7:14). It cannot motivate godly living.

The "new perspective on Paul" has raised an important challenge to how we understand Paul's view of the relationship between faith and law (see chap. 10).[5] According to this new perspective, Paul was not arguing against Jewish legalism in favor of his own theology of grace in Christ. Instead, the Judaism of that day was characterized by "covenantal nomism" (from Greek *nomos* meaning "law"): one gets into covenant relationship with God through faith by God's mercy, but one stays in that relationship through obedience to God's law as the working out of their faith.

There still remains a major difference between "covenantal nomism" and Paul's gospel message. Paul's gospel is characterized by covenantal "fideism" (faith) as opposed to covenantal "nomism." One is not only saved by faith but also sanctified by living the life of faith through the power of the Spirit—not by moving over to a life motivated by keeping the Old Testament law (see chap. 10).

---

[5]See E. P. Sanders, *Paul and Palestinian Judaism* (Minneapolis: Fortress, 1977). For a thorough analysis of this view and the various aspects of it, see D. A. Carson, Peter T. O'Brien, and Mark A. Seifrid, eds., *Justification and Variegated Nomism: A Fresh Appraisal of Paul and Second Temple Judaism*, vol. 2, WUNT 2/140 (Tübingen: Mohr Siebeck, 2004).

This was a danger among JMBs of Paul's day, and the same is true today among both Jewish and Gentiles believers in Yeshua. There is no power in the law. Leaders and believers within the messianic movement generally understand this, but at times, like the Galatians, believers in Yeshua can slip over into something like the covenantal nomism introduced above. The power for sanctification of believers comes from the work of the Holy Spirit in our human spirit, working the spirit of adoption into all the nooks and crannies of our hearts and minds. The same Holy Spirit who dwells within us uses the law that he originally inspired as a guide for our walk with Yeshua, but the law has no power for transformation of a life whether for salvation or sanctification.

Through our faith in Yeshua we are no longer under the curse of the law (Gal 3:10). There is no condemnation for those who are in Yeshua the Messiah (Rom 8:1). This is of primary importance, but it is also true and important that sanctification in the life of the believer comes about through the continued work of the Spirit, not through the works of the law. According to Paul, one is not only saved by faith but also sanctified by living the life of faith through the power of the Spirit—not by moving over to a life motivated by keeping the Old Testament law.

This applies to Jewish believers in Yeshua just as much as Gentiles. The Old Testament law applies fully to both, as I have argued in this volume, but it has no more power when Jewish believers live their faith in a Jewish way than it does when Gentiles live it in a Gentile way. There are two good reasons for Jewish people to live their life in a Jewish way and keep the law accordingly. First, it can be a wonderful way to turn the believer's Jewish background to their advantage in walking with the Lord. Paul, for example, found it useful and fulfilling to take a Nazirite vow (Acts 18:18). This was a meaningful spiritual exercise for him as a Jewish believer in Yeshua. Of course, this particular practice is no longer possible since there is no temple, but it illustrates how living life in a Jewish way draws on deeply imbedded background that the Holy Spirit can use to work deeply and powerfully in the life of the Jewish believer. One's Jewish heritage is important. Moreover, Jewish believers can benefit greatly from fellowship with other Jewish believers.

Second, living the messianic life in a Jewish way can help keep at least some level of connection to non-messianic Jews—family, friends, and all—in spite of the separation brought by faith in Yeshua. This is good for the believer and for nonbelievers as well. It provides a means of establishing, building, and maintaining relationships with fellow Jews and gives opportunity to share the gospel with them. Their need is desperate, whether they know it or not, whether they like it or not, and whether they will admit it or not.

CONCLUSION

To the end of his life, Paul continued to go vigorously to the Jews with the gospel as he continued his ministry as the apostle to the Gentiles (Gal 2:6-10). The last chapter of Acts ends with his appeal to the local Jewish leaders in Rome, where he lived with a Roman soldier guarding him (Acts 28:17-31). He forcefully proclaimed the gospel of Yeshua to them. In the face of their rejection of the truth, he ended with a quote from Isaiah 6 about their blind stubbornness and finally this: "Therefore I want you to know that God's salvation has been sent to the Gentiles, and they will listen!" (Acts 28:28). Luke concludes his history of the earliest church with this, "For two whole years Paul stayed there in his own rented house and welcomed all who came to see him. He proclaimed the kingdom of God and taught about the Lord Jesus Christ— with all boldness and without hindrance!" (Acts 28:30-31).

All believers, whether Jewish or Gentile, have a prophetic call to stand up and step out in the world as salt and light, living and proclaiming the gospel. My continuing involvement in messianic ministry has deeply impressed me with the boldness necessary in mission to the Jewish people. This is the cutting edge. There can be no backing off or backing down. Being a relatively shy "farm boy," I am often amazed at the boldness JMBs show in evangelism. They often relish the fact that they get sustained and forceful resistance to their preaching of the gospel. To them, this means that at least they are not being ignored! What an example this is to all of us.

In the end, all believers in Yeshua are first of all and above all worshipers. True worship is the most powerful and transforming experience a believer can have. It is all about getting impressed and overwhelmed with God and working this into and through our lives as individual believers and communities of faith. The reason worship is so powerful is that we live for what we are truly impressed with. Our biggest problem is that in so many ways we are more impressed with other things—fame, fortune, control, worldly power, personal comfort, and such. Worship can get us so impressed with God that everything else fades into relative insignificance. Worshiping God is not about leaving the regular struggles of our daily life behind but about bringing them before God and getting impressed with him as we stare them squarely in the face. The psalms tell us this and give good examples of it.

Some have argued that the apostle John had a relatively negative view of the Mosaic law, but this is highly doubtful.[6] He just had a different historical and experiential perspective. He seems to have been the youngest of the apostles and lived into the 90s. Although it is hard to be sure, he probably wrote his Gospel in the early 80s. If this is correct, it would have been after the destruction of the temple, which may shed some light on John's unique report of Yeshua's encounter with the Samaritan woman at the well in John 4.

He had a specific agenda with the woman. He wanted her to grasp the truth that "everyone who drinks this water will be thirsty again, but whoever drinks the water I give them will never thirst. Indeed, the water I give them will become in them a spring of water welling up to eternal life" (Jn 4:13-14). We know from John 7:37-39 that he was referring to what the Holy Spirit could do in her life. She did not

---

[6]W. Loader, "Jesus and the Law," in *Handbook for the Study of the Historical Jesus*, ed. T. Holmén and S. E. Porter (Leiden: Brill, 2011), 3:2745-72.

understand, at least not at first, and ended up trying to draw Yeshua into the Jew-versus-Samaritan controversy over the right place to worship: Gerizim/Samaria or Jerusalem (Jn 4:19-20). He responded by briefly affirming Jerusalem as the right place but refused to let her change the subject. He came back with this: "A time is coming and has now come when the true worshipers will worship the Father in the Spirit and in truth, for they are the kind of worshipers the Father seeks. God is spirit, and his worshipers must worship in the Spirit and in truth" (Jn 4:23-24).[7] This has always been true, of course, but here Yeshua's goal was to shift her attention back to the point—namely, the Holy Spirit welling up within the human spirit as the source of life with God and true worship of him.

Jesus and the apostles used the foundations laid in the Levitical regulations of the Mosaic law to teach and explain to the church who we are and what it means to be the kind of worshipers Jesus was referring to here. This is what the Levitical regulations were all about: worship. As Jesus put it to the woman at the well, this kind of law is most suitable for writing on the heart of the new covenant believer. This is how they applied these regulations to our lives as believers, whether Jews or Gentiles (see chap. 11). We are the temple of the Holy Spirit, individually and corporately (1 Cor 6:18-20; Eph 2–3; 1 Pet 2:4-5). Jesus is the high priest who offered himself as a sacrifice for us, and we are the believer priests who offer up spiritual sacrifices on the altar of service to him, including even our physical living bodies (1 Pet 2:5; Rom 12:1). In our worship we offer up sacrifices of praise to God and sacrificial aid to others (Heb 13:15-16).

Since worship must be in Spirit (spirit) and truth, we all join in this one way of worship and the worship of this *one* in this way. This is at the core of having the law written on the heart.

---

[7]For a full treatment, see Richard E. Averbeck, "Worshiping God in Spirit," and "Worshiping God in Truth," in *Authentic Worship: Scripture's Voice, Applying Its Truth*, ed. Herbert W. Bateman (Grand Rapids, MI: Kregel, 2002), 79-133 and Averbeck, "Worship and Spiritual Formation," *Foundations of Spiritual Formation: A Community Approach to Becoming Like Christ*, ed. Paul Pettit (Grand Rapids, MI: Kregel, 2008), 51-69.

BIBLIOGRAPHY

Albright, W. F. "The Hebrew Expression for 'Making a Covenant' in Pre-Israelite Documents." *BASOR* 121 (February 1951): 21-22.

Afulike, Caleb. "The Mosaic Vision of a Benevolent Society: A Study of Deuteronomy 10:12-22 and Its Implications for Deuteronomic Concern for the Most Vulnerable." PhD dissertation, Trinity Evangelical Divinity School, 2020.

Alexander, T. D. *From Paradise to Promised Land: An Introduction to the Pentateuch.* 3rd edition. Grand Rapids, MI: Baker Academic, 2012.

Allison, D. C. "Jesus and the Torah." Pages 75-95 in *The Law in Holy Scripture: Essays from the Concordia Theological Seminary Symposium on Exegetical Theology*, edited by Charles A. Gieschen. Saint Louis: Concordia, 2004.

Averbeck, Richard E. "A Rest for the Soul." *Journal of Spiritual Formation and Soul Care* 11, no. 1 (2018): 5-22.

———. " 'āšām, nom. guilt offering." *NIDOTTE* 1.557-66.

———. "The Bible in Spiritual Formation." In *The Kingdom Life: A Practical Theology of Discipleship and Spiritual Formation*, edited by Alan Andrews. Colorado Springs: NavPress, 2010.

———. "Breath, Wind, Spirit, and the Holy Spirit in the Old Testament." Pages 25-37 in *Presence, Power and Promise: The Role of Spirit of God in the Old Testament*, edited by David G. Firth and Paul D. Wegner. Downers Grove, IL: IVP Academic, 2011.

———. "Christian Interpretations of Isaiah 53." Pages 33-60 in *The Gospel According to Isaiah: Exploring a Deeper Understanding of Isaiah Chapter 53*, edited by Darrell Bock and Mitch Glaser. Grand Rapids, MI: Kregel, 2012.

———. "Clean and Unclean." *NIDOTTE* 4:477-86.

———. "Crucial Features of Sin Offering Atonement in Leviticus 4–5 and 16," forthcoming.

———. "The Cult in Deuteronomy and Its Relationship to the Book of the Covenant and the Holiness Code." Pages 232-60 in *Sepher Torath Mosheh: Studies in the Composition and Interpretation of Deuteronomy*, edited by Daniel I. Block and Richard L. Schultz. Peabody, MA: Hendrickson, 2017.

———. "The Egyptian Sojourn and Deliverance from Slavery in the Framing and Shaping of the Mosaic Law." Pages 143-75 in *"Did I Not Bring Israel Out of Egypt?" Biblical, Archaeological, and Egyptological Perspectives on the Exodus Narratives*, edited by James Hoffmeier, Alan Millard, and Gary Rendsburg. BBRSup. Winona Lake, IN: Eisenbrauns, 2016.

———. "The Exodus, Debt Slavery, and the Composition of the Pentateuch." Pages 26-48 in *Exploring the Composition of the Pentateuch*, edited by L. S. Baker Jr. et al. BBRSup. University Park, PA: Eisenbrauns, 2020.

———. "Israel, the Jewish People, and God's Covenants." Pages 21-37 in *Israel the Church and the Middle East: A Biblical Response to the Current Conflict*, edited by Darrell L. Bock and Mitch Glaser. Grand Rapids, MI: Kregel, 2018.

———. "*kpr*, to make atonement." *NIDOTTE* 2:689-710.

———. "Law." Pages 113-38 in *Cracking Old Testament Codes: Essays in Honor of Richard D. Patterson*, edited by D. Brent Sandy and Ronald L. Giese Jr. Nashville: Broadman & Holman, 1995.

———. "The Law and the Gospels, with Attention to the Relationship Between the Decalogue and the Sermon on the Mount/Plain." Pages 409-23 in *The Oxford Handbook of Biblical Law*, edited by Pamela Barmash. Oxford: Oxford University Press, 2019.

———. "Leviticus, Theology of." *NIDOTTE* 4:907-23.

———. "Offerings and Sacrifices." *NIDOTTE* 4:996-1022.

———. "Pentateuchal Criticism and the Priestly Torah." Pages 151-79 in *Do Historical Matters Matter for Faith: A Critical Appraisal of Modern and Post Modern Approaches to the Bible*, edited by James K. Hoffmeier and Dennis R. Magary. Wheaton, IL: Crossway, 2012.

———. "Priest and Priesthood." Pages 632-38 in *The Evangelical Dictionary of Biblical Theology*, edited by Walter A. Elwell. Grand Rapids, MI: Baker, 1996.

———. "Reading the Ritual law in Leviticus Theologically." Pages 135-49 in *Interpreting the Old Testament Theologically: Essays in Honor of Willem A. VanGemeren*, edited by Andrew T. Abernethy. Grand Rapids, MI: Zondervan, 2018.

———. "Reading the Torah in a Better Way: Unity and Diversity in Text, Genre, and Compositional History." Pages 21-43 in *Paradigm Change in Pentateuchal Research*, edited by Matthias Armgardt, Benjamin Kilchör, and Markus Zehnder. BZABR 22. Wiesbaden: Harrassowitz, 2019.

———. "Sacrifices and Offerings." Pages 706-33 in *Dictionary of the Old Testament: Pentateuch*, edited by T. Desmond Alexander and David W. Baker. Downers Grove, IL: IVP Academic, 2003.

———. "Slavery in the World of the Bible." Pages 423-30 in *Behind the Scenes of the Old Testament*, edited by Jonathan S. Greer, John W. Hilber, and John H. Walton. Grand Rapids, MI: Baker Academic, 2018.

———. "Spirit, Community, and Mission: A Biblical Theology for Spiritual Formation." *Journal of Spiritual Formation and Soul Care* 1 (2008): 27-53.

———. "Tabernacle." Pages 807-27 in *Dictionary of the Old Testament: Pentateuch*, edited by T. Desmond Alexander and David W. Baker. Downers Grove, IL: IVP Academic, 2003.

———. "The Tests of Prophecy and the Prophets." Page 1-17 in *"An Excellent Fortress for His Armies, a Refuge for the People": Egyptological, Archaeological and Biblical Studies in Honor of James K. Hoffmeier*, edited by Richard E. Averbeck and K. Lawson Younger Jr. University Park: Pennsylvania State University Press, 2020.

———. "The Three 'Daughters' of Baal and Transformations of Chaoskampf in the Early Chapters of Genesis." Pages 237-56 in *Creation and Chaos: A Reconsideration of Hermann Gunkel's Chaoskampf Hypothesis*, edited by JoAnn Scurlock and Richard Beal. Winona Lake, IN: Eisenbrauns, 2013.

———. "ṭmʾ, be unclean." *NIDOTTE* 2:368-70.

———. "Worship and Spiritual Formation." Pages 51-69 in *Foundations of Spiritual Formation: A Community Approach to Becoming Like Christ*, edited by Paul Pettit. Grand Rapids, MI: Kregel, 2008.

———. "Worshiping God in Spirit." Pages 79-105 in *Authentic Worship: Scripture's Voice, Applying Its Truth*, edited by Herbert W. Bateman. Grand Rapids, MI: Kregel, 2002.

———. "Worshiping God in Truth." Pages 107-133 in *Authentic Worship: Scripture's Voice, Applying Its Truth*, edited by Herbert W. Bateman. Grand Rapids, MI: Kregel, 2002.

Bahnsen, Greg L. "The Theonomic Reformed Approach to Law and Gospel." Pages 93-143 in *The Law, the Gospel, and the Modern Christian*, edited by Wayne Strickland. Grand Rapids, MI: Zondervan, 1993.

———. *Theonomy in Christian Ethics*. Nutley, NJ: Craig, 1977.

Baker, David L. *Two Testaments, One Bible: A Study of the Theological Relationships Between the Old & New Testaments*. 3rd edition, revised and updated. Downers Grove, IL: IVP Academic, 2010.

Balentine, Samuel E. *The Oxford Handbook of Ritual and Worship in the Hebrew Bible*. Oxford: Oxford University Press, 2020.

———. *The Torah's Vision of Worship*. Minneapolis: Fortress, 1999.

Banks, R. "Matthew's Understanding of the Law: Authenticity and Interpretation in Matthew 5:17-20." *JBL* 93 (1974): 226-42.

Barmash, Pamela, ed. *The Oxford Handbook of Biblical Law*. Oxford: Oxford University Press, 2019.

Barr, James. "Some Semantic Notes on the Covenant." Pages 23-38 in *Beitrage zur Alttestamentlichen Theolgie: Festschrift fur Walther Zimmerli zum 70. Geburtstag*, edited by H. Donner et al. Göttingen: Vandenhoeck and Ruprecht, 1977.

Bartholomew, Craig G. "Covenant and Creation: Covenant Overload or Covenantal Deconstruction." *CTJ* 30 (1995): 11-33.

Bartholomew, Craig G. and Michael W. Goheen. *The Drama of Scripture: Finding our Place in the Biblical Story*. Grand Rapids, MI: Baker Academic, 2004.

Belleville, Linda, Jon C. Laansma, J Ramsey Michaels, and Philip W. Comfort. *1 and 2 Timothy, Titus, Hebrews*. CBCS 17. Carol Stream, IL: Tyndale, 2009.

Bergsma, John Sietze. *The Jubilee from Leviticus to Qumran: A History of Interpretation*. VTSup 115. Leiden: Brill, 2007.

Berlin, Adele. "Numinous *Nomos*: On the Relationship between Narrative and Law." Pages 25-31 in *"A Wise and Discerning Mind": Essays in Honor of Burke O. Long*, edited by Saul M. Olyan and Robert C. Culley. Providence: Brown Judaic Studies, 2000.

Berman, Joshua A. *Inconsistency in the Torah: Ancient Literary Convention and the Limits of Source Criticism*. Oxford: Oxford University Press, 2017.

Block, Daniel I. *Covenant: The Framework of God's Grand Plan and Redemption*. Grand Rapids, MI: Baker, 2021.

———. *Deuteronomy*. NIVAC. Grand Rapids, MI: Zondervan, 2012.

———. "'The Meeting Places of God in the Land': Another Look at the Towns of the Levites." Pages 93-121 in *Current Issues in Priestly and Related Literature: The Legacy of Jacob Milgrom and Beyond*, edited by Roy E. Gane and Ada Taggar-Cohen. SBL Resources for Bible Study. Atlanta: SBL Press, 2015.

Blum, Erhard. "Issues and Problems in the Contemporary Debate Regarding the Priestly Writings." Pages 31-44 in *The Strata of the Priestly Writings: Contemporary Debate and Future Directions*, edited by Sarah Shectman and Joel S. Baden. Zürich: Theologischer Verlag Zürich. 2009.

Bock, Darrell L. *Acts*. BECNT. Grand Rapids, MI: Baker Academic, 2007.

———. *Luke 1:2–9:50*. BECNT. Grand Rapids, MI: Baker, 1994.

Bock, Darrell L. and Mitch Glaser, eds. *Israel, the Church, and the Middle East: A Biblical Response to the Current Conflict*. Grand Rapids, MI: Kregel, 2018.

Bosman, Hendrik L. "Sabbath." *NIDOTTE* 4:1157-62.

Brooks, James. *Mark*. NAC. Nashville: Broadman & Holman, 1991.

Brown, Michael L. *Answering Jewish Objections to Jesus*, vol. 2: *Theological Objections*. Grand Rapids, MI: Baker, 2000.

Bruce, F. F. *Commentary on the Book of Acts*. NICNT. Grand Rapids, MI: Eerdmans, 1954.

———. *Galatians: A Commentary on the Greek Text*. Grand Rapids, MI: Eerdmans, 1982.

Burton, Ernest de Witt. *The Epistle to the Galatians*. ICC. Edinburgh: T&T Clark, 1921.

Carmichael, Calum. *Law and Narrative in the Bible: The Evidence of the Deuteronomic Laws and the Decalogue*. Ithaca, NY: Cornell University Press, 1985.

Carson, D. A. *The Gospel According to John*. Grand Rapids, MI: Eerdmans, 1991.

———. "Matthew." In *The Expositors Bible Commentary*, edited by T. Longman III and D. E. Garland. Revised edition. Grand Rapids, MI: Zondervan, 2005.

Carson, D. A., ed. *From Sabbath to Lord's Day: A Biblical, Historical, and Theological Investigation*. Grand Rapids, MI: Zondervan, 1982.

———. *NIV Biblical Theology Study Bible*. Grand Rapids, MI: Zondervan, 2018.

Carson, D. A., Peter T. O'Brien, and Mark A. Seifrid, eds. *Justification and Variegated Nomism: A Fresh Appraisal of Paul and Second Temple Judaism*. 2 vols. WUNT 2/140. Tübingen: Mohr Siebeck, 2001, 2004.

Cassuto, U. *From Noah to Abraham*. Translated by Israel Abrahams. Jerusalem: Magnes, 1964.

Charles, J. Daryl. "Garnishing with the 'Greater Righteousness': The Disciple's Relationship to the Law (Matthew 5:17-20)." *BBR* 12 (2002): 1-15.

Chirichigno, G. C. "The Narrative Structure of Ex 19–24." *Biblica* 68 (1987): 457-79.

Civil, Miguel. "The Law Collection of Ur-Namma." Pages 221-86 in *Cuneiform Royal Inscriptions and Related Texts in the Schoyen Collection*, edited by A. R. George. CUSAS 17. Bethesda, MD: CDL Press, 2011.

Craigie, Peter C. *The Book of Deuteronomy*. NICOT. Grand Rapids, MI: Eerdmans, 1976.

Cranfield, C. E. B. *The Epistle to the Romans*. Volume 1. ICC. Edinburgh: T&T Clark, 1975.

Danby, Herbert. *The Mishnah*. Oxford: Oxford University Press, 1933.

Daube, David. *The Collected Works of David Daube*, vol. 3: *Biblical Law and Literature*. Edited by Calum Carmichael. Berkeley: University of California Press, 2003.

———. *The New Testament and Rabbinic Judaism*. Peabody, MA: Hendrickson, 1990.

Davidson, R. "Covenant Ideology in Ancient Israel." Pages 323-47 in *The World of Ancient Israel: Sociological, Anthropological and Political Perspectives*, edited by R. E. Clements. Cambridge: Cambridge University Press, 1989.

Davies, John A. *A Royal Priesthood: Literary and Intertextual Perspectives on an Image of Israel in Exodus 19:6*. London: T&T Clark, 2004.

Dempster, Stephen G. *Dominion and Dynasty: A Theology of the Hebrew Bible*. NSBT 15. Downers Grove, IL: InterVarsity Press, 2003.

deSilva, D. A. "Clean and Unclean." Pages 142-49 in *Dictionary of Jesus and the Gospels*, edited by J. B. Green, J. K. Brown, and N. Perrin. 2nd edition. Downers Grove, IL: IVP Academic, 2013.

Dorsey, David A. "The Law of Moses and the Christian: A Compromise." *JETS* 34 (1991): 321-34.

Dumbrell, W. J. *Covenant and Creation: An Old Testament Covenant Theology*. Exeter: Paternoster, 1984.

———. "The Prospect of Unconditionality in the Sinaitic Covenant." Pages 141-55 in *Israel's Apostasy and Restoration: Essays in Honor of Roland K. Harrison*, edited by A. Gileadi. Grand Rapids, MI: Baker, 1988.

Dunn, James D. G. "Law." Pages 505-15 in *Dictionary of Jesus and the Gospels*, edited by J. B. Green, J. K. Brown, and N. Perrin. 2nd edition. Downers Grove, IL: IVP Academic, 2013.

———. *Romans 1–8*. WBC 38. Dallas: Word, 1988.

Ellis, E. E. *The Gospel of Luke*. Grand Rapids, MI: Eerdmans, 1974.

Evans, Craig C. *Matthew*. Cambridge: Cambridge University Press, 2012.

Finkelstein, J. J. *The Ox That Gored*. TAPS 71/2. Philadelphia: American Philosophical Society, 1981.

France, R. T. *The Gospel of Matthew*. Grand Rapids, MI: Eerdmans, 2007.

Fredriksen, P. "Did Jesus Oppose the Purity Laws?" *BRev* 11, no. 3 (1995): 19-25, 42-47.

Gane, Roy E. *Leviticus, Numbers*. NIVAC. Grand Rapids, MI: Zondervan, 2004.

———. *Old Testament Law for Christians: Original Context and Enduring Application*. Grand Rapids, MI: Baker Academic, 2017.

Gentry, Peter J. and Stephen J. Wellum. *Kingdom Through Covenant: A Biblical-Theological Understanding of the Covenants*. 2nd edition. Wheaton, IL: Crossway, 2018.

Gibson, John C. L. *Textbook of Syrian Semitic Inscriptions*, vol. 2: *Aramaic Inscriptions*. Oxford: Oxford University Press, 1975.

Goldingay, John. *Old Testament Theology*, vol. 1: *Israel's Gospel*. Downers Grove, IL: InterVarsity, 2003.

Green, Joel B. *The Gospel of Luke*. NICNT. Grand Rapids, MI: Eerdmans, 1997.

Greengus, Samuel. "Covenant and Treaty in the Hebrew Bible and in the Ancient Near East." Pages 91-126 in *Ancient Israel's History: An Introduction to Issues and Sources*, edited by Bill T. Arnold and Richard S. Hess. Grand Rapids, MI: Baker Academic, 2014.

———. *Laws in the Bible and in Early Rabbinic Collections: The Legacy of the Ancient Near East*. Eugene, OR: Cascade, 2011.

Greenstein, Edward L. "Decalogue." Pages 164-72 in *The Oxford Encyclopedia of the Bible and Law*, edited by Brent A. Strawn. Oxford: Oxford University Press, 2015.

Hahn, Scott W. *Kinship by Covenant: A Canonical Approach to the Fulfillment of God's Saving Promises*. New Haven, CT: Yale University Press, 2009.

Hallo, William W. "Slave Release in the Biblical World in Light of a New Text." Pages 88-93 in *Solving Riddles and Untying Knots: Biblical, Epigraphic, and Semitic Studies in Honor of Jonas C. Greenfield*, edited by Ziony Zevit, Seymour Gitin, and Michael Sokoloff. Winona Lake, IN: Eisenbrauns, 1995.

Hallo, William W. and K. Lawson Younger Jr., eds. *The Context of Scripture*. Vols. 2-3. Leiden: Brill, 2000, 2002.

Haran, Menahem. "The Bərît 'Covenant': Its Nature and Ceremonial Background." Pages 203-19 in *Tehillah le-Moshe: Biblical and Judaic Studies in Honor of Moshe Greenberg*, edited by Mordechai Cogan et al. Winona Lake, IN: Eisenbrauns, 1997.

Hartley, John E. *Leviticus*. WBC 4. Dallas: Word, 1992.

Harvey, Richard. *Mapping Messianic Jewish Theology: A Constructive Approach*. Colorado Springs, CO: Paternoster, 2009.

Hendrix, R. E. "The Use of *MIŠKĀN* and *ʾŌHEL MŌʿĒD* in Exodus 25–40." *AUSS* (1992): 3-13.

Hess, Richard S. "The Book of Joshua as a Land Grant." *Biblica* 83 (2002): 493-506.

————. "The Slaughter of the Animals in Genesis 15: Genesis 15:8-21 and Its Ancient Near Eastern Context." Pages 55-65 in *He Swore and Oath*, edited by R. S. Hess et al. Grand Rapids, MI: Baker, 1994.

Hilber, John W. "Theology of Worship in Exodus 24." *JETS* 39 (1996): 177-89.

Holmén, T. "Jesus and the Purity Paradigm." Pages 2709-44 in vol. 3 of *Handbook for the Study of the Historical Jesus*, edited by T. Holmén and S. E. Porter. Leiden: Brill, 2011.

Houtman, Cornelius. *Exodus*. HCOT 3. Leuven: Peeters, 2000.

Huddleston, Neal A. "Ancient Near Eastern Treaty Traditions and Their Implications for Interpreting Deuteronomy." Pages 30-77 in *Sepher Torath Mosheh: Studies in the Composition and Interpretation of Deuteronomy*, edited by Daniel I. Block and Richard L. Schultz. Peabody, MA: Hendrickson, 2017.

Huey, F. B., Jr. *Jeremiah, Lamentations*. Nashville: Broadman & Holman, 1993.

Huffmon, Herbert B. "'An Eye for an Eye' and Capital Punishment." Pages 119-31 in *The Oxford Handbook of Biblical Law*, edited by Pamela Barmash. Oxford: Oxford University Press, 2019.

Hugenberger, G. P. *Marriage as a Covenant: A Study of Biblical Law and Ethics Governing Marriage, Developed from the Perspective of Malachi*. Leiden: Brill, 1994.

Huggins, Ronald V. "Marcion." Pages 855-56 in *Eerdmans Dictionary of the Bible*, ed. David Noel Freedman. Grand Rapids, MI: Eerdmans, 2000.

Hundley, Michael B. *God in Dwellings: Temple and Divine Presence in the Ancient Near East*. WAWSup 3. Atlanta: SBL Press, 2013.

————. *Keeping Heaven on Earth: Safeguarding the Divine Presence in the Priestly Tabernacle*. FAT 2/50. Tübingen: Mohr Siebeck, 2011.

Hurowitz, Victor. *Inu Anum Ṣīrum: Literary Structures in the Non-Juridical Sections of Codex Hammurabi*. Philadelphia: Occasional Publications of the Samuel Noah Kramer Fund, 1994.

Imes, Carmen Joy. *Bearing YHWH's Name at Sinai: A Reexamination of the Name Command of the Decalogue*. BBRSup 19. University Park: Pennsylvania State University Press, 2018.

————. *Bearing God's Name: Why Sinai Still Matters*. Downers Grove, IL: InterVarsity Press, 2019.

Jipp, Joshua W. *Christ is King: Paul's Royal Ideology*. Minneapolis: Fortress, 2015.

Kaiser, Walter C., Jr. "The Law as God's Gracious Guidance for the Promotion of Holiness." Pages 177-199 in *The Law, the Gospel, and the Modern Christian*, edited by Wayne Strickland. Grand Rapids, MI: Zondervan, 1993.

————. *Toward Old Testament Ethics*. Grand Rapids, MI: Zondervan, 1983.

Kaufman, Stephen A. "The Structure of the Deuteronomic Law." *Maarav* 1:2 (1978–1979): 105-58.

Kazen, Thomas. *Jesus and the Purity Halakhah: Was Jesus Indifferent to Purity?* CBNTS 38. Winona Lake, IN: Eisenbrauns, 2010.

——. "Theology of Law: New Testament." Pages 384-400 in vol. 2 of *The Oxford Encyclopedia of the Bible and Law*, edited by Brent A. Strawn. Oxford: Oxford University Press, 2015.

Kilchör, Benjamin. "Sacred and Profane Space: The Priestly Character of Exodus 20:24-26 and Its Reception in Deuteronomy 12." *BBR* 29:4 (2019): 455-67.

Kinzer, Mark S. "Messianic Jews and the Jewish World." Pages 126-35 in *Introduction to Messianic Judaism*, edited by David Rudolph and Joel Willitts. Grand Rapids, MI: Zondervan, 2013.

Kitchen, Kenneth A. *On the Reliability of the Old Testament*. Grand Rapids, MI: Eerdmans, 2003.

Kitchen, Kenneth A. and Paul J. N. Lawrence, eds. *Treaty, Law and Covenant in the Ancient Near East*. 3 vols. Wiesbaden: Harrasowitz, 2012.

Kline, Meredith. "Review of Thomas Edward McComiskey, *The Covenants of Promise: A Theology of the Old Testament Covenants*." *JETS* 30 (1987): 77-80.

Knoppers, Gary N. "Ancient Near Eastern Royal Grants and the Davidic Covenant: A Parallel?" *JAOS* 116 (1996): 670-97.

Koch, K. " ʿāvōn." *TDOT* 10:559-61.

Leuchter, Mark. "The Manumission Laws in Leviticus and Deuteronomy: The Jeremiah Connection." *JBL* 127 (2008): 635-53.

Levenson, J. D. *Creation and the Persistence of Evil*. Second edition. Princeton, NJ: Princeton University Press, 1994.

Levine, Baruch A. *Leviticus*. The JPS Torah Commentary. Philadelphia: Jewish Publication Society, 1989.

Levinson, Bernard M. "The Manumission of Hermeneutics: The Slave Laws of the Pentateuch as a Challenge to Contemporary Pentateuchal Theory." Pages 281-324 in *Congress Volume Leiden 2004*, edited by André Lemaire. VTSup 109. Leiden: Brill, 2006.

Lioy, D. *Jesus as Torah in John 1–12*. Eugene, OR: Wipf & Stock, 2007.

Loader, W. "Jesus and the Law." Pages 2745-72 in vol. 3 of *Handbook for the Study of the Historical Jesus*, edited by T. Holmén and S. E. Porter. Leiden: Brill, 2011.

Lock, Walter. *The Pastoral Epistles*. ICC. Edinburgh: T&T Clark, 1924.

Longman, Tremper III. *Genesis*. SGBC. Grand Rapids, MI: Zondervan, 2016.

Magdalene, F. Rachel, Cornelia Wunsch, and Bruce Wells. *Fault, Responsibility, and Administrative Law in Late Babylonian Legal Texts*. MC 23. University Park, PA: Eisenbrauns, 2019.

Mathews, Kenneth A. *Genesis 1–11*. NAC. Nashville: Broadman & Holman, 1996.

McCarthy, Dennis J., S. J. *Treaty and Covenant: A Study in Form in the Ancient Oriental Documents and in the Old Testament*. New edition. Rome: Biblical Institute Press, 1981.

McComiskey, Thomas Edward. *The Covenants of Promise: A Theology of the Old Testament Covenants*. Grand Rapids, MI: Baker, 1985.

McConville, Gordon J. "bᵉrît." *NIDOTTE* 1:747-55.

McDermott, Gerald R. *Israel Matters: Why Christians Must Think Differently About the People and the Land.* Grand Rapids, MI: Brazos, 2017.

Milgrom, Jacob. *Numbers.* The JPS Torah Commentary. Philadelphia: Jewish Publication Society, 1990.

———. *Leviticus 1–16.* AB 3. New York: Doubleday, 1991.

Miller, Patrick D. *The Ten Commandments.* Louisville: Westminster John Knox, 2009.

———. "The Ten Commandments." Pages 517-22 in vol 5 of *The New Interpreter's Dictionary of the Bible,* edited by Katherine Doob Sakenfeld. Nashville: Abingdon, 2006–2009.

Moo, Douglas J. *The Epistle to the Romans.* NICNT. Grand Rapids, MI: Eerdmans, 1996.

———. "Law." Pages 450-61 in *Dictionary of Jesus and the Gospels,* edited by Joel B. Green and Scott McKnight. Downers Grove, IL.: InterVarsity Press, 1992.

———. "The Law of Christ as the Fulfillment of the Law of Moses: A Modified Lutheran View." Pages 319-376 in *The Law, the Gospel, and the Modern Christian,* edited by Wayne Strickland. Grand Rapids, MI: Zondervan, 1993.

Morrow, William S. *An Introduction to Biblical Law.* Grand Rapids, MI: Eerdmans, 2017.

Nicholson, Ernest W. *God and His People: Covenant and Theology in the Old Testament.* Oxford: Clarendon, 1986.

Nihan, Christophe. *From Priestly Torah to Pentateuch: A Study in the Composition of the Book of Leviticus.* FAT 25/2. Reihe 25. Tübingen: Mohr Siebeck, 2007.

Noth, Martin. *Leviticus: A Commentary.* Philadelphia: Westminster, 1965.

Osborne, Grant R. *John Verse by Verse.* Bellingham, WA: Lexham, 2018.

Otto, Eckart. "The Study of Law and Ethics in the Hebrew Bible/Old Testament." Pages 594-621 in vol. 3.2 of *Hebrew Bible/Old Testament: The History of Its Interpretation,* edited by Magne Sæbø. Göttingen: Vandenhoeck & Ruprecht, 2015.

Paul, Ian. "Metaphor." Pages 507-10 in *Dictionary for Theological Interpretation of the Bible,* edited by Kevin J. Vanhoozer. Grand Rapids, MI: Baker, 2005.

Paul, Shalom M. *Studies in the Book of the Covenant in the Light of Cuneiform and Biblical Law.* VTSup 18. Leiden: Brill, 1970.

Peterson, David G. *The Acts of the Apostles.* PNTC. Grand Rapids, MI: Eerdmans, 2009.

Postell, Seth D. "Abram as Israel, Israel as Abram: Literary Analogy as Macro-Structural Strategy in the Torah." *TynBul* 67 (2016): 161-82.

Poythress, Vern. *The Shadow of Christ in the Law of Moses.* Phillipsburg, NJ: P&R, 1991.

———. *Symphonic Theology: The Validity of Multiple Perspectives in Theology.* Grand Rapids, MI: Zondervan, 1987.

Propp, William H. C. *Exodus 19–40.* AB 2A. New York: Doubleday, 2006.

Rendtorff, Rolf. *The Covenant Formulary: And Exegetical and Theological Investigation.* Edinburgh: T&T Clark, 1998.

———. *Leviticus.* BKAT 3/3. Neukirchen-Vluyn: Neukirchener Verlag, 1992.

Rochberg, Francesca. *Cuneiform Knowledge and the History of Science*. Chicago: University of Chicago Press, 2016.

Rom-Shiloni, Dalit. "The Decalogue." Pages 135-55 in *The Oxford Handbook of Biblical Law*, edited by Pamela Barmash. Oxford: Oxford University Press, 2019.

Rooker, Mark F. *The Ten Commandments: Ethics for the Twenty-First Century*. NAC Studies in Biblical Theology. Nashville: B&H Academic, 2010.

Ross, Allen P. *Creation and Blessing: A Guide to the Study and Exposition of the Book of Genesis*. Grand Rapids, MI: Baker, 1988.

Rudolph, David. "Messianic Judaism in Antiquity and in the Modern Era." Pages 221-36 in *Introduction to Messianic Judaism*, edited by David Rudolph and Joel Willitts. Grand Rapids, MI: Zondervan, 2013.

Sanders, E. P. *Jesus and Judaism*. Philadelphia, PA: Fortress, 1985.

———. *Paul and Palestinian Judaism*. Minneapolis: Fortress, 1977.

Sarna, Nahum M. *Exodus*. JPS Torah Commentary. Philadelphia: Jewish Publication Society, 1991.

———. *Genesis*. JPS Torah Commentary. Philadelphia: Jewish Publication Society, 1989.

Schenker, Adrian. "The Biblical Legislation on the Release of Slaves: The Road from Exodus to Leviticus." *JSOT* 78 (1998): 23-41. Reprinted on pages 134-49 in *Recht und Kult im Alten Testament: Achtzehn Studien*. OBO 172. Universitätsverlage Freiburg Schweiz; Göttingen: Vandenhoeck & Ruprecht, 2000.

Schmutzer, Andrew J. *Be Fruitful and Multiply: A Crux Thematic Repetition in Genesis 1-11*. Eugene, OR: Wipf & Stock, 2009.

Schwartz, Baruch J. "The Bearing of Sin in the Priestly Literature." Pages 3-21 in *Pomegranates and Golden Bells: Studies in Biblical, Jewish, and Near Eastern Ritual, Law, and Literature in Honor of Jacob Milgrom*, edited by David P. Wright, David Noel Freedman, and Avi Hurvitz. Winona Lake, IN: Eisenbrauns, 1995.

Sim, David C. "Sermon on the Mount." Pages 285-89 in vol. 2 of *The Oxford Encyclopedia of the Bible and Law*, edited by Brent A. Strawn. Oxford: Oxford University Press, 2015.

Sklar, Jay. *Leviticus: An Introduction and Commentary*. TOTC. Downers Grove, IL: IVP Academic, 2014.

———. *Sin, Impurity, Sacrifice, and Atonement: The Priestly Conceptions*. HBM 2. Sheffield: Sheffield Phoenix, 2005.

Snodgrass, Klyne. "Matthew and the Law." Pages 99-127 in *Treasures New and Old: Recent Contributions to Matthean Studies*, edited by D. R. Bauer and M. A. Powell. Atlanta: Scholars, 1996.

Sommer, Benjamin D. *Revelation and Authority: Sinai in Jewish Scripture in Tradition*. ABRL. New Haven, CT: Yale University Press, 2015.

Sprinkle, Joe M. *"The Book of the Covenant" A Literary Approach*. JSOTSup 174. Sheffield: JSOT Press, 1994.

Stassen, G. H. "The Fourteen Triads of the Sermon on the Mount (Matthew 5:21-7:12)." *JBL* 122 (2003): 267-308.

Stek, John H. "'Covenant' Overload in Reformed Theology." *CTJ* 29 (1994): 12-41.

Stern, David H. *Jewish New Testament Commentary*. 5th edition. Clarkesville, MD: Jewish New Testament Publications, 1996.

Strawn, Brent A., ed. *The Oxford Encyclopedia of the Bible and Law*. 2 vols. Oxford: Oxford University Press, 2015.

Strickland, Wayne. "The Inauguration of the Law of Christ with the Gospel of Christ: A Dispensational View." Pages 229-279 in *The Law, the Gospel, and the Modern Christian*, edited by Wayne Strickland. Grand Rapids, MI: Zondervan, 1993.

Strickland, Wayne, ed. *The Law, the Gospel, and the Modern Christian*. Grand Rapids, MI: Zondervan, 1993; republished as Stanley N. Gundry, ed. *Five Views on the Law and Gospel*. Grand Rapids, MI: Zondervan, 1996.

Stuart, Douglas K. *Exodus*. NAC 2. Nashville: Broadman & Holman, 2066.

Swiderski, Igor. "Sabbatical Patterns in the Book of the Covenant." Master's thesis. Trinity Evangelical Divinity School. Ann Arbor: University Microfilms International, 2013.

Tan, K. H. "Jesus and the Shema." Pages 2677-2707 in vol. 3 of *Handbook for the Study of the Historical Jesus*, edited by T. Holmén and S. E. Porter. Leiden: Brill, 2011.

Tigay, Jeffrey H. *Deuteronomy*. JPS Torah Commentary. Philadelphia: Jewish Publication Society, 1996.

Treier, Daniel J. "Typology." Pages 823-27 in *Dictionary for Theological Interpretation of the Bible*, edited by Kevin J. Vanhoozer. Grand Rapids, MI: Baker, 2005.

Tsai, Daisy Yulin. *Human Rights in Deuteronomy: With Special Focus on Slave Laws*. BZAW 464. Berlin: De Gruyter, 2014.

VanGemeren, Willem A. "The Law Is the Perfection of Righteousness in Jesus Christ: A Reformed Perspective." Pages 13-58 in *The Law, the Gospel, and the Modern Christian*, ed., Wayne Strickland. Grand Rapids, MI: Zondervan, 1993.

Vannoy, J. Robert. *Covenant Renewal at Gilgal: A Study of 1 Samuel 11:14–12:25*. Cherry Hill, NJ: Mack, 1978.

Veldhuis, Niek. *History of the Cuneiform Lexical Tradition*. GMTR 6. Münster: Ugarit-Verlag, 2014.

Waltke, Bruce K. *An Old Testament Theology: An Exegetical, Canonical, and Thematic Approach*. Grand Rapids, MI: Zondervan, 2007.

———. "The Phenomenon of Conditionality within the Unconditional Covenants." Pages 123-39 in *Israel's Apostasy and Restoration: Essays in Honor of Roland K. Harrison*, edited by A. Gileadi. Grand Rapids, MI: Baker, 1988.

———. "Theonomy in Relation to Dispensational and Covenant Theologies." Pages 59-86 in *Theonomy: A Reformed Critique*, edited by William S. Barker and W. Robert Godfrey. Grand Rapids, MI: Zondervan, 1990.

Walton, John H. "Exodus, Date of." Pages 258-72 in *Dictionary of the Old Testament: Pentateuch*, edited by T. Desmond Alexander and David W. Baker. Downers Grove, IL: IVP Academic, 2003.

Walton, John H. and J. Harvey Walton. *The Lost World of the Torah: Law as a Covenant and Wisdom in Ancient Context*. Downers Grove, IL: IVP Academic, 2019.

Watts, James W. *Leviticus 1–10*. HCOT. Leuven: Peeters, 2013.

Weinfeld, Moshe. "*bᵉrit*." *TDOT* 2:253-79.

———. "The Covenant of Grant in the Old Testament and in the Ancient Near East." *JAOS* (90): 184-203.

———. *Deuteronomy 1-11*. AB. Vol. 5. New York: Doubleday, 1991.

———. "The Loyalty Oath in the Ancient Near East." *UF* 9 (1976): 379-414.

Weisman, Ze'ev. "The Place of the People in the Making of Law and Judgment." Pages 407-20 in *Pomegranates and Golden Bells: Studies in Biblical, Jewish and Near Eastern Ritual, Law and Literature in Honor of Jacob Milgrom*, edited by David P. Wright et al. Winona Lake, IN: Eisenbrauns, 1995.

Wells, Bruce. "Law and Practice." Pages 183-95 in *A Companion to the Ancient Near East*, edited by Daniel C. Snell. Malden, MA: Blackwell, 2005.

———. *The Law of Testimony in the Pentateuchal Codes*. BZABR 4. Wiesbaden: Harrassowitz Verlag, 2004.

Wells, Bruce and Rachel Magdalene, eds. *Law from the Tigris to the Tiber: The Writings of Raymond Westbrook*. 2 vols. Winona Lake, IN: Eisenbrauns, 2009.

Wenham, Gordon J. *The Book of Leviticus*. NICOT. Grand Rapids, MI: Eerdmans, 1979.

———. *Genesis 1-15*. WBC. Waco: Word, 1987.

———. "Sanctuary Symbolism in the Garden of Eden Story." Pages 19-24 in *Proceedings of the Ninth World Congress of Jewish Studies*. Jerusalem: World Union of Jewish Studies, 1986.

Westbrook, Raymond, ed. *A History of Ancient Near Eastern law*. 2 vols. Leiden: Brill, 2003.

———. "Lex Talionis and Exodus 21:22-25." Pages 341-60 in vol. 2 of *Law from the Tigris to the Tiber: The Writings of Raymond Westbrook*, edited by Bruce Wells and Rachel Magdalene. Winona Lake, IN: Eisenbrauns, 2009.

Westbrook, Raymond and Bruce Wells. *Everyday Law in Biblical Israel: An Introduction*. Louisville: Westminster John Knox, 2009.

Westermann, Claus. *Genesis 1-11*. Translated by John J. Scullion, S. J. Minneapolis: Augsburg, 1984.

———. *Genesis 12–36: A Commentary*. Translated by John J. Scullion, S. J. Minneapolis: Augsburg, 1985.

Wildenboer, M. "Eckart Otto's Contribution to the Question of the Composition of the Sinai Pericope: An Appreciation." *Verbum et Ecclesia* 40, no. 1 (1974), https://doi.org/10.4102/ve.v40i1.1974.

Williamson, Paul R. "Covenant." Pages 139-55 in *Dictionary of the Old Testament: Pentateuch*, edited by T. Desmond Alexander and David W. Baker. Downers Grove, IL: IVP Academic, 2003.

———. *Sealed with an Oath: Covenant in God's Unfolding Purpose*. Edited by D. A. Carson. NSBT 23. Downers Grove, IL: IVP Academic, 2007.

Wright, Christopher J. H. *Deuteronomy*. NIBC. Peabody, MA: Hendrickson, 1996.

———. *Old Testament Ethics for the People of God*. Downers Grove, IL: IVP Academic, 2004.

Wright, David P. *Inventing God's Law: How the Covenant Code of the Bible Used and Revised the Laws of Hammurabi*. Oxford: Oxford University Press, 2009.

Wright, N. T. *Jesus and the Victory of God*. COQG 2. Minneapolis: Fortress, 1996.

———. *The New Testament and the People of God*. COQG 1. Minneapolis: Fortress, 1992.

Younger, K. Lawson, Jr. and Neal A. Huddleston, "Challenges to the Use of Ancient Near Eastern Treaty Forms for Dating and Interpreting Deuteronomy." Pages 78-109 in *Sepher Torath Mosheh: Studies in the Composition and Interpretation of Deuteronomy*, edited by Daniel I. Block and Richard L. Schultz. Peabody, MA: Hendrickson, 2017.

SUBJECT INDEX

SCRIPTURE INDEX